SEP 2003

Co ... very d
303 ... 6529

D0031887

Weingarten, Kathy

DATE DUE

NOV 22 2003

DEMCO, INC. 38-2931

common shock

Also By Kaethe Weingarten

Sooner or Later: The Timing of Parenthood in Adult Lives
(with Pamela Daniels)

The Mother's Voice: Strengthening Intimacy in Families

common shock

Witnessing Violence Every Day: How We Are Harmed, How We Can Heal

Kaethe Weingarten, Ph.D.

DUTTON

DUTTON
Published by Penguin Group (USA) Inc.
375 Hudson Street, New York, New York 10014, U.S.A.
Penguin Books Ltd, Registered Offices: 80 Strand, London WC2R 0RL, England
Penguin Books Australia Ltd, 250 Camberwell Road, Camberwell, Victoria 3124, Australia
Penguin Books Canada Ltd, 10 Alcorn Avenue, Toronto, Ontario, Canada M4V 3B2
Penguin Books (NZ) Ltd, Cnr Rosedale and Airborne Roads,
Albany, Auckland 1310, New Zealand

Published by Dutton, a member of Penguin Group (USA) Inc.

First printing, September 2003
1 3 5 7 9 10 8 6 4 2

Copyright © Kaethe Weingarten, 2003
All rights reserved

REGISTERED TRADEMARK—MARCA REGISTRADA

LIBRARY OF CONGRESS CATALOGING-IN-PUBLICATION DATA

Weingarten, Kaethe.
Common shock : witnessing violence every day / by Kaethe Weingarten.
p. cm.
ISBN 0-525-94742-6 (hardcover : alk. paper)
1. Violence. 2. Violence—Prevention. I. Title.
HM1116. W44 2003
303.6—dc21
2003004685

Printed in the United States of America
Set in Sabon
Designed by Leonard Telesca

Without limiting the rights under copyright reserved above, no part of this publication may be reproduced, stored in or introduced into a retrieval system, or transmitted, in any form, or by any means (electronic, mechanical, photocopying, recording, or otherwise), without the prior written permission of both the copyright owner and the above publisher of this book.

The scanning, uploading, and distribution of this book via the Internet or via any other means without the permission of the publisher is illegal and punishable by law. Please purchase only authorized electronic editions, and do not participate in or encourage electronic piracy of copyrighted materials. Your support of the author's rights is appreciated.

This book is printed on acid-free paper. ♾

To witnesses, everywhere

Contents

Part One

What Is the Matter?

By witness is meant a mode of responding to the other's plight that . . . becomes an ethical involvement. One must not only utter a truth about the victim but also remain true to her or him.

—James Hatley[1]

"The Thousand Natural Shocks . . ."

The other day I took my friend's daughter, age seven, to the park. While I was pushing her on the swing, a father smacked his small son in the face. Turning away from this man and little boy, I saw my young friend, Anna, riveted with attention to the same scene.

Within a few pushes Anna began to kick her feet to slow herself down, and soon she was able to reach her feet to the ground, where she scuffed her shoes, the better to stop. Turning her head toward me, she said matter-of-factly, "I don't want to stay here anymore. Can we go home?"

Had I been bending down to remove a leaf off my leg, had I been chatting with the woman pushing her daughter on the swing next to ours, had I even been yawning, eyes temporarily closed, I might easily have missed what Anna saw. The little boy had not made one peep, so no sound from him would have returned my gaze to the sandbox where he was playing.

Had I missed what Anna witnessed, I would not have known what had distressed her sufficiently to change her plans for our time together. Nor understood why this little girl, who herself had been scolded that morning for hitting her younger sister, now wanted to go home rather than play on every piece of the park's equipment. I wouldn't have known to take her hand and ask her how she felt about what the man had done to the little boy. I wouldn't have gotten her reply: "He was mean. It wasn't fair."

Anna experienced *common shock*. It is *common* because it happens all the time, to everyone in any community. It is a *shock* because, regardless of our response—spaciness, distress, bravado—it affects our mind, body, and spirit.

Had I not seen and not asked, I wouldn't have known that I needed to help her express and rid herself of the bit of violence she had glimpsed and was now carrying within her. I wouldn't have asked her, "Do you think there is something we can do, right now, by ourselves, to show that we don't like it when people hurt each other?"

"Like what?" she had said.

"I don't know. Like stamp our feet," I said stamping both my feet, "and saying, 'Don't hurt people!' "

Which is what we did. For two blocks. We stamped our feet hard, shouting, "Don't hurt people. Don't hurt girls. Don't hurt boys. Don't hurt mothers. Don't hurt grandpas. Don't hurt cats. Don't hurt dogs." Until it turned silly, and we were shouting, "Don't hurt the sky. Don't hurt the stars." And then, I think the episode was over for Anna. When her mom came to pick her up, I didn't remember to tell her what had happened.

Whether we want to or not, we cannot escape witnessing such events. Sometimes these events occur between people we know. At other times we may just happen to be somewhere—like in a neighborhood park—and see a gratuitous example of violence. Unexpected scenes may accost us when we are following our usual routines, like turning on the television moments before our favorite show, but on this occasion the horrific dramatic finale of the previous program assaults us. Or an extraordinary event creates a disturbance that ripples throughout our lives. For some, the *Columbia*'s white contrails streaking across a deep-blue sky will remain etched in their minds. For others, September 11, 2001—9/11—will be remembered forever.

The witnessing of violence and violation, events that fall on a continuum from the ordinary to the extraordinary, jolts us into a response I call common shock. While some react with obvious physical symptoms, many of us respond as if coated with Teflon; nothing sticks. That is the paradox of common shock. The more we witness, the less we register. Violence and violation become like the wallpaper, just there.

None of us escapes this kind of everyday witnessing, and yet many of us have never "noticed" it. After September 11, however, many more people have a reference point for understanding that the witnessing of violence can produce immediate and long-term distress. While the violence we saw that day was massive and extraordinary, there are also consequences to witnessing the small and ordinary forms of violence that occur in our lives.

Let's imagine that your town has a road detour and you are proceeding cautiously, navigating through unfamiliar streets. The girl behind you is tailing you so closely that you decide to slow down further, hoping she'll back off. Instead, you look in the rearview mirror and her face is contorted into a grimace and she's raising her middle finger at you. You are momentarily shocked.

Or, you're sitting in the bleachers during a Little League game, enjoying your son's winning streak. Kicked back, you're chatting with your neighbors, talking about this child's stance, that child's swing, another child's way of slapping his thigh before he puts the glove to his chest. To your far right a father on the other team is laughing good-naturedly at a child who has just slid into third base and is covered with dirt. "Oh, it doesn't matter," he says to no one in particular. "If he cleaned up, his parents wouldn't notice the difference anyway."

The child is dark skinned. You freeze. Should you walk past the folks between you and this man and say something to him? Ignore him, pretending that there are no racist implications? Should you comment to the person sitting next to you? Tell the coach? Or, just let it go? After all, it is one more thing you feel helpless to do anything about without causing a big stink you have no energy for anyway. "Life," you say to yourself.

Violence and Violation

What slice of life is it? These anecdotes are examples of violence and violation.[1] Even though violence and violation surround us, defining what they are is not easy. People are probably most aware of the category of *personal violence,* which occurs when we harm or injure another. We can observe the consequences, whether the harm is physical, psychological, spiritual, or material. We have no trouble grasping that a father will hurt his son if he beats him and will harm his daughter if he fondles her.

There is another kind of violence, though, that is both harder to notice and harder to discern how it affects us. This kind of violence occurs when the social system itself exploits some people to the benefit of others. It produces the same kind of harms, but to classes of individuals.[2]

The noted peace scholar, Johan Galtung, first proposed the term for this concept: *structural violence.* He provides a thought-provoking example of how personal and structural violence differ. If one husband beats his wife, that is obviously an instance of personal violence, he states, "but when one million husbands keep one million wives in ignorance there is structural violence."[3] Structural violence also creates social injustice.

Violation may be subtler and even more difficult to notice than violence. In fact, many people find themselves confused after an experience of violation, wondering what exactly happened to make them feel so awful. Violation occurs directly between people and indirectly through structural inequities and injustice. In addition, illness, disability, aging, discrimination, and immigration can set the stage for keenly felt experiences of violation. While violation may not leave a physical mark, there can be psychic traces, for violation disrupts our sense of meaning and makes us feel fear and dread.[4]

In this book I am particularly interested in the witnessing of everyday violence and violation, but I am keenly aware that what we experience as everyday depends on where we live and who we are. What I may witness in my daily life in a Boston suburb is different from what I would witness as everyday in rural Iowa, a South African township, a Palestinian refugee camp, or an Israeli city.

Everyday violence and violation can evolve from the small to the massive, from one beating to a gang war. Our responses as a society can also escalate, causing great harm. We may start by devaluing some people's worth, then stigmatizing them, then excluding them then, finally, controlling their lives.[5] A restriction here, an identity card there, may provoke violent protest followed by counter acts of genocide. But the cycles of violence and violation that cause common shock are preventable.[6] That's why our responses to violence and violation are also the subject of this book, since it is in understanding these responses that we have a chance to undermine them.

Common Shock

Witnessing violence and violation can produce common shock. I chose the word *common* to emphasize that the experience is widespread, it is collective, and it belongs to all of us.

Common shock is ubiquitous. Routinely, we experience events and exchanges that disturb us. Every one of us must metabolize daily jolts. Since few people are aware of the chronic debilitating effects of common shock, few people know how to deal with it themselves or, crucially, help children do so. This book will help you become aware of yourself as an everyday witness to violence and violation, and provide you with tools to cope effectively with its consequences.

Although trained as a clinical psychologist and family therapist in the early 1970s, my experience with witnessing violence and violation, and my sensitivity to it, long preceded my professional training. Throughout these pages I will be drawing on a range of experiences and sources to show that though unintentional witnessing of violence and violation is harmful, it can be transformed into intentional, compassionate witnessing, which has the potential for addressing and alleviating our misery and the misery of others. There are two sides to the witnessing coin: one in which we are shocked, and the other in which we know what to do.

But first we need to "catch" that we *are* witnessing violence and violation. Perhaps your teenage son, whose speech bears traces of the fact that he is a recent English speaker, and whose face is clearly Semitic, comes home and tells you that a shopkeeper in a music store harassed him and his Jordanian friends, warning them in a threatening voice that the store had surveillance cameras. Sure, your first concern is for your child. But, something has happened to you too. You are witnessing his violation. Your child has experienced discrimination and it has affected him and you both. You are upset and angry. How are you going to keep your rage from burning a helpless hole in your belly? This book provides ideas about this.

Many more people now than even a decade ago are comfortable thinking in terms of victims and perpetrators, whether as applied to how individuals, ethnic groups, or countries treat each other. However, we need to be similarly sophisticated about the effects of witnessing violence and cognizant of the witness.[7] We need to know when it is happening and what we can do about it. While many people accept that the situation is urgent with regard to catastrophic events, it is important for mundane acts of witnessing as well.

Common Shock Is Pervasive and Widespread

Like so many people I have a love/hate relationship to the morning newspaper. I am drawn to it because I care, and I feel an aversion to it because I care. I want to know what is happening in the world, the country, my state, and my town, but I am apprehensive also. I have friends in many parts of the world. I have worked in troubled regions—Kosovo, South Africa—and the news from these places is often upsetting. I worry about specific people I know and the problems that beset them. At home, broadly speaking, I work in the health and social-service sector. I anticipate with dread local stories about abuse and violence, for they are likely to affect the lives of people I know well, workers who toil in systems that grind them down as surely as the clients they try to serve.

Usually, my curiosity and responsibility win me over and I do read the newspaper. We have a joke in our family. Certain kinds of sharp inhalations of breath accompanied by short, staccato, suffocated sounds mean Mom is reading the newspaper. Actually, it means that Mom is experiencing common shock. The articles enter my consciousness. I am touched and troubled. However brief, the experience rankles, prickles, disturbs. The words are not just lines on paper, black marks on white. They transmigrate from there to here, so that—even for a moment—the story is now inside my internal world and I am upset. Then, I read on. To the next article, and the next. My reaction may happen five or fifteen times in one pass through the paper. Joke or not, my family is right; I am affected as I read the paper.

Or listen to the news. Try as I might, these days, I cannot make it background. I cannot make it just information. I have learned, finally, to turn the radio off when I feel my mood slip from whatever it was before I turned it on to whatever it must be to resonate with the pain and horror on the sound waves, lapping our psychic shores 24/7.

It is precisely this dimension of constancy that makes it so likely that there is an epidemic of gargantuan proportions in our world today. One with no name. A silent, all-but-invisible epidemic that is profoundly altering the course of our lives without our even knowing it.

By the time the average child is twelve years old in the United States, he has seen eight thousand murders and a hundred thousand acts of violence on network television. The problem with this isn't just quantity; the majority of these acts are presented as if there are no direct or physically or psychologically harmful effects, and without any moral judgment.[8] If common shock is an epidemic, these kinds of triggers are the pathogen. As in any illness epidemic, not everyone who is exposed to the pathogen will be negatively affected by it. Some people are hardier than others, either because they have had a lower lifetime exposure to violence and violation, making them less vulnerable to experiences that trigger common shock, and/or because their biological makeup assists them in restoring equilibrium more swiftly than others.

Adults observe violent acts, are affected by them, and yet may not even register what is going on. I am trained to recognize acts of violence and I am studying the phenomenon of common shock. Yet I have had occasions when others pointed out acts of violence retrospectively that I had entirely missed. In a self-inventory of my daily exposures to events and transactions that produce common shock, I would never have counted these instances. Which is exactly my point. Common shock is pervasive and we do not even know it.

Triggers and Effects

Common shock is triggered by our being witness to an event or an interaction that we appraise as disturbing, whether we are aware of this appraisal process or not. Triggers for common shock are ubiquitous and range from the garden variety to the rare. There is no way of predicting from the trigger whether everyone exposed to it will experience common shock. However, there are some events or interactions that are likely to produce common shock in anyone, such as witnessing a beating, a terrorist attack, or the unexpected death of a loved one.

Responses to these kinds of extreme events are likely to be severe, but not invariably so. Again, there is wide variation among people for many reasons, and responses will also vary over time. Some people who witnessed the planes hit the World Trade Center suffered from a severe form of common shock that most experts call a trauma response.[9] A trauma response disrupts our fundamental sense of who we are, who others are, and our sense of safety and security. It leaves us with feelings of horror, fear, and dread. It produces an "indelible mark" on our worldview.[10]

Eventually, most of the people who experience this severe form of common shock stabilize and go on to recover. Others do not. These people develop a complex response, which in the Western world may be diagnosed as PTSD, or posttraumatic stress disorder.[11] Their symptoms continue.

Although I am a mental-health professional, I do not believe that common shock should be solely understood as a mental-health problem. Common shock refers to human suffering, and we don't have to medicalize it to make it any more real or important to alleviate it. Most people in the world who experience even severe common-shock reactions never see a health-care worker. Most communities in the world deal with common shock through processes of collective healing that are as ancient as any of their other customs and practices.[12] In this book there are examples of knowledge that is widely dispersed in communities to help us deal with common shock.

Common shock includes these severe responses to extraordinary events, but the term directs our attention to something much more widespread: our witnessing a broad range of violation or violence that includes ordinary experiences that we may think have no impact but do. Imagine that you are standing in line at the pharmacy, and the person in front of you is hostile and rude to the clerk. You witness this interaction. Actually, in my neighborhood that is a fairly typical occurrence, especially at 6:00 P.M. when evening commuters are trying to complete errands and hurry home.

When it is your turn, imagine that you ignore what you have observed. In a sense you saw it, but you didn't take it in. You didn't think about the young cashier's feelings or the customer's behavior. It is a scene repeated many times before, and you are habituated or inured to it. You have done it yourself. If you had any response, it was "So what? No big deal." Or, "That's not my business." Or, "This is just going to make it take longer before I get my prescription and get home."

In responding this way you are a passive witness. You are aware that something happened, but you don't attribute any significance to it. You've been exposed to an event that could produce common shock, but it doesn't because it rolls right off you. In essence you are unaware that one person was hurtful to another. You have witnessed without awareness.

Witnessing without awareness, while it may have few immediate negative consequences for the witness, has profound negative consequences for the quality of life in our communities. Two other hypothetical scenarios in the line at the pharmacy will make my point even clearer.

Let us say that you observe the interaction between the irate customer and the clerk. You hear the customer berating the clerk for a problem that is clearly not of her making. The customer is blaming the messenger for the message. The customer's physician did not call in the prescription and the customer is blaming the clerk for not having called the customer to tell her so. The clerk is defending herself, trying to explain that the pharmacist had called again but that the physician had not returned the call.

You are appalled by what you hear, but you feel frozen. You look away as if averting your eyes can distance you from this unpleasant encounter you wish were not happening. You feel bad for the clerk, angry with the customer, sorry for yourself, and a little bit ashamed too. You wish you didn't need your item because you would like to vanish.

You are certainly witnessing with awareness, but you do not know what to do. You feel helpless. Even though this happens a lot, you have no clue how to respond. You take your turn in line and avoid the clerk's eyes as best as you can, pretending that the previous interaction didn't happen. You leave the pharmacy with a lingering bad taste in your mouth. You notice that your body feels jangled. You have butterflies in your stomach and although you want to listen to the music you have turned on, you cannot concentrate on it. You may be able to shake it before you get home, or you may arrive in a bad mood, responding with irritation at the nightly shenanigans of your children that usually amuse you. It is as if your head is still replaying the scene in the pharmacy and a part of you is still there, not in the present moment with your family. Later, in bed, you are surprised by a nightmare, an old-fashioned-type

Western movie, where a bad guy comes into town and bullies two women in a dry-goods store and then spills red paint over bolts of their cloth.

Being upset, not knowing what to do, and then being disturbed by it for a time afterward is an experience we have all had. Who among us has been taught how to respond to these kinds of situations? Even professionally trained therapists I work with tell me that they, too, are often at a loss for what to do. When I take them through the steps I have developed to help them learn how to witness, it is an enormous relief. These steps are not hard to learn, for adults or children, as I will make clear in Part Three of this book.

Here is the final hypothetical scenario: You hear the interaction between the customer and the clerk and it upsets you. It produces common shock, one side of the witnessing coin. But you have an idea of something to do; the other side of the witnessing coin. When it is your turn, you want to acknowledge what has happened, but you also must get home. You step up to the counter and you look at the clerk directly. You give her a smile of sympathy. "Gee," you say as you hand her your prescription, "that customer was really unkind. I'm sorry that happened to you. I hope the rest of your evening is better." She smiles warmly back at you and says, "Thanks."

You have made a human connection that feels good to both of you. It is comforting to the clerk, and your ability to comfort her comforts you. Your bodies relax. Your minds feel calmer. You have made your local community a kinder place. You go home feeling a little more energetic than you usually do at this hour.

We can learn to transform passive, inadvertent, or unintentional witnessing into active acts of compassionate witnessing. These acts need not be big, dramatic, or sustained. They can be short and small, "ant steps," as a South African colleague of mine labels them.[13] Even small ones can make a difference to our families, our communities, the world, and us. The steps can be learned and they can be taught. Habits formed in the here and now, in the ordinary comings and goings of daily life, create connections with others that can sustain us. Habits formed in the present will be there when we need them in the future.

Unwitting Witnessing

Globalization now encompasses exposure to violence and violation anywhere in the world. Through the sweeping reach of media we have the potential to witness disturbing events all over the planet. I read a newspaper account of a two-year-old girl who had fallen into a well in Romania. The paper reported that millions of Romanians watched the rescue effort, which was broadcast on all three of Romania's television stations over a period of six hours.[14] Surely many viewers, seeing the distraught mother, knowing a young, helpless child was down in a dark well, must have experienced common shock. At the same time, many people may also have watched this human drama as if it were a particularly exciting made-for-TV movie. They wouldn't let themselves fully connect to the pathos of the situation.

A recent study published by the *Journal of the American Medical Association* provides an example closer to home. In my state of Massachusetts one in five high school girls has experienced physical or sexual abuse from a boyfriend. The study explored the relationships between their abuse and the major areas of adolescent health risk that had previously been identified by comparing the responses of girls who reported abuse with those who did not. Not surprisingly, girls who had been abused were more likely to engage in such risky behavior as heavy smoking, binge drinking, multiple sex partners, and attempted suicide than their nonabused peers.[15]

I read about this study in the newspaper and made one of those sharp inhalations. I am married to a physician and so I was able to read the full text of the article in his medical journal when it arrived the next day. I know these girls; I see them in my office, where I practice as a psychologist and family therapist, and I hear about them in the various settings in which I supervise and consult to other clinicians. Having heard these stories so many times over the years, I can create a scene, extend the time frames, and feel what happens not just when the slap or shove or threat occurs, but after. I also know that the girl who is abused on one day is likely to be a witness to similar acts of abuse suffered by her girlfriends on another. Studies often fail to ask questions about what people have witnessed, even though this is such a common pathway of exposure to violence and violation.

I can easily imagine that this girl has driven up to the school parking lot with her boyfriend. They're joking around, listening to a CD, singing, feeling silly and fine, and happy to see a crowd still hanging around the school. He parks, tweaks her spaghetti straps affectionately, they get out of the car, and he says, "Come here." She doesn't hear him. She's seen a friend and has started to walk toward her. He calls over to her, "Hey!" Distracted, she turns her head, now several feet away from the car, and looks at him with a questioning expression on her face. His tone escalates. "I said, come here!" She misreads this cue, thinks he is joking, that they are still having fun. She gives him a big grin, meaning, *You're so cute,* tosses her head back, and continues walking toward her friend. The next thing she feels is his hand on the small of her back, shoving her and she, not expecting it, loses her balance and falls to the ground. Caught off guard, she is shook up.

And so are others. About half of the twenty or so boys and girls milling around are turned in such a way that they witness his push and see her stumble to the ground. The next moments are a blur for many of them. Some of them "see" her pick herself up, look wide-eyed at her boyfriend, and, with tears in her eyes, say, "What did you do that for?" Others "see" her look at her girlfriend, who runs toward her, saying to the boyfriend, "What did you do that for?" Or, they "see" her turn to her boyfriend and with rage in her voice say, "What did you do that for?" Some of these witnesses experience common shock.

According to the report, that push may affect her at the moment and beyond, for hours, days, weeks, months, even years to come. It can affect her relationship to her body (she may use harmful substances; she may have unprotected sex), and it can affect her state of mind (she may consider or attempt suicide). It can also affect the members of her community. Even her boyfriend, who may be startled by his own aggression, though he mught justify it to himself, to her, and to others.

The effects of one shove seep out. The girl tells her cousin, who tells her to break up with the jerk. The cousin tells her husband, who tells his wife it's not a big deal. As a witness to his wife's cousin's experience he has no reaction. Or, he does experience common shock. He tells his wife he'll settle the score, and then sets out to find the boyfriend. These young men are now engaged in a scenario that places them at great risk.[16]

There is a lot of violence. There are a lot of witnesses to it. We know that violence begets violence, and we are beginning to understand that witnessing violence does too.[17] Nor are all the aftereffects of violence immediate. I work with a man whose father was physically violent toward his mother. He witnessed his mother being hit and he overheard terrible fights when he should have been asleep, but he was too frightened to relax into slumber. Although he is well educated about trauma, it had never really dawned on him that many of his disturbing feelings and behaviors at that time—and later—could be attributed to his having been a witness to his father's violence. He would say, "But I wasn't hit." He also remembered his father specifically telling him he had no right to his feelings.

Legitimizing Our Common Shock Responses

This anecdote raises another issue. For many of us it is difficult to give legitimacy to our own suffering as witnesses when the victims clearly suffer more. My male client could not register his own pain when he saw his mother's pain.[18]

While it is absolutely essential that we be capable of registering differences in scale, of appreciating, for instance, the difference between witnessing a slap or an ethnic slur on the one hand, and suffering an assault or racial profiling on the other, it isn't useful to use that appreciation of the difference to trivialize our distress if it comes from a lesser cause. Critical judgments about whether or not we are "entitled" to feel distress make us less aware of our own common shock. The goal is to care about all kinds and degrees of suffering, mindful that they are not the same.

Many of us are inured to common shock triggers. There are probably many reasons for this. First, there is the obvious: we are saturated with scenes and stories that are upsetting and disturbing and we defend ourselves from letting each one penetrate. Second, we develop habits of screening over time, so that we only barely notice what we are keeping out of mind. Third, many of us were trained as children to inhibit our common shock responses, perhaps because we were humiliated by a parent or peer for our reactions. We learned that it was not safe to let ourselves register our common shock responses, or we felt shame when we did. Humiliation and shame are aversive, and strengthen self-anesthetizing, which for some people may actually permit a fascination with and enjoyment of violence that would otherwise be intolerable. Whether adults or peers stop us from expressing our feelings, we learn that our feelings make others uncomfortable. Silenced, we become silent.

There are potentially serious consequences, however, to blunting our experience of common shock. In a series of experiments first conducted in the early 1960s, Stanley Milgram designed an experimental study of obedience.[19] He invited people into a laboratory setting to assist him, supposedly, with an experiment on "learning." He wanted to observe the conditions under which someone would deliver a shock to a volunteer "learner" when the learner made a mistake. The learner was actually a confederate of the experimenter. No shock was actually delivered. However, the learner/actor grunted at 75 volts, complained verbally at 120 volts, and demanded to be released from the experiment at 150 volts. In the original experiment twenty-six people (65 percent) obeyed the experimenters' instructions fully and administered the highest shock possible despite hearing agonized screams from the learner. Fourteen people refused to do so after the learner began protesting. Although this was a research project undertaken in an academic laboratory, its applicability to real-life situations is evident.[20]

In the nearly forty years since this initial experimental procedure was published, there have been numerous replications of the study, many with intriguing variations. The findings have been remarkably consistent: A large proportion of individuals do administer shocks at higher and higher levels. They register the learners' minor distress, they witness it, but obey the experimenter and keep going, even tolerating their own intense personal distress. Those who administer the shocks are ordinary people, not aberrant souls at the margins of civil society. They are people inured to their own experience of common shock, with what would have been disastrous consequences to others had the electric jolts been real.

However painful it is to be aware of ourselves as witnesses to violence and violation, it is ultimately worthwhile to be so. If we are aware, we have choices. If we are inured, we can follow commands or take actions on our own that will horrify us later when we do let ourselves fully take in the reality of the situation. Aware of our common shock, we can work with it to mitigate violence in our lives.

Societal Implications

Common shock presents us with many challenges. The causes can be natural, man-made, or accidental; intentional or unwitting; insensitive or monstrous. Common shock experiences vary along a continuum from mild to severe and from normal to abnormal. We need to find ways to address all of these, not just the ones that "qualify" as significant. As a society we have collectively committed ourselves to deploy health-care and public-health resources to those events—like natural or man-made disasters—that produce massive disruption in people's lives. We accept that these experiences are problematic not just for the individuals involved but for society as well.

However, it is also important to attend to the milder distress responses to seemingly "minor" events and transactions that we witness. Some, certainly, will provoke transitory upset that vanishes, perhaps even out of recall. But some apparently minor upset isn't insignificant at all, nor will the long-term consequences necessarily be trivial. Paying attention to even mild common shock is constructive.

First, the effects of common shock cumulate. Even mild common shock, repeated over and over, may make us vulnerable to more major reactions at another time. Children who witness abuse in their families and people who are exposed to community violence are at risk for developing a variety of health and mental-health problems. In the early days after the terrorist attacks in America, many trauma experts accurately predicted that those who would suffer the most extreme reactions were those who were most directly exposed to death, injury, and loss. But they also cautioned that those who were sensitized to violence and violation by previous exposure to it would also be at high risk.

A second reason to pay attention to common shock experiences to seemingly minor triggers is that it may lead us to surprising, unexpected, and helpful insights into our lives. The triggers may be microcosms of larger issues. For instance, one time my family and I were having dinner with a black South African physician who was staying with us for a few days. In exile during the apartheid era, he had returned to the country at a time when there was still massive turmoil and unrest. He told us many stories, one of which I cannot shake, perhaps because *he* was so visibly shaken telling it to us.

He told us about an evening when a black five-year-old girl from a township who had been repeatedly raped had been brought to a clinic by her grandmother to be examined by him. "I have dealt with many victims of rape," he told us, "but it was one gesture she made that got me. I told her I would need to examine her, and before I could explain what I needed to do, she opened her little legs wide. It was utterly shocking."

That one small movement, spreading her legs apart, spoke for all the terrible oppressions that rocked her world and his. It was emblematic of the corrupting, destructive power dynamics that pitted white-skinned people against darker-skinned people, males against females, older people against younger ones, and stronger-bodied persons against weaker ones. Our South African friend wept, not just for the little girl, but also for the injustices her gesture expressed.

Empathy, the ability both to understand another's experience and to feel what she might feel, is a third reason to pay attention to common shock.[21] Experiences of common shock that result from minor matters help us appreciate the life circumstances of people whose common shock experiences are far more frequent and severe than ours, creating an empathic bridge. With such appreciation we are more likely and able to take action together with and on behalf of people whose lives otherwise have made them seem unlike us.[22]

A client of mine's son, age six, was taken to a local hospital emergency room for a severe asthma attack. While he was there, a man was brought in covered in blood from a gunshot wound. The child was clearly upset at the time, and subsequently he was more reluctant than before to return to the hospital for his treatment. His mother and I talked about ways she could help him, and eventually our conversation also turned to what she might learn from the experience herself.

We realized that her experience could help her create an empathic bridge to others. The task was to see if she could use her experience as a stepping-stone to understand the dilemmas faced by mothers living in communities where their children are often exposed to violence,[23] without equating their experience with hers, or her child's experience with theirs.[24] Again, the point is not that the situation is similar to community violence, but that we can use experience in one situation to gain an appreciation of another. We may be more motivated to do so. Or we may feel that we have more of a starting place from which to understand than we had before. In attending to even relatively minor common shock experiences, we practice the habits that will help us respond to our own and others' major common shock experiences.

How we respond to common shock has significant effects on our own lives, and our individual responses have ramifications for the society as a whole. The individual's response may be directly or indirectly precipitated by larger social events or movements, and the collective response of those individuals to their personal common shock experiences may have a significant impact on the public character of the social order.

I have seen this recently in Kosovo, where I spent time in 2000 and 2001, working with Kosovar Albanian mental-health clinicians.[25] In Kosovo, Albanian villagers were made to watch the massacres of loved ones and neighbors. Everyone I met had experienced common shock and, in some form, was continually exposed to reminders that produced common shock experiences. For most, the exposure was of traumatic proportions.[26]

In Kosovo the consequences of political decisions made at the regional and international level are writ large on the bodies and minds of the people. It can be felt, for example, looking in the eyes of a twenty-two-year-old Kosovar mother who rarely puts her toddler down, so vivid is her memory of the day a Serbian paramilitary soldier pointed his gun at her child and demanded her gold necklace. When I met this mother, it was fourteen months after the episode. She was living in a large extended-family compound in a rural community, spending the vast majority of her time with women relatives, all of whom were also severely distressed. The other women remarked on her inability to separate from her child and were concerned about it.

What effects will this have on the little boy, a witness to his mother's common shock at having witnessed a threat to his life? How will he interpret the messages he gets from his mother as she holds him tightly to her? What impact will this have on his subsequent actions as a young man in a land whose ownership and control have been contested for generations? And what of the other hundreds of thousands of children, those living now and those who will be born, whose experience of this time in Kosovo's history will definitively shape its future?

Precisely because effects go both ways—from citizens to society and society to citizenry—it is difficult to dissect neatly the private dimensions of those events and transactions from the public ones that give rise to common shock. This book is written in the hopes of changing our collective response to the witnessing of violence. First, we need to become aware of common shock experiences in others and ourselves. These are the "thousand natural shocks/ That flesh is heir to,"[27] Hamlet's phrase that gives this chapter its title. Next, we need to know what to do about them. Violence creates a social fabric that is both torn and degraded. This book offers an approach to repair that every one of us can undertake.

Overview of the Book

I present a way of understanding the two-sided phenomenon of witnessing, both its toxic power and healing potential. There is no point in trying to shield ourselves from witnessing violence and violation; we couldn't even if we wanted to. But we can act on the insight that witnessing violence and violation is harmful to us by learning more about how it affects our bodies, minds, relationships, communities, and world.

I am particularly indebted to the hundreds of children, adults, couples, and families I have worked with over the last thirty years for insights about both sides of the witnessing coin. Disguised, some of their stories appear in this book.* I have also served as the clinical director of a trauma evaluation and treatment team in the Boston area for a decade, and insights from those years inform these pages. In the last two years I have read over a thousand articles, chapters, or books, and spoken with hundreds of people in many parts of the world to synthesize what people know about witnessing, from direct firsthand experience as well as scholarly ideas about facets of it. Finally, I have paid close attention to the stories of my own life that have made me so interested in witnessing, and so sure that witnessing well can be healing.

In Part One I will show how certain kinds of witnessing harm us while another, compassionate witnessing, when conditions are safe and

*In order to protect clients' privacy and confidentiality, case material is either fictional or composite, drawn from my clinical and supervisory practice.

we have deliberately chosen our action, can be positive. As readers you face the challenges of witnessing even in reading this book. It is important to pace yourself at a rate that you can manage without getting uncomfortably upset or going numb.

Over the years I have come to understand that there are multiple pathways through which we are exposed to violence and violation, some of which I had been oblivious to. It has been sobering and exhilarating to realize the ways our lives are affected by witnessing. Part Two details four paths by which we are exposed to violence and violation and shows the connections between events happening on the global stage and those that happen within our families and inside our very cells.

Part Three addresses what we can do about this. My focus is on the ordinary and the everyday because I believe that we can make a difference, right now, right here, wherever we happen to be. Compassionate witnessing has the potential for transforming violence at every level, from the personal to the societal. Few of us are in a position to change the world dramatically, with one action, but all of us can change the world by transforming how we witness the violence and violation we observe daily. While the book addresses the shadows they cast upon our lives, it also shows us how to step into the light.

The Varieties of Witnessing Experience

Flarebombs bloom on the dark sky.
A child clasps his hands and laughs.
I hear the sound of guns,
and the laughter dies.

But the witness
Remains.

—Thich Nhât Hanh[1]

Many of the critical questions of our lives revolve around the questions: Why do we act? And, why don't we act? In a small New England town, population 1,800, a young girl reported that she was pinned to the ground by four third-grade boys and "humped" in the presence of several classmates. Most of the children did nothing to stop it.[2]

This is not an aberrant response. Researchers have found that nearly two thirds of all incidents of bullying and harassment occur in the presence of other people, and of these, in only a minority of cases does a child attempt to assist the victim or call for help.[3] According to a newspaper account, a young boy who witnessed the incident with the young girl and her four assailants did report it to a teacher, who told him to "mind your own business."[4] It turns out that teachers also intervene in a minority of bullying and harassment episodes they are told about or observe.[5]

From children and adults who are bystanders to bullying, to communities who are bystanders to ethnic or racial discrimination, people often behave as if paralyzed. And, in effect, they are. As we have seen in Chapter One, witnessing can produce common shock. People can behave as if they are physically frozen, psychologically afraid and helpless, and caught in complex relationship dynamics that trap them into silence and inaction. Bystanders are often people who are overwhelmed by what they witness. If we understand better the experience and consequences of witnessing violence and violation, we will be better able to assist those who witness violence and violation help those who are directly harmed by it.

When I was a child, I was often in the bystander position in my family. My father had outbursts of temper that seemed to come out of nowhere. He was a bold, passionate man who had excellent judgment, and, most of the time, he was lively and fun to be with. But sometimes he would explode. My sister, who is four years older than I am, was more often the target of his occasional rages. But I was a witness to the scenes. My sister was canny and understood my father considerably better than I did. When he would rev up and she could tell he was about to explode, she would take off running. He would follow suit. I would often miss the cues and think my father was playing a game of chase. Not wanting to miss the fun, I would run after my father, who was running after my sister. At some point I would grasp that he was angry with her. Sometimes I would stop and get out of the way as quickly as I could, but sometimes there was enough ambiguity in the situation that I would continue to race after my father. Partly, I didn't like being left out. Partly, I was curious. And partly there was always the chance they would end up laughing, and I wanted to be there if that happened.

One Saturday morning when I was about six years old, all three of us were romping on the living room floor when my father abruptly stopped playing. First, my sister got up and began running away, and then my father rose off the floor and began "chasing" my sister around the house. She sped ahead of him, and I followed him in hot pursuit of her. My sister ran down the basement stairs and bolted out the door.

Seeing my sister leave the house must have surprised my father. "Invisible" until then, I was just steps behind him. He wheeled around, grabbed me, brought me over to a couch, flung me over his knees, and he yelled at my sister, who was peering through the glass door, "If you don't come inside, I'm going to hurt your sister!" My sister looked stunned, but only momentarily. Then, out of her much superior understanding of our father than I had at the time, she began to laugh. Just as she had calculated, he let me go, the anger released from his body, and he walked away. I was left shaking and in shock on the couch, sure that I had narrowly escaped a beating.

This incident and the one about the girl in the small town illustrate a key point about violence. We are used to thinking about violence as a drama with two roles: the victim and the perpetrator. In fact, in the majority of cases there is a drama with three positions: a victim, a perpetrator, and a bystander. The bystander, or witness, the term I prefer, may be present during the episode or may learn about it later, as the teacher and my mother did. In either case, the violence between the victim and the perpetrator affects the witness as well. The witness may respond in ways that are helpful, equivocal, or harmful.

Nor are the roles of victim, perpetrator, and witness static. Sometimes roles shift, as my sister's and mine did. Occasionally, the witness occupies an "invisible" role to the victim and the perpetrator, and to the wider community as well.[6] Newspapers don't always mention whether there were witnesses present, and unless the circumstances are unusual or they are interviewed for their comments about what they saw, we generally have the impression that most events between victims and perpetrators occur without others watching.

In this chapter I pay close attention to the witness to see what we can learn about this role in daily life. We know a great deal about victims and perpetrators. We need to know as much about the witness. If we do, we will have a better chance of being witnesses who respond constructively. Witnesses can play a key role in transforming everyday violence.

Clearly, the dynamics of witnessing are complex, as these two opening anecdotes make clear. In my family story I started off as a witness to my father in pursuit of my sister, and the story ends with my sister as my witness, cleverly rescuing me from my father's threat of violence. I was a clueless witness, not thinking for a moment I could help my sister. She, on the other hand, shifted her position from victim to witness in a split second and acted instantly in a way that helped me. In this chapter I present terms for different kinds of witnessing that provide some tools for thinking about how we can turn unintentional witnessing into an actively chosen, constructive act of witnessing. Each of us has opportunities in our daily life to practice intentional witnessing, where we can assist others and avoid feeling helpless and overwhelmed ourselves. I call this compassionate witnessing.

Witness, Victim, and Perpetrator Roles

First, let's consider the three positions in the drama. The **witness** role exists in relation to the other two roles of victim and perpetrator. In this book the witness is always a person or a group of people.[7] There are many ways a witness sees or hears. Sometimes we see for ourselves or are told, and sometimes we read or see images created later that evoke the presence of the witness.[8] In any case we are always "on the scene," and we cannot escape being witnesses.

A **victim** can be a person, a group, a community, a building, a city or an ideology. For instance, a person can be shot, a community devastated by a hurricane, or a group targeted by ethnic hatred. Many people felt that along with the more than three thousand people who died in the September 11 terrorist attacks in the United States, the American way of life was also the intended victim.

Perpetrators produce victims by a variety of processes. Sometimes perpetrators are people: strangers or intimates; groups or corporations. For instance, a perpetrator may be your boyfriend, someone who claims to love you but reacts violently to perceived insults and beats you. Or, companies that knowingly discard their toxic waste into landfills or water supplies can be considered perpetrators.

Man-made or natural disasters produce victims. Wars create victims and the nations that wage wars or commit genocide are the perpetrators. Hurricanes, volcanoes, floods, and tornadoes are disasters that produce victims through force of nature. Insidious processes such as racism, poverty, sexism, anti-Semitism, and homophobia produce victims by threatening people's sense of security and safety.[9] These processes, manifestations of structural violence, often carried out by economic or technocratic methods, can produce millions of victims with devastating outcomes. The racism embedded in the American health-care system, for instance, illustrates this phenomenon, with African-Americans having suffered from inferior health care and consequently poorer health outcomes than whites for nearly four hundred years.[10]

Finally, illnesses create victims through biological processes that go awry. Probably the most familiar metaphor we have of a biological process as perpetrator is cancer. Colloquially, we use phrases like *cancer victim* and *cancer survivor* without quite registering that in doing so we are implying that the cancer itself, the erratic or uncontrolled growth of cells, is the perpetrator. When we call cancer a "killer," we are drawing on our feelings about perpetrators and victims, even though most people would probably feel queasy drawing out the comparison to its fullest conclusion. Certainly, a person with cancer might have an even harder time than she already does thinking she is walking around with a "killer" in her body.

The **witness** is in a position to observe the interaction between the perpetrator and the victim. Sometimes the witnessing happens at the exact moment of the interaction, and sometimes it happens far into the future. James Gilligan, the forensic psychiatrist who writes about extreme lethal violence, begins his book *Violence: Reflections on a National Epidemic,* with a family story, overheard as a young child and seen in "his mind's eye, when as a child he overheard the adults talking after dinner in front of the fireplace, describing events to each other that they considered unsuitable to tell a child even half a century after the events had occurred. . . ."[11]

He was a witness to a family tragedy of violence complicated by its commingling with mystery, love, and injustice. The plot: A mixed-race mother bakes a pie filled with rat poison, and her beloved son, target of her Irish husband's physical abuse, is found dead at the bottom of a well, his body full of the poison. Soon after, she disappears. The story, of course, has layers of complexity. Did she poison her son? Did she run away, kill herself, or was she murdered? Gilligan's book bears the stamp of the witness who "remains," who has known something at the deepest levels of awareness before he was even able to articulate it.

Sometimes we *are* present when a perpetrator harms a victim. We see or hear the violence, but act as if we don't or can't register it. Blind to our witnessing, we may nonetheless express symptoms. However, it is hard to manage distress if we cannot account for it. Many people seek elaborate explanations for their chronic jumpiness, anxiety, or unhappiness that I believe can be explained by understanding what they have witnessed, either as children or adults.

As a therapist I often see clients for whom there has been an exceedingly long lag time before they let themselves grasp that they were witnesses to violence or violation. The realization is often profoundly disturbing, as if one's carefully crafted life story will now have to be rewritten to replace the one that shielded the person from knowing what he was not ready to know.

One client of mine, an accomplished scientist, was estranged from his younger brother and had a difficult, competitive relationship with his father. For example, if my client told his father about something amusing he had done over the weekend, his father would always counter with a description of the even better time he had had. During one session my client was expressing anger at his father for failing to see him as a separate person whose accomplishments did not have to diminish his. In the midst of his complaint he paused, then burst into tears. Moments later he told me that he had seen an image of his father and younger brother playing tennis. In the image he could see his father prancing about the back court, gloating over winning a point from his twelve-year-old son. His brother's shoulders were hunched over as he walked slowly back to the serving line from the net, into which he had hit the ball.

Letting himself fully take in the implications of this scene, my client felt himself become a witness to his father and brother. My client realized that his brother, too, had been the object of his father's competitive struggles, perhaps in ways that were even more injurious than those that had made him feel diminished by his father. He began to wonder if his relationship with his younger brother might have been affected by his having been so caught up in his own relationship with their father that he had failed to see his father's behavior toward his brother. He wondered whether his insight that he had been an unaware witness would prove useful to their relationship, and whether he could take up the role of witness to his brother's experience in the present.

In another session this same client shared a disturbing thought. Had he, in some way, participated in his father's humiliation of his brother? Had he derived some relief, perhaps even pleasure, at not being the object of his father's competition at those times? Had he been a perpetrator himself?

The question is an ancient one, as is the answer. The three-role drama, in which victim, perpetrator, and witness are intricately related to one another, also plays out as a drama inside every one of us. We have the potential to occupy all three roles and we all *have* acted from each role. We may not like to face this about ourselves, but most of us know that this is true. It is part of the human condition.

An Egyptian myth illuminates this perfectly.[12] In the myth Osiris, a beloved ruler of Egypt, is murdered by his brother Set. Osiris is married to Isis, who is also his sister. Set is jealous of Osiris and plots against him, eventually succeeding in killing him. First, Set seals Osiris with molten lead into a coffin and then he throws the casket into the Nile. Isis grieves terribly for Osiris and determines to discover his casket. Eventually, she does, at which point Set chops the body into pieces and flings them to the far corners of the land. Isis journeys to collect Osiris, traveling the earth to find his pieces. A healer, Isis collects the pieces to remember her beloved Osiris.

Osiris and Set are brothers. In mythic and dramatic terms the relationship of brothers directs our attention to a universal truth: Set the murderer is an aspect of the "good" Osiris. All of us are both Set and Osiris, perpetrator and victim.[13]

The other day I spoke to a neighbor who told me a story about her eight-year-old son, Tom, that perturbed her. Someone in his classroom was scribbling on the children's drawings that hung on the walls. The teacher had called all the children together into a circle several times to talk about these disturbing deeds. No child in the class confessed to having committed them.

The teacher encouraged them to express how they felt about seeing their work defaced. The children were all upset; they felt violated and frightened. They discussed the importance of respect for others and also the property of others. They discussed the value of coming forward and telling the truth. Still someone sat among them and lied. My neighbor's son articulated that he felt creepy knowing that someone who might be a close friend of his was behaving secretly in a way that didn't fit with his public behavior.

My neighbor continued. The previous weekend she had been out doing errands and called home to talk to her husband. Tom had answered and told her that his father was napping and couldn't come to the phone. My neighbor thought that was strange, but she didn't say anything. When she arrived home a few minutes later, she was surprised to see her husband planting bulbs in the yard. She asked him if he had just gotten up from a nap and he looked puzzled. "No," he had said, "I've been outside." Why had Tom lied, she asked me, especially during this time when he was so upset about a child in his class lying?

While there may be many complex psychological explanations for Tom's behavior, I offered my neighbor a relatively simple observation. Tom was showing his family that he was affected by what he was witnessing in his classroom. A victim and witness at school, he did to his parents what the classroom perpetrator was doing to him. I told my neighbor that I thought it was as if a little piece of the toxicity of the violation Tom was experiencing had worked its way into him and he was trying to understand it by doing it himself. I suggested that she make that connection for him and see if that helped him.

This incident illustrates the point: We all have the potential to play out all three roles under certain circumstances. Of course, I wonder, too, about the child in Tom's class who is committing the acts of vandalism. What has he seen? What has been done to him?

Witness Positions

All of us, whichever role we are currently in, can witness ourselves. We can become aware of what we see—witnessing ourselves as witnesses. We can become aware of what has happened to us—witnessing ourselves as victims. And we can become aware of what we do to others—witnessing ourselves as perpetrators. More able to witness ourselves in each of these roles, we will be better able to witness others in each of these roles as well.

Awareness is a key element in developing the capacity for self-witnessing. However, awareness is not itself a panacea. It does not always yield a sense of control. Nor does it bring clarity about or melt obstacles to action. An aware witness may suffer. In fact, witnessing experiences may evoke a wide range of feelings. For instance, some people agonize when they observe a person's distress, while others take voyeuristic pleasure in it. Likewise, I have worked with children who were terrified by their parents' fighting and others whom it made furious. Some witnesses feel hostility. I was once crossing a street and overheard an elderly woman speak harshly to her young companion about a homeless man they were passing. The older woman said derisively, "Put away your money. He's been here for three years. He can't really be needy!" What might have elicited pity from someone else evoked scorn from her.

While the quality of witnessing experience has considerable variation, there are two dimensions that reliably influence it: context and perceived intent.[14] Regarding the context, it makes a difference if you are the only one who witnesses an event or if there are other people—even one person—with whom to share the experience. Witnessing violence or violation in isolation compounds people's distress. It also makes a difference whether the violence you witness is intentional or accidental. People have a harder time witnessing situations they perceive as maliciously perpetrated than they do a harm they perceive as unintentional.

Coexisting with this variation are a limited number of witness positions. I developed a model of witness positions by thinking about my experience witnessing my mother's cancer diagnosis and death. (We will see in Chapter Four the ways that witnessing the illness, dying, and death of a loved one can produce common shock.) Moving between my evolving scheme and my family story, I decided to represent my ideas graphically by drawing a two-by-two grid of witness positions that shows that one's position as a witness is influenced by whether or not one is aware and whether or not one feels empowered in relation to any aspect of what one is witnessing [See Figure One].[15]

These dimensions captured something essential about what happened in our family during the period of my mother's illness and death. My mother remained unaware of the implications of her condition throughout much of that time. She was an uninformed witness to her own death. One episode is particularly vivid, perhaps because it was the first, and emblematic of what was to come.

After learning my mother had a rare, invariably fatal and aggressive cancer, my father chose a physician to be my mother's oncologist. Although Dr. P. was clear that my mother's tumor was metastatic, he also believed that the secondary tumors had been successfully surgically removed. He strongly recommended that we only tell my mother that she was now cancer-free. He assured my father that technically this was so.

Figure One: Witness Positions

	Aware	Unaware
Empowered	1	2
Disempowered	4	3

They had been unable to find the primary tumor, he argued, so there was, in fact, no current evidence of cancer in her body. The year was 1974. Dr. P.'s approach was well within the norms of "benevolent" patient care as well as congruent with popularly held ideas about cancer as an inevitably fatal disease that ravages patients. At that time secrecy was considered protective and kind.[16]

My father did an excellent job of keeping my sister, her husband, my husband, Hilary, and me informed. However, when he told my sister and me about his disclosure game-plan the day before we were all to visit my mother, she and I were stunned. We had talked about what our mother "should" be told, and we knew we didn't want to lie or withhold the truth from her. On the one hand we felt that our father was putting us in an untenable situation. On the other hand we didn't feel that the time was right to confront him with our point of view. Further, we wanted to see what our mother's needs were. We wanted to assess whether her wishes seemed to coincide with our father's plans or our beliefs.

On the afternoon that we visited her, six of us were at her bedside. Thoughtfully, carefully, with compassion, Dr. P. did not tell her the whole truth. Nor did he lie. The five of us appeared to be accepting and endorsing what he wanted my mother to believe, and yet it turned out, each of us meant something a little bit different by our participation in that bedside ritual. I meant that I accepted that my father was in the lead. I respected his right to his point of view and I did not want to cause him more pain by challenging him. For me the moment was a starting place. I did not appreciate then that our family might be signaling my mother that *we* could not tolerate her knowing what we knew. Twenty-seven years later I fear that is precisely the message we sent. The rest of the bedside visit was loving and odd. For me it was also surreal, because it was real in a way I so profoundly did not want.

At that moment and in the months that followed, I was an aware and passive witness, helpless to get my father or my mother's doctor to change their views. I felt totally disempowered. I believed that my mother had no hope of a cure and therefore the one achievable hope she had—we all had—was to stay in authentic connection to each other throughout her illness and death. This required her being aware of what was happening to her. She couldn't be empowered with respect to a cure—there wasn't one available—but she could be an aware and active witness to the knowledge that she would die from this cancer.

This was not to be the case. My father and her doctor saw themselves as aware and empowered witnesses to my mother's fate. I saw them as empowered, but unaware of my mother's state. They remained in power, creating the most painful circumstance of my adult life to that point.

As this story shows, our witness positions were in relation to different aspects of the complex situation. My father was focused on shielding my mother from the certain knowledge that she would die soon. Dr. P encouraged him to press my sister and me to protect our mother from this knowledge. Unable to control the progression of her disease, my father felt he was acting in the most loving way he could: blocking the shadow of death from intruding on her enjoyment of the present. My father's decision was consistent with many cultures' beliefs and with norms of his and my mother's generation.

I felt helpless and enraged by my father's directives to keep the truth from our mother, and I tried all kinds of ways to abide by the letter but not the spirit of his decision. I was certain that our mother would have wanted the experience that would have come from facing her death together. I felt that the secret isolated my mother from me at the deepest levels of connection to which she and I had aspired since my young adulthood. I adored my mother and couldn't bear feeling separate from her in life in advance of what would happen soon enough.

We all played multiple roles in this story. Among other characterizations I could make, I would say that my mother was both a victim of and a witness to the machinations that surrounded her. My father was a victim of the doctor's superior knowledge claims, a perpetrator of the doctor's unyielding point of view, and a witness to his wife's factual ignorance and his daughters' frustrated rage. I was a victim of my father's demand, a witness to all of our pain at the imminent loss of our wife and mother, and a saboteur of my father's wishes.

My mother lived for twenty-six months, and as witness positions often do, ours changed over time (Figure Two). Eventually, following a second surgery, she was told by an intern that she had an incurable cancer. This disclosure shifted everyone's position. Ultimately, every witness position creates consequences for the individual, family, community, and society (Figure Three). Each carries possibilities, challenges, and risks. Although I think it is desirable to be an aware and active witness, this is often a difficult position to achieve.

I have presented this witnessing grid in many countries, asking for stories that illuminate the four positions in order to compile a Witnessing Archive to circulate to others for whom the stories might hold resonance, consolation, and inspiration.[17] A young woman from Australia sent one to the archive that well illustrates the poignancy of trying to take an active, aware witnessing position, not accomplishing your primary goal but achieving others.

Tracy is a social worker for a private welfare organization. One day she was at a staff meeting in which there was discussion of making a video for fund-raising purposes. They then began talking about how to select the families who would be showcased. Tracy offered a practical

Figure Two: Changes in Witness Positions

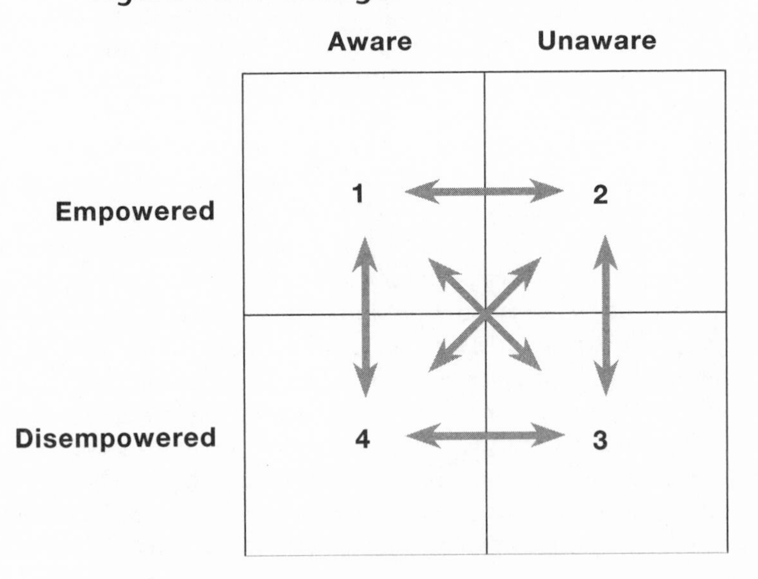

Figure Three: Each Witness Position Effects:

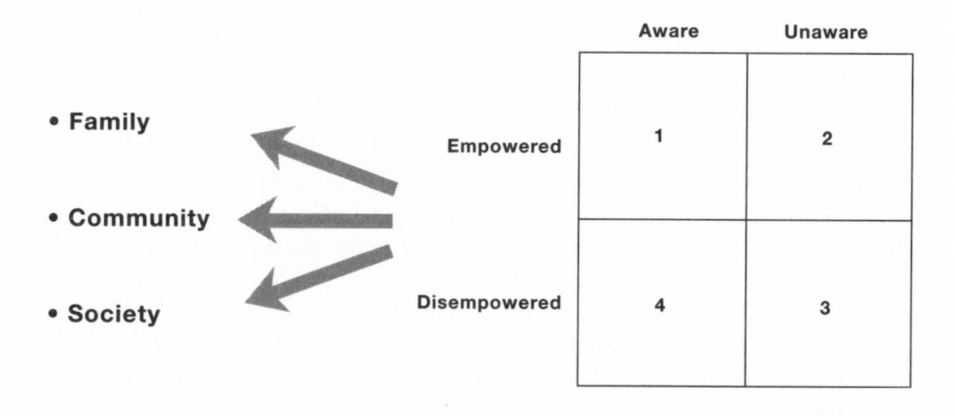

solution: "Why not film the children who attend one of the therapy groups next Wednesday?"

Tracy writes, "There was a long silence and then I was told that those children were Vietnamese and a decision had been made to use Anglo children, with whom the donor group could better identify.

"I sat with these words for several moments. I then asked my colleagues if everyone had agreed to this decision. Were racist practices going to be carried out in this agency? I asked them whether, as an Asian from India, that would mean that I would be excluded from the video?

"Colleagues responded in different ways: one said her silence was about shame; another that hers was embarrassment; another that my expectations of the agency were unreasonable.

"I was certainly aware of the agency's racism and I had spoken up to challenge it, but my looks and my racial background disempowered me. The management refused to change their decision and I refused to be silent within the agency and the community."

While Tracy was aware of the racism that influenced the production of the video, she had no power to change it. Management had a different agenda. They were focused on creating a video most likely to elicit financial support from their donor group, which, in the end, they felt would benefit the most people.

Tracy was focused on racism. From her perspective the management was unaware but empowered in relation to the racism they were perpetuating. Their practices were going to affect clients, staff, and the wider community whose interests they claimed to wish to serve. Witnessing their unacknowledged racism sickened her but strengthened her commitment to speak out against injustice. She spent time with colleagues discussing these matters with an honesty that went beyond everyone's comfort zone. Her colleagues responded by letting the management know that their racist workplace practices jeopardized the staff's ability to treat their clients, colleagues, and themselves with "care and respect." Although the video was filmed with Anglo children, Tracy and her colleagues engaged in powerful dialogues that expanded the community of people committed to antiracism in the agency.

One of the most powerful experiences I have ever had occurred in South Africa. I was giving a keynote address to a group of South African marriage and family therapists in Cape Town and speaking about one of my heroes, Nelson Mandela, drawing on anecdotes from his autobiography, *Long Walk to Freedom*, to illustrate the witness-position grid.[18] His personal journey through different witnessing positions—from being unaware of apartheid as a young child, to feeling helpless in relation to it, to being one of the principals who brought down the entire apartheid structure—is well known to millions and has affected the lives of all South Africans and the lives of people all over the world. The consequences of his different witness positions entailed twenty-seven years of imprisonment for him; his family's loss of their beloved husband, father, and son as well as constant attacks on the lives of family members; and turmoil and freedom for his country. He helped many people see their own role in the apartheid system, before which they had been unaware of the dangers they created for others while benefiting from innumerable advantages.

While preparing my talk, I had been particularly moved by the stories at the end of the book about Mandela's relationship to his guard. He had been imprisoned on Robben Island for twenty-seven years, during which he was confined to a cell whose dimensions did not allow him ever to stretch to his full height. He and his fellow political prisoners worked long hours in a limestone quarry, with little or no water to attend to their thirst or hygienic needs during the day. If they got stinging limestone dust in their eyes, they had nothing with which to wash it out.

In 1988, toward the end of his prison term, when talks with the apartheid government intensified, Mandela was moved to a one-story cottage set behind concrete walls at the end of a road, clearly a place where he could have secret meetings with government officials. Having lived through some of the grimmest circumstances contrived by man, he was now able to sleep when he was tired, eat when hungry, and even walk outside whenever he wished. He understood, however, that he was in a "gilded cage."

The prison provided him with a cook, a tall, quiet Afrikaner who, during their introductions, confided that he had been a warder on Robben Island. He told Mandela that he had sometimes driven him to the quarry and that he would make it a point to drive over the bumps to give them a rocky ride. Mandela describes his response in this way: " 'I did that to you,' he said sheepishly, and I laughed. He was a decent, sweet-tempered fellow without any prejudice and he became like a younger brother to me."[19]

In the next few pages Mandela describes the unique relationship that they developed for the time that he lived in Victor Verster Prison. His cook made the meals, but Mandela insisted that he wash the dishes, for it was "only fair." They helped each other improve their language skills: Mandela would speak Afrikaans to him and the cook would speak English to Mandela, and "in that way we both practiced the language at which we were weakest."[20]

Mandela had an extraordinary capacity to stay an aware and active witness under the most dehumanizing conditions imaginable. He is a prime example of a compassionate witness, one who is aware and takes action in relation to what he witnesses for the purpose of transforming, not exacerbating, violence. Faced with a guard who admitted to having found opportunities to make his life even more miserable, he saw the intention in the confession and was able to laugh with the man. They developed a mutually respectful prisoner-guard relationship, something I would have conceived of as a contradiction in terms.

I used this example in my talk in Cape Town. I described how the guard had been unaware of the insidious effects of apartheid and was in fact empowered by the apartheid system, whereas Mandela had such a complex vision of the apartheid system that he was able to act with respect, even kindness, toward his guard.

When I finished my talk a tall thin man walked over. He introduced himself to me and to my husband, Hilary, who was standing next to me. He said, "My name is Peter. I was one of Mandela's guards on Robben Island and I never understood what happened to me until your talk today. I was the one who made decisions about whether or not to give him his medicine. Being with Mandela, I came to understand apartheid in a way that I never had. When Mandela left the island, I left the service. I couldn't stay in the prison system anymore. I went back to my home and started to farm, but it wasn't enough. I decided to become a counselor and that is why I am at this conference."

The three of us stood there and wept. We were standing in the Huguenot Memorial Hall, a room still lined with the portraits of apartheid's architects and enforcers, a triracial audience milling around its austere benches. At that moment I believed I was looking into the face of a man whose life had changed utterly through observing the daily actions of a prisoner. Mandela's everyday witnessing of the apartheid system remained aware, active, and compassionate despite the fact that it threatened his life at every moment. This tall man beside us stood, literally, for the way everyday witnessing can transform violence, and for the importance of allowing perpetrators who repent to contribute to the restoration of justice.

Gearing Up to Witness Intentionally

A key to the transformation of violence in everyday life resides in how we witness it. In some instances awareness may be all that we can offer. Imagine we are reading the newspaper tomorrow and we see two articles. In one an eight-year-old child was removed from his home due to allegations of serious physical abuse, and in the other eighty passengers died in a bus crash eight hundred or eight thousand miles away. We have a choice. We can read as voyeuristic witnesses or quickly turn the page, anticipating that one more drop of sadness will do us in. Or, preferably we can pause, let ourselves sigh, feel sad, and then turn the page, not letting either story create so much distress that we will then have to spend time we may not have that morning to manage it. We can, in other words, practice simple awareness. It plants a seed. Awareness without action is neither irrelevant nor self-indulgent; it may be all that is called for at that particular moment. Action can be grafted on it far more easily than it can on lack of awareness. Further, awareness builds the platform for future action.

The temptation for most of us is to remain unaware. It wards off the pain of feeling helpless or confronting our uncertainty of what to do. Many people have the psychological makeup to deny the pain and violence around them, or they think they do. They may think they feel stress, have physical aches, and are irritable . . . just because. Or they may attribute these discomforts solely to immediate causes in their own lives, when they are actually reacting to their modest awareness of others' suffering.

Sometimes we are too keenly aware of the violence and violation in which we are immersed, and hate the feelings it evokes. We are disturbed or incensed but feel utterly helpless to make a difference. We imagine that only a person of heroic stamina and courage could make a difference and we know we are not that. In some ways the heroic image gets in our way, masking what ordinary action by ordinary people can accomplish. Gandhi, surely a hero, understood this. He said that "everything you do will be insignificant, but it is very important that you do it."[21]

To witness with compassion, to get to the other side of the witnessing coin, we have to recognize that we are witnesses. No mean feat. Nor is it comfortable to accept that we are always witnessing. First, witnessing takes a toll. As I will discuss in the next chapter, witnesses are subject to the same dynamics as victims, but often neither they nor anyone else appreciates this. Thus witnesses often do not take care of themselves as they need to do. If you see a man or woman in a mall strike a child in fury, you and that child may freeze. If you understand this, you may have an inner monologue: "I have just seen something that really upset me and I froze. I'm in shock and I didn't do anything. I feel bad about this, but I wasn't expecting it. I need to calm down, tell a friend what happened, and I need to keep myself from going numb so I can take care of myself. I know I'll have another chance in my life to respond differently and if I talk to people about this, I'll gather ideas from them to figure out what I want to do in the future. I was unprepared, but I can think about it so that next time, I am prepared and I know how I want to respond."

Second, all of us have walked in the shoes of the victim, perpetrator, and witness. These histories have an impact on how we witness. My hope is that this self-knowledge can create paths to compassion, knowing that we have been there and done that. I am certain that we can shift our positions in the three-role drama and that we can play, more than we do, the role of compassionate witness.

Third, we have seen that everyday witnessing occurs in complex interpersonal contexts, whether familial, organizational, or societal. Many forces constrain our awareness and our action. I desperately wanted my mother to know what we knew about her cancer. Yet, the dynamics of our family, the expert status of Dr. P., the fact that our mother trusted and came to love Dr. P., the zeitgeist of the early 1970s, my father's devotion to my mother, combined to confuse me about the right approach to take. I repeatedly argued with my father about the destructive power of secrets in families. His response was always the same: "If she wants to know, she will ask." I remained aware but helpless throughout the entire first year of my mother's illness.

Tracy took a stand against antiracist practices in her agency, assuming the risk that she might lose her job. Though her awareness and action had no effect on the fund-raising tape, she did feel more engaged with her colleagues, and confident that they had a different appreciation of, and a lesser stomach to tolerate, insidious racism within the organizational culture.

Peter left the prison system once he appreciated the injustices of the apartheid system that he was enforcing. He started out unaware but empowered to impact the prisoners' lives destructively. At the end he was unable to tolerate his perpetuation of injustice. A white South African guard, he was able to leave Robben Island.

While there are enormous constraints all the time on compassionate witnessing that can lead us to alienation or guilt, saying, "Oh, well, what can I do?" or "I feel so terrible about what I haven't done, I'm immobilized," there is also a middle ground. Appreciating the complexities of witnessing is part of establishing that middle ground.

No doubt, compassionate witnessing can be challenging, but it turns out that there is already a great deal we already know about it, and there are lessons to be learned in many places. Throughout this book, but especially in Part Three, I will be presenting stories suggesting ways people can transform unintentional witnessing of violence and violation into compassionate witnessing that helps others and themselves.

We are saturated with stories of victims and perpetrators but rarely read about witnesses.[22] When we do, they are often heroic witnesses: a man who saves his nephew from a shark; a woman who runs into a burning building and rescues a neighbor's child. While these are important stories, most of us don't consider ourselves potential heroes. We need examples of behavior *we* can emulate, that feel bite-size and doable. People who feel competent act more to help others.[23] We need to create histories in our families, communities, and nations not just of heroic action but of everyday ordinary actions that help. These instances of ordinary compassionate witnessing need to become as culturally available to us as heroic acts.

During World War II, in Le Chambon, in Vichy, France, villagers saved thousands of Jews, mostly children, despite threatened penalties of deportation and death.[24] The villagers have been the subjects of many studies. All have concluded that the villagers considered themselves ordinary people. Their courageous acts occurred incrementally and were not premeditated. Small acts of assistance predisposed people to help again. And in some instances, when it was clear that helping Jews would endanger their own lives at that very moment, they did not help, but resumed at another time.[25]

This form of responding to the plight of others has been found in other contexts. Helping tends to promote helping; harm tends to promote more harm; and inaction or turning away breeds more of the same. Critically, what happens early in a situation has a large impact.[26] I conclude from this that we need to promote, praise, and privilege the small and the ordinary.[27]

We all know how important it is to have heroes. However, we need to remember that heroes are not only those who act courageously alone. Heroes are also those who cooperate with others to do what must be done. Many of us can more easily see ourselves finding the courage to act with others than we can imagine ourselves responding to a problem all by ourselves.

In the aftermath of September 11 we had an excruciatingly painful but remarkably important lesson about how heroes can work together. We know that many lives were spared because of the actions of brave men and women who cooperated with each other to perform deeds whose consequences were indeed heroic.

In relation to witnessing, we place terrific burdens on ourselves if we believe we must act alone against injustices and violence we observe. Tracy understood this when she gathered colleagues at her agency together and began a process of dialogue about racism. It was difficult work but they did it together.

Sometimes one child can stop a bully.[28] He may be strong or popular or have a visible older sibling who is held in awe by the bully. Sometimes a David can fight a Goliath. More often the dynamics of the classroom, the schoolyard, or playing field make individual effort too tall an order for children who have not had the good fortune to go to schools that provide specific curricula on peacemaking or bully prevention.[29] As adults we can model that we value support from and alliances with others. We can teach our children that problems solved with others have as much merit as those solved alone.[30]

Certainly, it is helpful to have a repertoire of ways that we can witness violence and violation. In some instances we need to be able to respond individually. At other times we can turn to others and do compassionate witnessing together. In my community, interfaith dialogues proliferated after the terror attacks in September. Members of urban and suburban mosques gathered with church and synagogue groups, responding to the now glaring awareness that many in one community knew no one from the other community.

In the Boston area the need that was recognized was filled by people working in groups. For some Americans—for instance, those living abroad—the same need was harder to fill, initially, in a group. Jennifer Slack Gans, a young mother and close friend of mine who moved with her family from New York to Melbourne in 2000, wrote me a long e-mail after the eleventh about "feeling a strong need to be in the presence of Muslims with all that was happening. I was concerned about the acts of retaliation aimed at Muslims that were occurring all over the place. For the first time in my life I was aware of feeling disconnected from such a large part of society and the world, and was troubled that I didn't have a single Muslim friend. I was conscious in a new way of my own lack of knowledge about Islam, and this ignorance seemed somehow indicative of larger, global, problems. I felt a desperate need to form some connections."

Jennifer went on to establish regular meetings between Muslim and non-Muslim women in an effort to establish a meaningful dialogue process. She also established a pen-pal program for students in her oldest child's grade. Now, a year later, a group has formed to propel the process of community contact further. After a year of being pen pals the children as well as their parents are meeting each other.

There were many aftereffects of the September 11 attacks. For one, we saw that small steps by ordinary people could make a difference. People everywhere poured onto streets to offer comfort to those who wept. In New York a thirty-foot-high and thirty-foot-wide mountain of donated socks gave practical testimony to one way people all over the country had found to show their caring and support. Children sent drawings to firemen and police, not just in Washington, D.C., and New York City, but in their own hometowns. Something was so right about humanity even when something was also so horribly wrong. An intuitive grasp of compassionate witnessing burst forth from millions of people in the face of an extraordinary event. It provides a foundation on which to place more specific tools to help with the many opportunities we have to transform everyday toxic witnessing into witnessing that heals.

CHAPTER 3

The Consequences of Common Shock

On September 11, 2001, our nation was united in an eerie way. Millions of people watched television coverage of a plane flying through a brilliant blue sky into a tall glass building, recognizable to some as one of the twin towers of the World Trade Center in Manhattan. Many people could not comprehend what they had seen. Even when the flames engulfed the building seconds later, it was hard to understand what was happening, since it was unlike anything anyone had witnessed before—just as the concept of gas chambers was difficult to grasp before World War II, since no one had ever imagined such a thing. Within hours most people had learned something they never would have wished to believe: Hijacked passenger planes could be used as missiles.

The hijacking and crashing of the four planes was an extraordinary event that landed in the middle of an ordinary day. As a nation we were not mobilized and prepared for terrorist attacks. We were unwitting witnesses to extreme violence that had biological, psychological, interpersonal, and societal consequences. Yet barely two months later some people who lived in Lower Manhattan, who saw the second tower topple, who saw bodies falling from the building, were puzzled about why they felt so awful. A friend visiting New York reported to me that her friend had told her, "I don't know why I feel so bad. After all, nothing happened to me!"

Something did happen to this young woman. She was an unwilling witness to horror, death, and destruction. She experienced common shock. Even in the context of one of the worst disasters ever to hit our country, many people who were witnesses in one way or another—through living or working near the World Trade Center or the Pentagon, working in the airline industry, knowing people who lost family members, having seen endless hours of television coverage of the events[1]—could not account for their reactions.

It is not that they were ignoring something the rest of us all know. They were struggling to place their experience into the existing categories they had. They needed a different category—the concept of common shock—to explain that witnesses to violence and violation can experience painful reactions.

My friend told her friend, "Of course something happened to you. You were a witness."[2] My hope is that after reading this chapter, people will better understand why they feel the way they do after witnessing violence and violation and be better able to help others understand it as well. To accomplish this I describe the kinds of reactions witnesses may have in three main areas—the biological, psychological, interpersonal—and explore a few of the societal consequences. Other societal consequences will be addressed in the second and third parts of the book. Appendix Two provides practical applications of the ideas in this chapter for adults and children.

Reading this chapter may be evocative, since you may recall times when you were a witness to something that upset you. You may notice flutters in your stomach, tingles in your neck or arms, or a more rapid heartbeat. If you have uncomfortable sensations in your body or disturbing thoughts or feelings, pause and take a few deep breaths. You may want to orient yourself in the present moment to someone, some place, or some thing that is soothing or comforting to you, for instance calling to mind the face of your best friend or a serene pond or a favorite chair. If you notice more discomfort in your body, you might skip the pages you are reading or put the book down for the time being. Pacing is key.

In most situations, when we are not in danger, we can afford to pay careful attention to our bodies' language. It is a reliable guide. Helping people learn to understand the body's language is one of the goals of this chapter. Only you know when the time is right for you to read this material. Making these decisions throughout reading this book is good practice for the kinds of self-monitoring we need to do at all times. Noting when we feel distress allows us to make informed choices about how to meet our needs.

It is crucial that we learn how to do so. If we are all subject to the dynamics of witnessing, then, in every society, citizens are making decisions with bodies and minds that are often aroused and distressed. The young woman in Lower Manhattan was trying to think through what our country's response to the terrorist attack should be in a body and mind discombobulated by common shock. Kosovar Albanians returning to their country after the NATO bombing were trying to make decisions about where their Serb neighbors should live at a time when they were highly distressed. Israelis and Palestinians are trying to influence political processes in bodies and minds wracked with fear, terror, and rage.

The dilemmas faced by the young woman in Lower Manhattan, a Kosovar Albanian returning home, or an Israeli reservist are similar in that they must participate in the life of their country, supporting, defending, or protesting actions that affect great swaths of their society and even the world in bodies that are experiencing the effects of shock. Citizens routinely confront choices in both their domestic and political lives while they are dealing with the effects of common shock. How must violence be addressed? When, if ever, is vengeance just? How does the younger generation carry the legacies of the generations before, and with what effects for the generations that follow?

These are questions that people all over the world ask. Whether in New York or Washington, D.C., Kosovo or South Africa, Pakistan or Sri Lanka, our answers to these questions shape the world in which we live. We answer these questions as embodied humans, thinking and feeling about these hugely important abstract questions in bodies rattled by our brains. Common shock affects us biologically. Our biological reactions shape our psychological reactions and these in turn impact our relationships and the fabric of the societies in which we live.

The Biological Consequences of Common Shock

I heard the word *shock* used more times in the first week after September 11 than perhaps ever before in my life, although if I had been my current age and not sixteen in November 1963, when President Kennedy was assassinated, perhaps that occasion would have rivaled this one. On the morning of September 11 most people perceived their bodies reacting out of synch with their customary "mental" pace. Even FBI officials in Washington, watching television coverage at 9:06 A.M. with the deputy director of the agency, were described as so shocked they were unable to speak for a few moments.[3] Making sense of the events—then and now—was supremely effortful.

Recalling the events of September, you may be keenly aware that people's responses varied widely, not only at the beginning, but also over time. How rapidly and severely people responded had a lot to do with how close they were to the events and with their own personal histories of dealing with common shock.[4]

In Boston, away from the epicenters, the first child to rush crying into the office of one school was a ten-year-old who had been treated for a benign brain tumor the year before. Two days later I was in an electronics store buying an antenna for our ancient television so that we could watch more than one channel, and a man in combat-fatigue clothing, the age of a man who might have been a Gulf War veteran, was pacing up and down the aisles, visibly startling to ambient noise and customers walking by him. My guess is that both the child and this man were experiencing sensations in their bodies that were acutely uncomfortable for them.[5]

While there is less literature on witnessing violence and violation than there is on being a victim of it, and while some of the literature does not distinguish between being a victim or witness, what we do know strongly suggests that the biological experience of witnessing violence and violation falls along a continuum from mild to severe.[6] Stress is one designation for a mild reaction.[7] More serious common shock shades into what is designated as a trauma response.[8] Acute or chronic post-traumatic stress disorder may be the most appropriate label for the most severe common shock reactions.[9]

Fight or Flight

Stress is an alarm reaction to a stimulus the person appraises as emotionally charged or threatening. This state can range from exhilaration to mild or severe discomfort. It has also been called the fight-or-flight reaction; it produces hyperarousal, which is a normal and necessary response to threat.

The fight-or-flight reaction prepares the body for defensive action through a cascade of sympathetic-nervous-system firings and the release of stress hormones, the best known of which is epinephrine, or adrenaline. Our physical reactions match the potential demands on us. Our pupils dilate so that we can sense what is going on around us, and the hairs on our skin stand up so that we can sense vibration. The heart's output increases so that more blood is pumped to the extremities, readying our arms and legs to run if necessary. We increase our respirations as well, providing more oxygen for our tissues. At the same time blood is diverted from the digestive system, producing the sensation of butterflies in the stomach. Normally, once the perceived danger is past, the body will halt the alarm reaction and restore the body to homeostasis, or a state of rest.[10]

Following the terrorist attacks on America, many people did not get the relief that halting the stress response brings, or they did so intermittently, only to have it activated again and again, sometimes to surprising triggers. At the checkout counter of a local store on September 12, I asked the young clerk how he was doing and if all his "networks" were okay. He replied, "Oh, it's been a terrible day, but all the computers and phones are working."

"Oh, yes, it has been a terrible day," I said, "but I meant your social networks. Are your loved ones okay?"

"Mine, yes. But, my friend's brother called him from the roof of the World Trade Center and told him to tell their mother he loved her. Oh, these shakes," he said as tears streamed down both of our cheeks and he put his hand on his stomach as if he had a bellyache.

The story of the phone call brought him back into a witness position and it triggered his sympathetic nervous system to react again, so he was at once sad and aroused. Reaching out to him, witnessing his distress, I was sad, but comforting him kept my physical response to stress from being activated.

When stress is intense, when the way we understand ourselves, others, and the world is disrupted, and when we feel fear, horror, or terror, stress can produce a trauma response, which is a *normal* response to abnormal events and experiences.[11] Not only those who experience the violence or violation directly, but those who witness it—that is, see it or hear about it from others—may develop a trauma response.[12]

In the days that followed September 11, people reported a range of physical feelings: lethargy, yawning, tingles, hot and cold sensations coursing through their blood, shaking, tension in their muscles, aches and pains, difficulty falling or staying asleep, rapid heartbeat, and sweating, among others. Some people felt numb and spacey, blanketed in a kind of fog that seemed to insulate them from their own and others' terror. One woman described herself as protected within a turtle shell. Some people fed their terror, others starved it. Some people were unable to follow the news after the first few days, and others couldn't tear themselves away from it. The latter group had difficulty concentrating on anything else but the threatening images.[13]

Still others startled to the smallest unexpected sound and couldn't settle down. My husband and I, for example, startled awake at buckeyes falling from a tree in our yard, a noise we usually sleep through. Our bodies were hyperreactive and hypervigilant in the wake of recent events. There are biological explanations for these reactions, which can be moderated if attended to with care.[14]

In response to experiencing a life-threatening event, whether as victim or witness, some number of people's physiology will respond *abnormally* right from the beginning. It is possible that this is a group of people who will later develop posttraumatic stress disorder, PTSD, a disorder that is diagnosed when acute symptoms persist for more than one month and when there is also compromised functioning at work or in social relationships.[15] In relation to the attacks of September 11, a much smaller percentage of people developed PTSD than had mild common shock reactions or serious common shock responses suggestive of a trauma response.[16] Many people probably fell into some category that is still not defined. They had debilitating symptoms but could still function in their lives.

The Body's Trauma Center

The body's "trauma center" is a structure in the brainstem called the locus coeruleus (LC).[17] It has abundant connections throughout the brain to activate and alert a person, even interrupting an individual if necessary, to ensure that attention is paid to high-priority stimuli. When a person is repeatedly exposed to threat or is exposed to an extreme threat, the LC actually changes; it becomes hyperresponsive to stress signals. This produces the felt experience of hypervigilance for the individual. In effect this structure itself becomes traumatized.[18]

Under usual conditions of stress the body prepares for fight or flight, and when the threat is past (the threat ends or the person successfully fights or gets away), the reaction subsides. However, if the threat is extreme and the brain perceives that neither fight nor flight can succeed, the body may go into a freeze response. During the freeze response both parts of the autonomic nervous system, the sympathetic and the parasympathetic, function simultaneously. This has been likened to pushing your foot down on the accelerator and the brakes of a car at the same time.[19] Attention is narrowed and heightened. The limbs go limp; the body and mind feel numb; the person "goes dead" like a possum or mouse. This reaction cannot be consciously willed or chosen; it happens to us.

I have had many clients describe just this freeze response when telling me about watching a fight between their parents. One young man had always blamed himself for not running over to his father and pushing him away from his mother. But, he recalled, it was as if he were a frozen statue with enormous eyes, a good description of what the freeze response feels like.[20]

The Limbic System

Finally, the limbic system plays a key role in the body's response to extreme threat. Two structures of the limbic system are important to understand, since they can help us account for prominent psychological symptoms of severe common shock. The amygdala, named for its almond shape, assigns emotional significance to incoming signals.[21] The other structure, the hippocampus, evaluates, categorizes, and stores this information. Coordination between both structures is necessary for optimal functioning; the one reacts to information and the other makes sense of it. When severely threatened, a highly aroused amygdala interferes with and may shut down the hippocampus, resulting in a number of symptoms that are associated with the long-term effects of PTSD.

As the emotion center of the brain the amygdala is associated with the experience and expression of fear. Under extreme stress the amygdala can forge connections between elements in the threatening situation and a fear response, without the person having any conscious awareness that this is happening. Thus, people may be left with a fear response to triggers in the environment that make no sense to them.

Before the operation that revealed my mother's cancer diagnosis in 1974, her physician assured her that she had a 99-percent chance of being fine. I took the train from Boston to New York so that I could be there at the end of her operation. I was extremely upset during the train ride and cried frequently. I remember taking a taxi to my parents' apartment and telling the cabdriver that I was waiting for life-and-death news about my mother. During that trip I felt I knew my mother's fate, despite the physician's prediction that her tumor would turn out to be benign.

I did learn that day that my mother had a rare and lethal malignant cancer that had already metastasized throughout her body. Over the years I have had many reactions and feelings concerning her diagnosis, treatment, and death. Recently, I became aware of one more: I dread waiting for news. Any news. I understand now that I probably experienced a conditioned fear response to waiting, which was one element in the painful sequence of events by which I learned my mother would live a shortened life. These amygdala-based conditioned fear responses are very difficult to get over and, as I have discovered decades later, can be difficult to figure out.

Sensitization

These are just a few of the complex changes that occur in the brain as a result of exposure to extreme stress. The more the brain has to deal with, the more it will adapt and change. If circumstances shift, however, and there is no longer a threat, these changes can become maladaptive.[22] Thus, people who have been repeatedly exposed to the most troubling kinds of interactions and events, and who have done their best to meet the challenges, may find that they respond with such heightened reactivity that they are overwhelmed a great deal of the time. This is called sensitization. Indeed, their brains are so sensitive, that small matters that might not bother others present big hurdles for them. Children, youth, and adults who are exposed to domestic and community violence are a particularly vulnerable group to develop sensitization. For instance, a young mother who observed her father beat her mother may react with disproportionate anger to her son's hitting his younger sister, mistaking normal sibling fighting for dangerous violence.[23]

The Psychological Consequences of Common Shock

The preceding material on the biological consequences of common shock sets the stage for understanding psychological consequences of common shock.[24] In this next section I focus on the expected psychological responses for Americans who have been acculturated by Western values. One interesting and important point is that people's values and contexts shape the meaning they give to "symptoms," and therefore the various biologically based expressions of common shock are interpreted differently around the world, producing different psychological experiences.[25] In the United States, with peoples from so many parts of the world living here now, it is especially important to remember how culturally relative the psychological dimensions of common shock are.[26]

Categories of Events and Interactions That Produce Common Shock

A wide number of events and interactions can trigger common shock. Depending on the interpretation given to them, different psychological experiences will ensue. Several researchers have categorized types of victimization that seem to produce different qualities of experience in victims, and I believe this is the case for witnesses as well.[27] While referring to these categories, I will substitute *witness* for *victim*.

Researchers distinguish discrete versus chronic events, such as the difference between witnessing a murder, robbery, or fire and witnessing a child suffering a chronic debilitating illness or watching your parents fight each night. It is also different to witness something while alone—for example, seeing a pet dog struck by a hit-and-run driver—as opposed to witnessing as part of a group, for instance a group of neighbors watching a house on their street burn. Finally, there is a difference between witnessing a malicious perpetrator attack someone and witnessing an "act of God," like seeing a loved one attacked by a stranger while the two of you are walking in a park versus watching a tornado rip through your town.[28] While these different types of experiences are likely to be associated with psychological experiences that differ by category, it is important to remember that we are all unique. No two people will interpret or experience any event in exactly the same way.[29]

Numbness and Anger

Of the many psychological reactions to witnessing violence and violation, two are particularly common and also may be very familiar to us: numbness[30] and anger. When they resolve rapidly, they are normal reactions; when they persist, they may signal an abnormal response that may lead to the development of PTSD.

One Saturday, when my son, Ben, was about ten years old, he came home from playing in the park with a friend to report that an older child had poured gasoline on the ground and set the grass on fire. Hilary, Ben, and I dashed down to the park, but before we got there, the child had stomped out the flames. We could see the charred remains of a snakelike line, but there was nothing left to do . . . in terms of the fire.

Our son and his friend had witnessed the fire setting from a distance and each had run to his home to get help. A few minutes later Ben's friends' parents arrived on the scene. We were six witnesses, the boys having seen the grass on fire, the parents having heard about it.

Ben's friend's parents were livid. The father wanted to go immediately to the other child's house and either beat him himself or be sure his father did. Hilary and I, on the other hand, were hypercalm, even numb. I remember feeling that time was warped, both super speeded up and oddly slowed down. I felt like I was walking on the moon, trying to take in all that was happening, paying careful attention to how Ben was doing, and not feeling much of anything. I wanted time to collect my thoughts. I wanted to go home with just our family and figure out what we thought should be done. I wanted to get away from my neighbors' anger.

Both sets of parents had the same ultimate goal: the security of the neighborhood park. And both the father and I were having normal, albeit different, psychological reactions to witnessing a dangerous act that had jeopardized the safety of our neighborhood and involved our children as witnesses. However, at that time, I don't think any of us would have understood that as witnesses one step removed we had experienced common shock also, albeit mild, and were now subject to biological, psychological, and interpersonal consequences *because* of this.

Memory Effects

Witnessing also affects memory. Scientists have been working on the conundrums of memory for centuries, and in the last two decades a synthesis from several disciplines seems to be emerging. Scientists who work on the complex area of memory can now account for much of what I hear in my office. Memory is a phenomenon that has both neurobiological and psychological dimensions, although many people think of it as purely psychological. When they do not have perfect recall about things they think they should remember, they often believe that their lapses reflect badly on them.

When I was ten, my great-aunt Peggy died. My mother told me, but I forgot. I vividly remember coming into the kitchen and hearing my mother talking about someone's death on the telephone. Distressed, I interrupted her and asked her who had died. Somewhat puzzled, my mother turned from the receiver and said, "Aunt Peggy." Upon seeing her face and hearing her words, I remembered that my mother *had* told me my aunt had died. But in witnessing my mother's crying the first time she told me, I must have been so surprised and upset that I temporarily forgot what I had seen and what I had been told.

This episode illustrates an important aspect of memory. To establish durable memory people must select and transform what they see, hear, think, or feel into a memory.[31] This process is called encoding. It turns out that we remember better that which we have subjected to an elaborative encoding process based on what we know already, past experience, and our needs. In daily life much experience is subjected to shallow encoding and only very specific cues will retrieve those memories.

My great-aunt was the first person in my immediate family who had died. I had little past experience of death and no great sadness about her death. She was my mother's favorite aunt, but I had never been close to her. I also rarely saw my mother cry. In retrospect I would guess that I had encoded the information shallowly. However, seeing my mother's unhappy face and hearing her speak to her friend on the phone about funeral arrangements served as retrieval cues to recall that my mother *had* told me Aunt Peggy had died. I was then very upset that I could have forgotten.

I hear these kinds of stories from clients frequently. Like me they blame themselves for forgetting and develop negative self-judgments about what this says about them. People do forget a lot of what they witness; everything we experience is not stored in our brains ready to pop out if the right code is entered. However, given the chance to talk about something that has happened relatively recently, we probably remember it more accurately than if time has passed. If my mother and I had talked over her feelings about Aunt Peggy's death the first time she told me that Aunt Peggy died, I might have remembered it because it would have been more elaboratively encoded.

In general, memory is better for emotionally arousing events, and this benefit increases with the intensity of the emotional arousal—up to certain limits of intensity beyond which memory may be seriously impaired.[32] I worked with a six-year-old boy, Donny, over a period of two years. He would periodically come into our sessions and report in vivid detail events that had happened at home on the previous weekend, which clearly disturbed him. These accounts usually centered on fights he observed between his parents. His father was contemptuous of his mother and spoke in belittling tones, much of which Donny could mimic. When I would discuss the sessions with his mother, I would usually learn that although some details were inaccurate, his overall memory for the events was excellent. For Donny, although the household events were disturbing, they did not overwhelm him. In addition, talking to his mother and me helped keep the emotional intensity within a range he could tolerate and not have to shut out.

Under other circumstances, when events are highly stressful and do overwhelm us, conscious memory may suffer. Extreme fear can cause such high levels of stimulation to the amygdala that it blocks the hippocampus from working properly to evaluate and categorize experience. In addition, under conditions of extreme stress or threat, people may dissociate or "space out," which also interferes with their ability to accompany the intense sensory information they are experiencing with a meaningful personal narrative that makes sense of what is occurring.

When dissociation happens, experiences are poorly encoded, they are not compared to prior knowledge, and they are often disconnected from language. The hippocampus receives fragments of experience. Without the ability to evaluate, categorize, or supply context to experience, the hippocampus stores these kinds of memories differently from the way it usually does. These memories are stored without reference to time and place. Thus when they are retrieved, it is as if they are happening in the present. They are experienced as a contemporary terror. These types of memories are far different from ones we calmly recall about something that happened the previous day. They are usually set off by cues, triggers, of which we are unaware. We have sensations in our bodies, often accompanied by fear, panic, or anxiety, and no idea what is happening and no language to contain the intense emotion.

Thus extreme stress can also produce fragments of visual, auditory, kinesthetic, or visceral memory that are uniquely vivid. Many people call these experiences flashbacks. For most of us this is very disturbing, and we try to make sense of what is going on. Humans have an enormous capacity for interpreting and making sense of experience. One of the goals of this book is to increase people's resources to do this. Whether we can always do so accurately is a different question from whether we can do so in a way that is convincing and reassuring to us.[33]

I have a client who has flashbacks of fists and faces. He knows that his best friend's father beat his friend, but he cannot put together the haunting images of his flashbacks with any scene he remembers precisely. He isn't even sure he ever directly witnessed his friend being beaten, although he knows it happened because he has recently confirmed this with his friend. Over time in our work together he has constructed a story that makes sense to him of these fragmented images that plague him, and they trouble him much less frequently now.

Many parents wonder what to do about children who witness violence or violation. They are uncertain if children can remember or "know" what they have seen or heard. Again, researchers have studied this carefully and have concrete information about children's memory development that can guide parents about how to help their children if they are witnesses.[34]

Parents often rely on their children telling them what bothers them but, not surprisingly, children's ability to give verbal accounts of events they have witnessed is dependent on their verbal abilities at the time of these events. There is some evidence that before age eighteen months, children have memory of upsetting events because they express it in their behavior. If the event is one that made them afraid, their behavior will express fear. Between eighteen months and thirty-six months children give "spotty" verbal accounts. Children older than three are able to provide verbal accounts of ordinary to very upsetting events.[35]

But this description is incomplete; in the above description the upsetting event is unspecified. If the upsetting event is one in which a child witnesses someone she knows hurt someone else and is told by the person who has done the hurting that nothing has happened *and* that she must not tell, the child's memory for the event will be more consistent with how memory functions when we are massively overwhelmed and the events are stored in fragments of visual images, sounds, and sensations.

From the perspective of witnessing and its effects on memory, it is clear that for both children and adults who have witnessed disturbing events or interactions, they are reassured by the comforting presence of a person who is able to remain calm in the face of their distress and wants to know about it. The opportunity to talk with a reliable, kind person about their memories helps children and adults alike. Sharing our memories helps with later recall. It is profoundly comforting to children and adults to be able to tell a story that makes sense to them about events in their lives. Having the assistance of a thoughtful, soothing, kind caregiver to create a meaningful account of disturbing events is one important way to cope with common shock experiences.[36] There is also growing evidence that this has long-term positive effects on physical and emotional well-being.[37]

Sadness, Helplessness, and Shame

Other psychological consequences of everyday witnessing include sadness, helplessness, and shame. A client reported a story about taking her three-year-old daughter to a local emergency room after she had fallen while jumping on her parents' bed. The emergency-ward staff had treated the child's deep facial gash competently and been sympathetic to the mother, but she still felt awful. It was likely that her daughter's cheek would bear a permanent scar.

The mother had left her daughter in her bedroom while she had tended to other chores. She knew her daughter was jumping on the bed and knew that she often was too boisterous. She also knew that the bedroom was cluttered with items that were dangerous for a young child to be near. Nonetheless, she had not supervised her. Her daughter had fallen on a vacuum cleaner that her mother had not yet put away.

For several weeks she described a range of feelings. She felt sad that she had not protected her daughter, helpless that she couldn't turn back the clock and do something to avert what had already happened, guilty for not supervising her child, and ashamed. Of all these feelings the one that was most difficult for her to manage was her shame. She felt exposed as the sloppy, disorganized, selfish person she believed she was.

Shame is often the hardest feeling to bear for many reasons, one of which is that there is no obvious way to express it.[38] If we are sad, we can cry; if we are angry, we can yell. But pause a moment. You can mimic shame by looking down and averting your eyes, but how can you discharge it? In trying to discharge shame we tend to look for actions as straightforward as tears or shouting. Yet shame's release may take something more complex than this; it may take the making of amends if we have injured others, or a forgiving of the self, if we are unduly harsh with ourselves.[39]

Michael Lewis, who has been studying shame for more than thirty years, makes a crucial point. Usually the person who feels shame has made a global assessment that the whole self is unworthy. The self doesn't say, "What you *did* is bad." It says, "*You* are bad." It stops the whole works down. You can't do something else, because anything *you* do will be wrong.[40]

This sense of total abject worthlessness is unbearably painful. Many parents socialize shame from an early age. I have never worked with a person who suffered shame without learning about painful interactions that she had had with parents who made her feel diminished or debased. One client had a voice in his head that regularly screamed at him, "You little shit. You little shit." He could never believe that any family member had actually articulated those words to him, but eventually he came to understand that the tenor of his parents' ways of interacting with family members when they were angry was precisely summed up by that phrase. It is not a stretch to understand that children who are treated this way feel unlovable and feel that love is tenuously available to them.

Shame, then, is a feeling that usually has long historical roots back to childhood. It is triggered in the present, and we often feel paralyzed and uncertain about how to get over the feeling. However, as we have seen, this uncertainty is intrinsic to the very dynamics of how shame is experienced. Because we are convinced we are *all* bad, nothing we can do will be acceptable or right. Finding this intolerable, some people shut down and others react impulsively, as if to push the shame away and make others be at fault. Both behaviors are caused by how unbearably painful it is to feel shame.

Aggression

This leads us to the last psychological consequence of common shock that I will consider: aggression. Children or adults exposed to mild or moderate violence or violation often experience anger that can result in aggressive behavior. The aggressive behavior may be turned toward the self, others, or both. One adult client found herself eating compulsively after reading a newspaper article in which a therapist had been convicted of sexually abusing a patient. Only after she had eaten enough to feel sick did she realize that she had felt furious at the doctor's violating his patient's trust, her psychic and physical boundaries. Reading the story, she had become an emotionally involved witness to it.

When adults or children witness disturbing events they are often so distressed that they have difficulty moderating their emotions. When they feel angry, they may lash out at the very people they want to comfort them. One young woman described fighting with her boyfriend within moments of coming home and telling him about seeing a passerby kick a homeless man sleeping in the street. She knew she wasn't really annoyed at her boyfriend's having turned to the sink to refill his glass of water, but at the moment he turned away from her, she felt abandoned and enraged. During our session we were able to understand that she identified with this homeless man due to episodes in her chaotic childhood. When her boyfriend turned toward the sink, it felt like she was a helpless child being dismissed, "kicked," like the destitute homeless man.

Exposure to extremes of violence and violation can activate aggression in some people who are predisposed toward it and inhibit it in others.[41] There are numerous clinical accounts[42] and artistic renderings[43] of aggression gone awry in individuals who develop PTSD as a consequence of exposure to an extreme stressor. The neurobiological underpinnings of this phenomenon are now quite well understood.

Finally, shaming can also provoke aggression.[44] Shaming can occur between individuals, but there is a more insidious, invisible, and continuous source of shaming: systematic structural inequity, structural violence, which occurs between groups and classes of people. This form of shaming is really better understood as an aggression itself, sometimes a massive aggression and sometimes a microaggression,[45] which disproportionately affects the poor, persons of color, the elderly, women, immigrants, and others whose identities mark them as different from a hypothetical average or cultural ideal, such as homosexuals and people with disabilities. Some people do react to the continuous, esteem-eroding provocations of shame with aggression.

The psychological consequences of common shock that I have considered—numbness, anger, memory alterations, sadness, helplessness, shame, and aggression—are eased by sharing our feelings with others. Children or adults who are told to "buck up" or "keep a stiff upper lip" will actually have more, not less, difficulty over time adjusting to the effects of common shock. It is clear that silencing, stifling, suppressing, or stuffing our experience may make life easier for some in the short term but has corrosive effects for all in the long run.[46]

Although Western culture places a high premium on individualism, the evidence is clear that "going it alone" does not heal. Social support, however, does.[47] While in the West we tend to provide resources to individuals to help them heal from trauma responses, it has been observed all over the world that families and communities are just as important a resource for healing.[48]

At the same time, when families and communities themselves are stressed, the very people we may want to help us may be too distressed themselves to offer us assistance. Understanding the kinds of interpersonal and societal disruptions that violence and violation cause is a first step in addressing them.

Interpersonal Consequences of Common Shock

One of the ironies of common shock is that when we most need people to comfort and take care of us, we may be least able to receive this help. Common shock shuts people down. They turn in toward themselves, wanting others to realize they are hurting and to know precisely how to take care of them. Since this rarely happens, they may withdraw, get angry, become defiant, sulk, or have any number of other responses that make it less likely that others' responses will be a good match.

A client of mine was sent to an overnight camp one summer, where he repeatedly saw one of the counselors fondle the boy in the bunk beside him. He clearly remembers the first visiting day and recalls how desperate he was for his parents to comfort him. Instead, he said nothing. He acted as if he were having a great summer and was totally integrated into the camp community. At the same time he remembers wanting his mother to guess what had happened and how he felt. Needless to say, his mother thought he was "in great shape" and didn't think he needed anything in particular, or more than usual. Decades later he feels sadness at how far apart his inner reality was from the one he put forward.

Remembering that common shock reactions cover a wide spectrum and the situations that produce them vary enormously, we can still consider four typical interpersonal consequences of common shock that may help us make sense of the painful, if not invariable, reality that people's needs may not get met when they are suffering common shock: silence, shattered assumptions, inhibition of self-disclosure, and problems of fit. Further, as I have indicated, there is rarely a point-to-point correspondence between an event and a reaction. The same event can produce different reactions in people who have all, supposedly, been similarly exposed. For instance, I have worked for thirty years with people who have witnessed family violence. In that time no story has ever been the same, and no aspect of the experience has ever had the exact same significance in one person's life as in another's.

Silence

In many contexts one of the central consequences of common shock is that silence is invariably tightly braided into the experience. Children who witness family violence or women who watch boyfriends assault children rarely have to be told—although sometimes they are threatened—"Don't talk about this." It is obvious. Something bad has happened; everyone who has experienced family violence knows this, and the very people we might run to tell are those who are involved in the awful scene anyway. We are trapped in silence as surely as if we were held in a vise.

When violence occurs, it is as if the air changes; it feels charged. As a witness you want, if possible, to get away, and if you cannot, you want to be so still, so tiny, so compressed, that you become invisible. Or, you get superanimated. You feel surges of power, you are superman who will fly into the mayhem and set it all to rights. But either way, you will not talk about it.

I remember sitting at my dinner table, after a fight in which my father had yelled at my mother, and drawing a figure eight in my mind around my parents, perhaps a hundred times. It was as if the line in my mind could create an inviolate boundary between them and me where I could be safe. When I finally left the table, I went into my room and never mentioned the fight to anyone, not even my sister, who had also been there.

If someone had asked me if my parents fought, I would have said no. Not because I would have lied, but because those words wouldn't have captured the evanescent quality of discord between my usually loving and compatible parents. My father blew up at my mother. My parents didn't fight. Thus, the standard way of representing conflict wouldn't have evoked my experience. It is often the case that when terms fail to express people's experience, they have trouble articulating theirs, and silence becomes the default position.

While a child I never spoke to either parent about these outbursts. The figure eight I drew was permanent. It defined a territory too fearsome to pierce. My mother was a loving, kind, creative woman. I held back from telling her what I truly felt, although on the surface I told her everything. Nor did she ever talk to me, as a child, about my father's anger. The silence in our family about our father's intermittent and unpredictable rage trumped everything else, at least for me. It set limits on my trust, my sense of safety, and my sense of connection. Silence created an isolation that I have worked my entire life to oppose, with my own family and friends, and with my clients and colleagues.[49]

Shattered Assumptions

A second interpersonal consequence of common shock is that meaning can be destroyed when trust is violated in families, communities, or nations. Most of us have some rock-solid core premise that shatters when we experience violence or violation.[50] Often we don't know we had one until it's gone. Ronnie Janoff-Bulman has identified three beliefs that form core assumptions about ourselves, the external world, and the relationship between the two. These apply for many, but by no means all, people. "The world is benevolent. The world is meaningful. The self is worthy."[51] Any of these can be shattered, she believes, by a traumatic experience.

A pregnant woman, happy to be alive, hearing from the emergency-ward physician that her four-year-old son has diabetes, can feel herself leaving the world she loved and entering a world she thought was about other people, not her. This is a condition the child will have to manage for the rest of his life. In that one moment she has gone from feeling whole and confident to feeling frightened and lost. She knows she must summon the will to care for her son, herself, the unborn child, and yet everything now feels unfamiliar. Although she is surrounded by people, she has never felt so alone.

Or, a seventeen-year-old young man, a passenger in the backseat of a car, driving home with his two friends from an evening at Dunkin' Donuts, suddenly feels the car hit a stone wall, careen forward, and smash into a tree. Trapped in the backseat with a seat belt on, covered with blood, hearing an uncanny silence, seeing slumped bodies in strange formations, he realizes that he alone of the three is alive. He has witnessed the death of his two best buddies. It takes him years to restore his sense that the world is meaningful, so complex is the task he faces to make sense of his friends' deaths and his survival.

His life is also ravaged by isolation. Others may not see that; he goes on to college, sees friends, attends church. But he feels keenly that he has crossed a divide, traveled to a place others have not gone. He imagines that what he would have to say would be unbearable for others to know, that is, if he could ever find the words for what to say. Yet words are rarely available. His belief that others couldn't bear what he thinks or feels is both wrong and right. Some few could, but many could not.

Inhibition of Self-Disclosure

The intuition that others cannot bear to hear what we have to say when we have experienced common shock is confessed to therapists and clergy, and investigated by psychologists. James Pennebaker, whose work I will refer to again in Chapters Four and Nine, has been studying the effects of self-disclosure for several decades.[52] In one of his research studies he and his colleague, Kent Harber, interviewed by phone over a one-year period 789 people who had experienced the 1989 Loma Prieta earthquake that hit the San Francisco Bay Area, killing over sixty people, and, in 1991, interviewed 361 Dallas-area residents over a twelve-week period about their reactions to the Gulf War.[53]

They found clear social stages of coping with these disasters.[54] In the first stage people can't stop talking about the events and will even do so to strangers. There is an insatiable need to talk and a complementary willingness to listen. The conversations create a sense of shared community that is prized by most people. Phase two starts around four weeks on. Although people are filled with thoughts and feelings that they would like to share, they cannot bear to listen to others. It is as if people are saturated with their own and others' distress and believe that one more drop will be ruinous. They feel literally sick hearing others, and yet they are aware that they themselves are sick from *not* speaking. This is the point at which having a shared cultural map (which I will discuss in Part Three) of how to witness others' distress without becoming undone oneself could make a vital difference.

Problems of Fit

No two people will ever have the same reaction to witnessing an act of violation or violence, and no two people will ever be a perfect fit for helping each other with their responses to it. This consequence of common shock is an inevitable, often heartbreaking, confrontation with our differences from each other.

People whose nervous systems have been sensitized by previous traumatic experiences may be perceived by others as "making mountains out of molehills."[55] Their needs in a situation may be very different from those of the people to whom they turn for comfort. Often they are blamed as weak or defective for being more distressed than others. They may be spoken to in moral terms—"Where is your willpower?"—when this is like asking a bird to ride a bicycle. The one who is suffering and the one who is responding are speaking from two different domains, albeit ones that could meet if they understood the biological and psychological consequences of exposure to extreme stressors.

Even those whose neurobiological systems have not been altered by exposure to severe violence and violation can find it trying to take care of themselves after experiencing common shock. By the last week of September, 2001, I had worked with many couples who were describing these problems of fit. One young woman had been evacuated from her office building three times in the first four days after the terrorist attacks. On the third day she called her partner, suggesting they meet for lunch. She felt jittery and discombobulated, wanting comfort. Her partner demurred, telling her that she was in the middle of an assignment, and asking if they could meet as usual at the end of the day. The partner was then thunderstruck to hear this young woman's subsequent furious attack on her.

In my office, a few days later, the two were now calm, but the woman who had asked for comfort spoke about trying desperately to rebuild trust. In her view her partner's reluctance to meet her right away challenged her belief that she was loved. Her partner had thought they were in a straightforward negotiation about time. She insisted, "If I had known what this meant to you, I would have dropped everything and come."

Another couple I see had had a similar experience. However, this couple had twenty years of relationship under their belts, and had learned not to generalize from an instance of poor fit to a global assessment of their commitment to each other. They told me that the problem had surfaced over a phone call . . . or the lack thereof. With much trepidation the wife had taken her first plane flight in late September for a business trip she felt she could not postpone. The husband had failed to call his wife to check that her plane had landed safely, which the wife experienced as an emotional abandonment. However, she blamed her husband's habit of not attending to things that upset him for his omission, not a lack of love. The second couple was able to restore equilibrium more quickly. The husband was able to acknowledge that the cost of his protecting himself from his own anxiety—by spacing out on her flight—had been hurtful to his wife.

These four interpersonal consequences of common shock are suggestive, not exhaustive, of the many social dilemmas that witnessing violence and violation can create for individuals, families, and communities. They are built on biological and psychological underpinnings that are intricately intertwined with, and help account for, their occurrence. A first step in easing the relationship problems caused by common shock reactions to everyday witnessing is to find frameworks that make sense of the fluctuations in comfort and distress we cause each other.

Societal Consequences of Common Shock

Certain populations within any society are more vulnerable to the biological, psychological, and interpersonal consequences of common shock. Specifically, populations whose rates of witnessing structural violence and violation are high, and whose resources are few, are likely also to have high rates of exposure to interpersonal violence.[56] Put another way, areas with the poorest schools, worst medical care, and most poverty also suffer the highest levels of personal violence.[57]

Many of us may be able to imagine the effects of living in a war-torn society. We can grasp how difficult it must be to create a sense of safety or normalcy for children when bombs and soldiers roam the streets; when curfews are imposed; when schools are closed more often than they are open; and when food and water supplies are limited. We may wonder how we would be able to soothe a child when we are terrified ourselves. We can project ourselves into the bodies of those who are suffering and understand that with weeks or months of fear, disrupted sleep, interruption of work, we, too, might be screaming for retribution, wanting our leaders to defeat our adversaries.

The United States, however, is among the most violent countries in the industrialized world—this is borne out in community violence statistics. While people deplore, and express general concern about, the level of violence, it is harder to imagine the kinds of routine exposure to violence this translates into and the short and long-term consequences of it.[58] Studies conducted in several cities show that rates of witnessing violence are astoundingly high, especially among inner-city children. In New Orleans 91 percent of fifth graders had witnessed some type of violence, such as a shooting or a stabbing, as had 72 percent of fifth graders in Washington, D.C.[59] In a survey of 3,735 students from six urban and suburban high schools, the proportion of students who had witnessed someone beaten up or mugged at school ranged from 24 to 82 percent for both males and females.[60] Nor is it only inner-city dwellers who are exposed to high levels of violence. Recently, researchers have expressed concern that exposure to violence in rural communities and small cities is being overlooked.[61] Current research suggests that the likelihood of witnessing violence is higher even than being the victim of violence.[62]

At the moment we know most about the effects of violence on those who live in so-called urban war zones—citizens at especially high risk for common shock reactions.[63] James Garbarino, a man who has studied the effects of community violence on youth for thirty years, distinguishes acute from chronic danger, describing the incredible challenges posed by exposure to chronic danger. One six-year-old girl he interviewed told him that her job was to get her two-year-old sister to safety whenever the shooting started. "The bathtub is the safest place," she told him.[64]

There are clear developmental consequences for children exposed to violence and violation in their communities. These effects differ at different age of exposure, but also exposure to violence impacts on and alters the course of development.[65] If a six-year-old witnesses a father's friend murdered, he will have symptoms that are age appropriate for a young child, and these symptoms may then set his developmental path in particular directions.

Parenting children exposed to community violence is a complex process, exponentially increasing the challenges all parents face. It is especially challenging to parent children who have witnessed parental victimization.[66] For instance, a mother may feel worn down, helpless, and hopeless herself, unable to comfort or reassure a youngster that he is safe, since she is uncertain if this is true. When community resources are limited, there is inadequate assistance for parents who themselves are often too strapped to help their children.[67] Fortunately, schools, churches, and health-care settings are becoming more aware of the impact of witnessing community violence, and innovative programs are springing up that specifically address these problems.[68]

Whether in the home, workplace, or the streets, men are most likely to be the perpetrators and women and female children the targets of violence.[69] This is true for all measures of violence—threats, intimidation, physical, sexual, or emotional abuse. When a woman experiences violence, there is likely to be a witness to it at some point—a relative, a friend, or a professional, be it a police officer, an emergency-room nurse, or a shelter worker. And the gender of the witness is as likely to be male as female.

Children, boys and girls, are the primary witnesses to partner violence, and the effects on them are staggering.[70] As one client said, "I could always smell it coming." Another adult client's father was physically and emotionally abusive to his mother. The abuse created an atmosphere that never dissipated, even when his father was out of the home. My client described himself as always in a state of waiting, wondering when the next episode would happen, where it would occur, who else would be there, and whether he or one of his siblings would get hurt if objects were thrown. At night he and his siblings would huddle into one bed, for insurance's sake, in case the yelling began. Neither he nor any of his siblings was able to concentrate in school. He never brought a friend home.

While partner violence occurs at all economic levels, the experience may be distinctly different if you are a woman of color, with few economic resources—perhaps even an illegal immigrant—and have far more obstacles to obtaining protection than other women. One result of the decreased access to protection is that lethal violence is greatest among women of color.[71] Consequently, their children are also witnesses to the most profound violence, with the severest consequences to child well-being.

If a woman of color leaves her home under these circumstances, she may also be brutalized outside her home on the streets, and her children witness this too. Far from having an internal schema that the world is benevolent, the world is meaningful, and the self is worthy, women and children in these circumstances know otherwise.[72] These women and children, boys and girls, grow up and take their places in society. For many of them their chances for full participation in civic life is compromised by the early circumstances of their lives. We ignore at our peril the interconnections among the effects of structural and personal violence that take aim at vulnerable bodies and minds, that disrupt relationships, and damage the fabric of the society we need to work well for all of us.

From the Biological to the Societal

Shakespeare's Prince Hamlet is a privileged youth, heir to the throne of Denmark. But neither his wealth, status, education, nor superior intelligence or gifts protect him from the consequences of common shock. Confronted by his father, the Ghost, with the fact that his father's brother, his uncle Claudius, has murdered his father and then married his mother, he is stunned. His father commands him to both remember and revenge. Commanded, the ever-loquacious, articulate Hamlet is brought to a standstill. Hamlet is in shock. Common shock.

Hamlet was written in 1600–1601, based on a story that first appeared in the twelfth century.[73] Yet the sordid facts of his domestic situation are as contemporary as any in our day; his reaction as predictable; his dilemma as vexing; and the outcome of his actions as devastating for himself, his family, community, and country as they would be transposed to our time.

His symptoms are those of common shock. They are biological: He is paralyzed by the freeze position; he has difficulty sleeping and eating. He is hypervigilant and restless, pacing the corridors. Psychologically, he feels shame, helplessness, and worthlessness. He is overwhelmed by intrusive thoughts and feelings. His memory plays tricks on him and his self-care is shot. He looks like a lunatic.

These biological and psychological symptoms disrupt his relationships with everyone in the castle, especially his mother, Gertrude, and Ophelia, his erstwhile girlfriend. Though he has friends "in town," he doesn't go out with them. The predictable biological, psychological, and interpersonal consequences of common shock snowball to a horrifying denouement that affects the entire country.

As the plot unfolds, it confronts the audience, not just Hamlet, with the most profound questions of any time. Do we really want to root for murder? Does retribution end or create more conflict? Do we actually think it wise for the older generation to pass to the younger the task of vengeance? We have five acts to sit with these questions.

While seemingly an argument for vengeance, the play does reveal alternatives. In the final scene Hamlet apologizes to his peer, Laertes, whose father Hamlet has killed. We learn that there are codes of honor that regulate revenge. Even four hundred years ago there were diplomatic means of adjudicating violence.

But, in the end, vengeance prevails in Denmark. Laertes wounds Hamlet with a poisoned rapier and Hamlet, still innocent of the plot against him, picks up the poisoned rapier by mistake and wounds Laertes. They are now both doomed. Gertrude dies, having drunk from a poisoned chalice intended by Claudius as a backup measure for Hamlet should something go amiss with the duel. All is chaos. Laertes confesses the plot to Hamlet and tells him "the king's to blame" [5.2.302]. Hamlet stabs the king.

At last, at the very end of the play, the command to revenge is fulfilled. It is left to each of us to decide what *Hamlet* teaches us. Among the richness of the lessons, I believe that we have learned that the biological, psychological, and interpersonal consequences of common shock have played out catastrophically in Denmark. Further, I would ask a different question from the one that has intrigued so many others. For me the crucial question of the play is not why Hamlet delays, but why he acts. What is the tipping point, and what can we learn from it? Four hundred years later, all over the globe, we still live versions of *Hamlet,* with endings no less calamitous than Denmark's. What are *our* tipping points, what can *we* learn? Does the play point us in any directions?

At least one. Hamlet's good friend Horatio, upon seeing that Hamlet is mortally wounded, reaches toward the poisoned cup. Hamlet exhorts him to give him the cup instead. He has a task for him: "Tell my story" [5.2.338].

An unwitting witness to violence, Horatio has now been charged to turn his unintentional witnessing to intentional compassionate witnessing. "Tell my story." Indeed. Compassionate witnessing is one way, an always available way, to transform, not repeat, violence.

Part Two

How Do We Pass Along Common Shock?

We succeeded in taking that picture [from deep space], and, if you look at it, you see a dot. That's here. That's home. That's us. On it everyone you know, everyone you ever heard of, every human being who ever was, lived out their lives. . . . The Earth is a very small stage in a vast cosmic arena. Think of the rivers of blood spilled by all those generals and emperors so that, in glory and in triumph, they could become the momentary masters of a fraction of a dot. Think of the endless cruelties visited by the inhabitants of one corner of [the dot] on the scarcely distinguishable inhabitants of some other corner, how frequent their misunderstandings, how eager they are to kill one another, how fervent their hatreds. . . . [In my view] there is perhaps no better demonstration of the folly of human conceits than this distant image of our tiny world. To me it underscores our responsibility to deal more kindly with one another, and to preserve and cherish the pale blue dot, the only home we've ever known.

—Carl Sagan[1]

The Toll of Illness and Dying in Families

I have been so accustomed to think of violence and violation in terms of "force" that each time I experienced common shock in relation to illness, I had no idea what was going on. Already a trained psychologist, nonetheless I "missed" my condition. This meant that not only was I miserable, but I was confused. Further, it took me longer to figure out what to do than it would have otherwise. I wish I had known at those time what I know now.

Illness and disability are processes that can create the experience of violation through severe disruption. Thus, they create victims and witnesses. We might say, metaphorically, that illness and disability—even events that cause significant worry about someone's physical or emotional integrity—function as "the perpetrator" in the three-part drama I described in Chapter Two.

Thinking this way has helped me make sense of the intensity of violation that I have experienced in the many situations in which I have either witnessed a loved one ill or suffered illness myself. These episodes have been thrust upon me, just as unexpectedly as a mugging, and have truly thrown me for a loop. However, realizing what is going on, now, I can take steps to turn my unanticipated witnessing experience into one in which I am aware and active, with regard to those aspects of the experience over which I can exercise some control. I can also express my feelings, which turns out to contribute to health and well-being even in times of stress.[1] This way of thinking about illness and disability has helped me assist others.

The other day a client consulted me, bringing her month-old infant son with her. She was in love with her new baby, happy to have time off from her job to care for him, satisfied with the support she was getting from family and friends, and more anxious than she had ever been in her life. Having delivered a few days after September 11, she was certain that hormones and concern for her son Mark's future accounted for the intensity of her reaction compared to others she knew. She thought her response was normal, but wondered if I had any suggestions for her.

Certainly, I thought her anxiety was "normal" also. We talked, and at one point she began to tell me some details about her labor and delivery, caught herself, and said, "It was great, I really shouldn't waste my time telling you . . . but I'll just tell you briefly."

I settled back to hear a type of story I love to hear: a positive labor experience that ends with the delivery of a healthy baby. As Sarah told the story—without much detail; she really did have other things she wanted to discuss—she slowed down at the moment that Mark was put on her right breast. I felt as if she were taking me into the room with her, whereas just moments before I had felt like I was on an express train listening to a high-speed version of the story. Her voice even changed, became more confiding, as she narrated, "He nursed on that breast really well. He wasn't sleepy or anything. And then someone came over, switched him to the left breast, and as I looked down, I heard some sounds and saw he was turning a dusky blue. I called the nurse, she came over, saw it, too, and pulled Mark off my breast."

Sarah went on to tell me that within moments a decision was made to run a series of tests on Mark to see if he had a heart problem. Exhausted, she chose to wait in her hospital room rather than go with Mark for the tests. By this time many family and friends had gathered around her.

Mark returned in ninety minutes; all the tests were negative. He has been fine ever since. Sarah continued talking, asking me for specific suggestions of what she might do to manage her anxiety. She also repeated, "It's so unlike me."

Sarah was surprised when I chose to begin my summary reflections by talking about her postdelivery experience. I told her that I didn't think her experience was just about being a new mother and feeling the anxiety we all did about what's next in the post-9/11 world. Rather, her baby was pulled away from her breast. For ninety minutes she was apart from him, fearing that something might be terribly wrong. She went through a shocking ordeal at one of the most physiologically vulnerable moments a woman experiences. I had no trouble understanding why she was anxious.

Tears pooled in her eyes. "You know, other than one person that day who said, 'This must be hard for you, to be worried about Mark,' no one has mentioned what happened. I feel that you're validating something that I knew but I couldn't even put into words. It's as if, because Mark is fine, it never even happened."

From my perspective Sarah experienced common shock in a most dramatic way. Nursing her minutes-old son, she witnessed him turn blue. Pain, love, terror, disbelief, commingled in a fraction of a second, creating a gigantic wave in their oceanic calm. This sudden reversal of the plot—textbook-perfect labor and delivery of healthy baby—went virtually unremarked by the loving, celebratory crowd in her room.

Surrounded, Sarah was profoundly alone, caught in that particular silence that so frequently attends common shock experiences. She was aware that something was disturbing to her but couldn't name what it was. She lacked the concept of witness and thus she was unable to articulate clearly to herself and others what she had experienced during that hour and a half. She had been a witness to Mark's distress and its potential medical significance, helpless to help him, yet exquisitely aware of what might be happening. Had she not made the decision to "digress" and "waste time" in the session, she still might not have a way to express to herself and others her experience of waiting to learn if Mark was all right.

She and her husband were the primary witnesses to Mark's potential heart problem, but there were others there, too, apparently unaware of themselves as witnesses. Sarah was aware of her distress but unable to speak about it in the midst of the hubbub of excitement around her. Once she had been provided with the concepts of witness and common shock, Sarah's experience made sense to her, and this part of the anxiety—her confusion about why it was happening to her—subsided.

Witnessing Illness Can Produce Common Shock

I have probably had more experience witnessing illness and dying than I have had witnessing any other kind of violence and violation, and so I had more than the usual connection to Sarah's story. My life as a new mother in 1976 started with the confirmation of a heart defect in my son. I had been alone when the initial diagnosis was made and with Hilary when the definitive one was pronounced. Weeping, I asked the pediatric cardiologist if there was anything I could do for Ben. He leaned over his large desk, his eyes scanning the far wall on which photographs of smiling children were arranged, each one signed "with gratitude," and provided the following response: "There's only one thing you can do to be a good mother to Ben. Don't tell anyone about this. If you do, they may relate to Ben as if he is going to be an invalid and that will create additional problems for him later on."

In one brief sentence he equated goodness with secrecy, and agency with isolation. He undermined and cut off one of the most potent resources families have to deal with illness and disability: social support.[2] Last, he placed responsibility for Ben's care squarely in Hilary's and my hands, with no wiggle room should he and I have differences of opinion about what to do. The message was: Rely on yourselves, kiddos.

We did our best. Knowing nothing about the range of severity of these defects, I conjured horrible images of the hole in Ben's heart that was letting blood pass the wrong direction at high speed from the left to the right ventricle. I felt he was always at risk, becoming hypervigilant about telltale signs of blue around his rosy mouth. When Ben was about four months old, I was so frequently afraid that my pediatrician suggested I buy a few blue paint chips and always have one nearby to check whether indeed Ben had turned "blue enough."

I did not realize, for I lacked the concept, that I was suffering from common shock. My mother had died six weeks after Ben was born. I was drowning in grief, sleep deprivation, fear, actual and anticipated loss. It was summer. I was on maternity leave. My only friend with a child lived twenty minutes away, and we had just moved to a new community. I was isolated, and in the spirit of doing "the only thing I could do" to be a "good" mother to Ben, I, who thought secrets invariably problematic, was keeping one.

Ben's heart defect closed on its own when he was two years old. I suppose the positive spin on that difficult time was that Hilary and I were "prepared" when we learned four hours after our daughter Miranda's birth, three years later, that she had a rare, life-threatening genetic disorder. A senior pediatrician walked into our room, stood at the foot of the bed, and told us he would be brief:

"Your baby has a genetic syndrome. They were worried after the delivery and called me. As it happens, I diagnosed a baby with her syndrome last year, although it's pretty rare. I've made copies of four articles for you that pretty much cover what is known. If she lives, which is a question with these babies, she has a hefty chance of having some pretty severe problems. She's going to need to be in the special-care nursery until we see how she does. She may not survive; we don't know whether or not she'll be able to feed. In a while you can visit her there, if you'd like. Any questions?"

Hilary and I were stunned. I asked the pediatrician one question: "Did you say she might not live?" He replied, "Yes, that's right." Hilary, a physician himself, thanked him and asked if he would be available if he had questions after reading the articles. He gave Hilary his card and shook his hand.

It was 1979. We were in shock. We had just learned that our already beloved daughter might die from a disorder neither of us had ever heard of and the name of which I, in my postcesarean state, could not remember. At that time neither the diagnosis nor the ongoing care of a child with a serious chronic illness was considered a severe enough stressor to meet criteria for the diagnosis of a trauma response by the psychiatric profession.[3] Two decades later, as Sarah's story shows, we still do not have a clear understanding that witnessing the distress of a loved one caused by illness, accident, or disability—whether acute or chronic, speedily resolved or lingering—can cause symptoms of common shock. In fact, consideration of trauma (what I would designate common shock) as an aspect of the experience of patients' family members is a relatively new topic even for health-care professionals.[4] In the absence of a clear understanding of this, our ability to help ourselves and others is limited.

None of us will escape being a witness to a loved one who is ill or dying. This is an inevitable fact. Few of us, however, will appreciate the significance of our being witnesses. Illness is rarely simple and witnessing it isn't either. It is crucial to have some sense about what one can do to cope. We need to know how to stay aware without being overwhelmed; how to stay aware without feeling helpless about what we cannot control; and finally, aware and active in relation to those things we can do that make a difference. There are always openings for creating healing interactions and moments of beneficence. Such moments may never affect the medical outcome, but healing and cure are two very different experiences.

Above all, we need to be aware that witnessing illness and death takes a profound physical and emotional toll. For many of us, attention to the suffering of the person who is ill or dying eclipses our own distress, rendering us less, not more, able to manage our own pain. Ultimately, this inattention to ourselves boomerangs and interferes with our ability to help the person who is at the center of our attention.

What a difference it would have made if I had known that my reactions to Ben's defect were typical consequences of common shock. How helpful it would have been if someone had said to me, "Kaethe, you were in the hospital recovering from a cesarean section; your husband was at work; the rest of your family were attending to your mother, who was dying in New York; and a doctor you had never met examined your child and told you he had a heart defect. All the while he is examining Ben, you are so unsuspecting you are thinking he must be thinking as you are thinking how adorable Ben is. Talk about being caught unaware.

Talk about becoming a witness when you least expect it. Of course, you experienced common shock."

Further, Hilary and I were out of synch, one of the relationship consequences of common shock I described in Chapter Three as a "problem of fit." Had we understood this, we might have been spared months of suffering. I was terrified that Ben would die. Hilary, who had seen children with heart defects do well, was sanguine. I interpreted Hilary's lack of fear as a deficiency of love. I couldn't bear that the person I needed most to rely on seemed unreliable to me, since he did not share the sense of doom with which I lived constantly.

I couldn't bear feeling estranged from Hilary and yet I did. Finally, I consulted a close friend of ours, a psychiatrist, at his office. It was a beautiful crisp fall day. Bill's office was on the second floor and from his windows you could see trees with orange and gold leaves. I cried, he heard me out, and he gently challenged my perception that Hilary lacked feeling for Ben. He handed me a book of poems by Robert Frost and asked me to read one, "Home Burial."[5]

As a reader I could see what I could not see as a wife; I had a husband who cared. The poem begins with the husband asking the wife what she always sees from the window: "She let him look, sure that he wouldn't see, / Blind creature. . . ." But he does see. He sees his family burial ground and the mound that is their first child's grave. The wife accuses him of having no feeling about the loss of their son. He accuses her of shutting him out and refusing to teach him how to speak to "please" her and give "no offense."

Through Frost's poem I regained empathy for Hilary. I was able to hold his perspective alongside mine and not feel eclipsed or invalidated by it. In doing so I didn't reject him as unloving. In believing that the husband in Frost's poem cared about their dead child in his own way, I opened myself to learning how Hilary cared about Ben. I needed to understand Hilary's feelings, not feel the same way, to be in an intimate connection with him.[6] In retrospect I can see that we were both aware and feeling helpless, not knowing whether the hole in Ben's heart would close—but that the quality of our witness experience was significantly different. Estranged from Hilary, I felt alone, which compounded my fear and misery about Ben's health. Once I could perceive Hilary's love for Ben, I could fully ally myself with him. Reconnected, I gained resilience to manage my dread.

Again and again, having ideas about common shock and witnessing would have helped me. It is hard to witness your child in pain or suffering. Even a step removed—a neighbor, a friend, or . . . a reader—it is difficult to witness. There are many stories in this book, the next among them, that people have told me are painful to read. I tell this one because there are lessons to mine from it, we all came through fine in the end, and the outcome was good. It is, after all, one of those slices of life.

When Miranda was three years old, full of life, she caught her finger in a heavy drawer, forming a blood clot under the nail that did not dissolve over a period of days. Instead the finger swelled, the nail bed turned black, and thin stripes of color began dripping down toward the joint.

We called our pediatrician, who recommended that we wait and see what happened. By the third day, a Saturday, I was certain something was wrong and I insisted that we take her to the emergency room. Ben, age six, had soccer practice that morning, so he went off with another family while we took Miranda to the emergency room.

When Miranda was finally ushered into a room, the doctor looked carefully and explained to us that he needed to relieve the pressure in the nail bed, which he would do by using an electric drill to puncture a small hole in the nail. Miranda, who understood language better than she could speak, quickly withdrew her finger. She was sitting on my lap and I could feel the tension in her body and also feel a particular determination she had when she decided that, "no, sorry, that may be fine for other children, but that, thank you, will not do for me."

The doctor could also see she would have to be convinced. First, he explained that the procedure would not hurt. Next, he told her that he would spray something so cold on her finger that she would feel no pain. Then, he sprayed the anesthetic on his hand, and as this seemed to interest her, he sprayed it on her arm. He sprayed it up and down several times, from finger to elbow, while she visibly relaxed, intrigued by the cold sensation and the now apparent fact that she no longer had much sensation in her arm.

Without verbally assenting she stuck her finger toward the doctor and he readied his equipment, a heat probe for burning a hole in the nail. He bent over her finger, turned on the probe, and promptly ignited the coolant. A column of flames, perhaps a foot high and two inches wide, erupted out of nowhere, rising from Miranda's arm to the doctor's head.

The next seconds felt like hours. The nurse who was assisting the doctor with the procedure leapt toward the doctor as he turned to the only sink in the room and doused his head with water. Hilary, who was standing behind Miranda and me, dived for her arm and blew out the flames, snuffing them out in short order. I held Miranda tightly as I could feel her wrench away from Hilary's ministrations.

Within moments the episode was over. The doctor and nurse left the room. Many examinations later we were convinced that Miranda had not been physically injured by the flames, which had actually ignited a few millimeters above her flesh since the anesthetic spray was an alcohol-based one. It took us months, however, to believe that she, we, might truly recover from the episode.

Miranda was the victim of the incident and Hilary and I were witnesses to it. Within moments of picking up Ben at his practice, at Miranda's urging, the two of us told him what had happened. By telling him the story, he, too, became a witness to what he dubbed "the day the doctor set my sister's arm on fire." Unlike Miranda, Ben told this story several times a week initially, and he told it to strangers if he could. If he told the story when Miranda was present, she, who could not tell the story herself because she lacked the language skills to do so, would often correct him by saying "no" if he got a detail wrong.

Over time Ben settled on a story that usually elicited about three nos from his sister. He didn't act the story out in play with his friends and neither did Miranda, although I tried to engage her in drawing and puppet play about it. However, Ben's behavior took on a frantic quality; it was as if he had added another cylinder to his motor. At the time of the incident Miranda was toilet trained. Within days she had regressed to having frequent accidents. Usually a cheerful, even exuberant child, she was sad, more aggressive, and more disobedient. I was unable to set limits on her, unable to imagine causing her a moment's more distress.

We were all beside ourselves. Miranda would periodically say in halting cadences, "I know it happened, but I can't see it anymore." I had nightmares during my sleep and intrusive thoughts during the day. I kept seeing the column of flames shoot up from her arm, gorgeous and ghastly. I replayed if I could have averted it in any way. Should I have told the doctor not to spray her arm? Should I have acted on my thought that he was showing off for Hilary, another doctor, and that his swashbuckling style with the spray can was more abstract art than medicine? Hilary felt incomprehension that members of his profession had not only hurt his child but then emotionally abandoned her by leaving the room and never returning to talk to her, or us.

Miranda had experienced a violation and we had witnessed it. Ben, who hadn't even been there, was as affected as the rest of us. All of us had common shock and none of us knew it, producing a family crisis. We muddled through. Hilary recovered his sense of equanimity. My anger, helplessness, and vulnerability ebbed. Ben moved on. I gradually became able to discipline Miranda. A wise friend pointed out to me that my equating discipline with pain was depriving her of the structure that she had always needed to keep her exuberant spirits in some kind of manageable zone for life with others. He was right and she did better once I began setting effective limits again. As she did better, we all did. Her symptoms disappeared.

We had no contact with the hospital. Had I understood the dynamics of witnessing as I do now, I would have arranged for our family to return to the emergency room and for someone there to talk with us about what had happened. Unable to heal each other, too caught up ourselves in the same horrifying experience, we needed help from the outside. We needed to hear someone from the hospital say: "We are so sorry that happened to you. Tell me what it was like for each of you so I can learn from this terrible mistake. We want to be sure nothing like this ever happens to anyone again."

Six months later just such an acknowledgment happened spontaneously. Miranda developed croup in the middle of the night, and nothing we did at home was sufficient to get air into her lungs. We raced her to the same emergency room, where, ten minutes later, she was inside a gauzy tent, a small, clear plastic mask over her nose sending in humidified oxygen and epinephrine. The nurse never left her side and neither did Hilary or I. Her breathing started up on its own, became more regular, and then her chest muscles relaxed. About a half hour after we arrived, she spoke. Effortfully, stopping after each word, she looked directly into the nurse's eyes. "Are you," she said, with no emotion in her voice whatsoever, in a tone as flat as the desert, "Going. To. Set. Me. On. Fire?"

This particular nurse responded to Miranda's question dramatically. "Oh, my God! Are you the little girl whose arm got set on fire? No, no, honey, no. Nothing like that will happen. No. You are perfectly safe. We're giving you oxygen, special warm air."

She called to another nurse and told her what had happened to Miranda and what Miranda had just said. Thereafter, in her tent, breathing oxygen, it was as if she became a little celebrity, holding court to staff who came by to tell her how sorry they were that her arm had been set on fire. When we left, well into the morning and the next shift, after exams and X rays to be certain that her airway was sufficiently open, a piece of the terror of that spring morning six months before had dissolved, dissipated each time a doctor or nurse or orderly or physician's assistant came by to express regret, chagrin, and disbelief at what had happened to her.

It was a powerful experience. Being witnessed, months after the event, with compassion produced healing for Miranda—the victim—and also for Hilary, Ben, and me, the witnesses. Amends by people who had not caused the injury nonetheless diminished its effects. After that we were all essentially fine.

Challenges to Witnessing Illness and Disability

While it is advantageous for those who are ill to have witnesses who are comfortable and effective in witnessing illness and disability, this does not always or often happen. In fact, there are many personal, relationship, and societal obstacles in the way. Each barrier interferes with creating social support for the ill, disabled, injured, dying, and their witnesses, thus limiting resources for all. This is particularly unfortunate, since social support has been shown to have positive outcomes for physical and mental well-being. When social support is diminished, there are significant negative consequences.[7]

There are three common challenges that attend witnessing loved ones in the context of illness and disability: rendering the problem invisible; becoming silent about it; and finding words to account for the experience of observing another's pain and suffering.[8] While these are indeed hugely challenging, we can find ways of coping with each one of them. When we do, we diminish rather than heighten our common shock experiences.

Invisibility

Several years ago I consulted to a family in which the middle-aged son, John, had severe complications of diabetes. He had had diabetes from childhood and had managed it quite well, but as he got older complications arose. A gutsy, determined man in his late thirties, John had experienced successive setbacks, eventually having to leave his job and move back home with his parents. His father was in terrible pain about his son's compromised life and shortened life expectancy. This was reported to me by John and his mother, because the father had refused to attend the family interview. He claimed that it would only make things worse, by which his wife and son understood him to mean, "It will make me too sad to face what is happening here."

The father had lived with common shock provoked by John's diabetes for decades. He had never been able to bear his own pain and this had closed him off to his son's. The current crisis was precipitated by the father stating that there was nothing wrong with John that self-discipline wouldn't cure. He accused John of not handling his medical regimen properly and thus bringing upon himself the deterioration in his condition. John was enraged at his father for not seeing how hard he worked to manage his disease. Compounding the many losses with which John was dealing was the invisibility of his effort. To some degree John had become so identified with his effort that his father's denial of it was tantamount to denial of him. John was a victim of his diabetes, longing for his father to be a compassionate witness to him. The father was frozen in grief, unable to bear his son's suffering. He handled it in a particular way: making the son, not the diabetes, the problem. He could not face the devastation of the disease process itself and therefore attempted to render it invisible.

The attempt to render invisible that which we cannot bear is common, and thus invisibility is a regularly occurring problem faced by those who are ill or disabled. Their family members face this as well. Miriam Greenspan, a psychologist, author, and mother of a daughter with special needs, eloquently describes a time when her experience and her daughter's were both rendered invisible by a stranger.

In this encounter on a wide expanse of lawn, Miriam was watching her three-year-old daughter Esther, who has movement and coordination problems and who had just learned to walk six months before, take the gawky steps of a "newly born colt" while able-bodied children were running, jumping, and tumbling. Another little girl was practicing gymnastics a few steps away from Esther, showing off her near-professional skills. A man who was standing next to Miriam commented to her, "Isn't she just superb? Children are so graceful and agile, aren't they?"[9]

Miriam was speechless, feeling that he had erased her daughter and her experience of her daughter all in one fell swoop. By creating a general category about "children" within which Esther clearly did not fit, he rendered invisible the incontrovertible negative evidence in front of his eyes that not all children are "perfect."

Miriam was able to ignore this man and rebound from the experience. John, on the other hand, lived with his father. It was not so easy to ignore his behavior. During our consultation several things emerged. John felt greater appreciation for his mother's support. He strengthened his own internal witness, weeping about his medical condition. Last, he realized that he did not want to give up on his father without one more try. He decided to ask his endocrinologist to talk with his father, to see if she could explain to him the reasons for the deterioration in John's condition.

There are many ways people who are well can deny or dismiss the experience of those who are ill or disabled, making them feel invisible. While the reasons for doing so may be to avoid dealing with something difficult, there are unintended negative consequences. It heightens the distress of the ill and deprives them of full-hearted witnessing of their suffering.

Silencing

Lapsing into silence is another way we distance ourselves from truly witnessing. Kat Duff, in her collection of essays on illness, writes: "There came a point in the depths of my illness when I realized that the people closest to me could no longer bear to hear of my despair, which was inconsolable; it seemed to short-circuit their capacities for attention and compassion."[10]

In Chapter Three I discussed the work of James Pennebaker and his associates on the social stages of coping with a natural disaster. Pennebaker has also worked extensively in the area of health and illness. He has found that actively holding back or inhibiting our thoughts and feelings can have negative effects on the body, while expressing emotion by talking or writing can be healthy.[11] However, hearing the distress of others may produce one's own psychological distress. This is so much the case that it is a natural impulse for listeners to withdraw from the conversation or to downplay the sufferer's pain. Kat Duff's quote above describes this illness dilemma. Researchers conclude that the effect on the sufferers is invariable: at some point, sensing the listener's apprehension, sufferers stop talking.[12]

Peggy Penn, who has worked with families with chronic illness for over twenty years, notes that the loved ones of the ill person also experience stress from the inhibition of their speaking. Both the person with the illness, who needs to have her feelings compassionately witnessed to derive the health benefits of expressing emotion, and family members, who are overwhelmed by passively witnessing the pain of the ill family member and who also need an outlet for what they are experiencing, need a way out of the relational impasse: how to speak without causing the other to suffer; how to listen without suffering. Penn describes this relational impasse in this way: "*I am afraid that if I do not speak to you and tell you how I am, I will slowly withdraw and leave you; however, if I do speak to you, I am afraid that you will slowly withdraw and leave me.*"[13] Penn tells us that though conversation about illness is immensely difficult, it also "widens the soul," and in a circumstance in which we often feel "so done to: *we are also doing.*"[14]

Stigma as a Contribution to Silence

There are many ways the relational impasse Penn describes arises in families. In some instances social stigma is a part of the mix. Since 1987 the Preventive Intervention Project (PIP) has focused on preventing affective illness—for instance, depression or bipolar disorder—in young adolescent children of parents who are currently affectively ill. The clinicians and researchers affiliated with PIP want to help family members break through the silence that surrounds affective illness, particularly to release children who live in these families to notice and put into language that which they experience with their affectively ill parent.

Also influenced by James Pennebaker's work, they have as a founding premise that expressing emotion is important for psychological and physical health.[15] Yet in families in which there is one or more generations of persons who suffer affective illness, there is often a powerful silence, influenced by experiences within the family but also shaped by the intensely negative attributions about affective illness that circulate in popular culture. These negative attributions, such as that depressed people are "lazy, manipulative, childlike, 'bitchy,' and *responsible* for their own illness"[16] influence family members and health-care professionals as well. Not surprisingly then, the PIP staff have found most of the children and adolescents in their project have little to say to them initially about their parent's illness. By providing families with information about affective illness over a series of visits, the PIP helps families destigmatize depression and bipolar illness. It also helps families move from the private unshared views they have formed about the meaning of the illness to ones that can be made public, shared, and thus revised on the basis of what they learn from each other.

I work with a client who has been depressed for the last ten years of her young adolescent son's life. She has endured months and years of feeling as though she is walking through her life encased in concrete on the lower half of her body and covered with a glass shield on the upper half. Everything she tries to accomplish is exponentially harder for her than it is for others. She can see out toward what she wants, yet she feels she is out of reach for anyone to truly touch her. Finally, through medication and therapy, she is better.

My client has felt searing shame about the manifestations of her illness—her eruptions of anger, her overwhelming exhaustion, her despondency and unavailability—and been loath to talk about it with her adolescent son. He has mirrored her reluctance with a reluctance of his own. They have "solved" the relational impasse that Penn describes by withdrawing from each other and not speaking about the illness that dominates their lives, in order to preserve their connection. Dinner-table conversation is superficial, especially on evenings after my client has erupted with irrational anger at her son. These episodes sink into oblivion between them, remembered privately, but not discussable.

Now that she is ready to break the silence, he is not. As a witness to his mother's severe depression, trapped by a set of ideas about its cause that has brought stigma into the center of his family life, he cannot so easily dispel the stigma and silence, and speak.

My client and I are informed by and take heart from the PIP experience in believing that it will take time for her and her son to open up to each other. We have worked on her accepting brief conversations as progress and containing her disappointment from rebuffs. She consistently invites her son to talk about her illness and hopes that someday he will. They are inching their way out of the relational impasse, moving slowly from silence to speech.

Secrecy as a Contribution to Silence

I understand this relational impasse better than I wish I did. Secrecy, not stigma, was the complicating factor in my family. In the context of the secrecy that surrounded my mother's terminal illness, I felt that my not speaking created disconnection between us at precisely the time in our lives I most wanted to store up every morsel of connection for the long years ahead when, absent, gone, dead, my mother would not be available to see or hear or touch. Yet I feared that if I broke the rule and spoke, that she, sensing the rule (or my father's wishes), would keep it by withdrawing from me.

Treating Children as Too Young to Know

Fourteen years after my mother was diagnosed with cancer, I was diagnosed with a different kind of cancer. My children were young, nine and twelve years old. Never having had to tell my children I had cancer, I was unprepared. I assumed that we needed to be protective of them, but I didn't understand just how individually tailor-made "protection" must truly be to protect your children. Our children knew I had had a biopsy for breast cancer and they knew the day that Hilary and I were going to the doctor's office to learn the results.

After Hilary and I found out that I had a malignant breast tumor, and after we had spent time alone with each other, we called a family meeting and talked with the children at length. We thought we had done well. We rose to make phone calls to our families when we thought we had all finished speaking. As we got up, Miranda yelled at us that she wasn't finished talking. We sat back down and she made one point: "Why am I the only one in this family who is scared?"

Without knowing it, without wanting to do so, we, I, had shared my experience in a way that separated me from the children. In trying to take care of them, in trying to shield them from my fear, I had withdrawn my feelings from them. Miranda was *not* the only one in our family who was scared. I was scared that I was about to do the worst thing I believed a mother could do: die and leave her children without her.[17]

Miranda was my witness to my breast cancer saga, a harrowing year of treatment and then another recovering from it. Throughout she pleaded to break through the relational impasse of illness by speaking all that we felt, all of the time. Over and over, she wanted to know more than I wanted to reveal. She also wanted other people to witness her witnessing me.

One day she told me: "I feel like all my life I have been the kind of person who would jump in and help if she saw a person drowning in the river. And now I'm drowning in the river and people are prancing by." At nine she intuitively understood what at age fifty-five I now believe wholeheartedly: witnesses need witnesses.

Realizing that she would probably speak to her friends, I called the mothers of her closest ones and asked them to be available to support their daughters should Miranda's speaking provoke distress in them. I organized my women friends to witness her witnessing me. One evening a friend took her skating at the public ice rink. My friend reported Miranda saying, "It feels so good to get exhausted. It's like flopping on a mat. It's like your heart has been broken and then all of a sudden put back together again."

Illness continually breaks one's heart. But it can be put back together. Speech, breaking the silence, heals. There are rings of witnessing. I witnessed myself as a victim of breast cancer. Miranda witnessed me living with a life-threatening illness. Friends witnessed both of us. At each ring there is the potential for any of the four witness positions to be operative. One way of transforming the relational impasse of illness is to stay aware and active in relation to it, creating connections with others that everyone can bear.

Meaningfully, my father and I did just that. He was a loving and attentive witness to me. I called him when I needed encouragement and he tolerated my episodes of despair. His sustained support and optimism, his mantra for me—"Be of good cheer"—was both a joke and a profound commitment on his part to bring cheer into my life. Unlike my mother's illness, mine drew us together. I experienced his abundant loyalty, love, and comfort.

Illness narratives

There is a third challenge to aware and active witnessing that adds to those contributed by invisibility and silence and which makes it hard to connect with others around experiences of illness and disability. Illnesses are not all alike. One way they are unequal is a way people rarely consider: illnesses themselves generate stories.[18] The narrative one can tell about an illness is inextricably linked to certain parameters associated with the illness itself, and these parameters have real effects on the story that can be told, the storyteller, and the audience. In general it is easier to recruit witnesses to listen and help with an illness that will improve over time, an illness with what is called a progressive narrative, than it is to recruit witnesses to an illness that will only get worse, perhaps leading to death, an illness with what is called a regressive narrative.[19]

There are other dimensions of illness that affect the story that can be told as well. Imagine the narrative of an illness, condition, or disability that is common, widely understood, for which there is a treatment and a cure, produces no social isolation or stigma, and has no greater incidence in any particular gender, class, or racial or ethnic group. Now imagine the narrative for an illness, condition, or disability that is rare, poorly understood, has no known treatment or cure, produces stigma and social isolation, and has a greater incidence in a particular group. Which one is more likely to be rendered invisible and to be silenced? Which one to receive compassionate witnessing?[20]

Miranda's illness narrative of her syndrome and my illness narrative of breast cancer couldn't be more dissimilar, and the differences produce real effects as a specific consequence. I feel free to talk to whomever I wish about having had breast cancer, but all of us are cautious about speaking about Miranda's syndrome. We learned very early on that rarely had anyone ever heard of it; they found her symptoms confusing and perplexing; they wondered if Hilary and I, and then Miranda as she got older, were accurately reporting her symptoms; and they invariably felt uncertain as to how to help us. This was so for family, friends, and physicians alike.

Miranda's medical history is long and diffuse. Her symptoms varied over time and were unpredictable. Around high school age her joints dislocated easily. She sometimes fainted when she changed position from sitting to standing or lying down to sitting. She had terrible headaches. She had a quirky learning style that didn't fit with any defined learning disability but which required her to use compensatory strategies.

Miranda rarely spoke to any of her friends about medical issues or the frequent discomfort she was in. Teachers failed to understand or act on the instructional modifications recommended in her educational instruction plan, perhaps unclear why she would need them given her evident intellectual ability. During her sophomore year her discomfort began to accelerate and the lack of predictability became even more disconcerting to all of us. Living with the knowledge that she was in chronic pain wore me down. Her intermittent fainting terrified me. If she hit her head on a hard surface, as she had at home a few times, she might suffer a concussion or worse. I was always on the alert, cued in to the smallest variation in the sound of her movements. I lived in dread.

Here again the absence of a literature supporting the idea that people who live with those who suffer illness may suffer symptoms of trauma or, as I am proposing, common shock, was not available in the early 1990s. The situation is certainly confusing. Medical illness is not a good fit with the ways mental-health professionals have primarily thought about trauma. A person who suffers posttraumatic stress, by definition, is suffering symptoms after—post—an event. However, the parents' "trauma," their common shock, includes a fear of what may be in store in the future. Common shock isn't just "post," it's always also present and future.

In addition, caring for a family member who is ill or disabled—child, spouse, parent, sibling—can cause "compassion fatigue," a term coined by psychologist Charles Figley to convey the biological, psychological, and social exhaustion and dysfunction that can occur when a family member has prolonged exposure to "compassion stress," the "stress connected with exposure to a sufferer."[21] This concept makes abundant sense to those who have cared for ill or disabled family members over time, but is not readily articulated by them. As a culture we seem to minimize or forget how hard these times can be.

In March of 1995, on a Sunday afternoon, I was packing to go to New York for two days to work with my Australian colleague Michael White and a few colleagues, when Miranda's left hip slipped in the socket. In excruciating pain, she and Hilary headed to the emergency room and I headed to the airport.

Hilary kept me informed by voice mail. The next day one of Miranda's shoulders had slipped its socket due to the crutches the doctors had prescribed for her hip, and the other had incurred a strain. By the time I returned, I was as upset as I had ever been about her.

I couldn't bear Miranda's pain. I felt it in my own body. I had been able to concentrate on the work I was doing with Michael White because I believed I was learning something I could transfer to our own lives. Miranda was in bed when I got home and I sat with her until she finally fell asleep around 2:00 A.M. I didn't try to sleep. My mind was working overtime to integrate what I knew as a therapist with what I experienced in our situation. Why was the social support and medical care available to me as a woman living with breast cancer so much more abundant than that available to Miranda living with her problems?

I was determined to come up with a theoretical rationale. I was desperate to block Miranda's blaming herself for any of the difference that she perceived between us. The fact was that Miranda, by virtue of having a rare genetic disorder, was more isolated than me.

People who study narratives talk about whether they are coherent or not—that is, do they make sense to most people? Unlike my breast-cancer story, Miranda's stories about her condition rarely did make sense. They lacked coherence. When Miranda developed a symptom, Hilary and I were usually uncertain about what it meant. Sometimes we didn't even know whom to consult. Should we go to a geneticist or a pediatrician? Find a specialist for this particular problem? We didn't even know how to feel. Were we on the edge of a cliff, nowhere near, or had we fallen over?

Some illness stories are so familiar to us that most people have a clear idea of how to interpret what they are hearing. Breast-cancer stories are now commonly told and heard. It is improbable that a woman who has discovered a large breast lump would find a friend or physician who says, "Oh, gee, don't worry about that large lump you have." The stories have what is called high cultural resonance.[22]

On the other hand, Miranda's illness story has virtually no cultural resonance. Few people know how to respond to the name of the disorder or even the names of the physical manifestations. For instance, during the initial period when Miranda was suffering joint dislocations, before we had a term for why it was happening that most people understood, many friends were puzzled. When we were finally able to say, "Her ligaments are loose," there was almost a collective sigh of relief.

By virtue of having a rare genetic disorder that almost no one has ever heard of, Miranda is more isolated in her experience than me, who has a disease that affects one in eight women at some time in her life. At my age it is hard to imagine that I might know or meet an adult who does not know a woman who has had breast cancer. By contrast it is hard to imagine that Miranda will ever find anyone who knows someone with her syndrome.

The disparity shows up in the health-care community as well. In all the years that we have interacted with the medical profession over concerns related to Miranda's syndrome, only a handful have ever personally worked with a child with the same disorder. By contrast, all my medical providers have other patients with breast cancer. The differences go on and on.

I was determined to create a context in which the fact that Miranda's illness narrative was often incoherent and had little or no cultural resonance would not matter. The next day I told Miranda I thought we were all affected by her syndrome's uniqueness. In crises, such as this one, it was exhausting to cope with the pain, for her, and the logistics of care management, for us. When we added to this the effort of explaining to well-meaning family, neighbors, and friends what was going on, we were always frustrated. We never had explanations that were satisfying to us, much less to others. At precisely the moment we most needed empathic listening, we tended to isolate ourselves. We felt awkward explaining that although *something* was going on, we didn't know what or why.

I told Miranda that I had thought of a way of creating legitimacy for the story we could tell, coherent or not; of a way to increase its cultural resonance; and of a way to decrease her sense of isolation, even if it were to a small group of people.[23] I proposed to Miranda that we design a ceremony and invite a group of friends and helpers whom she would trust to share the history of her living with her syndrome. With an audience of loving friends and helpers as witnesses acknowledging all that she had learned herself over the years, I hoped that she would also activate her own witness role in relation to her disorder. I hoped that she would no longer feel solely its victim. Additionally, I hoped that the ceremony would enroll this audience as future witnesses as well.[24]

Open to anything, Miranda agreed. We planned the ceremony for one month, during which time she became more aware of all that she had lived through and all that she had mastered. Her invitation went right to the point:

Please join me and my family
at a ceremony
to witness the history of
my living with
my syndrome

I am hoping that you will become members of an
"opposing despair/nourishing hope" team to help me deal
with the ongoing trials of my life.[25]

Ten women, including her guidance counselor and her physical therapist, joined Miranda, Hilary, and me for the event. Before she began her talk, she introduced a ritual she had designed. At the beginning of the ceremony she gave each of the twelve people present a candle and lit the one in front of her. She began to tell her story. She asked people to light their candle from hers when they understood the magnitude of her experience. As people lit their candles, at different intervals of time, she said she felt that "each lit candle took some of the burden off me."[26]

Throughout the ceremony, at one time or another, people had tears running down their cheeks. Observing the effect of her story on her guests created as profound an emotion for Miranda as hearing them reflect on what she had shared. By creating a team I think we did "oppose despair and nourish hope." Miranda, Hilary, and I all had a form of support none of us had experienced before. It worked synergistically; the support each of us felt affected us all positively.

The team generated additional witnesses when the three of us were clearly unable to cope effectively with the continuing crises of Miranda's medical care. Witnessing individually or as a member of a team provides social support. Social support has consistently been found to have positive effects on adapting to illness, adherence to treatment for illnesses, and even on health outcomes themselves. Social support can reduce morbidity and mortality.[27] In a just world the resource of witnessing, as a form of social support, would be equitably distributed among us. But this is not the case, and the reasons are not primarily personal or familial.

I know that my idea of forming a team for Miranda was influenced by the example of gay men and women in the early 1980s who mobilized to care for those in their community who developed AIDS. Recognizing that social support was accorded not by the severity of the need, but by the acceptability of the individuals who suffered, the gay community organized to care for its own when existing structures failed to provide the services and support their loved ones needed.[28]

They organized themselves to cope with the most basic and with the most far-reaching needs of those suffering with HIV and AIDS. Their advocacy work influenced the way AIDS was understood by the culture at large, the way the medical community cared for AIDS patients, the way medical research was prioritized and conducted, and the way government responded to the epidemic. AIDS activists have served as a model for much of the organizing that we now see in relation to other illnesses, including my own, breast cancer.[29] This community understood as well as any other that while dying may be hell, and while witnessing it may be, too, it can also be a time of awe.

Witnessing Dying and Death

All of us will experience the death of a loved one. No one is exempt. How we witness and the support we have during and after will make all the difference not just to us, but also to future generations.

Carrie's grandmother died months before her mother, Judith, became pregnant with her six years ago. Judith has been my client for one year, during which time we have focused on Judith's angry outbursts at

Carrie, whose temper tantrums, her mother says, are matched by her own. In the last few months we have talked about Judith's mother's death, and these conversations have released Judith from daily ruminations about her beloved mother. Recently, Judith told me that Carrie's favorite game is playing "hospice at the orphanage."

Like Carrie, children are often the unintended witnesses to our own despair. Judith was an overwhelmed witness to her mother's illness and dying and Carrie, we would have to conjecture, is an overwhelmed witness to her mother's grief, although she may be unaware of just exactly what she is intuiting. Judith has begun talking with Carrie of her feelings about her mother's death in the hopes that breaking the silence will release Carrie from her preoccupation with other people's dying.

Judith is trying to intercede now in a situation that can have far-reaching consequences. Many people are unable to imagine that children can be affected at an early age by death, and yet many children are. In *A Death in the Family* James Agee writes about the death of a father from the perspective of his six-year-old son. Inspired by the death of his own father when Agee was six, the novel makes vividly clear the subtlety with which children can sense and feel death in their midst. In a passage in which his mother tells the boy and his younger sister that their father got "hurt and—so God let him go to sleep and took him straight away with Him to Heaven," Agee records the mother's "shattered breathing," her "whole body shaken as if by a wind, but she did not cry."[30] The entire book is a compendium of observations of what a child did, can, does, notice in the heightened awareness that learning about, and then living with, death brings.

Another client of mine, Gerry, has been suffering through the protracted death of his mother from disabling arthritis and worsening heart disease. Before I worked with him, he had seen another therapist, and in that therapy he had been able to articulate his experience of watching his mother watch her mother die from an accidental injury. As a young child, perhaps seven years old, his mother had taken him to the hospital, where she and other relatives surrounded his maternal grandmother as she lay dying. Gerry recalls feeling it was his responsibility to do something, but he is uncertain which person was the object of his conviction that he had to act. He also dates his mother's withdrawal from vital engagement with him—and life itself—from that period. He is sure that his relationship with his mother changed forever after her mother's death and yet this has never been spoken between them.

Now, his mother rebuffs all efforts to help her with the daily tasks of living and medical management, while at the same time her two diseases make her less and less able to care for herself or her small apartment. A nurse, Gerry has become severely depressed. He is a font of information and good sense, knows the social support system in his mother's community like the back of his hand, but is continually thwarted from activating assistance even as his mother informs him regularly of her complaints and calamities.

Gerry and his mother are frozen in a macabre dance that at once rekindles the common shock Gerry experienced as a child and produces new toxic interactions. We can only imagine what his mother feels, for she is unable and unwilling to talk about the past or the present. Gerry experiences his mother's implacable refusal of assistance, coupled with her evident desire to be released from pain and his willingness to help her, as a vise that is closing in, slowly torturing him. His experience in the present repeatedly slips back to the total helplessness of his seven-year-old self when he wanted heroically to save the day but had no means to do so. Today, he has every means, but feels just as helpless. He cannot bear the rage he feels toward his desperate mother, and so it turns back on him, sapping his own life of meaning and purpose. Cultivating caring with detachment is the goal of our work. I am trying to witness the dignity of Gerry's struggle to be present for his mother without becoming a target of her rejection.

Gerry's story, along with hundreds of others I know, fuels my belief that the circumstances surrounding dying and death can have long-reaching consequences. I try to assist people to be as present to death as circumstances permit. In Gerry's case the circumstances permit very little of what he most wants to provide, and this is a tragedy for him.

Sometimes my assistance toward others takes the form of my being a compassionate witness and sometimes I try to enlist others as compassionate witnesses. With Antonia, my colleague's five-year-old daughter, I proposed that she could be a witness to her friend Sam's death and thereby help other children as well.

I had read about seven-year-old Sam's death in our local newspaper. In the week before Halloween he was playing on the hanging rings when he collided with another boy. Both children fell to the ground, one landing on the other's head. A few hours later, Sam died at Children's Hospital from his injuries. This was a family's and a community's nightmare tragedy.

My colleague's and Sam's family were close friends. Sam and Antonia had known each other all of their lives. I knew from my colleague that Antonia was very upset. By coincidence I was writing an article for an Internet site on how children cope with death. I wondered if Antonia might want to be interviewed for this article. It occurred to me that she might find it comforting to think that her words would be read by other children and parents in similar situations who might be helped by what she had to say.

Her dad proposed the idea and she was interested. One Saturday morning, before her ballet class, Antonia came to my house. We went upstairs with her dad to my office and I turned on my computer, opening up to Planet Therapy's home page.[31] I showed her the picture of the spinning planet and she said, "Oh, the Earth." She hadn't understood the word *planet* before she saw the picture.

I opened to the page on the Web site where her story would appear and she was obviously pleased to talk with me. However, she was also very shy. She moved away from the computer screen and snuggled up to her dad, who sat down in a chair with Antonia on his lap.

I asked Antonia to tell me about Sam. Straightaway she volunteered this: "He taught me how to eat string cheese."

"Have you eaten string cheese since Sam's death?"

"I have," she said, and with a prompt, "I remembered Sam and it was a good feeling. I want to remember him because he was nice. It makes me happy to think about him."

I asked her if there were other ways she had of remembering Sam, and there were many. Antonia likes visiting Sam's family because there are lots of pictures of Sam on display, his room is "still there and so are his toys." Antonia said she thought it would be good if she were able to remember Sam always and if adults helped her remember by talking about him.

I next asked her about whether or not she had gone to Sam's wake. Many adults worry that young children will be frightened at a wake, especially if there is an open casket. Antonia's parents gave her a choice to attend the wake and to see Sam. Antonia chose to go and she is glad that she went. "I saw Sam in the box. His body and his face looked different. He was wearing a sweater I had never seen before. It was a good thing I saw him in the box because it was my last chance to see him. I said good-bye to him in my head, not out loud. But I said it to him."

Even though Antonia said her farewells, she continues to talk to Sam through her prayers. "I say prayers to Sam during the day. I tell him, 'I still know you even though you're in heaven.' "

At the end of our conversation I asked Antonia if she thought there were ways that children could be helpful to the parents of a child who has died. She thought hard. "Sometimes I hug Sam's parents to make them feel better."

I'll bet that does help Sam's parents a lot. On Monday, two days after our talk, Antonia came home from school with several drawings, all of planet Earth. She has told her dad she is glad she has helped other children.

The loss of a loved one is painful. I was able to provide Antonia with an outlet for personal pain to take on public purpose. While this was an exceptional opportunity for Antonia, the principle I was acting on was ordinary: I gave Antonia something to do.

There is no reason for children to know what to do unless they are helped to learn. I learned from my mother. When I was a freshman in college, a friend's father died. My mother called me at school, told me about his death, and reminded me to write a condolence note. At our next phone call she inquired whether I had. I explained that I was having a lot of difficulty, that I couldn't figure out the right thing to say, and that I had torn up several drafts. There was a pause. Then she said gently: "The point is not that you get it right, but that she hear from you. Anything kind you say will be fine, but it must get to her." These words have been touchstones for me.

When our neighbor's mother died, our children were four and seven years old. I told them that when they next saw Jack, who was away at his mother's funeral, it would help Jack if they went over to him, looked him in the eyes, and said, "I am sorry that your mother died." Miranda was so eager to execute these steps she headed for the window to watch for him. Older, Ben was wary. Eventually he did speak to Jack, but he had already picked up the hesitancy so many people feel, at first, about talking with the newly bereaved.

My friend's son Gabriel died the autumn he was eight years old. I addressed some of my remarks in my eulogy to the children in the audience. I had suggestions about what they might do, recognizing that for many of them, Gabriel was the first person they knew who had died. I told them that remembering something about Gabriel would be a way that his spirit would live on in each of us. It would also be a great comfort to his parents and sisters, knowing that others remembered their child and brother. I suggested that they should "seize life by the armful, as you would the colored leaves that are falling all around us." And third, I asked them to stay in touch with Gabriel's family, who I knew would want to be reminded of Gabriel by seeing his friends from time to time, and over the years.

In the gymnasium of Gabriel's school that morning, we were all mourning a child whose cancer cells had not only ravaged his body and ultimately caused his death, but had also been the occasion for creating a community of support, care, and compassion around his family, and the friends who loved him. Hundreds of people were connected through the rituals of mourning, which are times that most cultures have formal rites of witnessing.[32]

In some parts of the world there are elaborate rituals of support and mourning, but the sheer numbers of dying and the overwhelming numbers of dead make performing those rituals agonizing for their communities. In South Africa the AIDS epidemic is ravaging the black African community and a complex culture of denial has sprung up in relation to many factors—including the current national politics of AIDS—giving invisibility and silencing free rein.[33]

Unlike the United States most of the countries of southern Africa have strong traditions of community unity and collective care. There is an African concept, *ubuntu,* that provides an important philosophical context for African traditions of care. As Archbishop Desmond Tutu, a noted South African antiapartheid activist and chairperson of the Truth and Reconciliation Commission, has articulated it: "A person is human precisely in being enveloped in the community of other human beings, in being caught up in the bundle of life."[34]

In Malawi AIDS counselors use the image of a bundle of sticks to promote community support for the ill and dying, for it has clear cultural resonance. "One stick on its own is easily broken, but if you put sticks in a bundle, that bundle becomes very strong, so strong that you cannot break it. A spirit on its own can be easily broken. But bundled together we will not break. That is our power and our strength."[35] However, the official politics of denial, coupled with silence and stigma, hinder the creation of that bundle of sticks.

In the winter of 2002, following her graduation from college, Miranda accompanied her father and me to South Africa, assisting each of us in work projects we had there. In the Eastern Cape, Miranda visited three large hospitals and saw hundreds of people, mostly young, waiting in emergency rooms, the vast majority of whom were hours or days away from dying of AIDS. None was going to be admitted to the hospital. Although the medical burden of AIDS in the South African hospital system is unprecedented, she never heard one mention of AIDS in the three days of meetings she attended with Hilary.

A witness to the horrors of AIDS on the body and on the body politic, Miranda was devastated by what she saw. Her witness lacked a witness; she met no one who acknowledged either the disease or the effects of being so helpless in relation to it. She was truly in common shock.

Ten days later we were visiting friends who live in a rural part of Kwa Zulu Natal. Our friends took us to visit a local community center, where one single enterprising woman has given over her home and her small parcel of land to create a shelter for women who have been battered, children orphaned by AIDS, and those dying of AIDS.[36] On our tour we were taken into a small room, clean and bare, with an emaciated man and woman, both staring into space, their bodies already rigid, their eyes huge and glassy in their wasted faces. My first instinct was to hustle Miranda out of the room as quickly as I could without offending the two dying people or our guide. Moments later, outside and alone, I held Miranda and asked her how she was.

She was clear. She wanted me to understand that it was not seeing dying people that was terrible, but rather it was the lack of acknowledgment that people were dying that was horrifying to her. By contrast she felt that what we had just seen was as good as it gets. Everyone used the word *AIDS* and people were lovingly cared for in their community. Their death had witnesses.

And so it is. We cannot halt death, but we can acknowledge it, name it by its true name, and be present to it. The dying need witnesses and the witnesses need witnesses too. The peoples of the world are inequitably burdened by death and its witnessing. Those of us in parts of the globe whose witnessing capacity is not stretched to the limit have something to offer communities that are massively suffering. We can become a "community without borders,"[37] sharing in the essential human task of caring for those who most need care.

CHAPTER 5

Double Jeopardy or Do No Harm

A mother in my clinical practice reported that she had overheard her thirteen-year-old daughter and a friend speaking in dramatic tones and gestures about a recent incident at their suburban middle school. From what this mom gathered, a white boy had jumped an African-American boy in the locker room, who had beaten him up in return. Through the grapevine the girls had heard that the principal had suspended the African-American youth but only gave detention to the white youth. The girls believed that their principal had acted unfairly, and that his actions were racist. The girls had spent their afternoon on the computer, instant-messaging their friends about what had happened, getting more and more agitated.

Neither girl was present at the locker-room altercation. They were distant witnesses to the fight and to the disciplinary actions that followed. Rightly or wrongly, they perceived the principal's actions as racist and were troubled by this. Not directly involved themselves, they nonetheless experienced a tear in the social fabric of their school community.[1] Their distress, a mild common shock reaction, demonstrates their sensitivity to violation and their interest in social justice.

Their reactions point to another route by which common shock passes among members of a community—when professionals who have authority over certain areas of our lives have their own common shock reactions that they do not manage well. When this happens, their constituents get "sprayed," as it were, with their inadequate conduct.

As a society we place extraordinary levels of trust in certain professionals whom we have anointed to bear responsibility for key social functions. For instance, we entrust teachers with the task of educating our youth, doctors with diagnosing and treating our illnesses, clerics with ministering to our spiritual needs, police with protecting us, and journalists with informing us about our world. We expect these professionals to perform these tasks competently and with integrity. When we believe that a professional, for instance our school principal, has failed to perform his job adequately—of which acting in a racist manner would certainly be an example—we experience a betrayal of trust. We cannot ignore their reactions because of their positions in our lives. Thus, we must cope not only with our own reaction to events but also with the reactions of professionals to these same events. How they deal with their own witnessing has significant ripple effects outward to the wider community.

In the previous chapter we have seen that we can develop common shock when we witness illness, dying, and death. This can happen particularly easily in settings in which people know each other well, like families, but also in work settings or community groups. Features of certain professional relationships make them ripe for passing common shock on to the people they serve.

Double Jeopardy

Educators, health-care professionals, police, clergy, and journalists, the professional groups I consider in this chapter, by virtue of the roles they perform in our society, exercise significant power over our lives. They operate with a set of social privileges that go along with and are related to the authority they wield. Our deference to their authority and expertise is based on an implicit agreement between these professional groups and us. We turn to professionals to meet our needs and we trust that they will use their knowledge and experience to serve our needs in good faith. We believe that individuals who have trained to perform these societal roles have been selected by their professional associations because of outstanding qualifications to serve us. We trust that the individual professionals with whom we interact are dedicated, committed, and competent people who deserve our cooperation, respect, and obedience. Professionals have power over us, and we are vulnerable to the ways they wield this power. We expect and want them to use their power beneficently.

The vast majority of people who enter these professions do so because they have a calling to serve others. Police are motivated by the desire to protect the community from harm; reporters want to inform the community and change how people see the world; health-care professionals aspire to relieve suffering and enhance wellness in the community; educators hope to realize the potential in each person they teach to contribute to a knowledgeable, productive, and energetic citizenry; and clerics seek to guide us to transcendent values that diminish isolation and provide energy to tackle problems in our earthly lives.[2]

Few professionals are aware when they choose their careers that they may place themselves at great risk in the service of these lofty goals. For in caring for the people they serve they expose themselves daily, repetitively, and cumulatively to the violence and violation that permeate the lives of their constituents. As their constituents we need to be aware of two facts: First, we expose those who serve us to high levels of violence and violation; and second, we are then vulnerable to how these professional groups manage their reactions to witnessing violence and violation. A few examples will illustrate these points.

Policemen routinely witness violence in the performance of their duties. Since 1960 it is estimated that more than one million police officers in the United States have been assaulted, resulting in the murder of several thousand officers.[3] For every officer killed there is at least one police officer witness, as well as an entire department that learns in detail about the events leading to the officer's death.

On any day in the United States local news will cover violent crime in print, radio, and televised media. Journalists who cover crime beats are witnesses to these events.[4] They interview on-site witnesses, and sometimes victims as well; photograph or film the scene; and gather as much background information as they can to make sense of the particular crime. Other journalists cover wars. Day in and day out they place themselves in harm's way alongside military personnel who have received months to years of specialized training to handle situations that journalists confront with no comparable preparation.[5]

Teachers work among young people whose lives are beset with trials and tribulations, many of which they do not leave at the classroom door. Teachers are often chosen by students to confide their woes. While gratified by their students' trust, teachers are also burdened by the stories of hardship they hear. Teachers also are witnesses to students' treatment of each other. For example, national surveys consistently report that the majority of students experience sexual harassment in public spaces in schools, that is, the hallway, classroom, gym, or cafeteria. These surveys note that it is common for school personnel to be present during an episode of unwanted sexual attention and rare for the school person to intervene effectively.[6] One category of sexual harassment is antigay slurs. Research shows that students hear such slurs as many as 25.5 times a day; teachers often overhear this hate speech.[7]

Clergy assist congregants at times of suffering and transition.[8] They minister to the ill and officiate with the dying and their relatives. People confide their problems, both spiritual and mundane, to clergy. In some religions clergy hear people's sins and help them atone. Clergy may be first responders to problems of abuse within families. They are privy to the pain and woes of the community with whom they interact daily. For instance, it is not uncommon for clergy to serve on a committee with a congregant who has confided a tormenting secret. Their role requires them to keep the person's confidence; to provide comfort, support, and guidance; and to keep their private knowledge of the individual from changing their public behavior toward him.

Health-care professionals are exposed to physical suffering and all the disturbances attendant to the pain and anguish that illness and dying bring in their wake. We give health-care professionals privileged access to our bodies, which they see in all states of disrepair and breakdown. Depending on the state of medical knowledge and their own command of it, they may feel effective or helpless in the face of the complex challenges of the acute or chronically ill. For example, during the AIDS epidemic in the United States, and before the advent of effective drug regimens, it was not uncommon for house officers in urban hospitals to have a caseload dominated by young, terminally ill patients for whom they had little but palliative care to offer.

Professionals' Experiences of the Four Witness Positions

In one way or another individuals in these five professions are all witnesses to the pain and suffering that come from violence and violation. In addition to the exposure they have to violence and violation in their personal lives, as everyone has, they have exposure in their occupational roles. During the performance of their duties they may have any of the four types of witnessing experiences I described in Chapter Two (See Figure Four). In general a professional who witnesses violence or violation in the course of his work and feels aware and empowered in relation to it is likely to be someone who is practicing effectively and competently (Position 1). By contrast a professional who witnesses violence and violation, is clueless about its significance or implications, but nonetheless responds as if he knows what he is doing will be misguided, ineffective at best, and guilty of malpractice at worst (Position 2). A professional who is unaware of and thus passive in relation to the urgent need of a constituent has abandoned that client. This abandonment may

Figure Four: Witness Positions

	Aware	Unaware
Empowered	**Effective and Competent Position** **1**	**Misguided, Possible Malpractice Position** **2**
Disempowered	**Ineffectual and Stressed Position** **3**	**Abandoning, Possible Malpractice Position** **4**

also be a form of malpractice (Position 3). Finally, a professional who is keenly aware of the client's situation, but feels helpless to do anything about it, will be of little or no use to his client and highly stressed by his work (Position 4).

Position 1

We all have many examples of professionals who act competently and effectively. This is how professionals earn our trust, respect, and gratitude. These professionals manage their own witnessing in ways that allow them to thrive at their work. The teacher who creates a supportive community among her boisterous second-graders and virtually eliminates bullying, scapegoating, and exclusion from her classroom earns her weight in gold. The minister who organizes his congregation to assist those in the community who have been made homeless by a flash flood helps them all to feel they are effective witnesses. The journalist who interviews victims of crime for the evening news and does so in a way that helps them tell their story while promoting the audience's capacity not only to know the facts but understand the victims' experience is building the community's capacity to care. The policeman who arrives quickly at the scene of a domestic altercation in the courtyard of an apartment building where there are scores of onlookers, pulls the protagonists apart with no escalation of violence, and gets the perpetrator to agree to enter a detox unit, has protected the victim and witnesses. Finally, the hospice nurse who helps a large extended family manage the daily emotional, physical, spiritual, and logistical burdens of care for their terminally ill elderly father, protects that family from the despair and exhaustion that can make terminal care a nightmare. The nurse assists the family to witness their elder member's dying process effectively, helping them be emotionally and physically present for him.

Position 2

Although we may not have been cognizant of it at the time, most of us have also had experiences with professionals who occupied each of the other three witness positions. With each of these witness positions there is a breach in the professional-client covenant. The client is harmed by the professional's inability either to be aware of the significance and implications of what she is witnessing, or to take effective action in relation to what she has witnessed, or both.

At the time of this writing the country, indeed the world, is focused on the issue of clergy sexual abuse. As of January 2003 at least 1,205 priests in 161 of 177 Latin Rite dioceses in the United States have been accused of sexual misconduct against more than 4,200 people, mostly teenaged boys. Every region of the country, in large cities and small, has been affected by priest sexual abuse of parishioners.[9] While the harm done by priest perpetrators to their victims and allies is immense, the harm caused by those priests' superiors who were told of allegations of sexual misconduct—as reported, ranging from fondling to rape—and did not intervene to protect the victims is also huge. By being informed of the abuse, these ecclesiastical officials were witnesses to it. They had the power to act protectively of the victims and to help perpetrators take the necessary steps not only to change their own behavior but to acknowledge the harm they inflicted on their victims, their friends and families, and the community as a whole. But Church officials, for the most part, have not used their power in this way.

Oddly, for an institution whose very theology provides such exemplary parables of repentance, and whose scripture makes clear that Christ loathes abuses of power, Church officials focused on behavioral rehabilitation exclusively. That is, of course, if they took any action at all and didn't just reassign a priest—ignoring reports of sexual misconduct altogether. They never saw that they had the opportunity to enact Christ's witness in these circumstances. They didn't see that whereas the issue of whether the priest could ever safely minister would always remain ambiguous, the issue of whether the priest could repent and make amends could be answered by those he harmed. Church officials missed the opportunity to create healing for those who had been wronged. Victims remained victimized, perpetrators remained perpetrators, witnesses—families, friends, parishioners, and the public at large—were devastated, parishes suffered, and the Church itself was injured.

From media reports and analyses it seems that few in the Church intervened even to remove offending priests from contact with parishioners.[10] By allowing such priests to continue to serve, many in the Church hierarchy demonstrated that they protected the interests of the Church, not the faithful. In this way they were empowered, but their attention was directed to potential harm to the institution of the Church, not the immediate and long-lasting harm to the victims, their allies, and the community as a whole.

It may often be the case that the witness is aware of something, just not what others would want him to be aware of. As we will see later in this chapter, the harm to victims, allies, and the community that has occurred through the abuse of clergy, as is the case for any instance of sexual abuse, is far more devastating than it would otherwise be, because witnesses who could have prevented it failed to act decisively to protect and care for parishioners.

Position 3

Witness Position 3 combines lack of awareness with inaction, resulting in the professional's effectively abandoning his responsibility to his client. As with all the other witness positions, any of the professionals can occupy this one, with terrible effects. One example comes from schools.

I mentioned above that students hear antigay slurs approximately twenty-five times a day. Faculty, however, intervene in fewer than 3 percent of occurrences. In May of 2001 Human Rights Watch prepared a report titled "Hatred in the Hallways" to document the existence and the impact of violence and discrimination against gay, lesbian, bisexual, and transgender youth in American schools. The report puts a poignant face to those youth who are harassed in school and whose insult is compounded by the neglect of teachers and administrators. It is particularly sad to learn how often faculty fail to stop harassment or offer support to those who are harassed since, when teachers do respond effectively, they can make a considerable difference to the young person's school experience. In virtually every instance when these young people reported feeling good about school, they gave credit to a teacher.[11]

Students talked about several kinds of problematic faculty or administrative responses to harassment, of which the most common is no response. Youth describe teachers standing right beside them in the hallway when they are called "faggot" or other slurs and having the teacher say and do nothing. The youth attribute the teachers' failure to act to a number of causes, including their lack of awareness that it is harmful to the targeted child. A sixteen-year-old youth is quoted in the report as saying, "There was this underlying tone that boys will be boys or kids will be kids, but that's wrong."[12] The report cites other factors, including the failure of teacher training to address issues of discrimination and harassment based on sexual orientation or gender identity and also the absence of clear administrative guidelines either at the school or district level. In combination the portrait is drawn of teachers who are unaware, passive witnesses to the steady barrage of harassment faced in public and private spaces in schools. Sadly, these youth have exceedingly low expectations of their teachers, so much so that even a small gesture of support takes on great significance. For the most part they expect and encounter teachers who abandon them to the cruelty of their peers.

Position 4

When I teach, supervise, or lecture, I often hear heart-wrenching anecdotes from the health-care professionals with whom I work who are haunted by experiences in which they were painfully aware of what needed to be done, but felt helpless or lacking in resources or expertise to provide it. The corrosive effect of finding oneself in witness position 4 cannot be underestimated.

A case in point is handling death. Physicians face death as a routine part of their day, yet "good" doctors do not let death ever become routine. Strangely, many physicians have not been trained to deal with dying patients and find themselves ill equipped to communicate about matters related to death and dying.[13] Richard Peschel is a professor of therapeutic radiology at Yale University Medical School who cowrote a slim volume of essays describing experiences he had as a young physician during his medical training.[14] In the opening essay he describes an eerie encounter he had taking a patient who was in the middle of a heart attack through a long and narrow tunnel from the emergency room to the cardiac intensive care unit. Along the way a sheet-covered corpse, accompanied by several men in black suits and hats, passed them, presumably on their way to the morgue. Peschel looked down and saw his patient turn his head so that he was exactly eye level to the corpse. The patient then looked up at Peschel, who developed the certain conviction that his already terrified patient believed he had seen his own future.

One might think, given the sensitivity with which Peschel renders this encounter and the subsequent lingering effect it had on him for years, that he would have spoken to his patient in an effort to comfort him. But he did no such thing. He never initiated a conversation with this man, who did survive his heart attack, and only addressed their shared encounter with death when the patient himself inquired about it several days later. Confronted by his patient's question, he writes, "I cannot escape answering." He then affirmed the man's conviction that the shape they saw in the tunnel was a dead body.

Peschel is an aware but disempowered witness in that tunnel, emotionally overwhelmed by the chance meeting of a critically ill man and a dead one. Full of feeling, he cannot harness his sensitivity to break the silence and to speak into it with some words of care or consolation. Not trained to handle one of the most fundamental aspects of his work, he is struck dumb, incapable of using his rich inner experience as a guide to console his patient. Not surprisingly, he is particularly exhausted at the end of this shift, not registering the extent to which he has failed his patient.

Empathic Stress Reactions

Ironically, although individuals in these professional roles have especially high exposure to violence and violation in the performance of their roles, and are frequently witnesses, they may never have thought about themselves in this way. In fact, it may come as quite a revelation to conceptualize their experience using these ideas. "Oh," one physician said to me, "that explains it. It's so obvious, but I never thought of it like that." In fact, it is so obvious, like air, it is invisible. Yet there may be consequences of their not appreciating this particular path of vulnerability to common shock and the real possibility that this very vulnerability may have negative consequences for them, their family and friends, their constituents, and the wider community whose lives are touched by their professional practice.

For some of these occupations—for instance clergy, physicians, psychotherapists, and educators—the exposure to witnessing violence and violation often occurs in the context of ongoing and unfolding relationships in which knowledge and involvement develop over time. For police and journalists exposure is usually to different people in different situations, with little opportunity for relationships to develop with the individuals involved. Both kinds of exposure involve risk.

Just as family members can pick up or react to the distress of others in their families, professionals in performance of their occupational roles can pick up or react to the distress of their clients. No amount of training for the performance of their duties—be it surgery, citizen arrests, confession, therapy, or photographing a crime scene—changes the fact that these professionals do their jobs inside bodies that work the same way in their professional as their personal lives. That is, professionals are subject to the workings of the same biochemistry that makes all humans vulnerable to common shock.

People in these professional roles may also be particularly sensitive to the needs of others. As I have said earlier, most health-care professionals, police, clergy, educators, and journalists experience a call to service as a primary motivation for their choice of work. Yet, ironically, it may be their very sensitivity to others that opens them up to the kinds of "injury" that these professionals can sustain.

All of us have a capacity to feel empathy for the pain and suffering of others.[15] Professionals, naturally, do too. The dilemma, though, is that they encounter high levels and frequencies of pain and suffering in their work, day in and day out, year in and year out, decade after decade. We know that the effects of exposure to violence and violation are cumulative. Professionals may develop "empathic stress reactions" as a consequence of their attunement to those they serve.[16] When a professional feels empathically attuned to a client, wishes to relieve suffering, and feels satisfied that his response is helpful, he is less prone to empathic stress reactions. However, when the professional is dissatisfied with his response, he is more vulnerable to empathic stress reactions.

Empathic stress reactions are a severe form of common shock that persists over time.[17] There are two kinds of empathic stress reactions that may have significant job, constituent, and personal consequences for these five professional groups: burnout and secondary traumatic stress reactions.[18]

Burnout

Professionals in all of the occupations I am discussing in this chapter are subject to burnout. I have worked with several, of whom Carla is one. Carla consulted me at the suggestion of her best friend, to whom she confided how much she hated going to work. Her friend had put it succinctly: "There's something terribly wrong. You were the most dedicated teacher I know and now you're talking like our fantasies of the worst jerks in the school!" Indeed, Carla only brought herself to therapy when she caught herself having disparaging and demeaning thoughts about her middle-school pupils that startled her with their vehemence.

Carla was in her early thirties, unhappily single after having been engaged twice in relationships that did not work out. She had been teaching at the same school in a small city outside of Boston for the previous eight years, where she was hired after completing her master's degree in education. One aspect of Carla's story was the way dissatisfaction in her personal life had made the stakes at work higher and thus the disappointment keener when conditions at her school deteriorated. Like many small cities hers had experienced falling tax revenues, which resulted in larger classes and fewer resources to assist teachers. Carla not only had more students, but she felt that they were needier. Carla was a witness both to the deteriorating conditions in her classroom and to the personal difficulties of her large number of students. She felt helpless with respect to both.

Initially, Carla felt that she and her fellow teachers were welcome to express their frustrations to the school administration, but in recent months, she said, that had changed. "It's as if we are opposing parties in a conflict: My team leader acts as if I'm complaining because I'm spoiled and not because I am thinking of the kids and what we are *not* doing for them that we should be doing. If I have twenty-eight kids in a class, no aide, and kids who can't sit still, I spend my time setting limits, not discussing short stories. If I had wanted to be a disciplinarian, I would have become an animal trainer. That's what I feel like some days."

When I met Carla, her physician was evaluating her for an ulcer. She took analgesics for headache pain. She routinely took all of her sick and personal days—something that she had never done before—and found Sunday nights intolerable; her stomach would get into a knot around 6:00 P.M. as she contemplated reentering the school building. Most alarming to her was that her inner talk now consisted of mean and hostile thoughts about her students. "It's as if I have a giant chip on my shoulder," she said. "I don't trust the kids, and I don't think I even like them. I can't be doing them any good."

Carla suffers from *burnout*.[19] People with burnout feel emotionally drained by the work that they do. In most instances burnout occurs in a healthy person who has had no psychological problems beforehand and who has been drawn to her line of work out of the desire to help others. On the job, stresses gradually mount so that the person feels less and less able to accomplish the goals for which she entered the profession. Often there are institutional or structural barriers that interfere with the person's ability to work effectively. Carla was required to teach more students with more serious difficulties than she had when she entered her profession. Job conditions—the struggle to help students or clients, for example, in an institutional context that appears to thwart one's efforts to do so—produce a gradual erosion of the very idealism that motivated the person's occupational choice. When this occurs, over time, job satisfaction deteriorates and the person begins to develop symptoms of burnout.

Burnout consists of physical, emotional, behavioral, relationship, and work-related difficulties.[20] In a couple of sessions it became clear to both of us that Carla was suffering from many of the symptoms of burnout, compounded by feelings of guilt and depression that she felt the way she did. The first step in resolving her burnout was for Carla to gain some understanding of the circumstances that had produced her reaction. She had not suddenly become a bad person, as she had feared. The next step was harder: she had to decide whether she could respond differently to conditions as they were likely to remain in her school, and schools elsewhere, or consider another occupation. Eventually, she decided to stay in teaching and to work on changing her reactions to the challenging job conditions.

Secondary traumatic stress

Secondary traumatic stress is a concept that refers to the effects on the helper of being exposed to another person's trauma. It, too, is a severe common shock reaction. Whereas burnout usually emerges gradually, secondary traumatic stress can appear suddenly, in response to witnessing or learning about the primary exposure to a traumatic event of a significant person or a person whom one wishes to help. Secondary traumatic stress is usually accompanied by intense feelings of horror, helplessness, and fear. Crucially, the symptoms that accompany secondary traumatic stress may be profoundly disturbing to a professional who subscribes to the belief that his training renders him invulnerable to distress. Although he may know exactly what is occurring to him, he may be unable to respond effectively out of shame and disbelief that "this" is happening to him.

Police, like the other professionals I consider in this chapter, are highly vulnerable to secondary traumatic stress reactions, and yet the culture of policing and the institutional structures of many police departments make it difficult for officers to recognize, accept, and receive help for the painful symptoms they experience. Many officers anticipate negative consequences, such as second-guessing by fellow officers, discrediting by supervisors, and suggestions of unfitness by the administration, if they reveal their distress reactions.

On a daily basis police officers may be exposed to violence, directly as victims and through witnessing others. In reading dozens of accounts of police work researching this book, I was filled with compassion and respect for the job that officers do, the risks they take doing it, and the psychic toll their work exacts. An officer who arrives at a fatal traffic accident or responds to a call for backup at a shooting and must supervise the scene of a murder, may develop severe common shock, that is, a secondary traumatic stress reaction.

At first the officer may not notice anything. Then, he may realize a few days later that he is shaking on the way to work. He may notice physiological symptoms: sweaty palms, heart palpitations, or stomach pain. Next he may realize he is replaying the accident scene in his mind, like a slowed-down home movie, and he can't get away from the sight of blood that had sprayed on the victim's dog or the smell of smoking rubber. These elements recur unbidden as intrusions both in his waking and his dream life.

The officer may find himself quarreling with his family. An already strained relationship with his fourteen-year-old son may get more frayed. He may grill him on his whereabouts, challenge his choice of friends, tell him he is no good, and either believe he is within his rights to do so or feel out of control and terrible for his behavior. He may brush off his wife's efforts to comfort him, barking at her to mind her own business.

A few weeks into a secondary traumatic stress reaction, he may give up working out at the gym, stop going out with his partner for one drink after work, and instead take three alone at an out-of-the way bar, and wander into a strip club a few times. Gloomy, having trouble sleeping at night, he may feel the whole world is rotten.

At work, on the job, he may be curt with fellow officers and brusque with citizens with whom he interacts. Suffering more muscle aches than usual, when challenged on his behavior by his partner he may attribute the cause to his physical discomfort. He may find himself cynical about the very work he had heretofore loved. At some point he may question whether he's got "a problem," but worry that if he consulted a counselor, his supervisor would find out about it and he would come under unwanted scrutiny.

The officer is in a bind. He may feel worse and worse but be sure he has no way out. Plus, he may be telling himself he is weak and a hopeless case for not being able to snap out of it. Although an imagined history, I have drawn it from scores of descriptions I have now read. This hypothetical officer is suffering from severe common shock, secondary traumatic stress, compounded by his belief—which may be accurate—that he cannot get help for his condition without jeopardizing his job.

There are several areas of symptoms that are frequently, but not always, associated with these severe common shock responses in helpers. First, there are psychological symptoms. Chief among them are distressing emotions, such as sadness, rage, fear, or horror. Some helpers experience intrusive imagery of the victim's experience. For instance, a helper may have a nightmare that has elements of the other person's experience in it. On the other hand, some helpers are plagued by emotional numbing. They suddenly feel hollow, empty, dull, unable to feel anything about anything or anyone. They close up shop, as it were, not just on the job, but in all parts of their lives. In addition, they may find that they shy away or avoid any reminders of the victim's experience.

Then there are physical symptoms. The helper may notice a rapid heartbeat, sweating, a sense of alertness and vigilance, difficulty concentrating, and insomnia. These higher-than-usual signs of physiological arousal may be cues that the helper is reacting to the other person's trauma. Or, the helper may notice a range of somatic disturbances, especially headaches and gastrointestinal difficulties.

The helper may experience behavioral change as well. He may have trouble adhering to his usual schedule of activities, find himself overusing alcohol or abusing drugs, or forgo his usual routines of self-care, such as exercise or listening to music. He may throw himself into work but find that his performance is less effective.

Finally, there may be changes in the person's relationships. The helper may become irritable with people in his personal life, lash out, or withdraw. Usually, the helper must keep his victim's confidence and therefore he doesn't feel at liberty to disclose the situation that is so disturbing to him. Significant people in the helper's life, partners or children, may feel shut out at the same time that they feel adversely affected by the "spillover" from the empathic stress reaction of their loved one.[21]

Perhaps most difficult in terms of the helper's ability to relate to loved ones and friends is that secondary traumatic stress, severe common shock, provokes alterations in one's basic sense of meaning and purpose. Trauma disrupts trust. Helpers dealing with secondary traumatic stress, or reeling from it, are engaged with profound questioning of values and purpose that may be disruptive to ongoing relationships, especially if the helper feels unable to share what he is going through.

These two empathic stress reactions share characteristics but are also different. Burnout develops gradually over time and primarily affects one's job performance. Secondary traumatic stress reactions can develop acutely in response to witnessing another's trauma. The symptoms of secondary traumatic stress are similar to the symptoms of posttraumatic stress disorder and they remit to similar interventions. People can suffer from either of these empathic stress reactions or a combination of both. These responses are normal, common, expectable, and, still, often not recognized. Or they are recognized, but the person feels considerable shame about them. Sadly, these occupational hazards of witnessing violence and violation are interpreted by many people—both within and outside of these professions—as signs of personal failings.

Biases that Harm Service Providers

Objectivity

Westerners tend to split the personal from the professional and see it as a hallmark of professional competence to do so. This creates certain dilemmas of practice with regard to empathy. A reporter who was covering a series of child murders in Los Angeles wrote: "[I] kept seeing those tiny faces, even though I did the 'professional' thing and showed up for work every day, ready to deliver my reports without a shred of emotion. I didn't want my boss to know that these stories were ripping my heart out, lest she think I wasn't up to being a 'real' reporter."[22]

Professionals are socialized to believe that objectivity is possible and necessary to be effective in one's job. Authority is associated with detachment and emotional neutrality. Charlotte Aiken, also a journalist, reflecting on the toll that covering violence takes, describes the way detachment may show up in a reporter's life: ". . . I've been both police and courthouse reporter. I read autopsies every day on those beats. I flipped through them, glanced at the grim details, and tossed them aside in search of a news angle on crime and violence. That's how we survive in this business. We find it, read it, and report it."[23]

Emotionality

Westerners tend to view thoughts as superior to feelings and, more crucially, they are viewed as distinct, the way the body is seen as distinct from the mind. In fact, emotionality is frequently construed as being in opposition to rationality. Thus when strong emotions are aroused in the work that professionals do, this is often perceived as threatening. Strong emotions may be construed as a sign of weakness or incompetence. Still worse, expressing emotions may be viewed as leading to professional errors, either in judgment or performance. Consequently, feelings are kept private; silence is the norm.[24]

I have worked with many physicians, some still in training, some senior in their fields. All describe the necessity of maintaining control over their emotions lest they inadvertently display "inappropriate feelings." One doctor reported, "I've never heard a colleague of mine say, 'This patient made me feel *x*, *y*, or *z*. It's just not done. It's always 'this forty-year-old man came into the ER high on heroin with multiple lacerations across his face and arms.' If you vent, it's in private with someone you select and it's off in a corner. You don't want to be seen as emotional, or colleagues will think you won't be able to do your job."

To further complicate matters, many professionals have been socialized to believe that expressing emotion is key to well-being.[25] However, while they are supportive and sympathetic to colleagues who express emotions, they practice emotional reticence themselves. Only one form of emotional expressiveness seems to be generally acceptable: humor. In some contexts it may be more aptly termed "gallows humor," a phrase denoting a morbid or cynical joke about a serious, even tragic, situation.[26] When professionals employ gallows humor, it vents emotion without their appearing vulnerable. Bob Gassaway, a former Vietnam correspondent, recalls how he used humor in groups to cope with situations he found incomprehensible, such as the immolation of a Buddhist monk and nun. Not proud of it now, he writes that he referred to them as "monk flambé" and "nun flambé."[27] Further, the laughter that the group shares creates a temporary closeness that is comforting in and of itself.

The Dilemma of Empathy

Coping

Here, then, are all the elements of an intractable dilemma. Professionals in these five occupations have higher-than-usual exposure to witnessing violence and violation, with the attendant common shock. They are constantly dealing with situations that demand empathy. They are submerged in a wider culture that believes that the expression of emotion is healthy, yet they subscribe to professional norms that posit that emotionality on the job undermines performance. How do professionals handle these contradictions?

Over time accommodations can be complex and nuanced. Roger Rosenblatt, writing about journalists on the eve of covering the Rwandan genocide, describes three stages of managing feelings that might apply to any of the other professional groups as well. One can well imagine substituting the word *police* or *ER doctor* for *journalist.*

> In the first stage, when they are young, [journalists] respond to atrocities with shock and revulsion and perhaps a twinge of guilty excitement that they are seeing something others will never see: life at its dreadful extremes. In the second stage the atrocities become familiar and repetitive, and journalists begin to sound like Spiro Agnew; if you have seen one loss of dignity and spirit, or one loss of limb, or loss of head, you've seen them all. Too many journalists get stuck in this stage. They get bogged down in the routineness of the suffering. Embittered, spiteful, and inadequate to their work, they curse out their bosses back home for not according them respect; they hate the people on whom they report. Worst of all, they don't allow themselves to enter the third stage, in which everything gets sadder and wiser, worse and strangely better.[28]

Rosenblatt's third stage, sadder and wiser, is also probably safer, for the professional, their loved ones, their constituents, and the community. Before this stage, though, other methods of managing this professional bind exist. The consequences of some of these attempted solutions are destructive. Alcohol use is high for several of these professional groups. Physiologically and psychologically "wired" by their work, they know they need to bring their arousal down and some use alcohol for this purpose. For instance, in a sample of 140 war correspondents with an average of fifteen years reporting war, over 40 percent of the male correspondents and 50 percent of the female correspondents disclosed drinking habits that were rated as excessive.[29] These journalists used alcohol to "relax" and to help with sleep. Police and physicians also have high alcohol intake.[30] For many of those who drink, they, too, are using alcohol to "unwind" and they view it as a "coping strategy," ignoring the long-term negative consequences of this choice.

Depression and despair are also occupational risks. It is ironic that in those professions in which people serve others, needing help oneself is often seen as problematic. Many fear that they will be viewed as impaired if they seek help. Physicians in general have high rates of self-medication,[31] and some psychiatrists medicate themselves for depression.[32] Law enforcement officers worry that seeing a counselor will be construed as impairment and that their weapons will be removed.[33]

Clergy fear that if they admit depression they will be viewed as unfit to minister to their congregations.

Yet, the work they do constantly exposes them to human tragedy. Suicide is a significant risk for those with untreated depression, and yet professionals in these groups may avoid or delay getting help for fear of the professional ramifications. Elizabeth Neuffer, a foreign correspondent for *The Boston Globe*, described being unable to talk after returning from the Gulf War. She had seen "some very bad things." Chatting with a former FBI source one day, she describes herself as having been "appalled" when he sent her to the FBI psychiatrist. " 'What do you mean? I don't need any therapy. I'm fine, I'm healthy.' But his point was—and I think it was a wise one—Whenever [they] send an agent into danger, when they come out of the filed, [they] send them to a psychiatrist."[34]

FBI culture makes counseling a standard operating procedure. Neuffer and other journalists participating in a panel discussion about the emotional challenges covering war describe their colleagues as supportive, but their news organizations as indifferent or "clueless."[35] The lurking shadow is suicide. On an interview show with four photojournalists in December 2001, there was a discussion of covering the war in Afghanistan that turned poignant and pointed.[36] Tyler Hicks, a photographer with Getty Images, had taken a series of photographs of Northern Alliance soldiers who found and eventually killed a Taliban soldier. These photographs appeared in *The New York Times,* November 13, 2001. Asked whether he had considered intervening, Hicks gave a detailed and thoughtful account of the moment and its reverberations. He said that he thought about the incident every day and replayed what he might have done. With some distress in his voice and with evident concern for Hicks, another guest, Stan Grossfeld of *The Boston Globe,* entered the conversation: "Part of the problem of being photojournalists, we're witnesses and it's our job to record it, but we bear the baggage, and I don't want Tyler to be blaming himself for this man's execution because I'll tell you, Kevin Carter, who won the Pulitzer Prize in 1994 for a dramatic photo of a vulture hovering over a small child in Somalia, he carried that baggage and he committed suicide. Don't blame yourself, Tyler."[37]

The professional's repertoire for dealing with empathic stress reactions, severe common shock, is constrained by many factors, of which professional norms regarding appropriate management of emotions is an important one. When professionals in these key societal roles become overwhelmed, the problems ripple out. Certainly family and friends experience their distress. For one thing, it is difficult to be married to someone whose work is her "calling."[38] Many spouses feel that there are three parties in the marriage. But when that calling has negative consequences for the marriage, it is even more troubling, and perhaps for some, galling.

The Ripple Effect

In *Lantana,* an Australian film, the police detective, Leon Zat, is coming apart.[39] His emotional constriction creates distance in all his relationships and although he can feel the emptiness of his life, he doesn't know what he can change. A casual affair doesn't work. At one point, confronted by his wife, he lets out a short burst of concentrated pain: "I can't feel anything!" His emotional numbing, part masculine ideology, part professional police culture, part common shock, collide and collude to create an explosive mix.

As is so for professionals in all of the groups I have been discussing, Zat's troubles do not just affect him and his family and friends. They negatively impact the very constituents he is committed to serve. In one scene in the film he and his partner sweep into a house where they suspect there are drug dealers, and he uses what his partner later tells him is excessive force. Here, then, is the awful final segment in the common shock transmission sequence: professionals on the front lines of witnessing, who are not able to master their own common shock experiences, pass them to us. However, because they are in positions of authority and touch the lives of so many people, the negative effects of their unsuccessful coping efforts disperse widely into the community. The doctor, nurse, and orderly in the emergency room will mediate the witness experience of the son who brings in his dying father. If they are brusque, this will negatively impact the family's experience of the man's final hours. The teacher who yells repeatedly at the youngster in her classroom frightens the other students. The photojournalist covering a refugee camp in Macedonia, selecting which pieces of footage to air on the nightly news, will influence the witness experience of millions of people on the planet.

The sequence of common shock transmission I am proposing consists of two parts. However, it is exceedingly difficult to prove the link between the two parts; at the moment it must remain a plausible hypothesis—one, though, that I think is well worth pursuing. The first part of the sequence is that professionals have high exposure to witnessing violence and violation, on account of which they are susceptible to developing severe common shock or empathic stress reactions. They try to cope with what they witness, and they are more or less successful at it. The second part of the sequence is that because of their positions in society, if common shock impairs their job performance, leading them to commit acts of violence or violation themselves, they can spread common shock to us.

Their common shock derives from the same sources that everyone's does plus their occupation. They may have been witnesses to violence and violation in daily life, through caring for an ill or dying loved one, or through interactions in the families they grew up in, as I will discuss in the next chapter. But they also contend with job exposure to violence and violation. It can be too much.

One acquaintance, who grew up in a suburb of Washington, D.C., recently recalled an episode during the Cuban missile crisis in 1962, when people feared there might be a nuclear exchange with the Soviet Union, that graphically demonstrates the passing of common shock. One of her teachers terrified the entire class with descriptions of an impending nuclear holocaust. He distributed a diagram to the sixth-grade students that showed concentric circles from the center of the city, providing death rates per ring. The students were to go home, see where their houses fell on the chart, and then figure out how many of their family and neighbors would be killed. My friend remembers sobbing as she walked home from school, sure that she was about to die. This teacher's fear, coupled with insensitivity, leaked into his instructional curriculum, spreading *his* common shock to an entire classroom.

Perhaps this formulation can provide one additional strand to the complex set of factors that needs to be understood to account for the failure of the church hierarchy to provide an adequately protective response to victims and congregations against abuse by priests. It is clear that their failure to respond protectively has spread common shock to millions of people. I can read almost daily newspaper accounts in *The Boston Globe* describing parishioners' shock coupled with outrage and a sense of betrayal. Several people in my clinical practice who have sexual-abuse histories have noticed flare-ups in their symptoms whenever they hear about these situations; they must actively screen the clergy abuse stories.

Is it possible, though, that the church officials themselves are using mechanisms we associate with unsuccessful attempts to cope with common shock—denial, secrecy, silence, avoidance—to manage these allegations? Surely, church officials, learning about reprehensible acts of sexual predation and abuse committed by priests whom they have favorably regarded, find themselves in the witness position. Mightn't this provoke common shock in some church officials? Perhaps one factor, among what I believe to be many factors that contribute to church officials' flawed and damaging administrative responses, may be that they themselves are unsuccessfully coping with common shock reactions. Tragically, their unsuccessful efforts lead to more youth victims and spread common shock to countless others who become witnesses to these crimes.

One final anecdote will make this point. A physician colleague told me about a recent episode with a group of medical students that had an unusual, rather than what might have been a disastrous, outcome. She was co-teaching with a colleague of hers, an emergency-medicine physician, and toward the end of the fifth session the students confronted the ER doctor and told him that they found his teaching style to be unproductive and harmful to them. They said that they found his tone harsh, his comments critical, and his attitude toward patients demeaning. The students said that whether or not they were his targets, they felt violated by his treatment of their peers. My colleague had also been concerned about her colleague; she was trying to decide on an approach to talking with him.

To everyone's surprise the physician brought in a prepared statement to the sixth session. In this statement he candidly disclosed the struggles he was having with his job and thanked the students for giving him an opportunity to look at the effect his behavior was having on them. He told the students that he was having physical and emotional symptoms of distress, which he attributed to feeling overwhelmed by the violence, trauma, pain, and suffering that he saw daily in the busy urban emergency room where he worked. He described feelings of irritability, hostility, anger, and cynicism, which he said had gradually overtaken him. He no longer looked forward to work, and in fact, in recent months, he had reduced his hours. He had also tried to minimize the number of shift changes he had to do, as he thought that his difficulties sleeping might be due to lower tolerance for shift work. Overall, without using the phrase, he described himself as someone suffering from severe common shock.

The students were stunned by his honesty. The conversation quickly shifted from a tone of blame to one of compassion and curiosity. The students felt that they had been given a chance to be allies with this senior physician so that all of them could look together at the demands of medical practice and the possible ways of handling the challenges. The rest of their sessions went well.

The ripple effects of people in the five professions vary considerably in range. An elementary-school teacher can usually impact one classroom at a time. A physician can impact colleagues, students, patients, and family members. A member of the clergy who ministers to a large congregation may affect not only his own parishioners, but also congregants of his denomination in other regions. A journalist who publishes a sensational article on a horrific crime with lots of macabre detail can reach a wide audience. A police officer who uses excessive force against a victim can cause widespread distress, outrage, and anxiety among community members.

Amplification of the Ripple Effect

The ripple-effect phenomenon makes it particularly worrisome when professionals commit acts that are perceived as racist, sexist, homophobic, or discriminatory in any way. Their positions amplify the negative effects of their behavior, which may augment common shock for some witnesses.[40] Further, if these acts are reported and analyzed by the media—who are themselves reacting to the same acts—their accounts create witnesses not only to the facts but also to certain interpretations of these facts. Readers of different papers or viewers of different television stations can develop quite different perspectives on the same situation.

The events surrounding the beating of African-American Rodney King by three white Los Angeles police officers provide a clear example of these dynamics. On March 3, 1991, early in the morning, Rodney King was driving at high speed when he was spotted by a husband-and-wife team of the California Highway Patrol. They gave chase, flashing their lights at King, who ignored them. Finally, King stopped the car at an intersection off the freeway, and within seconds three Los Angeles police cars and a helicopter surrounded him. George Holliday, a plumbing-store manager, heard the noise and took video footage of the scene, which was about ninety feet away. The next day Holliday sold his videotape to a local TV station, which aired it on the evening news.[41] CNN played it the next day, and used it "like wallpaper."[42]

The film showed three white officers kicking Rodney King and beating him with metal batons while their white supervisor looked on and directed their use of force. Although 90 percent of Los Angeles residents who saw the videotape believed that the officers had used excessive force, and even the Los Angeles police chief, Daryl Gates, called the use of force "very, very extreme,"[43] the sergeant who had been in charge that night described the use of force as "managed and controlled."[44] Within a week a grand jury indicted all four officers who took part in the beating of Rodney King.

Subsequent to the beating, rifts within the leadership of Los Angeles opened up. Conflicts between the mayor, the police chief, the city council, and the police commission all became apparent through public statements that they made. Initially four separate investigations into the beating were undertaken. Four months later the Christopher Commission released its report about the Los Angeles Police Department, finding "an organization with practices and procedures that are conducive to discriminatory treatment and officer misconduct directed to members of minority groups."[45]

While the majority of Los Angeles citizens, politicians in Los Angeles and in the nation, and the local and national media portrayed the beating as brutal, unjust, and, perhaps, criminal, media accounts of the meaning of the beating and the events that unfolded subsequent to it diverged considerably. A month after the beating the *Los Angeles Sentinel,* a newspaper that primarily serves the African-American community, distinguished the reaction of "black America" from that of "America":

> While America pretended to be in shock, black America was not in shock at all . . . the attack on Rodney King is part of a historical pattern of violent oppression of Africans in America which has been visited upon our people ever since we arrived in conditions of involuntary servitude.[46]

The dominant themes of the mainstream press concerned the politicization of the crisis. While their analyses of the politics differed, they concluded that remedies were available. By contrast the African-American press saw the beating as part of a larger pattern of systematic oppression, requiring political and economic empowerment of African-Americans, for which adequate mechanisms did not exist. The mainstream press was essentially finished with the story after the release of the Christopher Commission Report, whereas the local African-American press continued to be engaged with issues related to failures of civil society.[47]

Despite different interpretations of the context of the beating, there was widespread agreement across color lines about the beating itself. Thus, while no one was prepared for the not-guilty verdict handed down by a predominantly white jury in nearby Simi Valley, its meaning to African-Americans and to whites was different. Whites largely disagreed with the verdict, but they did not feel betrayed by it. African-Americans, on the other hand, who were cynical in general about the ability of the justice system to respond fairly, had thought that in *this* instance justice would prevail. Through the videotape African-Americans had been witnesses to violence. Now, with the verdict, they were witnesses to violation, a miscarriage of justice that confirmed what they thought they had known, and which they felt more painfully, perhaps, for having relaxed their suspicion in this instance.

Within hours of the verdict protests and massive destruction broke out in minority communities throughout the nation, but particularly so in Los Angeles, where there were fifty-five deaths[48] and property damage estimated at between $785 million and $1 billion.[49] The African-American press criticized the rioters and condemned the violence as "pure folly," denouncing the self-destructive rage the rioters had unleashed against their own communities.[50] The white community was also shocked by the verdict, but since the analysis they had been privy to was largely a political one, to the extent that the rioters were seen to be protesting the jury verdict, at least initially, there was considerable sympathy expressed by the mainstream press while still condemning the violence itself.[51]

The rage of the African-American community, in part, was triggered by the two experiences of helpless witnessing. (Sergeant Koon, in his testimony at the state trial, says that he now looks at the videotape and sees it as "violent and brutal." However, he asserts that "it was done to control an aggressive combative suspect, and sometimes police work is brutal. That's just a fact of life."[52]) In the first, people witnessed the failure of the police to restrain themselves. In the second they witnessed the failure of the justice system to restrain the police. The media amplified the effects of the police officers' actions, so that the brutal assault reached millions of people who were aware but helpless witnesses to it. It is this witness position, number four, as we have seen time and time again, that is so devastating for those caught in it.

Reducing Harm

Professionals in these five occupational groups would undoubtedly all subscribe to the maxim *Primum non nocere*—"Above all [or first] do no harm"—associated with physicians.[53] It is a crucial foundational principle that guards and guides the covenant relationship professionals have with their clients. We all know that by virtue of the functions professionals in these groups serve, they have the potential for doing great good, but also great harm. Perhaps what is clearer now is that they are also exposed to situations that can place *them* in harm's way. As a society I believe we must look squarely at this reality and begin to shape professional training, societal expectations, and social supports to reflect the realities of the work that certain key professionals do for us. As a global village we cannot afford for those who are on the front lines of mediating violence and violation to be overwhelmed by it.

Much will have to change. And change is starting to happen. For all the horror of the attacks on America in September 2001, some good has also risen alongside it. Many people now understand that witnesses can experience common shock. They felt it in their bodies and they will never forget it. No one doubts that the rescue workers at Ground Zero, who probed the rubble for eight months looking for human remains, were at risk. People understand the reasons why posters went up around New York City that said "Even heroes need to talk." Now we have to seize the momentum of this understanding and transfer what we have learned about extraordinary circumstances to ordinary ones. For rescue workers are at risk, albeit not on the same scale, on a daily basis under what is for them routine circumstances.

The same may be said for journalists. Many people read the profiles of the missing and dead that appeared in *The New York Times* daily for months after the terrorist attacks. Fewer may have realized that they were reading a journalist's form of compassionate witnessing. According to Peter Applebome, deputy metropolitan editor of *The Times,* journalists were unable to manage the horror as they usually do. "Even if we tried to reduce tragedy to data, there was no way to reduce this tragedy to its component parts."[54]

Instead, reporters wrote 150-word portraits. Applebome continues, "They are the opposite of what most of us in journalism usually get rewarded for—tiny, anonymously written, and emotionally draining miniatures that offer the writer no glory. But they've become like our little sacrament. No one can do them for too long, but everyone has taken pride in doing them. They're our version of leaving flowers at the Vietnam Memorial."[55]

Hopefully, this experience will become a bridge for understanding with utter clarity that people who witness in the line of duty are at risk, not just in extraordinary circumstances, but in ordinary ones too. We will all benefit if professional training includes education about the dynamics of witnessing. Professionals need to have a clear understanding of the risks of exposure to violence and violation in the actual work that they do. For instance, in a survey of 875 photojournalists, only 11 percent were warned about risks to their mental health.[56]

Professional education must also include training in the recognition of and approaches to management of common shock reactions. Professionals need to be prepared to handle this occupational hazard with the same degree of competence as any other aspect of their job. Training that includes frank discussions of severe common shock reactions would reduce the stigma attached to them by normalizing these reactions and breaking the silence about them.

We cannot afford for people to believe that they must blunt their feelings to stay "sane." We need those who serve us to be in touch with their emotions as they perform their duties, for it's this comfort that allows them to express care and concern for others as they do their jobs. We want to preserve, not crush, this ability. Speaking about journalists, but making a statement that can be applied to any of these professional groups, a senior reporter wrote, "If journalists lose their souls, their work will be hollow and meaningless. So they should never leave their feelings at the front door."[57]

A great deal is known about how to manage severe common shock reactions, for the individual and the workplace.[58] Professionals who have support from their colleagues and the institutions of which they are a part perform better, with more confidence and enthusiasm, and stay longer in their professions. Yet, very few institutions devote the time and resources of their organizations to care for their employees, either preventively or after a problem has occurred, with the sophistication that current knowledge allows. Instead, concern is with productivity, as if empathic stress reactions will not eventually have a significant negative impact on productivity.

The mandate for change must come from an informed public. There is an old-time Maine story that I tell frequently in my practice. In it a farmer is telling his neighbor about a feeding experiment he is employing on his chickens in order to save money. He tells him how successful he has been, until, "just when I got 'em on pure sawdust, they up and died!" We are cutting perilously thin the feed of workers whom we need to perform with excellence and compassion; there is too much sawdust. Failing to address directly, specifically, fully, and compassionately the inevitable toll that working with others exacts is shortsighted and harmful. It is a way that we harm those whom we don't want to harm us.

At best, those who care for us are well cared for themselves. Here, altruism and self-interest extensively overlap. For those who do not have support to manage common shock can easily pass theirs to us. Helpers who minister to our wounds can be wounded themselves. It is not their wounds that jeopardize others, but rather it is the impediments to their taking care of those wounds. Henri J. M. Nouwen, an eminent theologian, mines a story from the Talmud to make this point. In it the Messiah sits among the poor, covered with wounds, as are the others. What distinguishes the Messiah is that he unbinds his wounds one at a time, not all at once, so that he will be ready if he is needed.[59]

Wounded helpers can still be competent ones. Acknowledging their needs can ensure continued effectiveness. As a society we must insist on no less; the price of doing otherwise is one we do not want to pay.

CHAPTER 6

The Blindness of One's Heart

What is a curse and how does one work? Why do oracles and prophecies come true? I used to ponder these questions when I was a child, and as this chapter will attest, I still do. The Greek myths threw me. If people were forewarned, why couldn't they avoid their fate? Oedipus did everything he could to elude his destiny, and yet it rolled out as if he had done nothing to escape it. Atreus cooked his brother's children and served them to him at a feast just as their grandfather, Tantalus, had served the flesh of his son, Atreus' father, at a banquet. Why did family history repeat itself?

Filled with these questions, as a young teen, I approached my mother. She steered me to the *Odyssey* and I memorized these lines, not from the text itself, but from her memory of them: "Lo you now, how vainly mortal men do blame the gods! For of us they say comes evil, whereas they even of themselves have sorrows beyond that which is ordained." That phrase—*even of themselves*—was packed with implication but remained confusing to me. I wanted to understand how those sorrows, "even of themselves," passed from one generation to the other, like a domino, hitting the one beside it with the force that had taken *it* down.[1]

Forty years later, researching these Homeric lines, I see that my mother or I—I have no idea whose memory slipped!—omitted a crucial phrase. The line she had memorized was from Butcher and Lang's translation of Homer's *Odyssey* and contains an additional phrase: ". . . whereas they even of themselves, *through the blindness of their own hearts,* have sorrows beyond that which is ordained."[2] Homer intended the phrase *through the blindness of their own hearts* to address a fundamental question that has plagued observers of the human condition forever: how *do* people bring suffering onto themselves and pass it from one generation to the next?

At first I was dissatisfied by the proffered explanation. The poet's phrase asks us to turn our attention to these considerations: "What does it mean to be blind to what one knows in one's heart or to not let oneself comprehend what one does know? How does one become blind to what is in one's heart?" Over a period of days, however, I came to believe that Homer gives us a vivid description of what it feels like to live with trauma and common shock brought about by those we love and who love us. The wound *is* to the heart and we, out of a mix of loyalty and self-protection, blind ourselves to it.[3]

Humans have always hurt each other. The targets are often those we love most and live with daily, our family members. The Greek myths and our own family stories are replete with evidence that life in a family is a 24/7 opportunity for some to witness the effects of violence and violation on others.

In Chapter One I have argued that the witnessing of violence and violation is ubiquitous and happens under the most ordinary of circumstances, for instance, standing in line at the pharmacy, watching TV, reading the newspaper, or driving a car. In this chapter I delve into the consummate example of ordinariness, life in a family, to show the ways that here, too, in what we idealize as a haven in a harmful world, violence and violation intrude.[4] The intrusion inserts itself not from the outside, from forces and people unknown, but from those closest to us, those we love and trust, or wish to.

In some instances we observe our loved ones struggling with the effects of their own traumatic experiences, for example, a son watching his father who served in the Gulf War set up his beach chair on the asphalt parking lot while the rest of the family frolics on the sand. Sometimes these struggles directly engage us—for instance, a daughter whose mother screams at her when she finds her older brother lying on her bed reading comics with her. Often these struggles are woven into the daily life of the family in such a way that no one identifies this thread of shared family experience: there is no talk about it and there are no reasons given for it. It is there, but not acknowledged.

Although the belief that family members can pass their fortunes and misfortunes to their children is ancient and nearly universal, social scientists have been publishing papers about this taken-for-granted belief mainly since the mid-1960s. Two areas of concern prompted scrutiny: observation of the experience of children of Holocaust[5] survivors and observation of inadequate parenting among adults who had themselves been maltreated. Subsequently, the phenomenon under study has been given several imposing-sounding names, among them "intergenerational transmission of trauma," "multigenerational legacies of trauma," and "vertical transmission of intergenerational trauma." All three names refer to the accepted fact that family members can "transmit" their trauma to each other.

While this belief is widely accepted and now documented,[6] precise explanations, as opposed to compelling descriptions, of the exact mechanisms by which the "transmission" takes place lag behind. I have identified four categories of mechanisms that seem promising to help us understand how family members "pass" trauma to each other: biological, psychological, familial, and societal mechanisms. None alone is *the* answer; none is incontrovertible; and none can be neatly separated from the others. But each opens up ways of understanding how traumatic experience in one generation impacts another generation. *Impacts* is truly the operative word, for what is passed is not the trauma itself but its impact, and as we shall see, while the impact may be life shaping for many people, it is not necessarily "bad." If you live with a parent who has suffered trauma, you may acquire vulnerabilities you might otherwise not have, but you also have opportunities to develop resilient coping skills that you might not have had either.[7] A great deal will depend on whether or not you are "given permission" to witness your parent's experience. If you are, the legacy of trauma will unfold differently than if you are not.

In this chapter and the next I consider the impact on children of living with parents who were traumatized, either from living through extreme violence and violation that occurred outside of their families, such as the Holocaust, or living with extreme violence and violation that occurred within their families, such as child abuse. As in the preceding chapters, I am focusing on the child's experience of *witnessing* the effects of the trauma on her parent, mindful that the child may also be a victim of the parent's insufficiently successful efforts to master his trauma.

The study of intergenerational transmission of trauma began in the 1960s, when social scientists were examining the psychological aftereffects of the Holocaust after a lull during the 1950s that some Holocaust scholars liken to a "conspiracy of silence."[8] The first several decades of work yielded contradictory findings, and many researchers and scholars raised significant concerns about these findings on methodological and philosophical grounds.[9] A review of the literature published in 1992 concluded that it was time to stop the research agenda of trying to prove that children of Holocaust survivors have more problems than other children, because it hadn't been productive. The author of this study suggested two new avenues of study: what is the meaning and impact of *any* parental trauma on a child, and do parents confer strengths to children due to their histories of traumatization?[10] These two questions have subsequently guided much of the work in the field.

Biological Mechanisms

Cortisol Studies

Rachel Yehuda and her colleagues in New York City have taken up the proposal for a new research direction. One outcome has been to integrate the study of Holocaust survivors and their offspring into the study of trauma more generally, a field whose development followed the initial work on the psychological effects of the Holocaust. Yehuda and her colleagues are investigating the neurobiological adaptation of Holocaust survivors and their offspring using research protocols similar to the ones that they used to study combat veterans, especially Vietnam veterans.

They want to determine whether there are commonalities in behavioral and neurobiological factors between the two kinds of trauma, combat and the Holocaust, that might explain basic characteristics of the response to trauma. Further, they want to see if they can identify core behavioral and neurobiological features that can explain an intergenerational "syndrome."[11]

In one study with Holocaust survivors and their adult children, the research team found that offspring shared some similar psychological symptoms as their parents. They then wanted to know whether a biological factor could account for this. They decided to measure the hormone cortisol because it is released in response to stress and it is affected by severe trauma.[12]

Their studies showed that symptoms described by offspring as related to *hearing about* the Holocaust corresponded to symptoms described by people who had lived through the Holocaust. Further, the offsprings' symptoms were associated with the same biochemical abnormality, low cortisol level, that is associated with firsthand experience of severe trauma.[13]

For those who have never heard the child of a Holocaust survivor speak about his or her experience, it may be difficult to understand how hearing a parent's recollection of an event, being a witness, could be so disturbing that it would produce symptoms. To understand this we have to imagine the world from a child's perspective. The young child's sense of security rests with his perception that his parents will and can protect him. Most children derive their view that their parents can protect them based in part on the belief that their parents can protect themselves. It is an immense blow to learn that one's parent has not always been safe, that terrible harm befell people just like him, and that one's parent might have been murdered but wasn't.

Horrific stories, anecdotes, and innuendos drop into the child's life.[14] The child cannot comfort himself by murmuring, as one child I know used to do at upsetting movies, "It's not true, it's not true, it's not true." It is true, and what's more, as the child matures, he appreciates that the horror he does comprehend is a minute fraction of the horror of the Holocaust.

Art Spiegelman, a cartoonist and artist, is the son of two Polish Jewish parents, Anja and Vladek, who both were interred in Auschwitz and survived. In his books *Maus I: A Survivor's Tale: My Father Bleeds History* and *II: And Here My Troubles Began,* Spiegelman uses cartoon frames to confine his father's telling of his life before and during the Holocaust and he uses open squares, ones without lines, to present the story of his experience of listening to his father tell his tale.[15] The story inside the cartoon squares is inexorably chronological, relaying and thickening the gruesome events his father lived through in Europe from the mid-1930s until after the war. The story outside the lines weaves back and forth across time, a maelstrom of emotion and passion, reaction and reaction to reaction, that undermines the linearity of the Holocaust story and takes us powerfully into the child's experience of living with a Holocaust survivor parent.

The son's aesthetic choices make clear to us that his life has been shaped by his parents' Holocaust experience every bit as much as the explicit textual vignettes inform us of this. We can see—literally—the effect on him of his father's wartime experiences, but we are also told in moments like "But I did have nightmares about SS men coming into my class and dragging all us Jewish kids away."[16] Or "Sometimes I'd fantasize Zyklon B coming out of our shower instead of water."[17] Or we read about interactions between Art and his father that are harrowing precisely because his father's ordinary, irritating present-day intrusiveness is also simultaneously, inextricably loaded with the pain of his past.

In one sequence his father is telling him about life in the ghetto. We have already learned that his father's scheming, vigilance, handiness, and practicality saved him many times. As Art and his father are walking on the street, Vladek retrieves a piece of telephone wire from a trash can and wants Art to take it. Art declines. Although Art may want his refusal to be interpreted only from the perspective of the current moment, he cannot control the links his father makes to the past, thus appearing to his father as disregarding his lesson that anything may be useful and one must always be prepared. The frequency with which those who have survived danger try to teach what they have learned to their children has led some researchers to speculate that there may be some survival value in it for the species—parents passing on to their children sensitivity to danger, to better prepare them for subsequent challenges.[18]

These kinds of experiences for children of Holocaust survivors draw the interest of researchers and clinicians who inquire into the experiences of Holocaust survivors and their offspring. They want to understand what precisely about the parents' experience affects the children. Yehuda's research group found that parents who have experienced a severe traumatic event themselves may confer a vulnerability to their offspring of developing severe trauma responses (PTSD or posttraumatic stress disorder) *not* by virtue of the parents' exposure to these events per se, but if the parents developed and were living with chronic PTSD. Adult children of Holocaust survivor parents who lived with chronic PTSD had atypically low cortisol levels, the biochemical pattern that reflects an abnormal response to stress, whether or not they themselves had PTSD.[19]

The adult children of Holocaust survivors whose parents had PTSD reported significantly more emotional abuse than the other groups of adult children to whom they were compared and they also had particularly low cortisol levels. In trying to understand how trauma is passed from one generation to the next, these studies provide another clue. Children may develop vulnerability to PTSD if they grow up in a home in which they are subject to emotional abuse, as those children sometimes did whose parents suffered from Holocaust-related PTSD. The vulnerability can be ascertained by the biological marker of low cortisol levels (which may contribute to subsequent biological abnormalities in responding to traumatic events) and may be related to distorted cognitions about the world and the self that develop in the home and predispose children to develop PTSD if exposed to a traumatic event themselves.[20]

Maus opens with ten frames that serve as a prologue and vividly portray the way in which such distorted cognitions are conveyed to children. Art is ten or eleven, he writes, and he has fallen while roller-skating with his friends. They leave him, while calling him names. Sniffling, he walks home and tells his father what has just happened. His father stops what he is doing and says, "Friends? Your friends? . . ." Speaking now about a world that is not Art's and breaking out of empathic connection to him as he does so, Vladek says more, imparting distorted ideas about the current world they both inhabit: "If you lock them together in a room with no food for a week . . . then you could see what is friends! . . ."[21]

Without laying a hand on Art, Vladek communicates vividly the dynamics of the frightening world that is his reference point. A childhood spat is transformed into a potentially life-threatening betrayal. Vladek intends no harm as he compels Art to witness his Holocaust past via his distorted interpretations of the present. Seared by it, Art, as an adult artist, transforms the past in his own way, creating a work of harrowing clarity about the impact of witnessing parental trauma.

Psychological and Interpersonal Mechanisms: Child Maltreatment

Have humans evolved to transmit a sensitivity to danger to their children? The idea is intriguing. So far the human studies I have mentioned have looked at dangers that originated outside the family: dangers such as combat or genocide. However, there are also dangers that come from within a family. What happens when the source of danger is your own parent, like Tantalus serving his son to the gods or Agamemnon sacrificing his daughter, or your neighbor, Joe, beating his son, Peter?

The Cycle of Abuse

Researchers and clinicians alike have explored this phenomenon for decades, calling by the name "cycle of abuse" the phenomenon that children who are treated badly—who are abused or neglected—go on to treat their own children badly as well. Fortunately, the cycle is not inevitable. In fact, many researchers now agree that, at least in the United States and the United Kingdom, where the cycle has been extensively studied, only about 30 percent of those adults who suffered maltreatment as children will go on to mistreat their own children.[22] While this percentage may not be extremely high, it is still six times the rate of abuse in the population at large.[23]

Social scientists have worked diligently to understand why and how the cycle of abuse occurs. In one comprehensive review of the literature on the cycle of abuse, Ann Buchanan organizes the findings into "four major cycles that directly or indirectly lead to intergenerational child maltreatment."[24] At the broadest level, the cultural cycle, the values and child-rearing practices of the society or subculture in which a family lives exert an influence on parents' behavior. While no society condones child maltreatment, most societies do tolerate violence directed against children by their parents. Actually, there are only sixteen small-scale and peasant societies in which no family violence and no physical punishment of children occurs.[25] In the United States, for instance, a national survey of disciplinary practices found that 97 percent of children had been physically punished.[26] Cultures also differentially approve mistreatment of certain categories of children. For instance, in some cultures girls are more vulnerable to abuse, and in others unwanted, illegitimate, or disabled children are at risk of maltreatment.

The second major cycle is a sociopolitical one. Child maltreatment is more likely to occur in environments in which families are impoverished; lack adequate food, shelter, and clothing; and have restricted access to decent health care, education, and employment. These features of family life coexist with state policies that inadequately protect women and children and fail to provide security from a host of social problems that are within the power of nations to effect, such as war.[27]

Psychological factors comprise a third cycle. This cycle includes the ways parents interact with their children. A wide range of such factors has been shown to influence whether parents mistreat their children—including parental IQ, familiarity with children's needs and developmental abilities, children's temperamental fit with their parents, the parents' degree of social isolation versus support, and the parents' prior history of relationships.

Finally, there is a cycle of primarily biological factors that may lower the threshold for child maltreatment, contributing to and interacting with the other three cycles. The health of parents and their children is a risk factor for child maltreatment, and this can be exacerbated or ameliorated by environmental conditions.

When you consider all the possible factors that contribute to parents' mistreating their children it can be overwhelming, and yet there are approaches to intervention that target every one of these cycles. What is lacking is not an understanding of what needs to be done or ideas about how to accomplish it, but rather a commitment at the international, national, and local level to dedicate resources to end child maltreatment.

While these four cycles provide a crucial context for understanding the causes of child maltreatment, they don't help us picture how a parent who was herself abused ends up repeating this behavior with her own child. We have already identified a possible biological mechanism, cortisol regulation, that may be altered by living with a parent who has developed PTSD following traumatic experiences. This alteration in cortisol level may predispose offspring to have more difficulty regulating their responses to their own stressful life events, including their parents' maltreatment and then, later, their children's behavior. We turn next to psychological mechanisms that have also been proposed.

Attachment

One of the most frequently used frameworks for conceptualizing the psychological path by which parents pass their own traumatic upbringing to their children is attachment theory. Attachment theory has dominated the field of child development for over two decades and has provided a generative theory of close relationships.[28] Based on the work of noted British psychoanalyst John Bowlby, attachment theory focuses on the period of utter dependence of infants on their caretaker, the first year or so of life. The theory attempts to account for continuities and variations in the system that develops between the mother and the infant in relation to the child's signaling distress (either within the infant—for instance, hunger—or in the environment—for instance, a frightening noise or strange person) and the mother's responding to it with protection, care, and comfort.

The theory is not without its detractors. Some cross-cultural psychologists challenge the premise that the theory addresses a universal law of human attachment.[29] Feminists challenge the theory's sensitivity to social context as a crucial influence on the attachment system, especially over time.[30] Many clinicians believe that the theory is used to support mother-blaming interpretations. Still, no one debates the importance of "attachments," that is, loving relationships that provide protection, comfort, and security.

However, sadly, it is often the people who love us who compromise our ability to form secure attachments to others, including, later, our own children. Further, if abuse (physical, sexual, or emotional) and neglect (physical or emotional) occur between a parent and child, then the very person who is supposed to provide comfort *from* danger *is* a danger. When this happens, feelings of security and comfort can coexist side by side with feelings of helplessness, terror, and lack of control. What is damaged is not just the child's relationship to one person, but the child's ability to use relationships in general to comfort and soothe.[31]

Jane is a client I have been working with for more than a decade. Her childhood was hell. Her mother was a charming femme fatale who divorced Jane's father when Jane was two years old. Jane went to live with her mother and her succession of husbands. Jane's mother had been physically abused by her own father and she chose men who were physically abusive to her. The household was in constant turmoil, either in the midst of or recovering from protracted pitched battles between the adults.[32]

Jane has no memory of her early years, but she imagines they were similar to the years she remembers vividly. Jane was a witness to marital fights and their aftermath. She was largely neglected by her mother and her partners, who were too wrapped up in their own dramas to concern themselves with a young girl. When her mother would turn her attention to Jane, she was invariably critical of her. Jane's experience swung from witnessing violence, feeling abandoned, and soothing herself following her mother's harshness. At age sixteen she was accepted to college without even completing her senior year in high school. Although brilliant, Jane had absorbed her mother's view of her as "stupid, ugly, and worthless."

She went on to establish a successful career in business, but her advancement always floundered around difficulties she had in managing her staff. Male and female staff alike would complain to company human-resource officers that Jane made them feel stupid and worthless. Jane had never had an intimate relationship, and when I began working with her she lived alone. Happily. She was "afraid" of getting too close to people, she told me.

Like some women and men whose primary attachment relationship has been unloving, Jane consciously chose not to have children. "I was terrified I would do to them what my mother had done to me," she said. "Sometimes I would be around my cousins' children and I could feel myself getting furious at them for some silly, truly minor thing they were doing—like picking a tomato out of the salad bowl—and I would feel a different persona coming over me, like being invaded, and I would turn into my mother when she was yelling. I could literally feel my mouth, this nasty snarl, become the mouth I used to see on my mother that I hated so much."

Other people who have been abused or neglected by their parents, or who have witnessed violence between their parents or between a parent and a sibling, and who go on to have children themselves, are vulnerable to repeat with their own children what happened to them or what they saw. Attachment theory provides very specific ideas about how this happens.

In Bowlby's view, now elaborated by hundreds of clinicians and researchers, when an infant perceives danger, he experiences physiological arousal and discomfort. He signals his distress to the parent in the hopes of bringing her near to provide protection and comfort. Over time the regulation of physiological arousal evolves into the regulation of emotional arousal as well, which occurs not just when the basic survival needs of the infant are met, but also when more complex psychological needs are met by attuned parental responsiveness.

Infants and young children begin to form mental representations of the ways their needs are met at a very early age. Bowlby called the infant's mental map of interactions between herself and others the "internal working model." Children who are treated consistently and with respectful attentiveness develop internal working models of relationships as pleasurable and dependable, and think of themselves as worthy. Children who are treated obliviously, or inconsistently and harshly, develop internal working models of relationships as ungratifying and unreliable, and themselves as unworthy, like Jane.[33]

The child's "internal working model" represents the pattern of significant caretaking relationships over time, and the themes that organize it.[34] Three themes are common in families characterized by maltreatment across several generations: rejection, role reversal, and fear.[35] If a child is rejected when he moves toward the parent for comfort, over time he will learn to suppress his awareness of his need for comfort or he will turn away from the parent when he is distressed. If the parent requires the child to take care of her, and indicates pleasure only if the child is successful, the child's internal working model will be dominated by role reversal and his sense of self-worth will depend on whether or not he has succeeded in comforting his parent. And if the parent behaves in frightened or frightening ways, fear will dominate the child's internal working model of relationship.

Infants whose parents behave in a frightening or frightened way are truly in one of life's horrible dilemmas. The infant is stuck with an unsolvable conundrum: The source of care and protection is also the source of threat. Infants trapped in this kind of attachment relationship don't show consistency in their behavior with their caretakers. They look disorganized or disoriented; their behavior reflects the bind they are in.

Researchers who have studied infants and children who display this kind of attachment behavior have found a number of other associated features. Their caregivers often have had a history of trauma or loss that is poorly remembered or remains unresolved. As for the children themselves, they often go on to develop far more problems than other children. They may have disturbed relationships with their peers, academic and social trouble at school, and, later, are at higher risk for delinquency.[36] Intriguingly, they have also been shown to have low cortisol levels[37] and to use dissociation[38] (See Chapter Three.)

These children show the effects of the parenting their parents received. Studies show that many of the parents were treated in similar ways by their parents. (Other parents who treat their children in this manner suffer from unresolved trauma or common shock related to experiences external to the family.) When parents are asked questions about their upbringing, adults who have children with disorganized and disoriented attachment styles give confusing and contradictory reports of their own childhoods.[39]

I once saw a man, Barry, whose wife insisted that he go to therapy because she was appalled by his periodic rage attacks at their three young children, all of whom were doing poorly at home and at school. I did not see him for long because his company transferred him to a distant city shortly after I began to work with him. However, I vividly recall my few sessions with him.

Barry was clearly uncomfortable seeing me. He had come because he knew that he was "wrong" to treat his children the way he did, "but," he said, looking down at my rug and talking very softly, "something just comes over me. I am myself, but I am not me. It's like I am a balloon filling with anger, but something or someone else is blowing me up. I have to let it out. When it's over, I feel horrible. I don't want to look at my children. I don't want to look at anyone. I walk away. Go to the bedroom. Slam the door. And then time just passes. I forget. But my wife won't look at me, so I know I did something."

I asked him about his upbringing several times. In the few weeks I saw him, I couldn't get a clear sense of what his experience had been like because, apparently, he hadn't yet made sense of it himself. When he spoke of his childhood, he talked about his father. On the one hand his father was interesting and fun to be around, and on the other hand he was mean and belittling, but maybe "only when he was drunk . . . or was upset about something . . . which happened frequently . . . well, maybe I couldn't tell."

Using attachment theory to account for this man's experience, it is highly likely that his feeling of something coming over him when he is around his children, and of anger filling him, is triggered by something in the present that rapidly shifts his state of consciousness—so that he is no longer in the here and now, but actually back in the past feeling what he felt as his father's son, not his children's father.[40] He then behaves with his children in ways that express the emotion that has "come over" him, in all likelihood a feeling that is totally out of proportion to what set off his reaction. We can imagine that his children feel in his presence the way he did with his father. The cycle recurs.

Putting together these descriptions with the biological data, it is likely that children who are chronically exposed to these unpredictable, out-of-control, explosive parental behaviors, whether as victims of them or witnesses to them, experience repeated brief states of arousal, with bursts of stress hormones circulating, that eventually become biologically toxic for them as well as psychologically distressing.[41] These biochemical imbalances may help account for the higher incidence of mood disorders among children exposed to early trauma or stress.[42] This may be related to the finding that children with disorganized attachment behavior are at risk for developing dissociative symptoms in childhood and adolescence.[43]

As I have indicated, research clearly demonstrates that the majority of parents with histories of abuse manage to treat their children differently than they were treated. In effect, they manage *not* to "pass" on their experience of violence and violation to their children.[44] Researchers and clinicians converge in accounting for what seems to make the difference. Parents who are able to face the pain and hardship of their own upbringing turn out to be less vulnerable to repeat the abuse and neglect they experienced.[45]

However, lest anyone think that this is solely a matter of will, moral fiber, or emotional risk-taking, remember that the children who experience the most negative caretaking—caretaking that induces fear—are also at higher risk for dissociating—that is, splitting off awareness of experience. As one leading expert has written, "dissociation is akin to mental flight when physical flight is not possible."[46] If mental flight occurs to protect the infant and child from intolerable terror, then parts of the child's experience will be unavailable later. Those memories of troubling interaction that *are* available may have elements separated off from them. For instance, there may be the memory of an event but no memory of a feeling to go along with it.

Dissociation will accomplish protection in the moment but at the cost of later compromising the child's ability to tell a coherent story about his life or to come to terms with his life in all its complexity. Dissociation may also compromise the child's ability to witness himself and others.[47] Vast numbers of sources from a range of fields—pediatrics, public health, anthropology, sociology, psychology and psychoanalysis among them—report the same finding: some parents who are currently mistreating their children and who were mistreated themselves tell anecdotes about their upbringing that are idealized, inconsistent, and fragmentary.[48] This prevalent finding provides the scientific backing for the poetic phrase *the blindness of their hearts.* We can now see the path by which this blindness becomes reality.

The scientific literature also points to a way out. Parents who are able to integrate their past experiences are less likely to repeat them. Parents who were "rescued" by friends, friends' parents or partners, or who were able to form connections to therapists are less likely to mistreat their children.[49] These allies are like witnesses from the outside, helping the parent develop the capacity to observe that they were treated badly. With the support of a nurturing and caring person, these parents are able to construct an account of their lives that acknowledges their pain. In the poetic metaphor, through witnessing themselves, their hearts can see.

Perhaps nothing is as poignant as hearing a story about a horrific childhood from someone who doesn't seem to realize that the childhood he has lived through was brutal. Rajiv was a client of mine who didn't realize that his distress in the present could be traced back to early mistreatment. A bright, sensitive man, working with delinquent boys as a community organizer, he was happily married with three young children. While adept at talking about the impact family violence had had on the lives of the boys he worked with, he made little connection between their lives and his own. He could dispassionately recount stories of violence he witnessed between his parents and of beatings from his father, but still not link his own feelings of worthlessness to these experiences. One bright spot was a friend's mother who had taken him under her wing when he was in high school, and he recalled with tears in his eyes her affection for him.

Following the months he spent in close contact with his friend's mother, he began to view himself and his prospects in a different light. He buckled down to his studies, and to his surprise he did very well. It was as if he was able to use her belief in him to motivate him to turn his life around. Eventually, his belief in himself kicked in.

Rajiv went on to college, then married a warm and wonderful woman, who supported him through his periodic crises of self-doubt. He found work that felt like a calling and a commitment, helping youth whose journey might have been his own.

He was a devoted father. It was critically important to him that he never frighten or hurt his children. Yet, he had a hovering dread that he might. If 30 percent of maltreated adults abuse their children, 70 percent do not. Yet, their parental experience is far from easy. They are constantly dealing with the residues of their own experiences, trying to stop themselves from inadvertently treating their children as they were treated. Parenting is effortful. Their children witness their struggles, and this, too, becomes part of the intergenerational pattern. The cycle of maltreatment is transformed, if not entirely broken.

Rajiv felt that he had been successful in keeping his anger in check; he had never harmed his children. He noticed, however, that he felt lethargic whenever he had to take care of his children alone. All he wanted to do was sleep. We came to wonder whether drowsiness made him feel safer around his children than alertness. If he were exhausted, he wouldn't have the energy to strike out and harm his children. His goal was to feel awake, energetic, and safe with his children when he was alone with them.

Shelley is a client who grew up in a household of almost Gothic chaos and malevolence, with extreme physical and emotional abuse and neglect.

She both witnessed and experienced firsthand severe violence and violation. Shelley had been in therapy for many years, having made a conscious decision to break the family legacy of abuse. When Shelley came to see me, she wanted help with her explosive temper, which she feared was harmful to her only child, a son, Jason, then fifteen years old.

Through the years Shelley had sought frequent guidance and support from child-care professionals at every developmental stage. She suspected that any instinct of hers would misguide her and she therefore committed herself to learning from scratch how to do everything. Exhausting though it was, Shelley was utterly committed to parenting this way. It was her way of trying to intercept the past repeating itself through her.

Shelley considered herself a good parent and was proud that she had never neglected or physically abused Jason. She was, however, deeply ashamed of her intermittent fits of rage. She was convinced that Jason's exposure to them would have lasting impact on him. She worried, that is, that she was exposing him to common shock reactions.

In looking with Shelley at the triggers for these outbursts, I was amazed that she navigated her life as well as she did. Shelley was triggered into rage when she saw her husband or son behaving or interacting in a way that jeopardized people's safety. It was as if she had become an early warning siren, and yelling was her way of sounding the emergency broadcasting system: "Danger. Danger. I know from experience this behavior will lead to someone getting hurt." Given her subtle understanding of just how people can hurt each other, it was remarkable that her outbursts didn't happen more often.

In therapy she gained more understanding and more control over her anger. One episode, when Jason was sixteen, stands out as a turning point. Shelley had been giving Jason a driving lesson when he began swearing at a man in the car next to them. Shelley screamed at him to pull over at the next corner and move into the passenger seat. Jason was incredulous and began calling her "crazy."

Although shaken, Shelley was clear that she couldn't allow Jason to be an abusive driver. In the car with Jason she had flashed back to times she had driven with her drunken father when he was cruising at eighty miles an hour on two-lane highways, or had been fighting with her mother while driving. Although she had been reacting to the past as well as the present, Jason's behavior in the present was unacceptable to her.

Through conversation she developed an approach. It was brave and consisted of doing something no one had ever done with her. She decided she would talk with Jason about what had happened and provide him with some context for her reaction to his yelling. She decided to tell him that his yelling in the car had brought back terrifying memories of times she had been in cars and her parents had risked her life with their out-of-control behavior. She wanted to apologize for her screaming, while holding to the limit she had set. She would let him know that she agreed with her judgment, but not the way she had communicated it to him.

Shelley was breaking the silence that all too often follows painful parent-child interactions. True to her commitment not to repeat the past, Shelley was willing to take the risk of talking about something still utterly terrifying to her. She believed that by talking about what had happened in the car, she and Jason could repair the rupture that had occurred between them.[50] She also felt confident that Jason was old enough to learn something about her frightening childhood history. By breaking the silence, by returning to the moment of disconnection between them, Shelley was letting Jason know it was all right for him to fully register what he did know about their life together.

Shelley was teaching Jason to let his heart see.

CHAPTER 7

Putting It All Together: Our Planet, Ourselves

What a different place this world would be if those who loved us looked us in the eye and mapped out clearly the terrain of their distress, as Shelley did with Jason. If a parent said, "I was terrified by my mother and now whenever you get angry, I imagine that you are going to treat me the way she did. I know I overreact and I don't want to do that. I am working really hard to see you for who you are." Or, if a parent were to say, "My parents neglected me my whole childhood. I know that sometimes I look to you to take care of me when I should be taking care of you. I'm trying. You can even call me on it, if you do it really gently and kindly."

Children can be achingly forgiving. They want their parents' love and will accommodate to the most difficult conditions, distorting themselves in the process, to remain in connection to their parents. Later, these patterns of accommodation and distortion can recur throughout their lives.[1] Having a map and being an ally with the parent who is struggling with her own issues can make all the difference.

Family Mechanisms of Transmission

Within a family silence is the polar opposite of having a map and an alliance. Whereas a map and an alliance puncture fear and confusion, allowing connection across difficult interactions, silence produces, maintains, and strengthens fear and confusion. Silence is a powerful force in families. Although an absence of sound, silence signals prohibitions. It is its own map: don't go there; don't say that; don't touch. But why the territory is as it is cannot be read from the map of silence. The essential reasons cannot be deciphered from that map and so we remain blind, wandering without a guide.

In the previous chapter, I discussed biological and psychological mechanisms by which parental trauma can pass to children who witness or are victimized by it. Here I will tell a personal story that adds familial and societal processes to the mix.

It is a story of how the world comes to be inscribed in our very cells. And, correspondingly, how our very cells come to impact our world. I use my story because I have a fifty-year follow-up on it and a lot of detail. It is unique, as every person's story is, but the processes I am describing are common and exist all over the world. My story is set in a context of privilege and physical safety; yet, even so, I harbored terror. It has made me cast my lot with those who know terror and were not so fortunate as I.

Child Witness

In some families, when parents have suffered traumatic experiences, children are inappropriately exposed to frightening accounts that exceed their abilities to manage their own reactions to the horrors about which they are told.[2] In other families, like mine, children are *not* told what their parents have experienced.

Like so many families in which something fundamental to family life is not discussed, our family avoided its taboo topic, not exactly keeping a secret. We just knew what we weren't supposed to mention. I had a few ideas to account for what I wasn't supposed to raise, but since I never spoke to others, my thoughts were muddled and insufficient for my needs. They certainly didn't prevent me from developing fear incubated by silence. While silence functions to protect some family members, it does so at a high cost to all members.[3]

As a child witness to my parents' traumatic experience, I imagined what they didn't directly tell me, creating scenarios and frameworks out of the bits and pieces I gathered from them and other sources. Whether a child is overexposed to traumatic material or kept in silence about it, the child may develop a "disrupted schema," a conviction that the world is not safe and she is not secure.[4]

I was such a child. I developed thoughts, feelings, and behaviors that expressed this frightened worldview. However, I was out of synch with my parents. My parents testified in the summer of 1955 in front of the Senate subcommittee charged with investigating the "strategy and tactics of world communism."[5] I believe that I carried my parents' fear related to this experience long after they had successfully resolved their own fear regarding these events and the times. That summer my mother explicitly told me never to mention the hearings to my father, a request I honored for forty-six years.

My parents' failure to share with me what was happening in their lives left me to my own imaginative devices. I imagined the worst. Faced with a frightened child, my mother did her best to comfort me; my father reacted with characteristic irritation, humor, and humiliation. This is the story I lived with.

One day, when I was eight, my mother appeared at the bus stop in a police car. To this moment I see the scene as if I am a camera about four feet above and two feet behind my head. Like other images that form in the context of common shock, I have retained inconsequential detail: The asphalt is worn, and it skids off into a ditch. Pebbles of all sizes obscure the transition between road and gully. The police car is parked almost as if it had stopped as an afterthought. Although this is a bus stop where lots of kids get off, I can see no other child.

My mother's torso is leaning forward and toward the window, her head cocked toward me, her mouth moving. The police are not hurting my mother, she is not in any danger at that moment, but the entire scene is threatening. She must be speaking to the officer because the blue door opens. The policeman allows her to tell me something, but what?

Cut. Now I am walking down the road that is unnaturally curved to the left, as if banked by an inspired race-car aficionado. Only, I am on Munson Road. Nothing happens here. Your mother doesn't get taken away by the police. And children don't walk home alone after seeing their mothers drive off in police cars.

The scene is suspended in time with no before or after. Was someone at the house, about to arrive? Am I frightened? Do I understand? Have I been expecting this? Had I been told? Where is my sister? Is my father on his way? Does he know? Is he afraid?

This event frightened me. Or something associated with this scene, perhaps now spliced to it, did. I try to make the scene have meaning by connecting it to events in my life that are a bit clearer. My mother went away for several days and then my father did. Their airplanes "crossed in the air" and so they did not know for sure what the other one had said at the hearings.

The above account is written in the present tense because that is how this memory is preserved. Whenever I think about it, I shift into a past which becomes a vivid present, as if someone had yanked the intervening decades right out from under me. These images hovered in my child's mind, never discussed with anyone. I have no idea how accurate or inaccurate they are.

I remember the name of the person who told on my mother as if another part of my brain is responsible for storing and retrieving it. This memory is crisp and sharp, like a banner snapping in the wind. I'll never forget the name of the *man who stabbed my parents in the back*.

A few days after my mother left, she returned from Washington, D.C., and had one conversation with me about what had happened.

"If the teacher is about to leave the room," she said, "and tells everyone to be quiet, if, when she is out of the room, some children talk, when the teacher returns and asks if anyone talked, do you give names?"

"No," I replied.

"And if the teacher says she is going to punish everyone in the class unless people tell the names of the children who talked, then do you tell the teacher who talked?"

Indignant, I said more emphatically, "Absolutely not."

"Good," she said. "That is what your father and I did. We went to Washington and someone asked us to give names of people who they accuse of doing wrong deeds and we refused to tell on anyone."

The implication was very clear. Ours was a family that did not tell names. We were willing to suffer the consequences, even if something bad might happen. And I was pretty certain I knew how bad that could be.

In 1953, when I was six years old, Ethel and Julius Rosenberg were executed for conspiring to provide stolen atomic secrets to the Soviet Union. The Rosenbergs' innocence, their execution, and their son's welfare were all topics in my home.[6] Like the Rosenbergs, my parents were Communists. Or had been. Or maybe had been.[7] I knew I wasn't supposed to ask. The Rosenbergs had not told names either.

And the Rosenbergs were killed. I couldn't have known that they were the only people who were put to death during the McCarthy era. Nor could I have known that of the roughly 150 people who went to prison, most were released within a year or two. The primary "punishment" that people who were believed to be Communists suffered was economic: About 10,000 people lost their jobs.[8]

Apparently, standing up for principles and imposing silence on oneself was of the highest value in our family. Given my mother's analogy, I had endorsed both. Only, the real-life consequences in the scenario she had proffered and the one I had imagined—silence even if death is the punishment—were wildly different. I had agreed to one, but in my imagination I had also acceded to the other. I was sure we were choosing silence, at the risk of my parents' execution. My mother, on the other hand, knew that she and my father were at risk of economic reprisals that were frightening but not life-threatening.

That month at a local swimming pool, I lost a ring I had gotten for my sixth birthday. About a week after I reported it missing I received a letter in the mail. "We have your ring. You can't have it because your parents are Communists."

The bad things I anticipated had started. We were going to descend into the chaos of loss. I had been holding together, clinging to the feeling of belonging to a collective purpose around a principle that my mother had articulated and embraced. That single conversation with her, remembered minutely, was my life raft. Afterward my mother withdrew into her own fear and worry. Her admonition never to speak to my father about what was constantly on my mind isolated me from him. Neither parent was emotionally available that summer when my anxiety and fear were at a lifetime zenith.

I clung to a commitment to a higher principle, which was so connected to my parents that it served as a stand-in for them. But no commitment to an abstract principle could sustain me through the terror that the letter from the owners of the pool triggered. I was convinced that the letter was the beginning of the unraveling of our family. To me the letter was as official and ominous as a letter from the federal government. They were both The Authorities. Emotionally disconnected from my parents, relying on my own woefully inadequate resources, I collapsed. No one knew. I didn't tell. I kept silent. I was good.

I stopped being easily able to fall asleep at night. When I did fall asleep I would have nightmares. Always the same one. A man came into my bedroom with a knife in his hand, ready to stab me in the back. I learned to fall asleep sitting up, with my back against the wall.

Then I began to have symptoms during the day. I couldn't walk frontward up the stairs in our house from the basement to the first floor for fear that the man would stab me in the back. Then I couldn't walk down the block. The man with the knife again. Variants of these symptoms stayed with me for four decades.

No doubt my fear was my own, but I believe its intensity was also produced by my identification with my parents' fears, unquestionably more rational than mine. I believe that they were concerned about whether my father's clients in his public relations firm for nonprofit organizations would leave him out of fear of political fallout from their own clients. Within a month or two my parents must have gathered what became the reality: None abandoned him. With this knowledge the greater part of their worry about their own safety must have been allayed.

Meanwhile, the search for the red menace lost some of its glory. Journalists exposed egregious injustices; the Supreme Court curbed certain practices as unconstitutional. The public obsession with anticommunism began to diminish, and by late 1955 Joseph McCarthy became politically isolated. The White House declined to let him attend social functions there and in 1956 President Eisenhower is said to have told his cabinet that McCarthyism is now "McCarthywasm."[9]

I knew none of this. I assume that these facts allayed my parent's fears. As I was not privy to them, they didn't allay mine. Instead, I scrutinized my parents, vigilant for cues about whether we were in peril. My mother's transient concerns became grist for my mill. If my father was annoyed, this became evidence. Never being as intimate with him as with my mother, not sharing a temperamental similarity with him as I did with her, I hovered around him for clues more than around my mother whom I was certain I could "read." Unable to ask, I relied on my father's nonverbal cues. While my identification with my mother was overt, with my father it was subtler.

Watched by an anxious and fearful daughter, my father got irritated and frustrated by me. We entered a painful dance in which my hovering vigilance produced his anger which intensified my fear which led to more hovering vigilance which continued the dance. Seeing my fear, my father was able to disown whatever fear he had: first, to distinguish it from my exorbitant and now groundless fear and second, to rid himself of a feeling that was not acceptable to him. In effect, he managed his residual fear by dealing with it in me.

I thus carried my own fear and some part of my parents' fear as well.[10] Whereas my mother tried to comfort me, my father shamed me. Neither parent persevered in trying to figure out why I was so afraid. Although they were aware of all my symptoms, they, we, never created a conversational context in which it was possible to reconstruct the process by which what happened to my parents became soldered to me, expressed in symptoms of fear, vigilance, attention to political events, rigid adherence to principle, and fervent empathy.

My parents' trauma was transferred to me through my witnessing it. I was shocked by seeing my mother in the police car and believed that she had been "taken away." I was further distressed by my own vivid imaginings in the context of my mother's single conversation with me and admonition never to speak about these events. This silence created a medium in which symbolic representations of real and imagined parental trauma flourished. I became symptomatic.

My symptoms were lifelong and life shaping. They contribute to vulnerabilities but also to qualities of which I am proud. To this day the two are interlinked, so that pursuing political passions and commitments can take a toll. This was in evidence as early as sixteen months after the hearings.

In November 1956 I read about the Suez Canal crisis daily and saw film strips about it in my fourth-grade classroom. I was convinced that another world war was about to begin. Moved to action by Gamal Abdel Nasser's nationalization of the Suez Canal, the French, British, and Israelis allied with each other to attack Egypt. One week later, the Sinai campaign waged by the British, French, and Israelis was an apparent "victory," save one crucial factor. The Soviet premier, Nikolay Bulganin, threatened France, Britain, and Israel with military reprisals if they did not immediately withdraw from the Sinai. World leaders seriously believed that an all-out global war might happen.[11] So did I.

I didn't sleep. I paced. I read and watched the news compulsively. Finally, I wrote a letter to Dag Hammarskjöld, who was the UN secretary-general. In it I pleaded with him to do all in his power to stop the impending catastrophe. I then made the following offer. "Perhaps," I wrote, "the delegates don't understand how devastating war is. I would be happy to address the general assembly if you think that would help them understand how terrifying war is to children." I signed the letter, addressed it, and gave it to my father to mail.

I went to our mailbox every afternoon. My ritual held me together during the tense days of waiting to see what would happen on the world stage. I firmly believed that my offer would be accepted and that I would have a chance to protect the world's children. In trying to take care of all children, I was also trying to take care of myself.

By the time my mother told me that my father had never mailed my letter, the global crisis had passed. A few weeks into my afternoon mailbox vigil, she took pity on me and told me that my father had opened and read the letter. He had decided that it was just the kind of letter that might attract attention. He feared that someone might arrange for me to go to the UN and then a reporter would discover that my parents had been investigated as Communists, exposing our family to danger once again. He did not want to take that risk. As requested, I never mentioned this to my father, nor did I ask my mother the many questions her compressed explanation raised for me. The unsent letter took on powerful meanings. Despite potential dangers, I would be a person who witnessed, never relying on others to deliver my message.

These combinations of vulnerabilities, sensitivities, and resources have provided enduring shape to my life. Passionate engagement with world events, intense empathy for people all over the globe, attunement to others, proneness to shame, and occasional overwhelming fear have been steady companions. They are characteristics of mine that friends, family, colleagues, and my children can observe.

Much of what I understand about the effects of the hearings on me has come about through writing this book, which started a few months after my father died at age eighty-four. Months before that, knowing he would die soon, I summoned the courage to ask him the name of the hearings he and my mother had testified before. I did it during one of our three- to four-times-weekly phone conversations. There was a long pause. The "Eastland hearings," he said. We continued our conversation as if the question and the answer had been spoken by two other conversationalists, not this father and daughter for whom the topic was still unspeakable.

About two months after my father died, I began researching the McCarthy era. So strong was the felt prohibition that I obeyed the injunction not to "know" embedded in the parental silence well into my mid-fifties and only after both of my parents were dead did I delve into this material.[12] I also sought the exact date of their testimony. I found a newspaper article in *The New York Times* referring to their testimony in front of the Eastland committee. I asked Miranda, then a college senior, to see if she could locate the transcript of my parents' testimony.

In November, 2001, Miranda, called from the library stacks. She said simply, knowing I would know what she meant, "I found it."

I heard my father's testimony read in my daughter's voice, forty-six years after the fact. I learned through the medium of her voice what had transferred from my father to me without a word spoken between us.

He is asked to give names. He refuses. Over and over again he is asked. They threaten. He refuses. He is ordered to testify against my mother and he tells them that he doesn't think he should be asked to testify against his wife. They threaten him with contempt of the Senate for that as well.

I am now sure that he was traumatized by these hearings. But I had more difficulty understanding why he wouldn't speak about it, especially considering his brave and principled stand, until I began reading articles in the fall of 2001 about some of the men who had been detained after the September 11 attacks.

One vignette was about Mohammed Irshaid, who has lived in the United States for twenty-two years. A Jordanian-born civil engineer, his three children are American. On November 6, 2001, he was arrested at his office by federal agents and led away in handcuffs. "It was absolutely the most humiliating thing to happen to me in my life," he said.[13]

Another concerned Dr. Al-Badr Al-Hazmi, a Texas radiologist, who was picked up by federal agents on September 12 and flown to New York City where he was interrogated by the FBI and physically abused. On September 19 he was allowed a court appointed lawyer. On September 24 he was released in prison garb, without his glasses and allowed to fly home. His son, age eight, cried the entire time he was in custody and three months later still wasn't back to normal.[13]

My parents were a generation away from immigration and they had a private lawyer to represent them. They suffered no physical intimidation. Still, the aftereffects of trauma were profound. These two vignettes helped me put some pieces of my puzzle together, especially with regard to silence.

The day after Miranda had located my parents' testimony, she and I were walking in the woods near our home. I told her what had been dawning on me. The circumstances must have made my father feel so humiliated that even though he behaved with integrity, he must have been traumatized and reacted with shame. He couldn't face those feelings and so he imposed total silence about the entire ordeal. But in doing so, he never really took care of himself. If he had talked about the experience, he might have gotten over it.

He had to have been in a bind. He must have feared that talking about it would have endangered us—we were so young, he couldn't possibly have felt confident that he could control what we said to whom—and so his silence, their silence, was also their way of protecting us. They may well have understood that I needed more connection to them, but believed that it was just too risky.

Miranda ventured, "Maybe they were sacrificing their needs to fully deal with their experience to protect you?"

Her comment stunned me. It struck me as so sad. The wish to protect, so noble. The means—silence, secrecy—ultimately so inadequate. I thought of all the men and women in my generation carrying their parents' unspoken traumas, from battles they had fought, abusive relationships they had had to leave, molestations they had suffered. I was flooded with thoughts of my peers who had been silent, too, about things they had done in battle, their own failed first marriages, their struggles with eating disorders . . . and I knew what their children were carrying. So many parents valiantly managing their experiences of violence and violation as best they could, leaving child witnesses in their wake.

Once home, I jotted a note to myself on a pad so that I wouldn't forget Miranda's revelatory suggestion. I wrote: "sacrificing my needs to protect others." A few days later, I read my hastily scribbled note and smiled wryly. Even so many years later, my attempt to capture my father's experience is written as if it were my own.

Societal Mechanisms

Silence plays a crucial role in passing trauma and common shock from one generation to the next. This is the case whether it is the silence left in the wake of dissociation, the silence imposed by implicit or explicit family rules, or the silence shared by communities of people overwhelmed by the task of facing what mass violence has wrought. Silence operates at the individual, family, and national level, often in an interlinked fashion such that the silence at one level takes on additional meanings by its associations with other levels.

For instance, my mother's imposition of silence in our family occurred in the context of a political era in which the silence of not naming names incurred risk, and speech was dominated by those who gave names rather than by those who spoke to challenge the witch-hunts taking place. The silence in families of Holocaust survivors takes on different significance depending on whether the country in which families reside is one that collectively commemorates the Holocaust, as is done in Israel, or only the Jewish community observes the event, usually on a single day.[14] It feels different to be the child of a Holocaust survivor in a nation in which everyone shares some aspect of this legacy and references to it are common, as compared with the child of a Holocaust survivor in a nation that periodically debates the very existence of the genocide itself.[15]

People may appear to choose silence, but the reality is much more complex. We do not all have an equal opportunity to be heard. The color of our skin, the accent of our speech, the shape of our body, the experiences we have had, all contribute to whether or not others listen to us or we are relegated to silence. Voice is principally an expression of what the audience can bear.[16]

Humiliation

Silence is multifaceted and is associated with numbers of other phenomena. Shame is one of them. As with silence shame exists at the individual, family, and national level. If silence incubates fear, shame incubates violence, often retaliatory violence.[17] Shame, thus, also plays a role in the transmission of trauma and common shock from one generation to the next.[18]

New research points to regional and national experiences of shame, perhaps more aptly called humiliation, as central to the ways that trauma and, by extension, common shock, pass collectively from members of one generation to the next.[19] When whole groups are humiliated and must swallow their resentment, the desire for revenge builds. Children who see their parents and grandparents humiliated are particularly vulnerable to developing retaliatory fantasies. When one generation fails to restore social and political equality, this failure forms the next generation's legacy.[20]

Evelin Gerda Lindner, a German physician and psychologist, and Vamik Volkan, an American psychoanalyst, have studied this phenomenon extensively. While humiliation is enacted and experienced by individuals, it is built into the structure of social relations and institutions. Persons or groups who are humiliated are meant to feel put down or taken down.[21]

Lindner is particularly interested in the links between human rights ideology and humiliation. In those societies in which human rights principles form a fundamental understanding of the human condition, and in which preserving the dignity of all persons is felt to be essential, humiliation can take on traumatic dimensions, not just for individuals but for the group as a whole.[22] Thus humiliation, trauma, and common shock can become linked at the levels of individual and group identity.

Vamik Volkan and his colleagues have worked for decades to understand how disasters caused by ethnic, religious, or national conflicts can massively disrupt individual and group identity, transmitting trauma from one generation to the next. Volkan asserts that each person has a core identity that is comprised of both a personal identity and a large-group identity. He likens the large-group identity to a canvas tent. Commonly, the people in the group choose a leader who acts like the tent pole and keeps the tent erect. Under normal circumstances one is not aware that one stands under the tent, but in the event of a threat to the tent, should the canvas start to shake, the individual is motivated to secure the stability of the tent. The individual is protected by and defends the tent with thousands or millions of other people who share the same large-group identity.

The "Chosen Trauma": Another aspect of the group's identity is what Volkan calls "chosen trauma."[23]

> Within virtually every large group there exists a shared mental representation of a traumatic past event during which the large group suffered loss and/or experienced helplessness, shame, and humiliation in a conflict with another large

> group. The transgenerational transmission of such a shared traumatic event is linked to the past generation's inability to mourn losses of people, land, or prestige, and indicates the large group's failure to reverse . . . humiliation inflicted by another large group, usually a neighbor, but in some cases, between ethnic or religious groups within the same country.[24]

I suspect that the "chosen trauma" passes from one generation to the next primarily through witnessing.

In 2002, when I was teaching in South Africa, people who came to my workshops had no difficulty selecting the large group under whose "tent" they stood. People identified as Afrikaners, Cape Colored, English, Indian, Nguni, Sotho, Xhosa, Zulu, among others. Nor did they have difficulty identifying their group's "chosen trauma," when I gave them Volkan's explanation of the concept. They were puzzled, however, by the use of the word *chosen,* since none of them felt that the group with which they identified would conceivably have "chosen" the horrific, traumatic event that they had suffered.

I explained that Volkan didn't mean *choose* in the sense that one would make a conscious selection. Rather, a consensus would just emerge, as it had, for instance, in the United States in 1941 when the Japanese bombed Pearl Harbor and as it had, it seemed to me, after the September 11 attacks. Still, as a Jew, having selected the Holocaust as my group's "chosen trauma," I was disquieted enough with the idea of choice that I read more of Volkan's work when I returned home.

I found a paragraph in a paper of Volkan's I had not read before my trip that expressly addressed this concern. Volkan's discussion of the word *chosen* points to two specific meanings. He writes: "Since a large group does not choose to be victimized or suffer humiliation, some take exception to the term *chosen trauma.* I believe that it reflects a large group's unconscious 'choice' to add a past generation's mental representation of an event to its own identity, and the fact that, while groups may have experienced any number of traumas in their history, only certain ones remain alive over the centuries."[25]

When a large group is not under threat by an enemy group, the "chosen trauma" is commemorated with traditional rituals designed for this purpose. Under threat, however, the group experiences the "chosen trauma" as if the past were in the present, and members of the group react to current events with an intensity of response that is fueled by the feelings associated with the "chosen trauma." Sadly, there are many examples of this, of which I am probably most aware of those associated with the Israeli-Palestinian conflict. Many first-person Israeli accounts of the current conflict mention the Holocaust and many first-person Palestinian accounts mention the *nakba* (catastrophe), the 1948 expulsion of Palestinians from what is now Israel. The Holocaust and the *nakba* refer, respectively, to each group's "chosen trauma." Current events in this region illustrate Volkan's thesis that when the "chosen trauma" is fully activated it can justify "otherwise unthinkable cruelty."[26]

In the Middle East, Palestinians and Israelis invoke historical events that occurred half a century ago as if decades had disappeared, and in the Balkans, Serbs, Croats, and Kosovar Albanians speak as if centuries had collapsed into the present moment. Volkan's work, like Lindner's, emphasizes the centrality of humiliation to the large group's experience of trauma, noting that psychic energy builds up in succeeding generations to reverse ancestral humiliation. Volkan suggest that it is as if later generations are assigned the "task" to avenge the honor of their ancestors. When there is a current threat, the motivation and energy available to complete the task is immense.

I have worked in Kosovo twice, in September 2000 and May 2001. I have sat with extended family groups, with women only and with men only, on pads on the floor of newly rebuilt rooms in homes that were burned to the ground by Serb soldiers. I have been served elaborate multicourse meals by families that have re-formed to incorporate the children and wives of sons and nephews dead and missing since 1999. I have talked with children in a school in which 80 percent of them saw the massacre of seventeen men from their village. I have thought about Volkan's ideas as I met with young and old Kosovar Albanians, wondering how their experience of this most recent war was being passed down, even as we spoke.

One month before my first visit, an article appeared in the *Journal of the American Medical Association, JAMA,* whose purpose was to establish the prevalence of psychiatric problems and to assess social functioning following the war among ethnic Albanians in Kosovo. Among other findings to which I referred in Chapter One, 89 percent of men and 90 percent of women reported having strong feelings of hatred toward Serbs; 51 percent of men and 43 percent of women reported strong feelings of revenge; and 44 percent of men and 33 percent of women stated that they would act on these feelings.[27]

The figures shocked but did not surprise me. Working in Kosovo, however, meeting with children, adults, and families, I did not find that expressions of hatred and revenge dominated the conversations I had. Rather, fourteen months after the NATO bombing had stopped, my colleagues and I heard stories, often told by adults in front of children, of piercing tragedy, of men hauled away by Serbian soldiers, paramilitary, or police and shot, sometimes in view of their families, sometimes in view of entire villages. Men were missing and their families were hostage to the pain of "ambiguous loss."[28] The people we met told us stories primarily from the period of March through June 1999 when, following the NATO intervention, Serbian forces expelled 1.3 million Kosovar Albanians from their homes, most becoming refugees in Macedonia, others internally displaced within the province itself.[29]

This brutal systematic ethnic cleansing included the separation of men from their families; the murder of thousands of men and boys; and the destruction of homes, property, and personal documents.[30] These events, some of which I had seen at the time on television, were described in heartbreaking detail by the Albanian Kosovars we met. Often the women's eyes, in particular the women's eyes, darted wildly, as if they could still see the scenes they were recalling. In family after family, children were at the women's sides, sensing, as we did, that the events of the previous year were somatically alive in their mothers' and aunts' bodies; the events were not receding into distant memory.

Will this war become the Kosovar Albanians' "chosen trauma"? If so, will Kosovar Albanian children be "assigned" the task of avenging the honor of their parents and grandparents? Were the Serb soldiers fighting against the Kosovar Albanians acting on behalf of *their* ancestors, fulfilling a task that they had been assigned? Did Serbs perceive the Albanian Kosovars as "perpetrators," when most of the world saw them, and the Kosovar Albanians saw themselves, as "victims?"

Many commentators see the war in Kosovo within a larger historical narrative.[31] This narrative goes back six hundred years, when the Serbian kingdom lost power to the encroachments of the Ottoman Empire. One battle, the Battle of Kosovo, fought on the Field of Blackbirds outside of Pristina in Kosovo, on June 28, 1389, came to symbolize Serb defeat and decline. During this battle Ottoman Turkish Muslims killed the Serbian leader, Prince Lazar. His body was mummified and buried near the site of battle. However, about seventy years later his body was removed to Serbia to keep it "safe."

The Battle of Kosovo became the Serbs' "chosen trauma." Prince Lazar came to represent both the Serbs' victimhood and also their glorious efforts to achieve independence in relation to Muslim oppressors.[32] Kosovo itself symbolized precious land that rightfully belonged to Serbs. In 1912 the Serbs won back Kosovo from the Turks. A Serbian soldier, standing on the Field of Blackbirds, was quoted as saying: "We feel strong and proud, for we are the generation which will realize the centuries-old dream of the whole nation: that we with sword will regain the freedom that was lost with the sword."[33]

In 1914 a Serb murdered Archduke Franz Ferdinand, heir to the Hapsburg throne, and his wife, Duchess Sophia, on June 28, the anniversary of the Battle of Kosovo. The archduke's presence in Sarajevo on that day was considered by many to be a provocation, considering how high Serb sentiment was against the Austrian-Hungarian influence in Serbia. Seventy-five years later the chosen trauma was activated again. In April 1987 Slobodan Milošović was attending a Communist Party meeting in Kosovo and Serb demonstrators were loudly protesting their treatment by the majority Albanian Kosovars. Milošović was riveted to the demonstrators' stories of victimization. He promised that the Serbs of Kosovo would never again suffer the experiences of a minority.[34]

In 1989, to commemorate the six hundredth anniversary of the Battle of Kosovo, the remains of Prince Lazar were exhumed. His coffin was placed on a wooden cart and sent to every village and town in Serbia, reactivating the multiple losses he symbolized and revivifying Serbian hatred of Muslims. Prince Lazar's ashes were brought to the Field of Blackbirds, where a large memorial had been erected. On June 28, 1989, Milošović flew into the site by helicopter. Although the words in his speech do not foment Serbian nationalism, the huge crowd, estimated between one and two million, many wearing T-shirts imprinted with Lazar's call to battle against the Turks, heard what it had been hearing: "Never again."[35]

Concurrently, Milošović and his party removed autonomy from Kosovo and began systematic oppression of the Albanian Kosovars, then 90 percent of the population. Albanians were removed from jobs, Albanian schools were closed, and Albanian health-care professionals were unable to practice in public institutions. Parallel education and health-care systems were developed to meet the needs of the Albanian Kosovars. Throughout the decade of the nineties the oppression by Serbs of the Albanian Kosovars had profoundly different meanings to each group. While the Albanian Kosovars experienced themselves as victims of the Serbs, the Serbs saw themselves as avenging their losses, and reversing their humiliation, at the hands of the Albanian, that is Muslim, perpetrators.

Victim-Perpetrator Oscillations

At the heart of many intractable conflicts—at the familial, community, and societal levels—is just such a radical difference in point of view, with each party to the conflict perceiving themselves as acting defensively from the victim position to correct injustices wreaked by a cruel perpetrator. Distortions in the perception of time create different temporal sequences for the two sides, such that what is seen as provocation by one side is seen as retaliation by the other. To the witness on the outside of the conflict it may look like the two parties are engaged in a victim-perpetrator oscillation, such that victimization justifies aggression, leading to activities that create perpetrators out of former victims.

Often these oscillatory swings occur between the same two groups over centuries, as is the case between Serbs and their Muslim neighbors in Bosnia and Kosovo. But sometimes the swings are enacted on a group that was previously not involved. In conversations with Afrikaners in South Africa we wondered whether the defeat of the Afrikaners by the British during the Boer War was acted out on the black population later in the century.

The Boer War was the most frequently selected "chosen trauma" for the Afrikaners with whom I worked. Most could recite the appalling statistics of the war, in particular the numbers of women and children interned in concentration camps (by September 1901 there were thirty-four camps for whites with 110,000 inmates) and the number who died (26,251 women and children died, of whom 22,000 were under the age of sixteen).[36] Most believed that Indians, colored, and blacks had supported the British during the Boer War, and growing up, few had known that blacks were also interned in concentration camps. In fact, by the end of the war there were a total of 115,000 black inmates living in "appalling conditions," and at least 14,154 had died, the majority of them children.[37] My Afrikaner colleagues and I wondered whether the humiliating defeat of the Afrikaners by the British in 1902 had influenced the next generation of Afrikaners, inspiring a need to avenge this loss. Had Afrikaners turned the psychic energy of perceived victimhood away from the British toward the majority blacks, creating a system of laws—apartheid—that perpetrated violence on the black and colored population, all the while perceiving that they were protecting themselves against threat?

This question, while a legitimate one, raises disturbing issues, just as the related concept of victim-perpetrator oscillation does. How often in the history of the world, whether in families or in nations, has a victim been able to amass the resources to turn from victim to perpetrator, within the same or the next generation? How often would victims wish to if they could? Is it possible to judge the moral equivalency of acts of violence, that is, aggressions and counteraggressions? How does a belief in the existence of these oscillations affect the behavior of bystanders and witnesses, with what effects?[38] What societal mechanisms impede these oscillations and interrupt cycles of violence, and who can play a part in implementing them?[39]

Constructive Action in Relation to Societal Violence

It is easy to become overwhelmed by the apparent enormity of many geopolitical conflicts, whether between Indians and Pakistanis, Israelis and Palestinians, Kosovars and Serbs, or the United States and the countries President Bush has designated an "axis of evil."[40] However, there is plenty of work for ordinary people to do, in our homes and in our communities, while politicians and diplomats work at their levels to solve these ferociously intractable problems.

Our job as caring individuals is to acknowledge losses, to support mourning, to humanize the enemy, and to witness individual and collective pain with as much heartfelt compassion as we can muster. In the immediate aftermath of societal violence this work is much more complex than it is decades later, but it is better to start, better to try than to not try.

Mourning

Many experts point to acknowledging and mourning losses as essential to the interruption of cycles of violence.[41] Clearly, this is not easy to do, either for individuals or societies. In the aftermath of societal violence people are left with intense emotions of fear and rage, hatred and humiliation. People must find ways of managing these charged emotional states at the same time as they tend to the tasks of immediate survival. Without support, both from people who have suffered the same losses and from those who have witnessed the losses from afar, it is common for people to suppress or deny the depth of the pain and the loss, as a short-term solution to the complexity of the realities they now face.[42] People who fail adequately to mourn their losses and to work through the pain of their suffering, as we have seen, are more likely to repeat their past.

This is as true for societies and nations as it is for individuals, who after all are the citizens of nation-states.

Mimoza Shahini, M.D., is one of two child and adolescent psychiatrists trained in Kosovo since the war. I heard her present a paper during one of my visits in which she was struggling with how to incorporate Western psychological ideas about grief into Kosovar Albanian culture, which values stoicism, especially in public. Children are also protected from death, and this means that they are often excluded from traditional rituals of mourning.

In her work with children who had had at least one family member who died during the war, Dr. Shahini held group sessions in schools in which the children were able to express their grief openly. To prepare the way for these sessions she talked with the children's parents and teachers, explaining why mourning together would be helpful to the children. To her surprise one teacher even asked to participate in the group! Dr. Shahini wisely noted that she was trying to balance the children's emotional needs as well as the "needs of our culture for its stability."[43] At the same time, by working with grief as she is, she is providing a path for another kind of cultural stability.

The parents and teachers who meet with Dr. Shahini all are learning that there is something that they can do to help themselves and children; they can allow themselves and their family members to grieve. In the context of massive societal trauma, mourning is hard to do, but crucial. Nor can mourning be done as easily alone as with others. Sharing grief with others makes the pain more tolerable.

Rehumanizing the Enemy

Decades, even centuries, after massive societal violence, there is still work individuals can do. In 2000 I was giving a workshop in Pretoria, South Africa, and was making a rather simple point: societal trauma leaves imprints on individuals in a myriad of ways. To illustrate I used an example that was not in my notes: the story of my name.

As I understand it, my mother named me Kaethe after the German graphic artist Kaethe Kollwitz, whose work greatly moved her.[44] Kollwitz primarily depicted workers, and mothers and children. She combined her professional work with devotion to family, a life choice that was especially meaningful to my mother. Apparently, when my father came to the hospital and she told him that she had chosen "Kaethe" for my name, he asked her to reconsider this choice, telling her that he feared it would be unwise for a post-Holocaust Jewish child to have a German first name. Persuaded, my mother and he decided to call me "Kathy." So, I had informed my South African audience, even a name can bear the imprint of macrosocietal traumas. I looked down, searching my notes for the example I had intended to provide.

From the back of the room a woman shouted at me: "But you are Kaethe." I remember freezing. This woman's father had been a leader in the South African Defense Forces during the apartheid years. She had chosen a different path, striving with dedication to improve the lives of all South Africans, and working to dismantle her own racism. Her comment stunned me.

I realized that I had an opportunity to dismantle my own family legacy, one of anti-German sentiment, to "rehumanize the enemy" by using my own name as a bridge between two peoples, German and Jew.[45] By reclaiming my originally given name—as inconvenient as that would be to family, friends, clients, and colleagues who were used to calling me Kathy—I could take a small step in resisting the ways societal violence and its aftermath seep into our lives.

Because massive societal violence abounds, there are plenty of opportunities to assist with healing. Americans learned this tragically following the heinous acts of violence perpetrated on September 11, 2001. It was incredibly moving to observe the rich and generative public response, the acknowledgment of pain and mourning of our losses. Citizens (actually people all over the world) spontaneously consoled each other and created rituals of healing on street corners, within neighborhoods, in church and school communities, and within branches of government. These organic processes of healing occurred alongside of official governmental responses that more quickly than the citizenry moved from mourning to gearing up for a war against terrorism and designating enemies.

In the fall of 2001, living with my own fear and confusions, I was reminded of the words of a South African friend and colleague who spoke about her family's response to the Boer War. She had said, "Our family divided in two. One side responded by saying, in effect, 'This shall never happen to us again.' The other side responded by adopting the view that 'this must never happen to anyone ever again.' I feel incredibly fortunate to have grown up nurtured by the latter side of the family."

Intercepting the Passing of Trauma and Common Shock from One Generation to the Next

As we have seen in Chapters Six and Seven, biological, psychological, familial, and societal mechanisms all contribute to the passing of trauma and common shock from one generation to the next. Given the array of ways that this happens, it should come as no surprise that there are many ways to intercept it. Intentional, compassionate witnessing is the one I propose. Part Three provides a detailed examination of what this looks like in practice. In those families in which trauma and common shock are passed, it is likely that qualities to manage it are also passed, for, as I have written in the previous chapter, it is not just vulnerability that trauma and common shock confer, but also opportunities for resilience.[46]

Witnessing Oneself as Victim, Witness, or Perpetrator

The ability to reflect on one's experience is a key capacity that fosters resilience.[47] It allows one to witness the self and to witness others. It allows one to be aware. Without this ability we are much more likely to repeat the past. If the past is replete with violence, violence will permeate our future.

The capacity to witness the self can be compromised at any point in our lives, and also nurtured. To develop the capacity to witness the self, the infant and young child must be treated with kindness and respect, by someone who recognizes that the child's needs are different from her own. Later, the capacity to witness the self is linked to having an appreciative listener, someone with whom one can share honestly. Sadly, horrific events and experiences can obliterate the capacity to witness oneself, as one feels that what one has suffered is too awful to bear.[48]

Some who have lost their capacity to witness themselves are fortunate to meet others who are dedicated to restoring the capacity to witness even to those who have endured unimaginable suffering. They do so by communicating their profound commitment to try to imagine what cannot literally be imagined and by acknowledging that what they suffer from imagining what the other has suffered in no way compares to the suffering itself.[49] The knowledge that some people are willing to bear witness reactivates the capacity to witness oneself.[50]

In all instances the ability to witness the self is linked to witnessing by others. Honing our ability to witness others is, therefore, something we can all do that actively affects the transformation of violence. Likewise, the ability to witness the self can have profound effects on others, be they intimate others or citizens whom one leads.

One evening in my friends' home in Pretoria, tired after a day of teaching, I was reading a book of commentaries on the Truth and Reconciliation Commission in South Africa. I was reading quickly and not carefully when suddenly I became electrified. I was reading a "confession" from F. W. de Klerk, "spoken" at Nelson Mandela's inauguration in 1994. Reflecting on his role during the apartheid era, witnessing his actions and those of his party, understanding that he had been a perpetrator of massive crimes against humanity, de Klerk makes explicit what he is asking forgiveness for "the harm and pain our policies had caused . . . that we were fundamentally and completely wrong. . . . I also ask forgiveness from the young people who died unnecessarily for an indefensible cause, and especially from their parents."[51] I burst into tears at the exact moment my skepticism and yearning, disbelief and hope, collided into the author's statement that the speech was his fantasy.

Such a witnessing of the self, had it happened, would have changed the course of the history of the world. I am sure of that. His apology, coupled with the evidence of his understanding of the heinous effects of apartheid, coming from one of its perpetrators and "architects," would have had massive repercussions on the lives of millions and millions of people. In the author's fantasy de Klerk and Mandela are in a relationship of mutual recognition. Mandela, the survivor of apartheid, also shares a heart-stopping reflection on his life during the author's depiction of an imaginary Mandela inauguration. He says, "What I and my people suffered under your party's rule we will never forget, but we forgive you, and I invite you, and them, to build a new country with us."[52]

These conjoined acts of self-witnessing are not just wild fantasy, as in this imaginary inauguration. They take place every day, in living rooms, on sidewalks, between ordinary people, fathers and sons, mothers and daughters, brothers and sisters, who confess to each other harms they have committed and endured, and who forgive and are forgiven. In this intimate scale of witnessing, all the way to the national level, disconnections that have sundered relationships can heal.

Repairing Relationships

The willingness to repair what has been rent in relationships is one of the most precious gifts we can give to others and ourselves.[53] Failure to do so creates a second injury. Parents are faced with this challenge and opportunity frequently. The vitality of family life and the well-being of family members depends on the ability of all members to reestablish connection after disconnections have occurred. It is especially the case that traumatized parents face daunting tasks of reconnection with their children, for their own traumas, whether from their childhoods or from external events, such as war or rape, predispose them to lapses with their own children that can produce suffering and pain.

My parents were both traumatized by external events during the McCarthy era. After initially providing some framework around what was happening, my mother withdrew into silence and warned me never to discuss these events. My father never spoke to me about it. I was a silent witness to my parents' suffering and felt separated from them.[54] They believed that talk was dangerous and silence the surest way to provide protection. They pulled out of connection at just the moment I most needed it. Without their comforting presence my terror mushroomed. This silence added to the silence surrounding my father's rages. Together they produced a profound sense of isolation. When I couldn't speak, I produced symptoms to talk for me, only no one knew how to interpret them.

Adults' reactions to their own trauma vary enormously. But in every instance, if a parent harms a child, a parent can help that child. Parents can witness the child's pain, offering validation of the child's experience, remorse, and comfort. When the parent has experienced trauma from circumstances that seem too awful to share, parents are in terrible binds. Their trauma leaks out; they feel that they are toxic to their children. Many parents believe that the best resort is withdrawal.

My personal and clinical experience tells me otherwise. Children do better knowing something rather than nothing. It is possible to provide a context for children without going into detail that will be overwhelming. A parent can gear his speaking both to his own capacity to bear it and the child's developmental capacity to understand and manage what the parent has to say. Parents may want an outsider present—a witness—to support this brave sharing.

Following such disclosures the parent may need to check in with the child to see how the child is doing with the information that has been provided. Many professionals suggest taking one's cue from the child and only responding when the child poses a question or makes a comment. While I think it is crucial not to intrude on a child—and many children require time on their own to sort out their feelings—I think that this sensitivity must be balanced by clearly communicating to the child one's readiness to return to the topic, to review what has already been brought forward, and to hear the child's reactions to it. Otherwise, the provision of private time is hard to distinguish from a return to silence.

Dialogue

At the societal level actions by individuals can have effects. Organizations in many parts of the world have taken up the work of promoting dialogue between groups of people who have had historical enmities, as a means to diminish polarization. These dialogue processes, as fraught as they are, as hazardous and miraculous, are a means by which the passing down of trauma and common shock from one generation to the next can be interrupted. The fruits of these dialogues radiate out into families and communities devastated by societal violence.[55]

In some areas dialogue participants are members of groups who have both persecuted each other over centuries. In others, for instance, dialogues between the children and grandchildren of Holocaust survivors and Nazi perpetrators, the victimization has been unidirectional.[56] In some instances violent oscillations form the larger background to contemporary struggles that have been genocidal by one side against another, as is the case with recent dialogues between Bosnian Serbs and Muslims.[57]

Whatever the historical and political context, dialogue between individuals who are members of groups that have caused or endured horrific suffering is a fateful enterprise. No one emerges the same, not participants, not facilitators.[58] The goal of such dialogue processes is to truly hear the other and, in doing so, to enter into some form of acknowledgment. Whether dialogue occurs between individuals who have recently survived catastrophic turmoil or takes place between descendents of those who did, people speak from bodies that are supercharged, that is, with nervous systems whose activation is easily accelerated and hard to slow down. In these exquisitively sensitive states people know that they each have the potential for "flying apart" or "coming together," just as they bear responsibility for harming or healing others.

Letting Successive Generations Witness

There are informal ways also that we can create opportunities for children and grandchildren to listen to the experiences of their elders so that honor is paid by actions that promote healing, not revenge. If witnessing becomes a method by which the assigned "task" of previous generations is fulfilled, then the task will be completed without perpetuating violence. This is devoutly to be wished.

Adults must consider carefully the effects of the stories they tell about the "enemy" group. When my children were young, thoughtlessly, I told them a story about my mother refusing to "set foot" in Germany after World War II. Years later, on the eve of a school trip to Prague, Miranda brought up this anecdote.

Looking downcast, she said, "We have a two-hour layover in Frankfurt. I'll have to set foot in Germany." I recognized that phrase. I know that my mother has a place of honor in our family, and I imagined that Miranda was concerned that she would not be living up to her admired grandmother's principles, since she was willing to step on German land in order to go on the trip to Prague.

I did many things. First, I told her more of my mother's story. I told her how during the Vietnam War she had named herself as "like a good German" for, after all, what besides protesting was she doing to stop the war? Second, I told her that when I was twelve, my mother had taken me to Berchtesgaden, the village in the Bavarian Alps where Hitler and his mistress had a wartime villa. She had wanted me to be a witness to the place. Finally, I suggested that she perform a ritual while she was there in which she could join her hopes for reconciliation between Germans and Jews with those of the German people. This fuller conversation and its conclusions were much more in keeping with, and honoring of, my mother's spirit.[59] It also softened the polarization between Jew and German, us and them, that my initial anecdote had created.

The successor generations to those who have suffered mass violence play a pivotal role in the interception of the transmission of trauma and common shock, for it is they who must find ways to let their hearts see. Let no one be confused: this work takes courage. Anyone does it with more ease accompanied. Compassionate witnessing, the accompanying of another, is a task for all ages, in all ages.

At the end of Aeschylus' trilogy, the *Oresteia,* Athena hopes to conclude a peace with the Furies, to end their persecution of Orestes, a grandson of Atreus, and to forestall their putting a curse on her city, Athens.[60] The Furies and Athena acknowledge each other as members of different generations of gods. Athena seeks to soothe them, through flattery, perhaps, but with the intention of ending the power of the curse that has plagued the House of Atreus and all who know them. Witnessing their lives, bearing their pain, she begs the Furies not to inflict the kind of rage on the young men of Athens that will make them not only lust for war, but also turn "their battle fury inward on themselves." No, she implores, let goodness and honor reign and let the citizens honor you for your devotion to justice, not revenge. Wise Athena is successful. The Furies tell her that they feel their "hate is going."

That is the work all of us must do. We can listen and care. We can act as compassionate witnesses to others, in the hopes that in doing so we help hate go.

Part Three

What We Can Do

There are those who are trying to set fire to the world,
we are in danger,
there is time only to work slowly,
there is no time not to love.

—Deena Metzger[1]

CHAPTER 8

Foundations of Witnessing

The Maasai warriors of Enoosaen, who live in a mud hut village in Kenya, are expected to respond effectively to any emergency. This was not the case for Willson Kimeli Naiyomah, a warrior and premed student at Stanford University who was visiting Kenya's UN ambassador at the time of the attack on the World Trade Center. Kimeli found himself in an unfamiliar position: aware that people desperately needed help, but unsure how to be helpful, the witnessing position that we have seen creates problems for many people. He said, "Being in New York, I could not respond and I felt a little uneasy having done nothing, so I carried this pain in my heart and I wanted to do something."[1]

Returning home in May 2002, Kimeli found that many of the villagers had not heard about the attacks. When they learned, and he explained to them that buildings could be so tall that people could jump to their deaths from them, they were deeply saddened and troubled. "They decided to give the gift of solace," Kimeli explained: fourteen head of cattle, the Maasai's most prized possession and precious gift.[2]

Tribal elders presented the cows to the acting American ambassador at a formal ceremony attended by hundreds of Maasai holding banners, some of which read, TO THE PEOPLE OF AMERICA, WE GIVE THESE COWS TO HELP YOU.[3] And the gift *did* help. The Maasai's witnessing of the American people was itself witnessed by people all over the world via an Internet site that documented the gift and its reception. One response is from the family of firefighter Jeffrey James Olsen, from Staten Island, New York:

> To the Maasai people, *Ashi oleng, Ashi naling* for having such compassion and respect for our son and his brother firefighters

> who gave their lives saving other lives and for the thousands of innocents who were murdered so brutally. We have read many things about the Maasai people, all of them indicating that you are a proud, intelligent, and honorable people. Your recognition of our son and the others, coming from so far away, means very much to us.[4]

With their gift the Maasai initiated a remarkable process of connection, dissolving both physical and cultural distance. While their daily lives may be far different from Americans', their feeling for the tragedy clearly was not. Their symbolic and literal act was understood all over the world as signifying a deeply felt sense of common humanity. Their acknowledgment of American suffering and sorrow evoked a reciprocal appreciation, drawing disparate peoples into a more intimate awareness of each other.

This chapter and the next focus on the foundations that can support us, and on the resources upon which we can draw, to become intentional, compassionate witnesses, just like Kimeli and the Maasai people. These share an essence: they help us recognize and express our common bond with one another. Crucially, this is not the same as feeling similar to or identified with the other. Quite the opposite.[5] Kimeli had no trouble feeling linked to the shocked New Yorkers he was among, but he needed his community to help him express the "pain in his heart."

In this chapter we will look at personal capacities, interactional practices, and universal knowledge that support compassionate witnessing. In the next chapter we will identify particular actions that embody compassionate witnessing. Each of these resources provides a solid foundation for compassionate witnessing by helping us recognize our shared humanity, restore our sense of common humanity when it falters, and block our dehumanizing others. They change our *perceptions* of the other, who remains just as he or she has always been, human, no more, no less.[6]

"Otherness": the Gateway to Dehumanization

I feel some combination of anticipatory excitement and worry when I am about to meet someone for the first time. Will we connect? Will we find something in common that will engage and delight us? Will what we have in common be enough to overcome whatever differences, or sense of otherness, we may have?

This sense of otherness does not arise only in the context of strangers. I have had it with those I love most. And I doubt I am the only person who, enraged at her spouse or child, has thought, *Who is this person? How did I ever live with him and how will I ever do it again?*

Whether in relation to people we will never meet, or strangers we are about to meet, or those who become "strange" through the wear and tear of everyday life, we are constantly confronted with the recognition or reaffirmation of our common humanity.

Witnessing violence and violation is challenging, whether at the moment that an act of violence occurs or later, when the acute situation has passed. It activates physiological arousal, as we have seen in Chapter Three. Let us say we see a neighbor yelling harshly at his six-year-old son. We are physiologically primed to withdraw, react aggressively ourselves, or numb out, responses that correspond to flight, fight, or freeze. Aware and active witnessing requires us to overcome these initial physiological reactions, staying mindful of what we have seen and developing a plan of action that is safe and compassionate toward all involved.[7]

If our neighbor is someone we know well and care about, it is more likely that we will be able to view his behavior with concern and imagine ourselves in some kind of dialogue with him. If, on the other hand, we don't know him well, but have been disturbed by the few encounters we have had with him, observing this interaction may produce negative ideas about him that further distance us from him. Repeated, such a sequence can lead us to turn our neighbor into an "other."

When we experience people as wholly different from us, other, it is possible to feel a wide range of negative emotions toward them, such as disgust, revulsion, contempt, rage, hatred, or terror. These feelings not only contribute to our experiencing them as other, but the experience becomes self-perpetuating, justifying continued expression of these feelings. Over time we dehumanize the other person. Dehumanization, the process by which people are viewed as less than human, a process that individuals, groups, and nations all do, obstructs caring about the other.[8] Perceiving someone's shared humanity is a prerequisite for compassionate witnessing.

Examples of dehumanizing abound. Read the newspaper, and one can find instances of dehumanization in the ways estranged family members speak about each other, members of one community talk about a rival community, and citizens of one nation speak about people from "enemy" nations. The dynamics that turn a ten-year-old's best friend into her worst enemy share elements with the process that pits one neighborhood against another. The parent at his son's hockey game who demeans the other team's players is engaging in speech acts that are similar to those of hostile governments.

These practices of dehumanization are ancient and remain with us. In the *Iliad* Homer shows us the process of dehumanization multiple times.[9] In Erich Maria Remarque's *All Quiet on the Western Front,* the narrator, twenty-year-old Paul, a German soldier during World War I, talks to a soldier he has stabbed and holds in his arms until his death. His speaking maps the process of dehumanization and the return through rehumanization.[10]

> Comrade, I did not want to kill you. If you jumped in here again, I would not do it, if you would be sensible too. But you were only an idea to me before, an abstraction that lived in my mind and called forth an appropriate response. It was that abstraction I stabbed. But now, for the first time, I see you are a man like me. I thought of your hand grenades, of your bayonet, of your rifle; now I see your wife and your face and our fellowship. Forgive me, comrade. We always see it too late. Why do they never tell us that you are poor devils like us, that your mothers are just as anxious as ours, and that we have the same fear of death, and the same dying and the same agony—Forgive me, comrade; how could you be my enemy?[11]

The very lesson that Paul learns in the trench is one that the military, now, meticulously counters. In order to overcome the natural resistance people have to killing—numerous studies have found that the vast majority of men and women are reluctant to kill[12]—the military exploits every aspect of distance that people can feel. They have perfected techniques that use physical, psychological, cultural, moral, social, and mechanical distance factors to turn enemies into "inferior forms of life," that is, to dehumanize them.[13] In addition, the military inoculates its personnel against hate while at the same time it manipulates their capacity to hate through the use of propaganda. It should not be too surprising that the core feature of most hate propaganda is the dehumanization of the enemy.[14]

Dehumanization depends on the felt experience of distance, which is subject to sudden reversals. A young Israeli who fought in the Lebanon war in 1982 told of an encounter when he and his comrades were shooting PLO fighters in a refugee camp. Two refugees came toward them carrying an object and shouting at the soldiers. Because the men were only twenty yards away, the Israelis could discern that the object they were holding was a crate of Pepsi-Cola and their shouts were "invitations to have a drink! The [young Israeli] later reflected: 'If they had been two hundred yards away, we would have shot them and been glad to hit them.' And he asked: 'How far does a human being have to be before he becomes a target? How close must he be before we see he is human?' "[15]

These questions are profound. While we may know a great deal about dehumanizing others, we know, or think we know, a lot less about rehumanizing others, a process that is absolutely vital to the survival of us all.[16] Yet, the practices that restore our sense of common humanity are well known; they are just not conceptualized as such, like the shell collection kept on beaches all over the world.[17] In this chapter and the next I am, in effect, making a tour of the world's beaches, pointing out shells that can help us experience our shared humanity.

Personal Capacities

A foundation for compassionate witnessing, of turning unwitting witnessing of violence and violation into something deliberately chosen, is a set of personal capacities, each of which can be developed. They are: awareness, safety, empathy, Aidos, and compassion. Awareness is the cornerstone of them all—a precondition, if you will. Without some combination of these five capacities no one can witness appropriately and effectively.

Awareness

Most of us lead lives in which we are bombarded with millions of stimuli each day. People, activities, events, causes, sensations, perceptions, objects, demand our attention, and we must sift, filter, prioritize, ignore, lose track of, and block out much—some would say, most—of what impinges on us, or we would immediately be overwhelmed.

Awareness is a constant in our lives, even though what we are aware of shifts continuously. Some days I am able to stay aware throughout the entire time I make my cup of coffee in the morning. I am aware of the round glass kettle getting heavier as I fill it with water from the tap. I feel my torso turn toward the stove and my outstretched arm adjust to the weight of the now cold kettle. While I wait for the water to boil, I take the coffee beans out of the freezer, hearing the suction around the rim of the compartment give way, sensing the shift in temperature as I put my hand into the freezer to grab the bag of beans, and then hear the sound of the door as it swings shut. If I am truly focused, the sound the beans make as I pour them into the grinder can be deafening and I may flinch as I push my finger on the button, anticipating the pulverizing of the beans. I could go on. Just as often I walk upstairs with a cup of coffee in my hand, knowing that I made it but having no memory of doing so.

Clearly, there are variations in awareness. Too much awareness—as in hypervigilance, for instance—tends to narrow our focus and shut out a great deal of what is happening at the moment. Too little awareness—as in denial or numbness—also limits our scope of attention. The right kind and amount of awareness produces calm and clarity, even in the face of stressful conditions.

Awareness is not a gift some people are blessed with and others are not. It is a skill that can be developed with practice. Buddhists have been practicing awareness through mindfulness for millennia, and there are wonderful books, tapes, and programs that teach their techniques.[18] A few minutes of practice a day can make a powerful difference in one's life.

Buddhists have long known the importance of regulating the breath, and therapists work with the breath as well. For one thing, our breath is always with us. Noticing it, slowing it down, regulating it by as simple a technique as inhaling to a count of three, holding to a count of three, and exhaling to a count of three can provide remarkable benefits both physiologically, in terms of calming the sympathetic nervous system, and of focusing our attention to enhance awareness. When a person is experiencing common shock, working with the breath is one of the best things to do to restore calm.

Looking at the origin of the word *awareness* can help us understand two of its essential aspects. According to work done by the eminent psychiatrist Robert Jay Lifton, awareness is related to words like *wary, beware, ward,* and *guard* as well as to others like *conscious, cognizant,* and *sensible.* Lifton explains: "Awareness, then, includes the ability to anticipate and realize danger on the one hand and the capacity for knowledge and transcendent feeling on the other."[19]

These derivations help us see how vital awareness is to witnessing. First, if we are not aware, we will not notice situations that involve violence or violation. We have seen the enormous investment some people have in diminishing or dismissing violence and violation as not important, even those events that directly impinge on them. Awareness provides the opportunity to stay present so that we can contemplate what we want to do. Second, awareness is a state of alertness that can reduce the physiological arousal that often accompanies seeing violence and violation, or can help us recover from mild common shock more quickly later.[20] Finally, awareness helps us do a 360-degree scan of the context we are in, both physical and interpersonal. Aware, we can observe whether or not we are safe, what else is happening, and who the potential allies are in the environment.

Safety

Safety is a fundamental human need.[21] Aware that something could be or needs to be done, we still need to assess our physical safety, and that of others who may be involved, before we decide to offer compassionate witnessing. In those situations of everyday witnessing of violence and violation in which we are certain we are physically safe, we must still evaluate whether we feel emotionally safe to take action. In a sense we must assess our readiness to be involved with others. Part of this assessment requires awareness of the degree of common shock we are experiencing. If we are safe, and we are sure we can manage our common shock, then moving from the disturbing side of the witnessing coin to the chosen side makes sense.

Many situations confront us with the need to make this assessment. If our witnessing action is listening to another's story of what has happened in the past, our assessment may be different than if it is confronting an angry relative who is verbally lacerating her children. In the latter case we may decide that the children have been exposed to the woman's anger many times before and that our best chance of making a difference in all of their lives is to approach the mother when she is calm and we ourselves feel less threatened. Or we may decide we just can't risk the confrontation, even though we feel certain that she is damaging her children. There may be other steps to take that feel less risky and are also constructive.

In the matter of safety, we look straight into the maw of a moral dilemma. When people are victims or witnesses to violence and violation, their sense of safety collapses on them for what may be a brief or a protracted period of time. All recovery from trauma and common shock requires the reestablishment of the sense of safety. This is the first step in all successful treatment approaches.[22] At the same time it is sometimes necessary to risk safety to help others escape exposure to violence and violation. This is true at the individual level all the way up to the international level. How does one person or one nation do the moral calculus to decide whether or not to risk her or its own safety in favor of others?

There are no easy answers; nor would my answer for myself be useful to anyone else. As I have written in Chapter Two, the dilemma needs to be presented to children early in their lives, with opportunities to brainstorm strategies that minimize risk to the self and maximize protection of others, as well as opportunities to talk about the consequences of strategies they enact in their daily lives. Jawaharlal Nehru once said; "To be in good moral condition requires at least as much training as to be in good physical condition."[23]

A decision we make one day does not enshrine that decision forever. One day I may join a march to raise funds for victims of domestic assault, and another day I may feel I can't bear to listen to the stories I will hear at the premarch rally. No action or inaction commits me to any course.

During the Holocaust the citizens in a small village in southern France, Le Chambon, rescued 2,500 Jews. Magda Trocmé was the wife of the village pastor, André Trocmé, who inspired the villagers to hide Jews. Interviewed about her choices, Mme. Trocmé is reported to have said that her decision to hide the first Jew who appealed to her required no thought. She said, "What else could I do?" Yet later, when she had been hiding Jews for a while, she watched the Gestapo round up a group of young Jewish men and did nothing. She knew that at that moment there was no "safe or effective response."[24]

To me, this is a lesson about context. It means that individual moral courage is not an absolute but a contingent virtue. The choices we make may be quite different if our bodies are flooded with adrenaline than if they are calm. If one has time to reflect and if, in assessing one's abilities and limits, one does not feel safe to act, the task is not to throw in the towel forever. The challenge is to select what one *can* do now, do it, and imagine that a different choice may be possible in the future.

Empathy

Feeling what someone else feels, or trying to, is a good definition of empathy. Empathy can be contrasted with sympathy. Whereas empathy is feeling what another feels, or would feel, if she knew her own situation, sympathy is our own emotional response to another's situation, often sorrow or concern.[25] Scholars who study empathy believe that it is universal, self-reinforcing, and expressed by children as young as a year of age.[26] Empathy certainly helps us experience our shared humanity.

Abby is twelve years old. She is not Muslim. Her father wrote a piece for National Public Radio about her decision to fast for Ramadan. "Abby felt the crashes hard. . . . The pain of the dead, the displaced, and the survivors became Abby's pain," her father said in his commentary. "But she also grieved for the abuses suffered by young girls in Afghanistan. Abby announced that she intended to fast for Ramadan. 'Why?' I asked. 'To demonstrate solidarity with Muslims,' she replied." Abby is keeping a journal; the family is planning to visit a mosque. Her father worries about her fasting without community support. Her teachers worry about her staying alert in class. "She is more subdued than normal. . . . Her spirit is boosted by the reality that she is doing something, something that she can literally feel every time a hunger pang ripples through her belly." Her father tells us that when they read the newspaper, they see pictures of people "praying, meditating, breaking the fast. They are no longer other people from other places. They share our same corner of the world. But they are more noticeable now. It is easy to see them simply because they resemble the people who brought us terror. It is more difficult to see them as Abby has, as people we should strive to understand by trying to feel what they feel."[27]

Sometimes we are invited to empathize with others in ways that produce startling shifts of perspective. The other day I received an e-mail from a member of a women's peace group in Israel, who wrote about a surprising request she had recently received from a university student, Ron, at a peace demonstration. Ron was asking for volunteers to have their living rooms "ransacked" to help him complete a project he was doing on the occupation of Palestinian territories. He passed her a note that read, in part, "I turn the living room into an arena where I demonstrate what takes place during a typical search by the Israeli army—I overturn the bookcases and shelves, dump everything onto the floor, overturn all the furniture, and create disorder. I also tie up the residents of the home in the usual army way, all for purposes of the filming (which takes about an hour)."[28]

My correspondent took Ron's request home and gave it serious consideration, but in the end decided not to participate. However, Ron had made his point to her . . . and to me, reading the e-mail five thousand miles away. Imagining a search of my own living room, I could empathize with the plight of Palestinians, and people anywhere, whose homes are torn apart. I wouldn't choose to have my home, much less my living room, searched!

This anecdote helps underscore a distinction between empathy and personal distress. Empathy stays focused on the other's experience, while personal distress, caused by having an emotional reaction to another's experience, is focused on relieving one's own anxiety or discomfort. When people choose to witness others, they usually do so out of empathy, not to relieve personal distress. In fact, compassionate witnessing is probably a rather inefficient way in the short run to relieve one's own distress, since one is moving toward, not away from, the source of that very distress.

Empathy seems to be linked to helping behavior, and most people think that, in and of itself, it is a good quality to have.[29] Children can be taught empathy, both in the home and in school, and this has a positive effect on their ability to cooperate with other children and to resolve conflict without fighting.[30]

In general, psychologists and educators promote empathy from the point of view that more is better, and certainly that more people feeling empathy is better. In general I agree. However, I also know that there is a danger of *too much* empathy. In Chapter Five we have seen that people in helping professions can place themselves at risk if they don't carefully manage their empathy, and that as a society we insufficiently support those very professionals on whose empathy and competence we count.

Another danger can affect anyone whose empathy leads her to take actions that jeopardize her safety. Years ago I took a women's self-defense and empowerment program that used a padded "mugger" in its innovative twenty-five-hour program.[31] For the first two five-hour sessions my efforts at fighting off the mugger were restrained. At the end of each evening I went home and pondered what was holding me back.

During the third class the mugger was attacking a young woman who reminded me of Miranda. I could feel my fury. One might say I felt empathic anger. At that moment I realized that for the previous classes my empathy for the mugger, my imagining the life that had led him to this point, had blocked my ability to protect myself, even with nonlethal force. After this insight, when it was my turn, I was able to fight with full commitment, saying to myself, "Empathy can wait until I am safe." Here we see the complex interplay between two of the personal witnessing capacities. Empathy for the mugger interfered with my ability to assess my safety, whereas protecting myself didn't preclude also feeling empathy . . . at a more appropriate time. Fighting back did not cut off the opportunity to witness the mugger later.

Aidos: The Greeks have a term, *Aidos,* named for the goddess of reverence and righteous shame, associated with concepts of inner integrity and personal honor.[32] The Greeks pictured Aidos as a butterfly; a touch of her wings could prompt feelings of remorse followed by apologies. Hesiod, the Greek poet who wrote in the eighth century B.C., predicted that there would come a time when mortals no longer responded to wrongdoing with appropriate shame and that Aidos, and her companion, Nemesis, righteous anger, would then "forsake mankind and go, their beautiful forms shrouded in white, from the wide earth to Olympus. . . ."[33]

Cara, a client of mine in her forties, illustrates the theme of Aidos. She can still vividly recall the sounds of her older brother going into her younger sister's room at night, often while she was simultaneously hearing her father screaming at her mother and breaking objects downstairs. As a witness to violence and violation Cara believes that she should have been able to stop her family members or bring in someone who could. She cannot understand why she didn't call the police, tell a teacher, or speak to a relative. Cara suffers from severe common shock—in her case, chronic PTSD. She believes that she was at fault for failing to halt the abuses that were perpetrated by her father and brother. Although we have gone over the circumstances with a fine-toothed comb, and Cara now has a much richer understanding of the constraints under which she operated, she is still vulnerable to self-blame, self-criticism, feelings of worthlessness, and shame.

As we have seen in Chapter Three, shame is common in the aftermath of violence or violation, for victims, witnesses, and even perpetrators.[34] It is a painful emotion, which, for many people, no matter how much they work on it, does not diminish much. In recent years, in my practice, I have taken another tack in the effort to ease the suffering that shame causes.

I make a distinction between righteous shame and toxic shame.[35] Toxic shame is what Cara carries. It is as if the shame that the wrongdoers deserve to feel has bypassed them and been taken in by Cara, where it wears away at her self-esteem.[36] Another possibility, I have decided, is to imagine that the shame she feels expresses deeply held values.

I proposed to Cara that she might not be able to free herself of the experience of shame, but she might be able to interpret its meaning differently and thus have a less painful reaction to it. I wondered whether she could think of herself as responsive to Aidos' butterfly wing? Touched, she felt Aidos, righteous shame, a shame consistent with her abhorrence of injustice and rejection of any form of abuse.

Cara is trying this on, and some days it works for her. She carries a picture of a butterfly in her wallet and I have several butterfly objects in my office to remind us both that Aidos can connect us to the deepest sufferings of others and prompt us to protest, to protect, to care, and to heal. By doing this we are turning the pain of shame into a reminder of values we hold dear.

Compassion: The last of the personal capacities that provide a foundation for action is compassion. While the dictionary tells us that compassion is a feeling of sorrow or pity *for* the sufferings or misfortunes of others, I think that compassion is better understood as suffering *with* another with the intention of relieving that person's suffering, not getting mired in it as well.

The Dalai Lama of Tibet tells a story of speaking to a Tibetan monk who had been in a Chinese prison in Tibet for eighteen years. He asked him what he experienced as the biggest threat to him while he was in prison. His reply: "losing his compassion for the Chinese."[37]

This exemplifies extraordinary compassion that few of us can ever hope to attain. The monk clearly was able to feel his common humanity even with his jailors. To practice compassion one has to have an open heart, but not an overwhelmed one. This is absolutely essential for aware and active witnessing. If we are going to witness others' suffering, we don't want to be shattered the first time out. Knowing our own limits is part of living a compassionate life. It helps us to use our resources optimally.[38]

In my experience compassion arises when we allow ourselves to have a rich and complex understanding of the materials out of which people forge their lives. Richard Moore, the director of Children in the Crossfire in Northern Ireland, has lived much of his life with just such an appreciation. I met Richard at a conference I attended in which twenty-four people participated in a three-day dialogue on the question of compassion and social healing.[39] Richard lost his right eye and his sight in the left eye at age ten in 1972, when a British soldier fired a volley of rubber bullets at him as he was walking home from school.

In talking about his experience he talked about both the past and the present. About the blindness itself he told us, "[I]t was very easy to accept. I cried once about being blind that night—because I wasn't going to see my daddy or mummy's face again."[40] He reported that he never felt bitterness as a child.

Later, his brother joined the IRA. Richard was able to use this further family tragedy to create a more complex understanding of the Northern Ireland "Troubles," and his place in relation to them.[41] "If my brother could join the IRA because of what happened to me," he told our group, "then I know the soldier who blinded me could have experienced something that led to him shooting me."[42] Richard now directs a program to create dialogue between, and to address pressing social, economic, and environmental issues of, the two communities in Northern Ireland. His compassion for all those caught up in the Troubles is palpable.

In South Africa, where I now have close colleagues and friends, I am privy to a dilemma that sometimes arises for white people of privilege with regard to compassion. Still reeling from the revelations of the Truth and Reconciliation Commission, throwing themselves into the work of building the new South Africa, guilty about continuing to reap the benefits of the apartheid system, my friends, many of whom are Afrikaners, frequently deprive themselves of care and compassion when bad things happen to them, because they continually minimize their suffering in comparison to the suffering of others, white or African. As a visitor to South Africa, but a "resident" to the practice of denying myself care and compassion because I trivialize my "suffering" in comparison to the suffering that exists in the world, I find their practices of deprivation familiar even though they upset me.

Visiting them the first time, feeling compassion for my colleagues, I had an epiphany for myself as I spoke to them about these matters. I understood that the solution was not to deprive oneself of compassion, but rather to be unflinchingly honest about the nature of one's circumstances compared to others while still behaving toward oneself with compassion. I realized that one has an obligation to tell as complex a version of one's circumstances as one can without losing sight of the plight of others. Thus compassion includes discernment, but not judgment.

After my first trip to South Africa several of my clients shared with me their fears that I would no longer care about their pain because it would not measure up to the pain of people I met in South Africa. In fact, I had no such experience. For me, placing restrictions on compassion—to self or other—is an "intervention" in the wrong location. The more one feels compassion, the more there is. Likewise, the failure to care for the self tears the fabric of the world as surely as failing to care for others, for we are also someone's other.[43] Compassion is served by complexity and discernment, not by qualifiers and conditions.

Interactional Practices That Transform Violence and Violation

There are several interactional practices that support compassionate witnessing. I will discuss nonviolence, forgiveness, reconciliation, and restorative justice in some detail because they promote ways of relating to others that foster a complex vision of the other, while diminishing a sense of "otherness." Like the personal capacities, these are practices. Performed, they become richer and more reliable.

Betsy had to sit down when she learned from her daughter, Tanya, that her "best friend" had failed to invite her to the first boy-girl party of their lives, telling Tanya that no boy would be interested in dancing with a girl without "headlights." Having caught her breath, Betsy lost control and screamed at Tanya, "She may never come to this house again. Period."

When Bob learned from Anne, his wife of twenty years, that she was leaving him for another man, he was very clear: "I give you one more chance to change your mind. If you do, I will work hard on this marriage, forgive and love you, but if you don't, I'll hate you and make your life a misery."

Michael's thirteen-year-old stepson has been rude and hostile to his mother since she married one year ago. Michael has decided to give the boy the silent treatment, refusing to talk to him or interact with him in any way. He hopes this will teach the boy a lesson.

All three people have been witnesses to violence and violation. Witnesses, their personal capacities are insufficient to sustain empathy or compassion for the person or persons who have injured them or someone they love. They have responded by shutting down interest in the other's subjective experience.

Hate, revenge, and retaliation promise relief and yet they do not provide it.[44] Rather than protecting the self from attack, they make the self vulnerable to future aggression. Nonviolence, forgiveness, reconciliation, and restorative justice are all interactional practices that offer the possibility for long-term security because they do not mirror violence but transform it.[45] A commitment to nonviolence, whether implicit or explicit, also underlies forgiveness, reconciliation, and restorative justice.

Nonviolence

A common misperception about nonviolence is that it is passive. Nonviolence is neither passive nonresistance nor submission in the face of violence and violation. Rather, in pursuit of one's objectives, nonviolence is the refusal to participate in any kind of harm, be it direct or systemic, and the commitment to treat people fairly and respectfully.[46]

For example, in July 2002 hundreds of unarmed village women in southeast Nigeria staged a nonviolent protest against oil companies in their region, trapping hundreds of workers inside five separate facilities. Demanding jobs and community improvements, the women, ranging in age from thirty to ninety, used an unusual threat to maintain control over their hostages: They said they would take off their clothes, a traditional shaming gesture that humiliates the onlookers.[47]

Whether in mass protests or individual action, nonviolence works not by manipulation or coercion, but by a much subtler form of persuasion, more like the workings of compassion. As Thomas Merton has written in an essay on Gandhi, "The only way truly to 'overcome' an enemy is to help him become other than an enemy."[48] This is just what two people in Lincoln, Nebraska, did.

In June 1991 Michael and Julie Weisser were moving into their new home when Michael answered the phone and heard a harsh voice threaten him: "You'll be sorry you ever moved in [to that house], Jew boy!" Two days later hate mail came from the KKK. Following up with the local police, they were told that the hate mail looked like the work of

Larry Trapp, the state leader of the Ku Klux Klan, a man known to terrorize African-Americans, Vietnamese, and Jews, and also known to have used explosives.

Diabetic and wheelchair-bound, Trapp at this same time started a white supremacist series on the local-access cable channel. In response Michael Weisser began leaving messages for Larry Trapp on the KKK hotline, debating his racist, anti-Semitic, and Nazi propaganda. One evening Trapp answered the phone and screamed, "What do you want?" Having prepared with Julie what he would say, Michael replied, "Well, I was thinking you might need a hand with something, and I wondered if I could help."

A few months later, following regular calls from Michael, and a number of other caring interactions from Vietnamese and African-American strangers, Trapp agreed to meet with the Weissers. At their first meeting, taking off his two silver swastika rings, Larry Trapp broke into tears, declaring that he wanted to get out of the Klan but he didn't know how. With the Weissers' help Trapp resigned from the Klan in November 1991, five months after the Weissers' first nonviolent response to Trapp's hateful messages.[49]

Hate dropped into the Weissers' lives, and they responded to it with compassion and nonviolent action. In everyday life there are countless opportunities to respond to harm with nonharming action. The ten-year-old who links arms with a classmate who is teasing another child and gently pulls her away, distracting her with a story, is using nonviolence. The health aide at a clinic who brings an irate patient a cup of coffee while she is waiting for her appointment is using nonviolent action, whether she knows it or not.

Most of the world's religions have traditions that support nonviolence and peace,[50] while at the same time there is ample historical evidence that these same religious traditions have been used to justify war.[51] Whether an Eastern or Western religion, all "link the transformation of social and political violence to the transformation of inner violence."[52]

Forgiveness

Forgiving someone who has harmed us is one way we can experience and express the transformation of *inner* violence. When we have been injured or harmed, our attention is often riveted to the act that caused the injury or to the actor or actors who perpetrated harm. When we consider forgiveness of the perpetrator, a subtle shift occurs. We initiate a process of self-reflection that is very much like witnessing ourselves. We may ask ourselves questions such as "Can I do this?" "Am I ready to let go of this pain and anger?" "Do I truly no longer want the other person to suffer?"

There are many definitions of forgiveness, and scholars do not agree among themselves on how best to define it.[53] Most definitions include the idea that forgiveness is a response to an injury or violation in which the person overcomes the "natural and predictable" feelings of rage and hatred as well as the desire for revenge and retaliation[54] in favor of feelings of "compassion, benevolence, and love" toward the offender who has no right to expect this.[55]

For the most part, models of forgiveness and public discourse about it assume that the person who considers forgiveness is the direct victim of an injury or wrongdoing. However, as we have seen, witnesses to violence and violation are often greatly impacted by what they experience, even when they are not the targets of an offense.

A client of mine was stunned when his adult daughter confronted him one day and told him she had never forgiven him for having an affair and leaving her mother ten years earlier. An exemplary father by the daughter's account, he was flabbergasted that she thought she was in a position to forgive him—or not—for his infidelity and decision to leave the marriage. "Of course, I understand that she was upset about the divorce," he told me, "but where does she come off thinking she has a right to forgive me? Only her mother has that right," he fumed.

There is a tension among theological and psychological models of forgiveness with regard to whether or not forgiveness should be independent of the offender's attitude and behavior, or tied to it. For instance, in Judaism, victims are not obligated to forgive offenders unless the offender goes through a process called *teshuvah,* which means "return," although they may do so. The process of *teshuvah* is clearly spelled out in Maimonides' "Laws of Return"[56] and, interestingly, the steps are similar to those recommended by certain therapists who work with families in which abuse has taken place.[57] Of note, the process of *teshuvah* and the psychological work of an offender are not considered complete until, faced with the same or a similar situation, the person acts differently.

Christian, Buddhist, Islamic, and Hindu positions on forgiveness are different from this. Christianity and Buddhism endorse forgiveness without repentance, while Islam and Hinduism offer a range of acceptable practices of forgiveness and nonforgiveness for relationships.[58] When people of different faiths and religious traditions encounter each other, as happens all the time, these differences play out in remarkable ways.

Eric Lomax, born in Scotland in 1919, served in Malaya during World War II and was taken prisoner by the Japanese in 1942. In his memoir, *The Railway Man,* he describes working on the Burma-Siam railway, during whose construction 250,000 men died. He was also tortured by the Japanese after they found a map of the railway that he had clandestinely made.[59] Like many victims of torture he has some memories that are incredibly detailed and vivid, and others in which scenes suddenly go blank. Although he knows events took place, he can recall nothing.

He remembers one period of his imprisonment particularly well: There was an interpreter who stood alongside the officer who was torturing him, firing questions at him that alternated staccato with terrible blows from a tree branch. The interpreter became an obsession for him in the early 1980s when he retired. He was consumed by the desire for physical revenge on his torturers, especially on the interpreter.

Lomax suffered from PTSD, but he didn't know there was a term for his cluster of symptoms and daily experience until 1987, when, after encouragement from his second wife, Patti, he sought an explanation for the rages and withdrawals that so marred their loving relationship. Learning he was still suffering from his wartime trauma, he began to work with the Medical Foundation for the Care of Victims of Torture in London.[60]

In the fall of 1989 a friend's wife handed him a photocopy of an article in an English-language newspaper published in Tokyo about Mr. Nagase Takashi, a man who became an interpreter for the Allies after the war when they attempted to find their dead along the railway. In this article he described his charitable deeds on behalf of those who died working on the railway and his decision to dedicate his life to their memory and their survivors. A short, frail man, seventy-one years old and in ill health, he wrote that every time he experienced the pain of a heart attack, he "has flashbacks of Japanese military police . . . torturing a POW who was accused of possessing a map of the railway. . . . 'As a former member of the Japanese army, I thought the agony was what I have to pay for our treatment of POWs.' "[61]

Lomax's response was immediate. The man he had wanted to find was nearly in his hands. He knew who and where he was, and Nagase didn't know either. The tables were turned; he felt, finally, that he had the power. He shared the article with many people, all of whom could feel his excitement, some of whom suggested that it was time for him to forgive and forget.

Lomax had other ideas. He planned to visit Nagase as part of a film crew and then surprise him by revealing his identity. This fantasy of a surprise confrontation came to an abrupt end after he, and then his wife, read a memoir of Nagase's in which he describes his first visit in 1963 to the cemetery in Thailand, after the Japanese lifted foreign travel restrictions, which is the site of seven thousand graves of men who were found and buried after the war. Deeply moved, Nagase describes laying a wreath with his wife at the base of a white cross, praying, and then feeling his "body emitting yellow beams of light in every direction and turning transparent. At that moment I thought, *This is it. You have been pardoned.*"[62]

For Patti, Nagase's audacity was unbearable. She asked her husband's permission to write Nagase. In a carefully crafted, controlled letter, Patti identified herself and Lomax. She told Nagase that her husband was interested in meeting with him, and that she hoped that the meeting might be a healing experience for them both. She then posed the question that had impelled the letter: "How can you feel 'forgiven,' Mr. Nagase, if this particular former Far Eastern prisoner of war has not yet forgiven you?"

Her question, arising out of the pain of witnessing her husband's suffering from the effects of massive trauma, goes to the heart of critical dilemmas raised by the multiple, conflicting ideas about forgiveness that circulate among individuals from different cultural, ethnic, and religious backgrounds. Who has the right to forgive?[63] Who has the right to feel forgiven? Is justice served by forgiveness? Is forgiveness necessary for "healing?" Can conscious choice of nonforgiveness in the face of nonatonement of the offender also heal? What difference does it make, to whom, if forgiveness is freely chosen or a response to interpersonal or theological coercion?

Within days Nagase responded to Patti's letter. He understood precisely what Patti had wanted him to face. He repeated her sentence to him. His brief letter contained acknowledgement, tenderness for Lomax, appreciation of Patti's "taking care of him until today for a long time," and only in a second "P.S." did he explicitly reveal his feelings: "The dagger of your letter thrusted [sic] me into my heart to the bottom."[64]

A witness to Lomax's torture, but the human symbol of it, Nagase had spent forty years atoning for his part in the brutality of the Japanese army. He felt his witnessing of Lomax as pain in his heart, but at least in his letter, he didn't lose sight of the fact that his imagining of Lomax's suffering could not compare to Lomax's suffering.[65]

Nagase's letter moved them both. Nagase was the perpetrator; Lomax, the victim; Patti, the witness. All had developed a robust witnessing of themselves in relation to the events and aftermath of the war. Lomax and Patti had worked with the Medical Foundation, understanding the effects of trauma on their daily life. Nagase had embraced Buddhism, which had promoted continuous self-reflection. Their correspondence in 1991 came at a time when they were all "ready" for it. Nagase's scrupulous, unflinching witnessing of himself grounded his witnessing of them and was utterly convincing. Lomax and Patti were flooded with sadness and softness: Forgiveness became conceivable.

Forgiveness can transform inner violence, the painful preoccupation with past injuries that keeps the sufferer engaged with violence and violation despite the desperate wish for release from it. Sometimes forgiveness is private, known to nobody else. Sometimes it plays itself out in front of many witnesses, as Lomax's eventually did. When the offense that must be forgiven involves violence and violation, power dynamics are always at work. Whether a political regime that has committed atrocities and other human rights abuses or a father who has sexually molested his daughter, the one who wielded the power is often more interested in forgiveness than the person or persons who have been violated.[66] Certainly, their time frames may be different.

Lomax's story is instructive about time horizons and the processes that have to be in place for forgiveness, the outer expression of the transformation of inner violence, to occur. In 1991 both men were capable of witnessing themselves with integrity and honesty. This made forgiveness possible. Nagase's feelings of remorse and acts of reparation felt genuine to Lomax. If they made Nagase feel better, that was a by-product, not an objective. The objective was his authentic concern to make amends to the people he had harmed. How different this is, for example, from an abusive father who wants his daughter to forgive him so that he can be reunited with his family. Nagase had worked with sustained effort to become other than a perpetrator. The abusive father remains confused between personal pain and genuine remorse. As long as his own feelings are at the center of his concern, he cannot be other than a perpetrator.

The conditions for true, noncoerced forgiveness take time. We forget this at our peril—even more so, if forgiveness is followed by attempts at reconciliation, a next, but not invariant, further step in the forgiveness process.

Reconciliation

There is no inevitable relationship between forgiveness and reconciliation, although they are often discussed together, as if the former always precedes the latter.[67] In fact, reconciliation may proceed without forgiveness, or be viewed as irrelevant to it.

Nourit Pelet, whose thirteen-year-old daughter was killed by a Palestinian suicide bomber in 1997, describes a complex view of how forgiveness and revenge connect with peace and reconciliation: They don't.

> As for revenge, I don't think the dichotomy of forgiveness versus revenge is right. I don't think there is forgiveness. You don't forgive. But we have a very strong line by a poet, Bialik, "Even Satan hasn't invented the revenge for the blood of a child." This is not because Satan has no means. It's because after the death of a child the only thing that you want to do is protect the child, and since you can't protect your child, you want to protect all other children. I don't think that any mother would be satisfied to see another mother's child dead. So there's no forgiveness but there's no revenge. The only thing that drives me is this forever unsatisfied need to protect my child and any other child.[68]

Ms. Pelet's comment goes to what many scholars believe is the heart of reconciliation: the restoration of wholeness or harmony. Ms. Pelet feels this as a need to protect all children.

Reconciliation creates community where people can live together in mutual respectful relationship with each other, recognizing the other in his or her uniqueness. In the process of reconciling, trust must be repaired and justice addressed. For reconciliation between individuals as well as between societies the truth of people's experience must be acknowledged. Truth emerges when the context has been prepared by practice in listening carefully to each other, without defensiveness. It emerges when people understand that the purpose of revealing one's pain is to forge new relationships that can endure with less tension and conflict in the future. This is so for individuals and societies.[69]

Maryhelen Snyder is a family therapist and poet living in New Mexico. In her memoir, written after the death of Ross, her husband of forty years, she searingly describes their complex relationship, particularly her dissatisfaction with the emotional distance between them.[70] Toward the end of the marriage they had developed a practice of talking a minimum of one hour a week to see if they could reestablish their former intimacy.

Earlier in the week Maryhelen had told Ross that she was angry with him for replacing the basket in which she displayed their fruit with a green bowl that he had bought at the local discount store. "It's the wrong color for the kitchen," she had told him when she first saw it, "and it looks plastic, artificial, and cheap."[71]

Now, during their talk time, she brought the bowl up again and Ross responded by telling her that he felt "a 'deep hopelessness' about ever being accepted as he was."[72] Quietly, he shared his feeling that he might not deserve her acceptance, coupled with his belief that talking about it wouldn't make any difference. After a while, eyes filled with tears, he said, "Mel, I *am* that bright green bowl, and it's good."[73]

Committed to witnessing each other's pain, willing to engage in "deep listening," Ross and Maryhelen allow truth to be spoken and acknowledged.[74] Grieving her years of not fully seeing Ross's goodness, Maryhelen sets the green bowl in the center of her kitchen table, and it looks beautiful to her. This moment of reconciliation has been prepared by years of goodwill and practice with rupture and repair. Many relationships, communities, and nations must start from scratch, with little shared positive history on which to base their efforts.

In Tulsa, Oklahoma, efforts at community-wide reconciliation between white and black Tulsans with regard to the massacre of black Tulsans in 1921 has faltered around reconciling accounts of what happened during the day of, and the days and weeks following, what is called the Tulsa Race Riot. Reconciliation has been tied to requests for reparations by the African-American community, as a means of seeing that justice is done, and this has alienated many in the white Tulsan community, polarizing what has also been, at times, progress toward social healing.[75]

Tulsa's experience is in no way unique. Reconciliation is famously and fiercely difficult. People or peoples who are hurt naturally resist placing themselves in a position to be hurt again. Opening to the other, opening to hear another's account of how things really were, or how *you* really were, is incredibly painful. W. S. Merwin has a long prose poem in which he describes unchopping a tree, reassembling it leaf by twig by branch by trunk.[76] Many people, in the context of family or communal rupture, experience reconciliation as equally daunting and misguided.[77]

One set of objections to reconciliation efforts comes from those who study situations in which violence has been allowed to flourish with impunity. Whether within families, where power imbalances are usually configured by gender,[78] or between large groups, either within or between nations—also often configured by gender—reconciliation may reinstate and legitimate postviolence impunity.[79] For reconciliation to contribute to the transformation of violence it must "foster a culture in which transparent process, equitable distribution of social resources, and widespread involvement are normalized."[80]

Despite all the dilemmas associated with reconciliation, whether familial or societal, many people argue that healing through reconciliation is the only way to prevent future violence between injured parties.[81] Martha Minow, who has written eloquently about these matters in the context of mass violence, writes that while no response is adequate, people "wager that social responses [like reconciliation] can alter the emotional experiences of individuals and societies living after mass violence. . . . The wager is based at least in part on the recognition that some past responses seem linked to subsequent horrors. . . . Ultimately, perhaps, responses to collective violence bear witness: to it, and to the human beings destroyed by it."[82]

Restorative Justice

A Navajo husband, while drunk one evening, battered his wife. She decided to use the traditional Navajo dispute-resolution system to confront him. After the traditional ceremony the wife told her story. Then, eight of her husband's friends and relatives told stories about the husband, letting him know how much they respected him. In addition, they talked with him about his duties as a Navajo man to his family and to the community. Since the hearing, his wife has said, her husband has acted differently because he "knows that people think of him as a special person."[83]

For the Navajo, conflict represents a disruption of *k'e,* that force that speaks to one's reciprocal relationship to the community and to the universe. *K'e,* like *ubuntu,* encourages "respect, solidarity, compassion, and cooperation so that people may live in . . . harmony."[84] The Navajo use restorative justice principles to return individuals to a state of harmony among themselves and with the community.

Whether within a family or a nation, when we open ourselves to witness a person who has harmed us or a member of our community, punitive justice remedies are usually incompatible with our goals, which are, as for the Navajo, the restoration of harmony among all. For instance, if my neighbor's sixteen-year-old son Carl were to scrawl graffiti all over the old boat my husband has repainted and left out in the yard, I might be angry and frustrated, I might feel violated on Hilary's behalf, but I wouldn't want him punished. I would want to understand why he had done it. I would want him to tell me what he had been thinking the night he had done it. What was going on? Had he been high? Alone or with friends? Had it been premeditated or a spur-of-the-moment idea? Was he getting back at us for something we had done, or not done, to him or to his family?

Then, I would want him to understand what the boat meant to our family. I would want him to understand that it wasn't just a dinky boat, but a prized family heirloom that Hilary's father had made. I would want him to set out on the Charles River with Hilary looking for turtles so that he would experience the pleasure we do. I would want him to learn how to paint the boat so he could repair the damage he had caused.

My wishes fall pretty neatly within the restorative justice paradigm, which looks at "crime" not as a violation of the law, although it is, but rather as a violation of people and relationships in which the victim, witness, offender, and community are all harmed and must be involved in setting things right.[85] Although there are many models now for implementing restorative justice principles, they all rely on similar principles:

1. Invite full participation and consensus
2. Seek full and direct accountability,
3. Heal what has been broken,
4. Reunite what has been divided, and
5. Strengthen the community to prevent further harms.[86]

These principles are common to the justice traditions of many indigenous and first-nations people all over the world. In the last thirty years governmental judiciaries are learning from and consulting with indigenous peoples to assist them in developing robust restorative-justice programs to handle cases that previously would have gone to state courts. In New Zealand, for instance, all juvenile cases with the exception of murder and manslaughter are now handled using family-conferencing methods, a procedure adapted from the Maori, New Zealand's indigenous peoples.[87]

Knowledge of restorative justice principles provides a resource for thinking through the kinds of actions we can take that will enact compassionate witnessing in the aftermath of harm. It can provide ideas for ways to make amends.

In 1948 Dalia Landau, aged eleven months, emigrated to Israel from Bulgaria and settled with her family in Ramle, in an empty Arab house that had been taken over by the government in the course of the war. Nineteen years later, in 1967, after the conclusion of the Six-Day War that made travel of Palestinians living on the West Bank possible, three young Arab men knocked on her door and asked if they could visit the house that the father of one of them, Bashir Al-Khayri, had built in the 1930s. The three men walked through the house reverently, asking to go into the garden to see if a lemon tree Bashir's father had planted was still producing fruit. It was, abundantly. Dalia was moved by their feelings about the house, and Bashir's invitation to visit his family in Ramallah, which she did. At that meeting Dalia learned that Bashir was involved in political activity on behalf of the Palestinians and that the Israeli government had detained and interrogated him.

Some months later Dalia read that Bashir had been convicted of complicity in a terror attack and sentenced to fifteen years in prison. Deeply disturbed, she nonetheless pursued information about her house. She learned that the Arabs of Ramle had not fled their homes, as she had been taught in school, but that they had been expelled on order from Prime Minister David Ben-Gurion. Years passed. Dalia married; her parents died; she inherited her beloved house. In the 1980s after Bashir's release from prison, Dalia and her husband, Yehezkel Landau, sought out Bashir and told him that Dalia now owned "their" house. What would he like her to do with it? She could sell it and divide the proceeds with him or they could use it for some constructive purpose. Bashir was moved by the acknowledgment implicit in Dalia's gesture. He suggested that the house be used to serve the needs of Arab children. Dalia and Yezhekel said that they would like to use part of the house for Palestinians and Jews to meet each other in shared activities. Bashir concurred.[88]

This conversation laid the groundwork for what is now a flourishing community center in Ramle, Open House, which serves Arab children in a day-care center and Arab and Jewish youth and adults in a range of activities whose purpose is to foster intercommunal understanding and to promote peace. Jointly run by the Landaus and a Palestinian Christian, Open House has been in operation since 1991, still active through the most recent intifada and upsurge in terror and violence between Israel and the Palestinians. On a recent tour to the United States one Palestinian youth from Open House articulated the sentiment of the assembled youth group and the aspiration of the adults working with them, saying, essentially, "Our leaders cannot do what we can. We cannot leave peacemaking to our leaders. We want to get along and we do."[89]

Open House embodies the spirit of restorative justice in action. Moved by her witnessing the meaning of the house to Bashir, Dalia Landau responded creatively to set things right for the sake of the two families, the community of which they were members, and the nations to which they belonged. In doing so, with the collaboration of Bashir Al-Khayri, Open House now provides an example that other people in other communities can emulate.[90]

Nonviolence, forgiveness, reconciliation, and restorative justice are all interactional practices that can assist us in facing a situation permeated with violence and violation, and not responding in kind. Just knowing that there are options helps align us with a nonmirroring response.

While we read so much more about violence, nonforgiveness, retribution, and punishment, there is every reason to believe that nonviolence, forgiveness, reconciliation, and restorative justice are as ancient and basic as their counterparts. In fact, many of the world's major religions either explicitly support these four practices or have elements on which they can be based.[91] For some people, knowing that there are religious texts to consult and religious communities that will support actions based on these interactional practices is essential to undertaking the challenge of compassionate witnessing.

Universal Knowledge

As we have seen in the previous chapter, societies—large groups of individuals—have the potential for creating massive, horrific, traumatic disruption, making victims and witnesses out of combatants, civilians, and their descendents. WHO estimates that in the twentieth century, 191 million people died in the twenty-five largest instances of collective violence, 60 percent of whom were civilians.[92] At the same time, groups of people have the power to protect, to support, to inspire, and to console. In the best of circumstances groups can mediate the effects of violence and violation.[93]

Clearly, the forces that encourage large groups to act with malevolence or beneficence are complex. In broad strokes they include political, social, economic, and demographic factors.[94] Most of the causes are out of the reach of any individual, and yet, paradoxically, it is only by taking action as individuals that we can create effective collective action. As the old union song says, "Drops of water turn a mill/Singly none, singly none."[95]

Several kinds of universal knowledge have been deployed for good and ill. The ones on which I focus—ceremony and ritual, the power of the community, art and nature—have provided extraordinary healing, while, at the same time they have been misused to foment violence and violation.[96] It is up to each of us to resist such corruption and support the proliferation of these collective resources for the common good. I start at home, making the links from the personal to the societal.

Ceremony and Ritual

Ceremony and ritual are not necessarily formal, elaborately planned occasions, although they can be. Because all cultures have ceremony and rituals, most of us are familiar with their elements and the feelings they can inspire. We can make use of what has touched us to create our own home-style celebrations and rituals.

In 1995 my mother, who died in 1976, would have turned eighty years old. For months leading up to the anniversary my thoughts about her were more pressing, my connection to her more vivid. I realized that I couldn't bear that she would be missing what I knew would have been a gala party of friends and family who adored her, celebrating her rich and loving life.

Eventually, the shape of a ritual took place that felt modest enough to suit her and symbolic enough to satisfy me. I invited a few friends and my immediate family to a dinner party in *their* honor on the occasion of her birthday. I bought each of my guests a gift I thought would express my mother's uncanny ability to perceive the heart of other people's longings and wrote a letter to them from her. In the letters, "channeling" her through me, I witnessed my friends and family through her love, appreciating the qualities she would have noticed, cherished, and nurtured.

My mother died twenty-seven years ago. She was a woman who gathered stories, people, rocks, facts, newspaper clippings, ideas. . . . Nothing changes the ache of her loss or fills the stubborn, persistent hole left by her absence. Nothing makes her have more time to live what would have continued to be a shining, quirky, tender life. Nothing. But my homegrown ceremony helped. In that it felt true to her spirit, and those assembled could share her with me, the evening softened my devastation in a way that has lasted.

I mourn one mother. Although grief is not a sum one derives by multiplication, I am awed when I consider what it means to grieve loss produced by the deliberate ruthlessness of people, not by the indifferent ruthlessness of disease, killing not one beloved person but hundreds or thousands or millions of people who were just as loved. In December 1990, three hundred Lakota rode on horseback 250 miles over a two-week period in temperatures that dropped to eighty degrees below zero, covering the route that their ancestors had taken to the Pine Ridge Reservation in South Dakota hoping to escape starvation. This ride, the Big Foot Memorial Ride, was planned to commemorate the four hundred Lakota men, women, and children who were massacred at Wounded Knee one hundred years before; to help the Lakota people collectively mourn these deaths; to bring back the spiritual ways of their ancestors and fulfill their visions; and to celebrate the survival of the Lakota people and their hopes for the next seven generations.[97] The Lakota prepared for four years until they were able to undertake the memorial ride in right relation to each other, their ancestor spirits, and the universe.

There has been a memorial ride each year since 1990. Karen Duchenaux first participated in the ride at age sixteen and has now taken part eleven times. In 2000, she said, "The things you learn about yourself, how strong you are, are invaluable in real life. The things you learn on this ride stay with you forever."[98] Through this memorial ride, with all the harshness of its conditions, they transformed the victimization of their ancestors, their identification with and toxic witnessing of it, into a sacred witnessing of the strength and endurance of the Lakota people.

Although the two witnessing rituals I have discussed are ones that mark deaths, ritual and ceremony can be used as a resource in the context of any kind of violence and violation. Miranda's ceremony celebrated living with a chronic condition. I have helped create ceremonies for battered women and their children living in shelters that celebrated the power of love to overcome abuse.

While the purpose of ritual is to connect people, to reduce isolation and vulnerability, to disperse meaning widely by symbolically linking elements of space and time, the danger is that forging cohesive bonds with those who partake deepens splits with those who do not participate.[99] Nazi torchlight ceremonies are a good example of how one can use a shared cultural repertoire of meanings associated with light for malignant purposes, and carrying the Olympic torch from Greece to the country hosting the games is an example of light used as a symbol of peace and harmony.

For ceremony and ritual to function as collective resources for witnessing and represent a beneficent use of universal knowledge, they must support those who are present, but not at the expense of those who are not. As is true of every other practice I have described as providing a foundation for witnessing, ritual and ceremony are resources to the extent that they promote a vision of shared humanity rather than constitute an "us" who is not "them."[100]

Community

In the suburban community outside Boston where seven-year-old Sam Cichello lived before he died of his head injuries (See Chapter Four), people mobilized quickly to respond to the tragedy. School personnel called every parent to tell them about the tragedy and to invite them to a meeting led by a therapist from the "Good Grief" program at Boston Medical Center.[101] A food chain was started to provide the family with meals for months to come. The school decided to go forward with its annual Halloween parade, but each child was given a balloon and told to release it in Sam's name. The parade spontaneously marched to Sam's house singing "This Little Light of Mine."[102]

The community that formed around Sam's death had been working together for a long time. Connections and partnerships among people and institutions that were already in place were able to respond to Sam's tragic death with a number of witnessing activities. In Lower Manhattan, within sight of the remains of the World Trade Center twin towers, on September 11, stunned parents at PS 234 realized that their school community would need to come together—experienced with this or not—to support each other through the healing and advocacy that lay in store for them over the months, and perhaps years, to come. Witnesses to those tragic deaths, school members knew that there had to be another kind of witnessing they could harness to assist them with recovery.[103] They believed that unwitting witnessing of horror could be transformed into deliberate witnessing that had the potential to bring healing. They intuited the two sides of the witnessing coin.

Of course, violent events can also overwhelm communities, but communities can mobilize to become the center of and container for resilient recovery.[104] Even in situations of war and political violence, when the community itself may be targeted along with the individuals who reside there, communities can be the context for as well as the recipient of healing.[105]

Community can only be a healing resource for witnessing when there is trust between individuals and groups within the community. In 1990 a diverse group of citizens living in Richmond, Virginia, decided to turn their informal network of relationships that crossed race and class into a formal organization. They launched Hope in the Cities, which brought together political, religious, business, and community leaders to address issues of racism that manifest in daily interactions as well as systematic institutional barriers and economic inequalities. They understood that a lack of trust at the wider community level was blocking change in their community, and that challenging conversations about race would need to take place for progress to be made.

Richmond, with a city population of fewer than 200,000 people, largely African-American, and a surrounding, largely white population of 600,00 in several counties, has a racial history that has deeply divided its populace. For instance, Richmond was a major importer of slaves (approximately 100,000 slaves in the eighteenth century) and a major exporter of slaves (approximately 350,000 slaves) after the General Assembly prohibited importation in 1786 for economic, not humanitarian, reasons.[106] The former capital of the Confederacy, Richmond has four statues of Confederate generals lining its principal avenue, creating a discrete focus for the different meanings of the Civil War to citizens.[107]

Hope in the Cities sponsored public forums to address race, and the proliferation of issues tied to it, such as unemployment, housing, education, religion, taxes, and communication. In 1993, under the sponsorship of a local committee that included virtually the entire elected leadership of the region as well as religious, corporate, and community leaders, a conference took place that drew over 1,000 people from fifty cities and twenty countries to engage in dialogue with each other on the conference theme: "Healing the Heart of America: An Honest Conversation on Race, Reconciliation, and Responsibility."

While the conference was a stunning experience for many participants, they also understood that while relational change was necessary for structural change, it was not sufficient. The group from Richmond continued to meet. In 1996 they established Richmond Metropolitan Day to spread and build the vision of a healthy community, and in 2001 they began a new community initiative, a series of forty-eight-hour residential dialogues on "Race, Economics, and Jurisdiction."[108]

In Richmond, as in other cities that have used the Hope in the Cities model, a vision of a vital, just community sustains people through the heartache of difficult conversations. The aspiration for such a community, captured for some by Martin Luther King Jr.'s ideal of the "beloved community," makes a constructive outcome for these dialogues more likely.[109] While individuals witness each other, they do so for themselves and on behalf of the community. Thus, the dialogue is infused with public purpose, creating a powerful investment for people to struggle through their individual pain to forge partnerships that will strengthen their community. The universal knowledge that community can be a beneficent resource supports this challenging endeavor.

Art

It has been suggested that Tolstoy had intended to condemn Anna Karenina, but that in imagining her, through the process of writing, he came to understand and empathize with her predicament, a thoughtful woman with few options.[110] As writer, Tolstoy became a witness to his character. Art makes available to its audience the artist's witnessing—of characters, situation, colors, or scenes—such that art then also witnesses us.

This is one way of understanding the distinction the poet Adrienne Rich drews when an interviewer commented that she seemed "acutely aware of [her] responsibilities as an artist."[111] She said, rather, "For me it's less about the responsibilities of the artist than about the need for art in many kinds of lives, a need shared with others we may never know."[112] Another name for that "need for art" is witnessing. We need both to recognize ourselves in art, to find a faithful, illuminating witness there, and to discover a path out, what Rich calls " 'a wick of desire' that helps keep alive in us the capacity to resist, to imagine, to change."[113]

Seamus Heaney has deeply considered the artist's responsibility as witness, to "point out and redress evident social wrongs."[114] Poetry can do this directly.[115] But there are other ways poetry can bear witness, according to Heaney. One is to "create an image or symbol that will prove adequate to our predicament,"[116] and the other is to create a "counterweighting, of balancing out the forces, of redress—tilting the scales of reality toward some transcendent equilibrium."[117] In this sense poetry not only exposes how things are, but imagines a "satisfactory comeback." When poetry is successful, "the coordinates of the imagined thing correspond to and allow us to contemplate the complex burden of our own experience."[118]

Popular cultural forms can also help us imagine a satisfactory comeback to the pain and complexity of our lives. Musically, perhaps no one did this as well with regard to September 11 as Bruce Springsteen and the E Street Band in their album *The Rising*. Placing multiple images of rising up alongside the horrific images of falling, of the collapse of the Twin Towers, Springsteen and his band offered a requiem, not revenge, as the antidote to this violence. The fourteen songs capture the pain, rage, and terror but also a path out. The music and lyrics tell us that human connection will help us rise above the loss and the hatreds that threaten to consume us. The album bears witness to his own and our witnessing.[119]

Many artforms perform the function of bearing witness. In situations of social inequality, social unrest, and political turmoil, when it is possible to make art, art plays a crucial role in addressing brutal realities and assisting with witnessing.[120] In South Africa art under apartheid spoke directly to the pressing need for liberation. Today, postapartheid, in the midst of the AIDS pandemic, art can be judged, says Marilyn Martin, Director of Art Collections at the Iziko Museums of Cape Town, by the "extent to which it is a catalyst within society."[121]

In February 2002 the national art museum of South Africa mounted an art exhibit, "Positive Lives," featuring a photojournalistic study of AIDS in Africa by Gideon Mendel.[122] In addition, Mendel collaborated with the Treatment Action Campaign (TAC) and people living with HIV or AIDS to create "a positive activist environment in the national art museum on the doorstep of Parliament. . . . Together [Mendel and the art museum] broke new ground in our shared vision—and commitment—to making a difference, to offering solutions in a crisis."[123]

One component of the exhibit was the display of memory boxes, projects created by HIV-positive women. Memory boxes are containers made from recycled materials to explore and store personal and family stories, usually in the form of objects and photographs. For people with HIV and AIDS, memory boxes help them think about living affirmatively with the virus. For those who want to be prepared in case of death, memory boxes assist with bereavement and create a legacy for loved ones. Since HIV is a chronic but manageable condition, and its social context is highly politicized in most places in the world, groups who work on memory boxes also use them to address political issues.[124]

Each week during the exhibit women from Cape Town's poorest townships shared their memory boxes with the public. The presence of the boxes in the South African National Gallery was a triumph, and an expression of "terrible determination," as Judge Edwin Cameron put it in his remarks at the closing ceremony for the exhibit. This shows "a determination to defeat untruth and misrepresentation and distortion, and to assert hope. That is the ultimate significance of the unforgettable images of this exhibition: that untruth and inaction are the greatest crimes of all. Let us take an angry inspiration, and deep determination, from that."[125] "Deep determination" is a hoped-for outcome of the power of art to witness us and in so doing inspire us to witness others.

Nature

On my first visit to South Africa, Hilary and I were met at the Cape Town airport by a colleague and driven to the Cape of Good Hope, where the waters of the Indian and Atlantic Oceans meet. Feeling the fog speeding across my face, revealing, as it did, rugged sandstone cliffs rising 249 meters above sea level, I felt immense awe. At the same time the mundane pragmatics of life inserted themselves, even here: I had to find a phone so that I could participate in a radio talk show about my upcoming keynote address for the South African Association of Marital and Family Therapy. Looking out on this magnificent vista, but talking about witnessing violence, I turned what might have been a moment of mind-boggling contradiction into one of enduring comfort. The place became not contrasting backdrop but benevolent ally. My knowledge that it had been there for forty million years conferred a sense of perspective. These cliffs had seen, absorbed, and survived: nature, as counterweight and consolation.

The title of my talk was "Witnessing, Wonder, and Hope."[126] On the cold, gray January day I wrote it, I could never have known how apt the title would be: for the gorgeous scenery of South Africa, but also for the extreme poverty of the townships. Wherever I was, in the newness and strangeness of it all, the vast clarity of sky helped me to stay centered. Days later, in Cape Town, taking a break from the intensity of the workshops, stepping outside, I could gaze at Table Mountain and look into a physical manifestation of endurance, concretely representing what I was observing inside as I listened to the stories people told. The mountain soothed me.

Nature offers consolation for us as compassionate witnesses. It knows nothing of our tragedies.[127] Its silence is deep and complete. We are in it, but not of it. Like our breath it can always accompany us.[128] It inspires awe. A pebble, a leaf, a cloud, all richly reward our observation. The smallest sample has the power to draw us into the center of its stillness. Writing this book has been challenging, excruciatingly so at times. Throughout, the natural world has provided consolation, no more, but no less, than my social one.

In the next chapter I describe specific actions that people have taken to transform common shock through compassionate witnessing. The resources I have discussed in the preceding pages are foundation and backdrop, tools and treasures, that support the kinds of actions we can take to turn unwanted witnessing into intentional compassionate witnessing.

CHAPTER 9

Steps to Compassionate Witnessing

And action is the only remedy to indifference, the most insidious danger of all.

—Elie Wiesel[1]

Compassionate witnessing rests on a foundation of resources that range from the personal to the universal. Daily there are opportunities to turn unintentional witnessing into intentional witnessing of others who are distressed or suffering. On the return flight home from Kosovo after my second trip, pleased with the work that our team had accomplished, spirits high, my close friend and colleague, Corky Becker, and I sat for eight hours and talked. We had made a list of topics we wanted to discuss and we talked our way through the list.

Upon arrival, during the last moments on the ground when we were taxiing into the gate, a middle-aged woman who had been sitting across the aisle from me asked in accented English whether we were psychologists. Stunned, we replied that we were, but, puzzled, inquired what had given her that impression. "The way you listened to each other," she said.

Without any provocation, with no overture from us, she then proceeded to tell us that she and her friend had come to the United States to attend a memorial service for her son, who had been killed by a stranger several months before. As she spoke, she pulled out a photograph of her son, a handsome young man in his twenties who had been working in a job he loved at the time he was murdered. She spoke despairingly about the violence in our country.

We exchanged a few more sentences and then tried to respond in a way that would witness the little she had told us, using her words as well as the nonverbal cues we could discern by watching what she did and the ways she turned to her friend as she spoke.

We told her how sorry we were that her son had died and that her family had to suffer this way. We reflected that it must be especially painful to have a child murdered in another country, and to have to deal with feelings about the violence there in addition to your grief. We remarked on her friend's presence and how good it was that she wouldn't have to be alone in the next few days. Finally, we told her that we hoped she would remember all the wonderful things people would tell her about her son so that they would become part of her memories of him.

"Good luck," we said, as people in the aisles began jostling us, eager to exit the plane. "We will hold you in our hearts the next few days. Take care."

This unfortunate woman's revelation jolted me out of the bubble of mutual absorption that Corky and I had created for each other as a way of making the transition home from Kosovo. The woman's speaking was an uncanny reminder of how often we are confronted with terrible stories of violence and violation and how many, then, are the opportunities to turn the coin, as it were, and respond with compassionate witnessing. We did not have to be in Kosovo to use our skills. Across the aisle someone had noticed we were good listeners and intuited that she could use some of that. Thinking we were "off duty," Corky and I found we were not. We did what we could.

This story captures the three key elements in compassionate witnessing, which can be learned and practiced in small incremental steps. First, it is important to select a focus for one's witnessing that is doable. We could do nothing about this woman's son's murder, but we could acknowledge her pain about it. We could also comment on the wisdom of bringing a friend for support. Second, listening carefully and responding thoughtfully can make a difference. We hoped that letting her know that we were moved and disturbed by even her brief rendition of her circumstances might make her feel less alone. Finally, it is necessary to create transitions between compassionate witnessing of others and ourselves. In daily life few of us can devote ourselves to witnessing others for prolonged periods of time. We have to find ways of witnessing others and then making the transition into our other activities. In this situation, for the sake of all the passengers, we had to make our comments quickly and then return to what we needed to do: pack our items and leave the plane. However, even in such a short exchange, by selecting our focus carefully, listening well and reflecting compassionately, and then moving on, we felt what we often do with witnessing: It creates a synergy of recognition, support and action that is affirming, restorative, and energizing for everyone touched by it.

Selecting a Witnessing Focus

In Parts One and Two we saw that we are all everyday witnesses to violence and violation whether we like it or not. Starting to do something about it requires us first to notice when we are witnesses. Hopefully, having read this far, you now feel much more able to observe this. The next step is to contemplate whether or not you are in a situation that you want to address and whether or not you feel safe doing so. Noticing and deciding to act are steps that precede selecting a focus for witnessing.

Choosing a focus takes some thought. However, it is not about selecting the correct answer to an exam question. It is about a creative process of connecting one's understanding of a situation with one's response to it and bringing this into alignment with one's resources, commitments, and values. Scanning to see whether any of the widely used interactional practices or universally known resources might be useful is part and parcel of the preparation. Selecting a witnessing focus is a process that begins to shift our sense of passivity and helplessness, disempowerment and numbness, into (more of) a sense of effectiveness and competence.

Sometimes selecting a witnessing focus is a spontaneous process that we do on our own, once, and sometimes it is a planful process, done collaboratively, that evolves over time. Or it may be anything in between. Likewise, a witnessing focus can be simple or elaborate.

When Ben was about four years old, he loved walking to the violin repair store around the corner from us and then hanging out at the fire station. One evening, driving home from work, I saw that there had been a fire in the group of stores that housed the violin repair shop and I knew that Ben would be devastated. I diverted him from our usual walk until a few days later, when it was our breadmaking day.

Upon seeing the store, Ben reacted just as I thought he would. He was distressed and then stunned that his admired "firepeople" had not saved the violins. We talked about his feelings regarding what he had seen. He felt bad that the violins had been destroyed. I asked many simple questions, including "What do you want Jim and Alice [the store owners] to know?" In time he said, "I'm sorry that the violins burned."

In this situation there were many elements that could have become a focus. I was scanning for ones that would undercut his sense of helplessness, and make him feel that he had made a positive difference. I also wanted him to do something and then move on. A focus on the lost violins themselves would have maintained his awareness of the destruction of the violins but left him feeling disempowered. After all, he couldn't make the violins reappear. Instead we chose a focus that supported Jim and Alice's feelings about the burned violins.

Picking up on his sad feelings, I said, "How would you like to shape our bread today into a violin and bow and give the bread to them after it's baked? We can show them we're sorry about the violins by giving them a bread violin." Ben thought that was a fine idea.

Bread takes about four hours to make from the time you mix up the ingredients through its several risings to shaping and then baking it. Ben punched the air out of the dough with particular vigor that day, and then helped me form it into the shape of a violin and bow. We called the store owners, and as luck would have it, they were home.

We drove the bread over while it was still hot from the oven. With my help Ben held the cookie sheet with its bread violin and bow as we rang the doorbell. Alice answered the door. Too shy to speak, he thrust the cookie sheet into her hands. I had already spoken to Alice on the phone and told her we would be bringing something for them to express our sorrow about the fire. Exclaiming at the rudimentary but unmistakable violin-shaped bread, she thanked Ben profusely.

Ben was four. Making the violins reappear was not a realistic focus of his witnessing. Had he been an older child, he might have wanted to raise money to repair the damaged violins; he could have initiated an "adopt a violin" activity in our community. But he was too young for that. I wanted him to express his feelings in a productive manner with an involvement proportionate to his life circumstances. The bread violin conveyed that violins mattered and that we were sorry that Jim and Alice had lost many of them in a fire. We were able to adapt a concrete activity that was part of our weekly routine to send this message. If bread-making hadn't been part of our normal routine, Ben could have drawn a card or picked a flower and given these to Jim and Alice.

Sometimes we select a focus of witnessing to help *ourselves* stay present, since the conditions for us to slide into passivity, helplessness, or unawareness are ever present. One day, while working on this book, I had a familiar, disturbing experience. I had been listening to the news of the American bombing in Afghanistan while driving to the institute where I teach, and felt overwhelmed by the pathos and suffering implicit in the story I was hearing about scores of civilian deaths and injuries. Knowing that I would be out of sorts—physiologically aroused, distracted, sad—if I continued to listen to the story, and believing that if I did listen, I would have to space out and numb myself temporarily, I wished to disengage so that I could recompose myself. However, turning off the radio felt callous. I wanted to take care of myself but not feel disrespectful to the people whose disrupted lives I could imagine. I decided to turn off the radio and just say a sentence: "I am really sorry this is happening to you."

My sentence arose as a spontaneous act done privately to respond to the impact of hearing "bad" news on the radio. Clearly, this is not an action that has concrete, immediate impact on the lives of others. It is a gesture intended to help *me* not sink into despair about the world's ills and my own insignificance in relation to them. My words acknowledge that I have been touched by what I have heard at the same time they reflect what I can honestly give. Not much, but nonetheless, what I am doing is a small act of resistance against the feeling that I—global citizen *x*—can do nothing.[2] I can let myself feel the impact of the news, if only for a moment.

While these two examples show the selection of a witnessing focus as an individual act, selection can develop in any number of ways, including collaborative processes that evolve over time. My friends Pat and Glenda called together about thirty friends to be with them in the hospital the night before Pat had an operation on his brain to determine if a tumor was malignant. The effect of everybody's loving presence was so powerful that they convened what became known as "the healing circle" every month following Pat's diagnosis with a malignant brain tumor. Over the four years of its existence there was constant inventiveness to meet the changing challenges of their situation as well as rituals that remained the same.

Together with their friends, Pat and Glenda created a form of compassionate witnessing that uniquely fit them. Another couple might have designed something different. Their healing circle acknowledged that they needed support and their friends and family needed to help them. Coming together in community served the purpose of marking the changes that Pat's terminal illness was bringing into their lives. The circle was a formal occasion of compassionate witnessing of Pat and Glenda and, by extension, others in the circle whose lives were also changing through their love of, and connection to, this family.

I attended several of the healing circles; some family members and friends attended nearly all. No one held the belief that Pat would survive his cancer. Everyone was aware at the outset that death would be his fate. The purpose of witnessing was not about suggesting alternative approaches to his care that might extend his life, but rather about being fully present to the experiences Pat and Glenda were living each day, minute by minute.

People shared and responded with open hearts. The circle of family and friends created a container for the pain and the sadness, at least temporarily, so that it was possible to feel buoyed on the currents of care circulating in the room. The buoyancy did not rest on false optimism, but rather expressed the feeling that sustained connection through catastrophic loss mattered. The healing circle never lost touch with its focus on witnessing—and perhaps having some part in influencing—Pat's dying and Glenda's loss.

There were many elements of the healing circle, but none can account for the alchemy of inspiration and solace that emerged each month. People brought wonderful food to share. There was informal chat, silent meditation, and song. Pat and Glenda shared their experiences in powerfully simple and eloquent words and later, when Pat could no longer speak, his essential spirit was always recognizable as grace, thoughtfulness, and love. People in the circle reflected on what moved them and on what was changing for them as they touched in so closely to immutable mortality. Awe always arose, although no one set out to make this happen. People were able to sustain witnessing because within the framework of what was hoped for, there was always hope and always something one could do. The witnessing focus of "being present to what was happening" was always doable. It is precisely this element that makes the selection of the witnessing focus so crucial: the focus has to feel and be doable.

Elements of Witnessing

Re-membering

In Chapter Two I introduced the myth of Osiris, Set, and Isis. In that myth Osiris is chopped into many pieces by his brother and scattered over the world. Isis travels the world to collect his pieces and to remember him. Earlier, I made the point that we all have the potential for enacting any of the three roles in this myth: the victim, the perpetrator, and the healer/witness.

In thinking about what witnessing does, re-membering is a rich metaphor. As we go through our lives, any of us can become separated from vital aspects of ourselves. Life circumstances, troubling interactions, oppressive conditions, common shock, negative relationships—our reactions to any of these—can produce disconnectedness from our feelings, beliefs, values, and commitments, and then disconnection from others and our communities. When we are witnessed, or when we witness ourselves, we are remembered. Parts of ourselves that have been scattered, shattered, or forgotten are brought back together.[3]

A friend of mine told me about a recent conversation she had had with her older brother, who was having trouble with his teenage son. Demoralized by his son's defiance and apathy, her brother was alternating between withdrawal from and angry outbursts at him. My friend heard her brother out and then began to share memories of him as a camp counselor, recalling stories of the campers' antics and her brother's ingenious disciplinary tactics that earned him everybody's admiration. Without deliberating setting out to do so, she remembered the part of him that used to have a feel for adolescents and a knack for handling them. A week or so after her visit her brother called to tell her that things were much better. He said he no longer felt paralyzed, as if he was a helpless bystander waiting for some big accident to happen with his son.

Remembering, then, restores possibilities. If someone witnesses us by remembering qualities of ours or aspects of our life experience that we have put aside, but which have bearing on our current circumstances, that witnessing will produce a greater sense of wholeness. When we feel more whole, we have options for action that we did not have before.

Listening

In order to give this gift we do have to hone certain skills, the most essential of which is listening. It turns out that although we hear others all the time, few of us truly listen. Listening to others is difficult to do, but fortunately we can all get better at it. It is easy to identify a rationale for improving one's skill as a listener. Recall a time when someone listened to you well. What was that like for you? Now recall a time when you were not listened to well. What was that experience like?

Nonjudgmental, Accepting Listening

Listening as a foundational skill for intentional, compassionate witnessing requires a willingness to be deeply touched. For that to happen we have to open our hearts as well as our ears. This kind of listening is nonjudgmental and accepting.[4] It gives space and time for the other person to drop down into herself to see what is there that wants to be brought forth. It creates an opportunity for the speaker to plunge into confusion and uncertainty, knowing that she will be accompanied by a steady companion who will listen to her story without taking it over.

Perhaps the hardest thing for any of us to do when we listen intently is temporarily to wipe clean the slate of our own preconceptions, ideas, and assumptions so that it is truly quiet inside our heads. We want to be sure that we are really listening to the other person and not to ourselves making sense of or interpreting what the other is saying. In the previous chapter I discussed awareness as a precondition for witnessing. It is central to listening as well. Awareness keeps us in the here and now, able to be fully present to another person.[5]

As we have seen in previous chapters, witnesses suffer similar physical and psychological experiences as victims. When we listen to stories of violence and violation, we can have stress reactions that may interfere with our listening. Listening then requires monitoring our reactions, particularly the signals our body provides, such as tightness in the chest, a knot in the stomach, or a lump in the throat. As described in Chapter Eight, attention to our breath can restore us to our own equilibrium, returning us to our ability to listen to others.

Listening to others is not only about listening to the words they say. Often we sit beside children who communicate their experience to us without words. A six-year-old boy I was watching in the playground was rejected on the tire swing by the two other children who were playing on it. He came over to his mother, who was sitting on a bench, and nuzzled up to her. Without words she hugged him and started playing finger games with him. A few minutes later he jumped off and headed for the hanging bars. The momentary exchange condensed a sequence of support, validation, and re-membering of his competent, fun-loving self that renewed his interest in play, even if by himself. His mother repaired his experience of rejection by her kindness and belief in him, expressed through the nonverbal witnessing of her little boy.

Questions That Serve Listening

Questions are an integral part of listening that serve it in very specific ways. There are questions that seek clarification, when we are not certain we have understood what the person has said, and there are questions that seek elaboration, when we want to encourage the speaker to develop his meaning. Both of these types of questions must come from a place of curiosity, of not presuming to know what the speaker means but wanting very much eventually to understand.[6]

Many people feel that asking questions from a position of curiosity is pointless, since they are already good at understanding what people mean. They think that understanding another quickly makes a positive contribution. I think not. People often develop what they mean as they realize that their listener has no preconceptions or preunderstandings. It may seem contradictory to the task at hand, but in order to listen well to another, we have to be able to extend our *not* understanding as long as possible so that the people we are listening to can themselves develop an understanding of their meaning.

There is a simple exercise that can be used with children and adults that usually helps people see that meanings evolve in conversation and are not objects stored on shelves to be retrieved when given the chance.[7] Person A thinks of a sentence that conveys something of middling importance to him and which he believes is true. It should have the word *I* but not *you* in it. Person B hears the sentence and starts each response to Person A with "Do you mean . . ." and then fills in the sentence with a possible meaning. Once Person A says the sentence out loud to Person B, Person A can only respond to Person B with three options: yes, no, or maybe. The partners switch roles when Person B gets three yeses, or five minutes pass, whichever comes first.

Most people who do this exercise find that it is not so simple to get three yeses. But the more intriguing learning comes from realizing that their understanding of what they did mean develops in response to the questions Person B asks! This is often revelatory for people.

Here is an example of how this exercise might work:

Person A: I am feeling grumpy today.
Person B: Do you mean you didn't feel grumpy yesterday?
Person A: (Hmm. I hadn't thought about that. Did I feel grumpy yesterday? Maybe I did a little also. I wonder if something is going on with me?) No.
Person B: Do you mean you are unhappy?
Person A: (Am I unhappy or just grumpy? Out of sorts. Well, I must be a little unhappy.) Maybe.

You can see that Person B's questions prompt reflections on Person A's part that provide richer and more complex understanding than Person A intended or understood when Person A made the original statement. This is not an artifact of this exercise, but rather a possibility for all of us at any time if we are fortunate enough to have a listener who wants us to understand ourselves better rather than show off his ability to guess at our meanings.

Something else can be experienced from this very simple exercise. Listening is definitely a skill, but when practiced well, speaker and listener begin to feel in relationship to each other. Thus the skill of the listener fades into the background and becomes the foundation for something much more profound to take place. For people who are suffering from witnessing violence and violation, being listened to in this way is like being thrown a life preserver in choppy seas. The life preserver is a connection to another person; the experience of aloneness abates.[8] This is particularly important for people experiencing common shock, who often isolate themselves, believing that their feelings are too awful—weird, disturbed, gruesome, pathetic, shameful—to share with others.

In this kind of listening the speaker is kept at the center and the listener does not intrude his thoughts, feelings, or meanings into the process. At the same time the listening process is a collaboration between listener and speaker. The listener is informed by the speaker so that he can ask questions that serve the speaker. Since the witnessing I am addressing is that which is deliberately chosen to transform experiences of violence and violation, it is important that the listener pay close attention to the effects his questions have on the speaker.

Above all we want witnessing to diminish, not increase, people's common shock. We don't want people to be retraumatized in the process of telling their story. I have worked with the staff of a domestic-violence shelter program to introduce compassionate witnessing to battered women.[9] In one shelter we were planning an event for the mothers and their children that was similar to convening a healing circle. The children, ages seven to seventeen, were terrified that the event would remind their mothers of the time when they were unsafe and scared. The children were insistent that their mothers not participate.

We knew that the children were telling us something important and we agreed with them. Had we designed an event so that their mothers would speak publicly about what they had suffered, we could very well have made them feel frightened, resourceless, and helpless again. We could have placed them at risk.

Instead the focus of the witnessing event was on what they had learned about their values and commitments from their suffering and how this informed their future goals for themselves and their families. In addition we planned to monitor carefully the mothers' physiological and emotional arousal by noticing their breathing, skin tone, and their ability to sit still (but not too still) and attend to each other. We intended to pace the event to the ability of everyone there to stay present to each other. Monitoring these signs is another aspect of the collaboration between listener and speaker, the one who witnesses and the one who is witnessed.

The one who witnesses must balance the need of the one who is witnessed to tell her story as it happened, with the equally crucial need not to reproduce the experience of common shock for either of them. Certain kinds of listening can inadvertently replicate the experience of violation, albeit at a different level of intensity. Listeners should avoid:

- Interrupting
- Interrogating

- Making judgments or pronouncements
- Offering advice or conclusions
- Minimizing
- Denying the veracity of the speaker's account[10]
- Sharing one's own problems[11]

Questions That Promote the Development of Alternative Meanings

Instead, the listener can focus on staying present to what the speaker wants to communicate; asking the speaker questions that help him understand himself better; and pointing out alternative meanings that are present in what the speaker is saying that may not be evident to the speaker, but which are nonetheless there.

This last point bears some consideration. We all have lots of experiences all of the time. We also all tell stories about our lives. Our experiences are far more complex and various to fit into any one or even all of the stories we tell about ourselves. Our experiences are like dots on the page; we have many options about which dots to connect and how to connect them.[12]

For instance, let us say that over dinner Hilary asks me how my day was and I tell him that I had a really good day. I then tell him about a number of experiences I have had: I wrote three pages; the printer didn't work; I had a great walk with the dog but it took me an extra fifteen minutes to get the burrs out of his coat; I got a parking ticket because I didn't put enough money in the meter when I met my friend for lunch; I had a wonderful time at lunch; and I had four productive clinical sessions with clients, although one is severely depressed, which is worrisome. The story of my day has several elements in it that might equally well allow me to tell a story about a "bad" day, but that isn't how I experienced it.

As a listener Hilary could respond by telling me he is glad I had such a good day. However, he has an opportunity to reflect back something more useful to me. He can point out to me that there were also some annoying and upsetting things that happened. He might then ask: "How do you understand that you didn't get bogged down by the negative things in your day?" This question would spur a different level of consideration on my part than my recitation of the day's events. It is quite an interesting question to contemplate.[13] In exploring his question I may come to see myself in a new light and think about aspects of myself to which I was not paying attention.

Compassionate witnessing benefits from this kind of listening and questioning. Daily life provides many opportunities to practice these skills so that when we are in a situation in which we learn that someone has witnessed violence or violation, we will be able to use these skills to help her recover from the experience.

Of course, situations do not come with labels that say, "Yes, this is a situation in which there is violence and violation." Some situations are all too evident. Others are ambiguous, at least to the outsider, and occasionally to the person herself. Still others are just plain confusing.

When my friend Jen was leaving with her family for Australia to live there for several years, I called her on her last day in the States. She was very upset. She told me she was feeling awful about leaving and that maybe it was a terrible mistake. "How did you come to that conclusion?" I asked her.

She told me that many friends had come by the house, called, or sent cards to tell her how much they would miss her. She felt guilty that she was leaving behind so many people who loved her and relied on her as an important support person. She couldn't bear how "wrenching" her departure was for so many people. She was connecting the "dots" into a story about causing others pain. In her mind her leaving had become an unintended act of violation toward people she loved. In some irrational way she felt like a perpetrator, instigating her friends' grief, but then, also, witnessing it.

Something significant was implicit in Jen's words: People were telling her not only that she was important to them but how. I asked her to tell me more about this, to connect "another set" of dots, as it were. She replied, "I'm hearing the same things from many different people and from people who don't even know each other. I'm a lot of people's best friend. Their soul mate. One friend said I'm her safe place in the world. I'm the one person who really gets it about whatever it might be. I understand."

I reflected back to her that although people were sad that she was leaving, they were also giving her a rare gift: letting her know how she mattered to them. I wondered what it would be like for her to take in what her friends valued about her? A few weeks later Jen sent an e-mail from Australia. She wrote, "To some extent I feel as though I carry myself a little differently. I have a different awareness of myself than I had before."

Our conversation was an example of everyday witnessing. It shifted Jen's attention to include not only that her leaving was causing people pain, but also the reasons she was important to their lives. It illuminated for both of us that daily life is often a jumble of experiences with many strands. In this instance Jen was feeling so many different things that it was hard to figure out all of what was going on. Our conversation helped her to see that as a person who helps others, she couldn't bear being the agent of pain. By focusing on what her friends were also telling her about her positive contributions to their lives, she was able to place the episode of her leaving in the broader context of her ongoing supportive role with her friends.

Describing the Effect of the Story on You

I have now described several activities that go into witnessing another. They are:

- being fully present, even if the connection will be brief
- listening deeply without preconceptions
- asking questions that serve the speaker
- recognizing what is implicit but not articulated in what is spoken
- reflecting back to the speaker what one has heard

In addition:

- One can also tell the speaker what her story has meant and why.

Based on the work of Australian therapist Michael White, Corky Becker and I have distilled three subjects that guide our compassionate witnessing and how we teach it.[14] Imagine that you have just heard someone tell a story about how violence has had an impact on her life. You are truly moved and want to say something to the person. These three areas can be a point of departure for your comments. You may cover all three or just one.

1. Tell the person specifically why hearing the story was moving, powerful, or eye opening for you. (You might want to share something about your own life to account for your being particularly touched by something the speaker said. If you do, though, keep in mind that the point of sharing something about yourself is to make your response to the speaker more credible to her. It is not so that she turns her attention to, and tries to take care of, *you*.)
2. Provide specific detail about what the speaker said or did that helped you understand her experience. (Supplying this detail helps people not discount what you have said about them. This is not at all the same as praising a person or pointing out positives in what she has said. Rather it is reflecting back to the person exactly what she has already done or said that has made a difference to your understanding her situation.)

3. Let the speaker know how having heard her story will have an impact on your own life. (Again, be as specific as possible about how the person's story may contribute to your life.)[15]

The focus in each of the three areas is the other person. If you tell too long a story about yourself, it is likely that the person will get confused about who is at the center of the exchange. You want to be sure that the person is clear that she remains the focus.

To illustrate, imagine that your neighbor, Janet, has confided in you that her father was abusive to her. She tells you some details about his abuse and also some of her struggles to overcome her pain and to forgive her father. You are stunned. Janet has always seemed so upbeat and energetic. She is a terrific mom and does a lot for others in the neighborhood. It is hard to imagine that she spent her childhood terrified about what her father might do to her depending on how drunk he was when he came home. You want to say something now, and also know you are going to need time to think about what Janet has revealed.

Based on the three topic areas above, here is a hypothetical witnessing of Janet:

"Janet, I am so glad that you trusted me to talk about your fear of your father. It makes me appreciate even more how respectfully you treat your children and mine. You must have really made a commitment to parent differently. I could feel it even in the way you talked about your father. You didn't show any bitterness toward him. That makes me think about people in my life I'm still angry at and whom I haven't forgiven. You've given me a lot to think about."

Notice, I didn't go off into a long story about those people I am angry at myself. If I had, Janet might have felt that she needed to witness me, which would have defeated the purpose of what I wanted to do, which was witness her.

Practice with everyday situations stands us in good stead when we face situations that are more dramatic. The following incident occurred on the trip home from my first visit to Kosovo on September 10, 2000. Four American members of our project set out from Pristina with a driver and an interpreter to go to the airport in Skopjie, Macedonia, after a week of intensive clinical work with families and mental-health colleagues. We were driving on the road that was one of the main escape routes for those fleeing the Serbs. About fifty minutes into the trip we passed a large gravesite on our left and asked if we could take a closer look at it. We crossed the two-lane road and were let through by the few KFOR soldiers and municipal police who were guarding the site.

The site is located on a hill with views over barren fields into a town in one direction and to the highest mountain ranges in Kosovo in the other. We walked on a gravel path toward a middle-aged gentleman who later identified himself as Izet, a KLA (Kosovo Liberation Army) fighter and teacher. With our backs to the road we could see about sixty mounds of plastic flowers that had been placed over graves, many of which held more than one person. To the right three thin men were in the process of digging graves, in rows, each of which already had a small slate marker.

Our interpreter translated Izet's words. First, Izet thanked us for walking over to look at the work that he was doing. It was his job to exhume bodies and to oversee the proper burial of each person who could be identified. In this area 230 persons had been killed, of whom 90 were KLA. Approximately 83 people would be buried here.

Izet knew many of the people who would be buried at this site. His eyes grew moist as he answered our questions about his work. He pointed to different graves, showing us a mound in which four members of one family were buried and another containing two brothers. Moments later he unfurled a set of architectural plans that lay at his feet. Plans for this site include paths, a museum, and a memorial.

As our group listened to him, I noticed that we moved closer to each other and to him. The tone shifted and he stopped telling us facts and began to share more of his experience doing this work. He told us how much easier it was for him when people actually gave him an opportunity to talk about what he was doing and offered their condolences. And then, in a low voice, he confided that at times he was so stirred up that he slept in the cemetery rather than go home. "Sometimes," he said, "I cannot bear to be away from my people."

This conversation was punctuated by the sounds of birds overhead, the sharp percussive sound of the shovels hitting the dirt, and the swooshing sound of earth thrown into nearby piles. At this point we were in a close huddle, eyes moist. I wanted to acknowledge the generosity of his sharing his story with us and to tell him what his work would mean to me in the future.

I said, "We will take your story back with us to America, and I suspect someday we will turn to your example and you will help and inspire us." I then recalled I had my Polaroid camera in the jeep and ran back to get it. I took three photos: two for him and one for me. He looked at the photos and said, "I will put these pictures in our museum."

On September 22, 2001, I placed his picture below my computer monitor. That day I had been speaking to a woman whose husband had worked for a company that lost hundreds of employees in the World Trade Center attacks. Her husband's life was concentrated into one activity: preparing for, going to, and recovering from funerals. She was beside herself with grief and worry about her husband. I told her about Izet.

How could I possibly have known the year before that Izet would become my symbol of hope and that I would tell his story to many people? When I look at his picture, I see a fighter who has decided to mourn, not fight. I see a man who has decided to care for the dead and create a memorial to them. I imagine that his work means that he wants the cycle of revenge to end and that each stone he places on the path through the graves and each one that slopes toward the museum, he positions with a prayer for peace. It was a fateful encounter that day. It makes me believe that the stones in our hearts can be set on a path to peace.

Illustrations of Witnessing

There is no right way to witness. Although I have presented one framework for it, we all know that life is messy and doesn't lend itself to following protocols. Protocols do, though, provide initial structure, which can help until we get comfortable with our own ways of applying an idea.

As someone who has had the privilege of seeing a wide variety of witnessing acts and who has been told about many more, I know full well that there are many ways to do it successfully. In each, though, the spirit of re-membering, of reflecting back shining qualities and of letting someone know that sharing her experience makes a difference, is integral to the act of witnessing.

One of my favorite anecdotes is about Jane Goodall, the noted primatologist who worked, lived, and learned among chimpanzees in Tanzania for more than thirty years. Her knowledge of chimpanzees is so great, she is able to enter into a cross-species witnessing that does not rely on words.

In 1986 she watched a videotape that showed the ways monkeys were treated for biomedical research purposes. She was horrified at seeing their conditions of confinement in small cages, in noisy antiseptic rooms, as different from their native habitat as one could conceive. Their plight called her to action. She began to visit these research laboratories.

On one visit she was shown a room of cages that held ten adult chimps, one each along with a car tire in a five-by-five-by-seven-foot steel cage. As per the laboratory's regulations she was masked and gowned, wearing a cap, shoe covers, and rubber gloves. She knelt beside one cage occupied by a chimp named JoJo and looked into his eyes and talked to him. "Very gently JoJo reached one great finger through the steel bars and touched one of the tears that slipped out above my mask, then went on to grooming the back of my wrist."[16]

This is the essence of compassionate witnessing, compressed to its simplest elements. Kneeling, Jane Goodall looked JoJo in the eye and spoke to him in a tone and cadence that made him feel seen and understood. Her every move, gesture, and utterance was a reflection to him of his current existence. Small though they were, her gestures communicated to him that she grasped what his experience was like. Touching her tear, grooming her wrist, JoJo showed her what this meant to him, using the primate signal system they share.

Across species, within species, the task is the same. We must learn about and become familiar to each other, so that we can tell each other's story in a way that makes us each feel understood. When we acknowledge each other's despair, we transform it. This is the essence of compassionate witnessing. That is why even a small gesture can have great impact. Feeling seen, feeling known, we can change. This kind of chosen witnessing goes to the heart of the matter.

Few of us may ever be as skillful as Jane Goodall, who is able to witness across-species (although some of us probably believe we do this regularly with our pets). However, in everyday life we have opportunities to witness *people* who are in situations similar to our own and people whose life circumstances are different. The former is like looking into a mirror; the latter like looking through a window. In both cases, however, the task is the same. We want to convey that we understand and that our understanding makes a difference to us. In each act of witnessing we give a gift: in effect we say, "Your suffering has mattered. Knowing about it changes me. Your pain is not in vain."

We can give this gift whether we are witnessing an individual or a nation. I think of it as a continuum: from an individual witnessing an individual; an individual witnessing a group of which she may or may not be a member; an entire group or community witnessing itself or another group or community; and a whole society witnessing itself or another society.

In some instances the distinction between ordinary witnessing and extraordinary witnessing is difficult to make: what is everyday for one person or a group of people may be unusual for others. As we have seen, violence and violation are not evenly distributed, nor is terror.[17] Whether we live in chronic conditions of structural violence that produce daily experiences of racism or chronic conditions of collective violence that produce terror from lethal acts of a regime, the ability to witness oneself and others can be compromised.

The capacity to witness cannot be taken for granted. The more totalitarian the context within which one lives—whether it is an abusive system, partner, parent, or regime—the less likely it is that one can hold on to a reality separate from the one being imposed by the repressive person or authority. Dori Laub makes the point in *Testimony: Crises of Witnessing in Literature, Psychoanalysis, and History* that the loss of the ability to witness oneself may be the essence of the meaning of annihilation.[18] The costs to all of us of this annihilation are grave. When those who are oppressed lose the capacity to tell what is happening, those on the outside who "see" may not understand. Without understanding we have insufficient will to help.[19]

Looking into the Mirror

Witnessing the Self

KEEPING A JOURNAL

While it is true that any of us may find ourselves in extreme circumstances in which the ability to witness will be crushed and of no avail, this should not deter us from having the skills of witnessing in our repertoire. Despite and because of these extreme circumstances it remains essential to learn and practice ways of witnessing oneself. Writing in a diary or journal, or writing letters or e-mails to close friends or family members, is one way.[20]

People have always written for their own private purposes. We seem to have a need for completion of events and for meaning, and writing helps us organize our thinking into more coherent narratives.[21] Researchers have found that if people write for just a few minutes every day about the same disturbing, or even traumatic, event, over time their rambling writings become more coherent, until a summary form appears and the writer feels "finished" with the event. Certain kinds of writing styles are associated with health benefits, especially styles that reveal an increase in the number of words indicative of insight or understanding.[22]

Interestingly, in the program of research that has been done about the health benefits of writing by James Pennebaker and his associates, the researchers found that writing about events that had happened in the distant as well as the recent past could have health benefits for the individual.[23] That is, it was possible to go back in time and use writing to come to terms with events for which no meaning had ever been found. Writing allowed people to put the distressing experiences out of their mind, as if the writing had transferred them to another place and the experiences were no longer a subject for rumination.

MEDITATION

Meditation is another practice that promotes self-witnessing through the development of awareness, the capacity that is a precondition for all compassionate witnessing, as we have seen in Chapter Eight. Contrary to one popular version of meditation as a practice that removes people from the mundane realities of life, meditation can provide just the opposite: a sharpening of one's perceptions about "what is going on—in our bodies, in our feelings, in our minds, and in the world."[24] As presented by Thich Nhât Hanh, meditation is not about removing oneself from the cares of the world, but rather seeing the cares of the world in every breath one takes.

Many people feel stymied about how to act when they have unintentionally witnessed an act of violence or violation. They may feel physically or emotionally threatened. Even if people are safe and the situation is over, they may still be afraid of saying or doing something for fear that their words or deeds will be inadequate or that they will be overwhelmed by painful emotion if they get involved.

Practicing meditation helps prepare us for just these kinds of concerns. During mindfulness meditation one is encouraged to let thoughts, feelings, sensations arise and pass, noticing but not getting captured by them. One may get distracted a thousand times in a session, and yet the approach is always the same: "No problem. Start again. Nothing is ruined." This attitude can seep into the rest of one's life, softening the internal critic that gets in the way of doing things for fear that what one does won't be adequate.

There are many benefits of meditation.[25] Among them, meditation improves the ability to see oneself, and thus to see others with more clarity. As we have noted in Chapter Six, the capacity to witness the self seems to be a prerequisite for witnessing others. For instance, the parent who cannot acknowledge his abusive upbringing is likely to have distorted views about his children. If you cannot see yourself, you cannot see others.

But what do we see? Sharon Salzberg is a Buddhist practitioner who teaches loving-kindness meditation, known as *metta*. She writes that when one practices metta meditation, one opens "continuously to the truth of our actual experience. . . ."[26] According to Buddhists the truth that we discern is that our own suffering is no different from the suffering of anyone else on the planet. This insight eventually develops compassion.

In trying to convey what difference it makes if people truly feel compassion toward themselves and others, Salzberg quotes Galway Kinnell's poem "St. Francis and the Sow." When we practice metta, we "reteach a thing its loveliness."[27] What an eloquent way of describing an outcome of witnessing the self with compassion: one recovers the sense of one's own loveliness. Walking around the world with one's sense of one's loveliness intact is surely an antidote to violence and violation!

REPAIRING AN EVENT IN THE PAST

There are other ways as well to witness the self. I have designed an exercise that assists people to self-witness that is predicated on the belief that one can imaginatively return to the past, change how events unfold, and then experience resolution in the present. It is based on an experience I had bringing closure to a car accident I saw when I was a young child.

When I was three and my sister seven, we were walking on a sandy beach road and we both saw a car hit a teenage girl. My sister insisted that we continue walking to the store as we had been instructed to do by our parents, but I broke away from her and ran home screaming to my mother, who I feared would punish me for being on the road myself.

As a child, I scarcely understood what I had seen. In fact, I remember seeing legs sticking out of tires and it taking me a few seconds to form the concept of *accident.* When I did, I got hysterical and I was impelled to flee. As I was running, my focus shifted from the horror of the accident to my fear of punishment: I was doing something wrong.

I recall with total clarity locking my legs around my mother's waist and burying my face into her chest when she bent to pick me up. The moment was one of intense relief because I could tell that she was worried about me, not angry. The accident vanished. I told her about it, but the episode morphed into "my mommy comforted me."

But the accident didn't really vanish. Over the years, periodically, I felt bad about it and confused. I didn't know what had happened to the teenager. I didn't understand why I had run away. Much later I wished that I had done something after the fact to acknowledge that I had been there and seen it. I wished my parents had talked with me about it in the days that followed. Fifty years ago I doubt they would have thought I'd have a memory of it. They did what they believed was needed; my mother held and comforted me until I was calm.

I was a barely aware witness to an accident about which I took no action. In retrospect I wish that I had revisited the spot on the road the next day and placed some flowers there or I had made a drawing in the sand and had my parents write the words *I'm sorry you were hurt.* Neither of these would have changed the outcome of the accident, but rather my relationship to it.

In the context of my work on witnessing I designed an exercise for myself that I have subsequently used with hundreds of people, both in the United States and in other countries. In this mental exercise I placed myself back in the scene, but as my current self, my age now, with my present repertoire of skills, abilities, and resources.

I stop. I register what I have seen and dash across the road to the young person who has been injured. Others are present and they call the police and the ambulance. I sit quietly by the young woman, keeping her warm and still until the medics come. I speak in a soothing voice while I gently stroke her hand. I move aside when the ambulance arrives and report what I have seen, as do others. I find out what hospital they are taking her to and I call a few hours later to see how she is. In my fantasy she has a simple leg fracture, which has been set, and she has been discharged home to her family.

In this exercise I address what was unsettling for me about the original event and then, in the imagined past, I use my current self as the means to take the action that my three-year-old self could never have done, but has carried as unfinished anyway. Imagining myself as a compassionate witness releases me and provides completion to the event. People who have done this exercise, which takes about ten minutes, have reported powerful effects. (See Appendix Two for the exercise).

An Individual Witnesses a Group of Which He or She Is a Member

Farther along the witnessing continuum is an individual's act of witnessing a group of which he or she is a member. We can all appreciate the courage of the act when the person who witnesses others has recently been in the same predicament, and returns to the scene of her former victimization. Flora Brovina, a physician, poet, and human rights activist in Kosovo, provides just such an example. She transformed her medical work into a political movement for social change in 1992, during the years when the Serbs forbade Albanians in the province to use public services or be involved in government.

During the NATO bombing in April 1999 the Serbs arrested her and charged her with conspiring to commit acts of terrorism against Yugoslavia and aiding the Kosovo Liberation Army. She was sentenced to twelve years imprisonment, at the beginning of which she was subjected to physical and psychological torture, including beatings and mock executions. Following intensive international pressure she was released in November 2000 by Yugoslav president Kostunica.

Her husband, son, and several hundred people met her at the Kosovo border. As she crossed into Kosovo, she dropped to her knees and kissed the ground. She then spoke out on behalf of the 818 Albanian prisoners remaining in Serbian jails. She said, "I cannot feel myself free until all those mothers, fathers, and brothers feel the same as I do. I am tired, and upset, full of emotions. It is not easy to leave your friends behind, even though I have promises they are going to be released soon."[28]

Meanwhile Serb prisoners, angered by the news that authorities were considering amnesty for all the remaining Albanian prisoners accused of being involved in the Kosovo independence movement, began rioting. Just one week after her release, Dr. Brovina, spurred by her concern for the safety and health of the Albanian prisoners in jails, returned to Serbia to visit four prisons in which riots had broken out.

Just as she had articulated at the time of her release—a nanosecond in terms of her recovery from her own imprisonment—she could not "feel free" until she herself had seen the jail conditions that her comrades were now experiencing. Entering the prisons, she spoke to hundreds of Albanian men, ascertained their current living conditions, and determined that many were being held in appalling squalor, were ill, and needed medications.[29] Because of her own imprisonment she was able to identify which of their living conditions had been caused by the riots and to make an appeal for ameliorating those conditions immediately.

Despite her own release from prison, however, she couldn't enjoy her freedom until all the prisoners and their family members felt free as well. Going back into Serbia and visiting the prisoners honored this heartfelt conviction. A victim of the Serbs, by witnessing the prisoners she also restored the public dimension of the poet/physician/human-rights-activist part of herself that had been dormant during her imprisonment.

The ability of the victim to witness herself is an essential part of the victim's healing. Whereas it can take considerable time to venture even a rudimentary first step in this direction, for Dr. Brovina it did not. Since her release Dr. Brovina has remained active in efforts to rebuild Kosovo. In 2001 she was awarded the Millennium Peace Prize for Women, an award created by the United Nations to recognize women's contributions to preventing war and building peace.[30]

A Group Witnesses Itself

Again, moving along on the hypothetical continuum, groups can witness themselves. This is one way of thinking about the self-help movement, in which people facing a similar challenge come together. In the United States, approximately 3 to 4 percent of the population is in a self-help group within any one-year period, and it is estimated that around twenty-five million people are involved in self-help groups over a lifetime.[31] Perhaps the best-known self-help group is Alcoholics Anonymous, which provides expert-free, anonymous, no-cost, lifetime support for people coping with alcohol addiction.

With the advent of the Internet new opportunities for forming groups whose members witness each other have opened up. These on-line groups may be particularly appealing for people who are stigmatized or marginalized in their "real" lives, whose access to compassionate witnessing is limited by any number of factors, and for whom a virtual community provides the only way of witnessing others and being witnessed themselves.

Perhaps as different from the anonymity of an Internet support group, in which members of a group provide the experience of being witnessed to others who self-identify as members of the group, is a drawing our team saw in the southwestern town of Gjacova/Djakovica, Kosovo. According to our colleagues Gjacova, with a prewar population of approximately 61,400, 89 percent of whom were Albanian Kosovars, had a history of active resistance to the Serbs. During the months leading up to the NATO bombings and during the bombings themselves, the town and its surrounding villages endured significant violence from Serbs, much of which has been documented by the Organization for Security and Cooperation in Europe—Kosovo Verification Mission (OSCE-KVM).[32]

During the latter half of 1998 and the beginning of 1999, there were large numbers of reports of human-rights abuses, including arbitrary arrests, beatings, and execution-style murders by unidentified perpetrators. Often the victims were taken from their homes so that the entire family saw their loved ones abused, removed, and in some cases shot. These events happened with considerable frequency and few residents were unaffected or unaware of the violence.

By the end of March the killings and terror had accelerated in the region. Homes and stores were torched, and on some days dozens of people were killed. Women and children were beaten and killed along with the men. In April convoys of tractors and trucks from other parts of Kosovo went through Gjacova, and these convoys were subjected to violence by Serb police and paramilitaries as well.

Thus, murder became a daily sight for children in the town and surrounding villages. Driving through Gjacova's market eighteen months after the war ended, we could see the work of rebuilding in progress. Carts loaded with sacks of bright peppers provided eye-catching color in the midst of the still-ruined streets. We were en route to the Center for Crisis Management, a community mental-health facility that uses expressive arts and relaxation techniques, like meditation and writing, to work with community members suffering from trauma and common shock.

Staff members greeted us and we made our way to the large meeting room along drawing-filled hallways, where we were served refreshments while we learned about the programs they offered at the Center. At the far end of the room, fifteen feet away, leaning against the wall, was a large drawing, perhaps three by five feet in size. It was impossible not to look at the child's drawing that, even at a distance, evoked the feelings behind the descriptions of events that had become familiar to us from our conversations with our colleagues and the reading we had done before our trip.

After a while we were invited to view the drawing. We walked slowly, almost ceremonially, toward it. Up close the artist's rendering of the massacre that had taken place on April 27, 1999, was uncannily real, even as the technique was more Grandma Moses than photographic. At the bottom of the paper is a convoy of tractors pulling carts laden with families and a single horse-drawn cart filled to the brim with people. Guns from three tanks are trained on the convoy and small groups of men are on the road, surrounded by uniformed men with machine guns. As the eye moves up the page, there are men walking the short distance to a hillside, one of whom being beaten by his guard.

The hillside is lushly drawn with long grasses, orderly fences, and swooping lines of trees heavy with new leaves. Into this pastoral scene the men walk, but they are headed for the top of the hill, in full view of those in the convoy below, where other men squat in three neat rows, heads down, with uniformed guards training their guns on them.

That day, the OSCE-KVM report states, Serbian forces abducted 119 men and their fate remains unknown. The drawing represents the events of this day, but also the collective experience of the Albanian Kosovars of Gjacova during a period of many months. In the moments that we ringed the drawing, Kosovars and Americans together, we Americans were not only observing the child's gift of witnessing to her community, but also witnessing this dedicated staff's work with the children they had helped to give expression to the terror, grief, and rage they all felt. The drawing memorialized these tragic events, but its very existence and placement in a position of honor conveyed the resilience of the children who had created art in this center and of the adults who had encouraged them to do so and recognized its communal value. In this instance a group witnesses its own history through art. In the doing and the viewing, healing happens.

A Society Witnesses Itself

Whole societies can also witness themselves. Truth commissions, of which the most famous may be South Africa's Truth and Reconciliation

Commission (TRC), contribute to nations' accounting for and ending past abuses through processes of public inquiry that allow witnessing at the national level.[33] In South Africa the TRC was established by Parliament based on extensive study of previous truth commissions, public discussions, and negotiations among major political parties who had been adversaries before.[34] The TRC's primary goal was to assist in the peaceful transition to democracy and its methods were based on three key concepts that I discussed in previous chapters: *ubuntu,* restorative justice, and forgiveness.

Chaired by Archbishop Desmond Tutu, the TRC heard testimony from twenty-two thousand victims and seven thousand perpetrators, of whom 80 percent were black.[35] The hearings were public, covered by print and broadcast media. The national audience was brought into the most shattering experiences of people's lives. They saw people's struggles to make sense of what they felt in the context of the known objective of the TRC to promote national reconciliation. The TRC promoted an assiduous process of establishing truth about gross violations of human rights and granted amnesty under certain conditions.

People with a wide spectrum of feeling and belief came before the TRC: repentant and unrepentant perpetrators; forgiving and unforgiving victims; people like Lucas Baba Sikwepere, shot and blinded by a member of the security forces, who said: "I feel what—what has brought my sight back, my eyesight back, is to come here and tell the story";[36] and people like Nomonde Calata, who wailed so piercingly during her testimony that someone who heard it said it was to "witness the destruction of language."[37] Calata eloquently stated that she could not yet forgive the man who had murdered her husband, but "I'm a human being. I'm just a person like him [the perpetrator]. I will also want to overcome this thing. I don't want to live with it my whole life."[38]

The TRC provided an opportunity to learn what some people in South Africa had endured at the hands of others. Although not complete, it covered more territory than some could bear, and less than some wanted to have aired.[39] The public testimony prompted dialogue, dissension, and silence; remorse, repentance, and denial. It provided an opportunity for remembering, which was taken up by some, but not all.

Cynthia Ngewu, mother of a young man set up, framed, and murdered by the government, provides a profound understanding of remembering as it links perpetrator, victim, and witness. She speaks of it in terms of reconciliation, a central aim of the TRC: "This thing called reconciliation . . . if it means the perpetrator, this man who has killed [my son], if it means he becomes human again, this man, so that I, so that all of us, get our humanity back . . . then I agree, then I support it all."[40]

Ngewu articulates more generally a particular view about the profound interrelationship among perpetrators, victims, and witnesses. If perpetrators are committed to witnessing what they have done to harm others, then, in Ngewu's phrase, they can become human again. The effects of this ripple out to the victims and witnesses. Further, though perpetrators in South Africa carried out political acts of violence against individuals, the ramifications of their acts were also always societal. Thus reconciliation among individuals has the potential for repairing the social fabric.

Testimonies like Ngewu's contributed to moving the country from its brutal past toward hope. Less well known in some circles was a moment of hope and national healing that occurred six months before the TRC began its work. In June 1995 the World Cup rugby finals match took place in South Africa between the South African national team, the Springboks, and the New Zealand team. The South African team, largely white Afrikaners, had been denied international play since the 1970s as part of the international community's sanctions. With the unification of the segregated teams in 1992 and Mandela's presidency in 1994, the slogan was "one team, one country." That day in June when the Springboks faced the New Zealand team, about seventy thousand mostly white fans were in the stadium. South African rugby player Chester Williams, who had been designated colored under the apartheid system, went in to replace Pieter Hendriks, an Afrikaner who had been banned for "foul play" during a previous game. The stadium went wild cheering Williams.

The Springboks won. Nelson Mandela, wearing a Springbok jersey and cap, long racist symbols, walked onto the field and began waving his cap. Although we cannot know this, the crowd's cheering of a colored player must have been moving to Mandela. It may well have contributed to his decision to wear the Springbok jersey and cap. When the crowd saw him so outfitted, they began to shout, "Nel-son, Nel-son, Nel-son."

Interviewed about the event, Archbishop Tutu said:

> I believe that that was a defining moment in the life of our country—this sport being so white and really so Afrikaner. And with everybody baying for the Springbok emblem to be destroyed, and that he should come out wearing a Springbok jersey . . . it was an electric moment . . . it was quite amazing how many of those who were present would have been white, mainly Afrikaner, who had known this man to be a terrorist, that the government had done one of the stupidest things to have released him, and to have them yelling, "Nelson, Nel-

> son, Nelson." . . . It had the effect of just turning round our country . . . it is unbelievable that when we won, people could be dancing in Soweto. If you had predicted that is something that was going to be happening in 1995, most people would have said, "I think you are crazy. You have been sitting in the South African sun too long, and it's affected your brain." But the incredible transformation, really a metamorphosis, was an extraordinary thing. It said it is actually possible for us to become one nation.[41]

Tokyo Sexwale, who had been a prisoner on Robben Island with Mandela and was premier of the province in which the games took place, had this to say about that day:

> For him to go there and be associated with the Springboks . . . to stand with them, to move his hands in the air, to wear that jersey, to have that cap, to lift the cap for them and to greet the people—you sit there and you know [all] the years in underground, in the trenches, denial, self-denial, away from home, prison, it was worth it. . . . The liberation struggle of our people was not about liberating blacks from bondage, but more so it was about liberating white people from fear. And there it was. Fear melting away.[42]

Mandela's humble gesture was rich with symbolism. It acknowledged that he had heard the Afrikaner crowd cheer a colored player. Waving the cap sent several messages: "I am changed because of what you just did. Therefore, together, black, colored, and white, let us look to a future when we are one people caring more about reconciliation than revenge, more abut unification than separation." That day, blacks, coloreds, and whites witnessed each others' hearts bursting with pride as the Springboks' victory created a national release from international shame. Together, they entered the community of nations and within months, with the start of the TRC's work, they embarked upon a process of national healing as moving and risky as any at any time anyplace on the planet.

Looking through the Window

The hypothetical continuum I have been illustrating so far is one in which witnessing occurs within the context of similarity, from individuals witnessing themselves to a group witnessing itself to a whole society witnessing itself. It is equally common to witness those who are, or seem, different from us: other individuals, groups, or societies.

An Individual Witnesses Another Individual

Most of can probably imagine witnessing a victim or a witness to violence. Fewer of us may think ourselves capable of witnessing a perpetrator with an open heart and mind. Yet, perpetrators are profoundly in need of such witnessing if they are to develop the capacity first to honestly reflect on their injurious actions and later to witness those they have harmed. In many communities and societies, however, there are no means by which perpetrators can be assisted to repent and change. They are frozen as evildoers.

I am familiar with this situation from my years working with victims of sexual abuse. All too often perpetrators are moved immediately into the criminal-justice system or moved too swiftly through the mental-health system, in neither case developing a robust witness position based on a solid, nonself-serving understanding of how they have harmed their victims and why.

A group in Australia has been working for two decades with adult men and youthful male offenders, helping them understand the effects their abusive actions have on others, and helping them change their behavior.[43] Larry is a fifteen-year-old in the Australian program who wrote to his mother about sexually abusing his seven-year-old half sister. He writes:

> I sexually abused Suzie and I let all of you down in the worst way. . . . She didn't know what I was doing because I tricked her into it. She was little and didn't know what was going on but I did know. . . . I think I picked on Suzie because she was easy to pick on and I was only thinking of what I could get and I didn't think about her feelings. . . . I feel heaps disgusted and so sorry for what I have done to you all. I've caused you hurt and I know this will last a long time and that you won't trust me for a long time. . . . In counseling I'm trying to understand what I have put you all through and trying to change so that I think of other people's feelings. I will never treat you or anyone else like this again.[44]

Men and youth who stay in the program develop a capacity to witness themselves; they are able to transform their explanations of what they have done from accounts that blame others and express self-pity to ones that accept responsibility and express empathy toward those they have hurt. The capacity truly to witness themselves opens up the capacity to witness others. This provides the opportunity of becoming other than a perpetrator, which is urgently needed the world over, whether the perpetrator is a sexual offender, a child soldier, or a brutal dictator. Perpetrators must be given ways to take responsibility for what they have done, express remorse, and perform acts of apology, restitution, and restoration so that they can live in the world no longer as perpetrators. We need to develop practices, and language to match, so that people are not forever doomed to think of themselves as perpetrators or to be regarded as such by others. It is the hope of the world, of all of us, that perpetrators, through their own acts of acknowledgment and restitution, and witnesses and victims, through their acts of acknowledgment, can reintegrate those who offend into the community of those who contribute to the common good.

An Individual Witnesses a Group of Which She Is Not a Member

So far I have provided examples in which the witness's goal is to understand what someone has suffered. Sometimes witnessing requires the suspension of this premise. The point is not to communicate that one does understand or empathize, but rather that one grasps "the impossibility of suffering the other's suffering."[45] Witnessing, then, becomes action undertaken with an exquisite awareness of the disjunction between what one can testify to and what one can claim to understand.

I first learned about Jan Karski, the pseudonym of Jan Kozielewski, when I read his obituary in the summer of 2000. A Polish Roman Catholic, who joined the Polish cavalry in 1939, he was soon captured by the Soviets, but escaped and joined the Polish underground, for whom he worked as a liaison between the Polish fighters and the West. In this capacity he was approached in the summer of 1942 by two members of the Jewish underground to "argue, convince, do anything I could, use every available proof and testimonial, shout the truth till it could not be denied" that the Jews of Poland were being systematically murdered."[46]

To prepare for this assignment he went into the Warsaw ghetto twice and once to an extermination camp near Warsaw. Interviewed in Claude Lanzmann's film *Shoah,* Karski expresses both his total separation from what he observed—"This was not this world, this was not mankind . . . it was a kind of hell"—and his commitment to faithfully describe what he saw but could not grasp.[47] His own testimony emphasizes this excruciating disjunction, as he repeats to Lanzmann his Jewish guide's description of the experience of being unable fully to comprehend the horror: "The Zionist leader [said], 'No one in the outside world can possibly understand. You don't understand. Even I don't understand, for my people are dying and I am alive.' "[48]

Karski was given hundreds of documents on microfilm soldered to a key to take to the West, as well as five points to pass on to the Allies. Fearing that his Polish-accented speech would give him away, he had several teeth pulled so that the resultant swelling would provide an excuse for him not to speak should the Germans stop him.[49] He made it to the West. He spoke to his superiors in the Polish underground, the British, and the Americans, but it was his assessment that while every individual was sympathetic, no one was willing to save the Jews at the risk of compromising the military defeat of the Germans.

He continued to tell what he knew, and a secret meeting was set up with President Roosevelt. This, too, he deemed a failure. John Pehle, who later became head of the War Refugee Board, disagreed. He believed that Karski's meeting "changed U.S. policy overnight from indifference to affirmative action."[50] Karski, however, believed his mission a failure and became in his own way a *"bearer of the silence."* Speaking thirty-five years after the war, he tells Lanzmann: "I have been a teacher [at Georgetown] for twenty-six years. I never mention the Jewish problem to my students."[51]

Karski chose to witness that which neither he nor anyone else could encompass, but which was the daily reality of millions of Jews in the ghettos and camps of Europe. He was an individual witness to an entire society that the Nazis were systematically destroying, trying to enlist other witnesses who would be in a position to act. Whether or not he was successful is obviously a matter of interpretation. What is not is that the world has the example of Jan Karski: a man who indefatigably brought the news of what he had witnessed to others.

Karski's failure to move the Allies to action can be likened to the failure of Major General Romeo Dallaire, a Canadian in charge of several thousand UN peacekeeping forces, to motivate the UN to act to prevent what turned out to be the massacre of eight hundred thousand Tutsi Rwandans by fellow Hutu Rwandans. Philip Gourevitch, a *New Yorker* staff writer, who wrote a book that explores the Rwandan genocide, *We Wish to Inform You That Tomorrow We Will Be Killed with Our Families,* spoke with many UN officials in an effort to understand the UN's failure to give Dallaire a mandate to act. Gourevitch says, "They were trying to make me understand the burdened life of a bureaucrat and how a high-level bureaucrat is swamped with information and can't be expected to recognize unusual information except in hindsight. They were describing themselves as having become numbed, blinded, deafened, and indifferent, which struck me as not entirely encouraging."[52]

These characteristics—numbed, blinded, deafened, and indifferent—are signs of common shock, and the consequences of ignoring it, as we have seen over and over again, can be catastrophic, not just for individuals but, as in the case of Rwanda, hundreds of thousands of people. Gourevitch was stunned by the officials' attributing their failure to respond to the genocide to something ordinary, the difficulties of the "overburdened" bureaucrat's work life.[53] In his book Gourevitch hammers home this point. He records a chilling conversation he had with an American military intelligence officer at a bar in Rwanda. The officer says to him: "I hear you're interested in genocide. . . . Do you know what genocide is? A cheese sandwich. Write it down. Genocide is a cheese sandwich. . . . What does anyone care about a cheese sandwich?"[54]

The statement is chilling, as it should be. The ordinary has gotten mistaken for the trivial. If we practice awareness, if we notice when we are becoming "numbed, blinded, deafened, and indifferent," we will lessen the chances that we will let the ordinary pass without questioning whether or not it is also heinous.

A Group or Community Witnesses Another Group or Community

In Cambridge, Massachusetts, Cathy Hoffman has been working with youth in the Cambridge Youth Peace and Justice Corps (PJC) for a decade. Founded to foster nonviolent social change through the promotion of youth leadership for peace and justice, the program helps youth use their own experiences to understand others. The program encourages the youth to imagine that small acts of witnessing are worthwhile.

In the fall of 1996 Hafsat Abiola, then twenty-two and a senior at Harvard, addressed them. According to Hoffman, Abiola began her talk by holding up her necklace, a silver outline of Africa. She told them that Nigeria is home to one out of four Africans and one out of seven black people. She then proceeded to tell them the story of her country through her own family's experience.

The country, she told them, has been led by one military government after another since 1966. In 1990 a new constitution declared that the country would return to civilian rule in 1992. Pressure mounted on the government to allow elections, which they did, but then they annulled the results, claiming fraud. The next year elections were held again. Hafsat's father, Chief Moshood K. O. Abiola, a wealthy businessman and philanthropist, ran in June 1993 and won by an overwhelming 60 percent of the vote. These were believed to be the first fair elections in the history of the country, but again the government claimed fraud.

Despite demonstrations against the government, within four months there was yet another military dictator, Sani Abacha. Abacha terminated all democratic assemblies, banned all political activity, and suspended the constitution. In this climate Chief Abiola proclaimed himself president in 1994, on the anniversary of his election the previous year. He was imprisoned for treason and in 1996 placed in solitary confinement.[55]

After his arrest his wife, Kudirat Abiola, defying the military orders and inspiring people all over the world, campaigned for human rights and democracy. In June 1996 she was assassinated. Students listening to Hafsat were mesmerized by her story, her dignity, and her conviction that "you can silence a person who speaks the truth, but you cannot silence the truth."[56]

The PJC asked Hafsat what they could do. She told them, "Boycott Shell Oil," a company that she believes violates human rights in Nigeria and contributes to the degradation of the environment. The students arranged for her to speak at the city's public high school, where she addressed two assemblies of riveted students. Later, the PJC youth circulated a petition calling on the city council of Cambridge to boycott Shell Oil, urge President Clinton to impose sanctions on Nigeria, and write the president of Shell Oil to demand that Shell change its policies in Nigeria and become accountable to Nigerians.

With seven hundred signatures on their petition the PJC and Hafsat Abiola went to the city council in May 1997 and made their case. The youth gave the councilors a standing ovation when they passed a resolution to restrict the city of Cambridge from "doing business with companies doing business in Nigeria or who have business relations with the current military regime."[57] Inspired by Hafsat Abiola the students took steps for their community to witness the plight of the people of Nigeria. They learned that simple actions—listening, witnessing, spreading the word, circulating a petition, requesting a municipal resolution—cumulatively, can make a difference.

Creating Transitions Between Witnessing the Self and Witnessing Others

For compassionate witnessing to remain robust, one must be able to move flexibly between witnessing others and witnessing oneself. As I wrote in Chapter Eight, using our personal capacities wisely is part of the self-knowledge we need to extend ourselves to others in ways that we can sustain. Throughout this book I have emphasized the grave individual, interpersonal, and societal consequences of being oblivious to the fate of others. In Chapter Five I showed that problems also arise when we attend to the suffering of others but neglect the effect this has on us. Attending to others and to oneself are both necessary.

Sharon Salzberg writes of time she was doing loving-kindness meditation in Burma, directing *metta* to herself, a benefactor, a friend, a neutral person, and an enemy. At the end of intensive six-week practice her teacher called her into his room and posed the following question: "Suppose you were walking in the forest with your benefactor, your friend, your neutral person, and your enemy. Bandits come up and demand that you choose one person in your group to be sacrificed. Which one would you choose to die?"[58]

She was shocked. Through her practice of *metta* she had ceased any longer to feel a distinction among any of those people, including herself. Through metta she had come to feel an equality of loving feeling toward herself and all others. As she told her teacher, she could not choose. "Everyone seems the same to me."[59] This is a desirable by-product of *metta* practice.

It is also a spiritual basis for observing compassionate witnessing toward the self in a world so filled with the suffering of others that it is easy to lose one's way and diminish the needs of the self in an effort to feel more aligned with the suffering of others. Attention only to the suffering of others is a sign of common shock, of dysregulation and disharmony. On a purely pragmatic basis it is essential that we know our limits so that attending to the suffering of others does not insidiously produce common shock in us. Whether a trauma specialist, a peace activist, or a New York City firefighter, we need to set up our lives so that self-care naturally arises as an outcome of compassion for all beings.

Cultivating loving attention to the self equal to that cultivated toward others may be harder to do for people immersed in belief systems that rely heavily on notions of individualism, in which the self is viewed as separate from others. *Ubuntu* and interbeing are religious and philosophical orientations that propose a fundamentally different conception of the self. Thich Nhât Hanh describes interbeing in this way: "My well-being, my happiness, depends very much on you, and your well-being, your happiness, depends on me. I am responsible for you, and you are responsible for me. . . . Therefore, in order to take care of you, I have to take care of myself."[60] In this way of thinking, caring for ourselves is an aspect of caring for others and vice versa.

On my second trip home from Kosovo, due to flight connections, our team of four left Pristina on a Monday afternoon but had to spend the evening in Zurich before we could fly out the next day. Although in Kosovo we had spent hours with each other preparing for the day's work and then debriefing at the end of the day, and while the conversations had been intense, intimate, and productive, they had not been lighthearted. Now, in Zurich, we reminded me of tops unwinding. We strolled along the canals, walked up the steep streets in the old city peering into windows, and swung our bodies loosely as if we were on the verge of dancing.

Dinner was a lively affair. We ate with gusto, laughed through the evening, and were the last to leave the restaurant. My mood was so cheerful that I reflect back on that time months ago as a measure of what feeling good feels like for me. Our unwinding was part of the necessary shedding of the layers of tension that work in Kosovo inevitably brings to our bodies and minds. Our evening on the town was a way of coping with the common shock residues that linger anyway, but which can also be put temporarily aside with people who totally understand that the levity is not disrespectful.

We were not unaware of the suffering we had just witnessed, but rather aware of it *and* now attending to ourselves in ways we could not have done while we were working. We were not blocking out the suffering of the Kosovars: their experience and ours coexisted without tension. Nor did we feel that in having fun we were being insensitive to the plight of the Kosovar people. Rather it was one manifestation of what all of us were striving for in our work together: to release people from suffering to feel joy again.

One matriarch in a family we visited twice explicitly articulated this. She has suffered greatly since the war when, along with fourteen other men in her village, her husband and two sons were murdered in front of her and other family members. She responded to a question my colleague and I posed her about what she wanted her grandchildren to understand from what she had learned in the last year about coping with loss. She did not hesitate in replying: "I will tell them it is important to take care of each other, their home, and those who are alive. Most of all, to live well with those who are alive."

Witnessing others with compassion needs a solid foundation of witnessing the self. We must know when we need to care for ourselves and also when we must disengage from the sorrows of others to live our lives fully, joy and all. Experiencing joy does not profane suffering: it is part of living life well. Compassionate witnessing makes living life well more likely.

CHAPTER 10

Transforming Violence

In Louise Erdrich's story "The Shawl" a young man recounts a story that is told "on the road where he lives" about a family breakup.[1] An Anishinaabeg woman, Aanakwad, falls in love with a man who is not her husband, has his child, and then falls ill from the grief of not living with the man she loves. Aanakwad's nine-year-old daughter takes over the mother's work of caring for her five-year-old brother, the baby, her parents, and their cabin, but it is too much for her. Each night she falls asleep exhausted, wrapped in her red-and-brown plaid shawl.

The husband, although he loves his wife, understands that their life together is over and sends for the other man's uncle to take her to him. After bitter fighting over who will get the older children, Aanakwad, the daughter, and the baby leave with the uncle in his horse-drawn wagon, fitted with sled runners to travel over the deep snow. The little boy, upon realizing that he is being left behind, runs after the wagon until he collapses from the exertion, watching the wagon, with his beloved mother and sister in it, recede. "At that moment he truly did not care if he was alive or dead."

A year later the little boy's father, weakened by tuberculosis and grief, recounts what happened, "far too often and always the same way." A pack of wolves had attacked the horses and the people in the wagon. When the father arrived, he had seen his "treasured" daughter's shawl, and a few scattered remains, and "ravens, attending to the bitter small leavings of the wolves." He tells the story incessantly, "because the father had to tell what he saw, again and again, in order to get rid of it. . . . He told how when the wolves closed in, Aanakwad had thrown her daughter to them."

The little boy vividly imagines the scene and knows that he is broken, never to be "mended, except by some terrible means." He grows up, marries, has three children, and it is his eldest son, the narrator of the story, who provides the "terrible means" by which he recovers.

Aanakwad's son manages to keep his demons at bay until his own wife dies and the government moves the Anishinaabeg from rural parts of the reservation into housing in towns. At that time, when his older son is ten and his twins are six, he begins drinking heavily and beating his children, sometimes binge drinking for days, leaving the children to fend for themselves. When the older boy turns thirteen, strong, but not as strong or as heavy as his father, he challenges him. During the fight, experiencing a "frightful kind of joy," wanting to "waste him," he is also dissociated, watching the scene from the far wall, "pitying us both."

At some point during this one-time-only fight, the father falls and stops fighting. The son "wins." He sits beside his father and tenderly wipes the blood off his face with a bit of blanket the older man always has with him. The father eyes his son closely, taking the "frayed piece" of shawl and pressing it to the middle of his own forehead, "as if he were praying, as if he were having thoughts he wanted to collect in that piece of cloth. For a while he lay like that, and I, crouched over, let him be, hardly breathing. Something told me to sit there, still. And then at last he said to me, in the sober new voice I would hear from then on, *Did you know I had a sister once?*"

The son and his siblings have been victims and witnesses to their father's violence, precipitated by a convergence of losses that overwhelm the father's ability to cope. He cannot adequately mourn the loss of his wife, recapitulating the earlier losses of his mother and sister, coupled with the loss of place, through the government's forced removal of the Anishinaabeg people. He turns to alcohol, compounding his losses by losing a loving relationship to his children. His children stop seeing him as human: "We survived off him as if he were a capricious and dangerous line of work."

At thirteen the older son takes on his father. The fight and the tenderness after, the sitting still, are all, in their own ways, acts of compassionate witness to the father, who feels this. They release the father to witness himself, to touch his broken place, and to know he must share his grief. He asks a question—*"Did you know I had a sister once?"*—intuiting that his son's negative reply will invite him to start the story in the place where he has gotten separated from his own life's narrative.

Years go by. The son's younger siblings marry and "get away." His father is with a woman. He, however, "prefers to live alone." When his father next brings up what has become the "old days," no longer a past that mercilessly invades the present, but a story of a time gone by, the son tells him "at last the two things [he] had been thinking."

First, he tells his father he must burn the shawl so that it can "cloak [his sister's] spirit." The Anishinaabeg, he reminds his father, do not keep the clothing of the dead. Second, he poses his own question to his father, one that offers an alternative interpretation of the "facts" embedded in the story that the father's father had told *his* son. The grandson's version, told to his father with exquisite compassion for all, incorporates cultural meanings into the story in a way that the grandfather's story—a story of extreme loss, rage, helplessness, and betrayal—does not, perhaps cannot. The new version of the story, posed as a question, maybe forty years after the event, and fifteen or twenty years after the reconciliation of this father and son, is produced by imaginatively entering the mind of the nine-year-old girl, riding in the wagon, seeing that the wolves were "only hungry" and that "their need was only need." It adds yet another layer of witnessing.

The son speaks to his father: "She knew that you were back there, alone in the snow. She understood that the baby she loved would not live without a mother, and that only the uncle knew the way. She saw clearly that one person in the wagon had to be offered up, or they all would die. And in that moment of knowledge, don't you think, being who she was, of the old sort of Anishinaabeg, who thinks of the good of the people first, she jumped, my father . . . brother to that little girl? Don't you think she lifted her shawl and flew?"

The story within the story, and Erdrich's story, both end there. The question has changed everything. For the reader as well.

I absorbed the original story, lulled into accepting as truth the spare description that the mother had thrown her daughter to the wolves. My experience should have made me cautious—knowing that pain, rage, and grief would thread distortion into a tale—but it did not. The retelling struck me as a revelation, and made me weep. It struck me with the force of hope.

Compassionate witnessing can do this. It can transform everyday violence by threading hope into its fabric. Not always with powerful results, and not always in ways that ripple out, touching many people. But both its promise and potential arouse hope.

What constitutes hope varies across situations. Hope is not unitary but specific to people and place, the past, present, and future. In the previous chapter I wrote about children I met in a domestic-violence shelter who were cautious about their mothers' recounting their stories of abuse. Eventually, these children did join their mothers in a witnessing event. The mothers sat in an inner circle surrounded by their children and the shelter staff and spoke about the kinds of values they hoped the children were learning in this safe setting. At times one or another mother would cry.

When it was the children's turn to respond to their mothers, to sit themselves in the inner circle, their mothers' tears were central to their reflections. Daniel, age nine, remarked: "Everything they said was interesting. But their crying . . ." His sister broke in: "They weren't upset!" "No," Daniel picked up. "They were crying because they really like us." "They care about us," another child chimed in.

The mothers' tears, dreaded initially, were no longer a sign of terror and misery, but of love and concern. The children could feel the difference. In the closing moments, the children each offered words into the circle. These were their choices: "Love, love, love, it was good, understanding, affection, mommy, happy day of love, peace, respect, gratitude, crying, gifts, tears are caring."

I drive a car with one bumper sticker on it. It was made by my friend Glenda's family after her son died, and reproduced when her husband died. It is a statement by Dorothy Day, who cofounded the Catholic Worker Movement and was a tireless peace activist. The bumper sticker says: LOVE IS THE ONLY SOLUTION.[2] The night I drove home from the shelter after that witnessing event, I utterly believed that hope's name was love.

Everyday violence and violation surround us everywhere all the time. It is as "natural" as the air we breathe. What constitutes our daily diet of violence and violation depends on the circumstances of our lives. Life in an American urban war zone affords different sights and experiences than living in my suburban community a scant five miles away. Life in a South African township is different from life in a middle-class section of Cape Town, which is different still from a refugee camp anywhere in the world. Our different "places" provide different opportunities for witnessing personal and structural violence and violation.

Our "place" intersects with other factors. For instance, television, song lyrics, radio, film, comics, and video games provide equal-opportunity bombardment of violent content to viewers, whether in Manhattan or Malaysia. Media are the great levelers of our time. Yet the answer to this media bombardment is not to censor it, but to question it. More than ever we need a free press.[3]

Witnessing is not all alike. Some kinds of witnessing are highly problematic for others and ourselves. If we witness without awareness of what we are seeing, we may turn away from a situation in which inaction contributes to the misery of the violence itself. The child who is bullied on the playground in full view of his teacher who does nothing is abandoned as well as harassed. If that same teacher laughs at the bully's taunts, the child is violated by the teacher as well as the bully. The teacher who looks on, concerned for the child but unsure of how to respond, has been abandoned by her school system. It has not provided her with the training she needs to respond appropriately.

The relentless witnessing we are subject to—whether we like it or not—produces common shock, which may range from minor to major. Common shock is not a medical term, because the phenomenon it describes isn't either. In some instances people do have responses to what they have witnessed that meet the criteria used to define a medical condition, for instance "posttraumatic stress disorder," but often they do not. Further, current medical criteria are not always a good match for the social or cultural context in which violence and violation occurs, either in the United States or in other parts of the world. For instance, as we have seen in the chapter on illness, there is nothing "post" about worrying that your child's cancer will return or, as we have seen in the chapter on intergenerational transmission of common shock, in the concern that another group of soldiers will invade your village.

Common shock is a condition that is widespread but all too often unrecognized. There are biological, psychological, relational, and societal consequences of common shock that affect us individually and collectively. Only if we understand how common shock operates are we in a position to do something about it.

I have identified four pathways by which we are routinely exposed to the conditions that produce common shock. These four pathways—coping with illness and dying, living with relatives who are significantly distressed by their own trauma or common shock experiences, coming into contact with professionals who are having difficulty dealing with their own trauma or common shock, and living in communities that have suffered political violence—are by no means exhaustive of the ways we are exposed to common shock, but they are significant ways. While the exposure may be inevitable, there is much that we can do to mitigate the effects, if there is collective will to do so.

Fortunately, we can turn inadvertent witnessing into compassionate witnessing. There are numerous resources available to us to support the shift. I hope that the ones I have described in Chapter Eight will stimulate readers' recognition of others that can be of assistance in their particular circumstances.

Compassionate witnessing, aware and empowered witnessing, of which there are infinite expressions—as many ways of doing it as there are people and situations—provides a platform for a response that is helpful to others and to us. While it may be awkward at first, people come to appreciate doing it. I think of Ben, age seven, avoiding the back door for fear that he would see our neighbor whose mother had died, necessitating him to offer his condolences. He wasn't less empathic than Miranda, who was plastered to the window, but more cautious and uncertain that he would "say the right thing." Younger, Miranda didn't even entertain that possibility!

Sometimes I fantasize a social movement, a citizenry going about its day alert for moments that can be transformed by compassionate witnessing. I imagine motorists smiling at the honking, agitated drivers beside them in traffic jams; coaches lecturing their soccer players that ultimately it is the caring they show each other on and off the field that matters, not winning, although that would be nice too. I imagine parents apologizing to their children for angry outbursts, telling them that they were not to blame and promising to work to control themselves. I could go on.

Once, I was taking care of an eight-year-old while her mom was recovering from day surgery. My young friend had found a penny on the sidewalk where we were walking, and was so excited. "Did you ever think about how the pennies get there?" I asked. "How would you like to be a penny dropper so that other children can find yours?" She was thrilled with that idea and I gave her three pennies to drop. She held on to them, carefully planning the best place to release each penny, the more likely for it to "find" a child.

I've always felt fondly about this outing, and I see now that it links with my ideas about how small compassionate acts of witnessing performed routinely could have a significant impact. Daniel Schacter's work provides a rationale for this. In his comprehensive and fascinating book *Searching for Memory*, he cautions us that our thoughts, feelings, and behaviors are pervasively influenced by implicit memories that are out of our awareness. Implicit memory can bias our judgment and affect our emotional state.[4] The viewing of violence and violation is so routine that many of us are actually no longer aware of what we are seeing; we have stopped registering it. However, as Schacter makes clear, the absence of conscious awareness does not mean that it has no effect. In my fantasy the citizen throng of compassionate witnesses are creating alternative implicit memories for onlookers, ones that, like the penny droppers, "find" and fill our minds with images that bias us toward caring and concern.

People sometimes tell me that while they see the need to do compassionate witnessing, they don't think that they can do it. They raise two kinds of objections. The first is that they don't know enough. Actually, to be a compassionate witness you don't have to know a lot about any subject at all, except yourself. We are so used to experts who give advice that we fear that if we don't have *the answer* we can't be helpful to others. In fact, just the opposite is usually true. While we may want the experts to have answers for us, we usually want our friends, family, and acquaintances to help us find our own answers. On the other hand, hearing from those people how our lives have affected them is usually gratefully received. This is expertise everyone can acquire. It requires knowing how we feel and what we think. Whether we develop these skills for compassionate witnessing or for other purposes, these are important life skills to have.

The other objection that people raise is that they don't have the stomach or the heart to show concern for others. They fear that they will be overwhelmed by what they hear and need to back off hastily. They often invoke a mechanical image of a bucket that has only so much water in it and indicate that compassionate witnessing would be like a hole puncturing the bucket, draining them dry.

I don't try to argue with this fear, because the person may know something about him or herself that I need to understand and respect. On the other hand, I do offer a contrasting analogy that comes from my experience doing compassionate witnessing and watching hundreds of others do it as well. I liken compassionate witnessing to exercise; the more you do it, the stronger you get from it. The expenditure of effort yields gain.

Further, compassionate witnessing feels good. Let me leap to qualify this. It is certainly the case that listening intently to people's stories of violence and suffering is painful. I would even go so far as to say it must be or we are not hearing what we are being told. But the pain of deeply registering what we hear coexists with our perception that the speaker is benefiting from being heard, even though the act of telling the story may be difficult.

This point can be easily misunderstood. I do not subscribe to the idea that suffering can be redeemed. Rather, I believe that suffering is always terrible, often tragic. I do not believe that suffering serves a purpose, although many people, and I am one, have used suffering to serve a purpose. I used to tell people who asked me whether cancer had changed my life that *it* hadn't, but *I* had. I wasn't being a smart aleck, but rather expressing a distinction I thought was critical then, and still do. Cancer brought me nothing but *tsuris,* the Yiddish for trouble. I, on the other hand, worked mightily hard to make some good come of it, for myself and others.[5]

In a similar vein, listening to other people's suffering does not redeem it or make it less than it is. If something changes, it is not the suffering per se that does. Speaking to a compassionate witness releases something else that can be felt as a presence in the space between the witness and the speaker.

This coexistence of states—suffering alongside compassion—is not unusual. One often encounters a commingling of states of vulnerability and states of resilience.[6] Several couplets have been identified, the first member designating a state of vulnerability and the second a state of resilience. They are: despair paired with hope, helplessness with agency, meaninglessness with purpose, isolation with communion, resentment with gratitude, and sorrow with joy.[7] It has been my experience that compassionate witnessing first invites a telling of the story that allows people to express the states of vulnerability. This story is often one that has been silenced, blocked, denied, or forbidden. As difficult as it is to put this story into words—and as painful as it is to feel the states of vulnerability—it is also the beginning of an antidote to the violence that inspired it.

The person who tells the story to a compassionate witness is inhabiting the role of witness in the very act of telling the story, even if just for a few moments. Receiving witnessing from another as well as enacting it oneself may contribute to the mechanism by which the second state in the couplet is brought into being. For that is also my experience. During compassionate witnessing states of resilience are activated, for both the witness and the person being witnessed. Thus, far from the experience of compassionate witnessing draining a person, it seems to replenish and restore.

There are several ways of understanding this enhanced sense of well-being. Research on the neuropsychology of the brain suggests that social cooperation—and I would argue that compassionate witnessing is a form of social cooperation—has been shown to be "intrinsically rewarding to the human brain."[8] Whether the compassionate witnessing happens between two people who have never met before or between groups of people who have ongoing affiliations—for instance, at the shelter—people do feel more bonded with each other, even if transiently so, and happy about it.

Compassionate witnessing may also be an expression of what psychologist Shelley E. Taylor calls the "tending instinct," a biologically hard-wired response to stress that may be as natural as fight-or-flight, particularly in females.[9] When humans are threatened, the sympathetic branch of the autonomic nervous system is activated. However, females are more likely to tend and to turn to others than they are to fight or flee under certain circumstances of threat. Oxytocin may be a key factor in this "tend-and-befriend" behavior.[10] Oxytocin is associated with the parasympathetic branch of the autonomic nervous system, and reliably produces a calm state. In fact, it is associated with a reduction in the biological systems that produce the fight-or-flight response.

By speculating that there may be a link between the mechanisms that account for the sense of well-being that people get when they do compassionate witnessing and the "tending instinct," I am not implying that compassionate witnessing is more suited to females than males. Taylor's work offers a radically different, refreshing, and I think credible, view of men that reveals the ways that tending is vital to men's relationships also, especially in men's groups. Rather, I am suggesting that there may be a biological substratum to account for the felt experience of well-being rather than misery that seems to accompany compassionate witnessing for many people. The release of oxytocin is one such candidate. Oxytocin is released during stress and is associated with a feeling of calm. Oxytocin may be present when people do compassionate witnessing.

There is one final mechanism that intrigues me in this regard. When compassionate witnessing occurs among a group of people, for instance during designed witnessing events, such as at the shelter, or in spontaneous events with assemblies of people, such as at the rugby stadium in South Africa when Mandela wore the Springbok cap and was rhythmically cheered: in addition to the enhanced sense of closeness to others that many people report, there can also be an experience of awe or wonder.

Not surprisingly, there is a neuropsychological basis for these perceptions also. Researchers who study spiritual experience propose a unitary continuum, such that either fast or slow ritualized behaviors can provoke the brain to experiences of unity, sometimes mild ones and sometimes very intense ones. Examples of slow ritualized behavior are common in daily routines. Reading a poem, preparing a cup of tea according to an invariant set of steps, listening to a love song, all may trigger feelings of unity, a decreased sense of the separateness of the self from the external world, and an increased sense of connectedness to others.[11] So, too, fast ritualized behavior, for instance repetitive dancing, drumming, or clapping at a stadium may trigger these unity states.[12] Even intense absorption in nature, art, a romantic partner, or our work can produce mild states of unity, what psychologists call flow.[13]

I believe that compassionate witnessing can set off the brain's capacity to experience unity. I think that this is what I am experiencing when I feel awe and wonder following compassionate witnessing. If this is what is happening, then there is a biological, as well as a psychological, explanation for compassionate witnessing diminishing the perception of us versus them and contributing to a perception of our common humanity.

Unfortunately, we live in a world more organized to support the brain's ability to perceive binary oppositions, us versus them, good versus evil, than to support its ability to perceive unity. This can be both futile and dangerous. Alexander Solzhenitsyn succinctly points out the absurdity of such arrangements: "The line between good and evil cuts through the heart of every human being."[14] Mark Twain makes explicit the embedded, often unrecognized, implications of thinking in binaries in a short story he published posthumously, since his family and publisher found it too controversial to be printed in his lifetime.

In "The War Prayer" he describes a church service in which the minister is giving an impassioned sermon to young men who are about to leave for a war [Probably the Spanish-American War, a war of imperialism that Twain vehemently opposed].[15] The minister recites a prayer in which he calls for God to watch over the men as they do their patriotic duty and help them "crush the foe, grant to them and to their flag and country imperishable honor and glory. . . ."

Before the minister concludes his prayer, an "aged stranger" walks down the aisle and faces the congregation at the pulpit. He tells them he comes from "Almighty God" to tell them that He will grant this prayer if the congregation still desire it after they have heard the "full import" of the prayer, which is really two prayers, not one, "one uttered, the other not." The stranger then puts the implicit prayer into words:

> O Lord our God, help us to tear their soldiers to bloody shreds with our shells; help us to cover their smiling fields with the pale forms of their patriot dead; help us to drown the thunder of the guns with shrieks of their wounded, writhing in pain; help us to lay waste their humble homes with hurricanes of fire; help us to wring the hearts of their unoffending widows with unavailing grief; help us to turn them out roofless with their little children to wander unfriended the wastes of their desolated land in rags and hunger and thirst, sports of the sun flames of summer and the icy winds of winter, broken in spirit, worn with travail, imploring Thee for the refuge of the grave and denied it—for our sakes who adore Thee, Lord, blast their hopes, blight their lives, protract their bitter pilgrimage, make heavy their steps, water their way with tears, stain the white snow with the blood of their wounded feet! We ask it, in the spirit of love, of Him Who is the Source of

> Love, and Who is the ever-faithful refuge and friend of all that are sore beset and seek His aid with humble and contrite hearts. Amen.

The story ends with the narrator stating that the congregation thought the man was "a lunatic, because there was no sense in what he said."

Thinking in binaries is common and is also a frequent outcome for people who have experienced fear and reacted with common shock. It tends to cause a kind of mental shutdown, which restricts access to new ideas.[16] Cognitive restriction as a consequence of fear diminishes our interest in the workings of other people's minds as well. In Chapter Six we saw how fear as a consequence of maltreatment could produce a withdrawal of interest in others. This happens internationally as well as interpersonally. In some instances aggression becomes more likely,[17] and in other instances silence does. In some situations both occur together. When silence develops, it is as if it permeates the ruptured relationship like a mist seeping into every cranny.

The antidote to silence is the creation of story, whether at the interpersonal or the international level.[18] However, not all kinds of stories are equally useful to repair relationships and to promote peaceful coexistence. Those stories that maintain the binary oppositions of us versus them, or good versus evil, are insufficiently complex, or accurate, to assist people in revisioning their relationships. They do promise a quick stress release from the fear that gives rise to them. In the long run, however, these kinds of stories generate more, not less, stress, as they provide a flawed basis for improving the situation. Only a coherent narrative that makes sense of the fundamental propositions of both parties' points of view can ever promote peace between people or peoples.

Here, then, is another attribute of compassionate witnessing. It assists in the development of a coherent narrative for those who take the risk to bridge the pain and suffering caused by violence and violation. Whether there is an outsider who witnesses the parties in conflict or each person is able to witness himself with compassion, the steps that we have seen in Chapter Nine can be effective in moving toward a shared narrative that renders an account with which both sides can live.

The transformation of violence and violation always entails bridging the discontinuities, disruptions, and disconnections that violence and violation inevitably leave in their wake. Whether a new story must be generated for Joe, who sees his friend Bill push their colleague Wendy against her will at the water cooler and feel her breasts; or it is a story for Daniel, who sees his new stepfather hit his mother; or a story for Serbs riding a commuter train who see a NATO plane return to drop more bombs on the bridge where their train is crossing,[19] violence and violation disrupt the old story. Only a new, revised, honest narrative that accounts for each other's feelings, motivations, and actions will prove resilient enough to sustain an ongoing relationship or put right an interaction that has been disrupted by violence or violation.

Compassionate witnessing assists in the telling of stories that begin to do just this. Filaments of truth get spun and laid down across gaps caused by acts that may have been horrific and horrifying or difficult and damaging. In the interplay among telling, listening and reflecting, rudimentary coherence, continuity, and connection can form. Repeated, they take hold.[20] Acts of compassionate witnessing, helping others revise their stories, can make a difference at the micro and the macro levels. Individuals, families, communities, and nations can all do compassionate witnessing, and we would all benefit if compassionate witnessing were widespread. Most of us will never be in a position to solve the problems of the world. We will live ordinary lives, faced with daily challenges that will greet us in our homes and neighborhoods, not in the White House or the United Nations. Yet, it is precisely what we *can* do in our homes and in our neighborhoods that can make a difference. The effects of recognizing others' experiences of common shock and responding with compassion to them have profound biological, psychological, and relational consequences for those individuals who are witnessed well. So, too, recognizing our own common shock and responding with compassion to ourselves is important. Finally, witnessing our own acts of violence and violation, whether or not they have produced common shock in others, can be salutary.

The other day I behaved rudely to a customer service representative of my Internet server. Our server had been down for several days, and I had been promised that they would correct the problem in forty-eight hours. When I called on hour forty-nine to report that the server was still down, the representative told me that I needed to go through a series of steps for them to reinstate my service. Apparently, she informed me, the person to whom I had originally reported the problem had failed to tell me this, and consequently the company had done nothing to solve the problem. Since I rely on the Internet daily, and was inconvenienced by not having access to it, I was frustrated and annoyed that their oversight had resulted in my further inconvenience. The young woman who assisted me was patient and competent, and was not provoked by my abrupt and irritated manner.

A few hours later, now calm and remorseful, I decided that I should call the young woman and apologize to her. But I was tired, so I took a nap instead. Then I forgot. Then I remembered, but it was inconvenient.

A week later I decided to call her supervisor. In praising her attitude and skill I was witnessing my own bad behavior, transforming my rudeness into an action that might benefit her, the person I had treated unfairly. The fact that time had elapsed was not material.

It is often the case that compassionate witnessing must take place after the fact, not in the moment. A young family friend recently revealed that her father had been emotionally abusive to all the family members during the time that she had lived in our neighborhood and visited us regularly. She had known that something "bad" happened in her family, but she had no vocabulary for it at the time. Five years after she had moved away, now a young adult, she sat with us and told us pieces of her family story. The conversation was rich, clarifying, and poignant, providing an opening to continue discussion.

Compassionate witnessing often transcends normal time frames. When we help a child draw a picture of the man who hit him, the flat sheet of paper collapses the past into a hoped-for future in which the child has some measure of control, not unlike choosing the crayons to color the man's clothing and choosing to confide in us. When we write a letter to the IRA supporting their open letter of apology and urging them to back it up with continued support of the peace process and commitments to nonviolence, we are witnessing the past and present with a pointer to the future.[21] No day goes by that I don't see, whether or not I take them, opportunities to do compassionate witnessing.

When my father was dying, I initiated a conversation to witness him that unfolded into one of mutual compassionate witnessing. His imminent death pressed on us both, although I doubt either of us thought it would be our last conversation. We were witnessing each other in highly vulnerable states; my father, not wanting to die; I, facing the death of my second parent. Both of us were experiencing common shock.

Hilary and I were visiting him in Florida in what turned out to be a visit three weeks before he died of congestive heart failure. His scope of action had gradually been decreasing over the years, and his accommodation to his limitations had been remarkable and unforeseen, at least by me. Rather than depression characterizing his demeanor, acceptance and sweetness did. He was being taken care of by his wife, who was devoted to him.

I had seen him with my sister two weeks previously when he had been hospitalized for kidney failure, and been toxic from his own circulating fluids. This day I entered the apartment and saw for the first time that he was sitting in a wheelchair. He was frail, and his large hands lay folded loosely in his lap, occasionally moving as if he were agitated.

He looked up and saw me. His eyes filled with tears, and with a frankness for which I had always longed but he had never revealed to me, he said, "It's near the end. It's so barren. I don't know what to do. I try to do what people tell me to do." He paused. "People call. But they will get bored."

I walked over to him, kissed his head, and knelt down, looking up at his face as I talked. I told him that I thought he was wondering how to have this last phase of his life have meaning, but that I thought he was doing things right now that were living his life the way he wanted it to be. For instance, I pointed out, he was cooperating with everything that was asked of him and he was trying to help the people who were helping him.

"I am."

I reassured him that that was an important form of doing. It made life easier. And that wasn't all he was doing. I reminded him that he was talking on the phone to people who loved him and that he was staying in touch with what *they* were doing.

"But I want to walk. I can't walk."

At this point his wife interjected. "You can walk." She brought over his walker, and for the next twenty minutes or so we stood by while she helped him walk down the corridor outside their apartment. He was exhausted when he returned to the den, but pleased.

He and I resumed our conversation alone, while Hilary and my father's wife discussed medication issues in another room.

I asked him if he remembered what we had been talking about before.

"Not really."

So I summarized for him that he had been telling me that he found it hard to find meaning in his life now. Then I reflected that I thought that might be the case because he had always seen meaning as consisting of working on a goal and accomplishing it.

"That's right."

I shared with him that there might be another way of thinking about what was meaningful at this time in his life that could be available to him. He could think about the people whose lives he'd influenced, and the way his work and values lived on as a legacy. But, I acknowledged, that wasn't his style.

"As a child, Dad, I was hurt by your saying that nothing I did, no accomplishment of mine, had any impact on you; that what mattered was what you did. . . ."

"I was an arrogant son of a bitch, wasn't I?"

"Yes, you were. Some of the time. But not all of the time. Now, this could be a way for you to experience meaning in your life. If you think of your children and your grandchildren and you think of how we are living our lives. And if you realize that you are a part of that."

I told him that I was working on a project that I saw as directly related to his work, an aspect of my connection to him and to his legacy. I asked if I could tell him about it.

"Sure."

So I did. I told him about the Witnessing Project. And I told him I was going to write a book. He was quiet. Then I told him a story.

I told him about an event that happened during a cruise we had taken the December before I turned seven. My mother's father had been furious because he thought my father was going to ruin us by spending his earnings on a cruise when things were so precarious. But my father believed that it would be a memorable adventure; and he had been right. On one of the days we had driven around Havana, seen slums, and then driven through a middle-class neighborhood. I had asked if we could stop the car so that I could play in the park, which my parents had let me do.

The next day I had been invited to an afternoon birthday party by a little girl I had met on the boat. I had gotten all dressed up and my mother had bought and wrapped a present for me. I went by myself up to the salon, but they wouldn't let me in because we were on D deck and the party was on B deck.

I flew downstairs, sobbing my head off. I was so humiliated and angry. I told my parents what had happened. He and my mother had said, "Remember yesterday when we were driving around Havana? And there were some people who lived in nice houses and some people who lived in terrible-looking houses? Well, the people who live in nice houses often do just what happened to you on B deck to the people who live in the poor houses." They made the connection to class in a way that informs me to this day. They helped me link my experience to a wider context of injustice and created a lifelong commitment to be a certain kind of person.

"My current project is an expression of that commitment, Dad, which goes back as far as I can remember to you and Mommy, the work that you did, and the loving way you treated me."

He shook his head. His voice was weak. He was clearly tired. "That's beautiful. That's very, very beautiful. That's lovely."

"Do you want to take a nap, Dad?"

He was too tired to do more than just nod.

Long before this conversation with my father I had pondered the potential of children or grandchildren witnessing their elders'—even their ancestors'—lives. I thought of the healing the Anishinaabeg son conferred on his father and of the hero in *All Quiet on the Western Front*. He, while recovering from his wounds in a hospital, seeing the men who will not, reflects on the abyss of sorrow surrounding him: "What would our fathers do if we suddenly stood up and came before them and proffered our account?"[22] Ironically, sadly, the children's account of war would be no different from their fathers', if both would tell the truth. I thought of Miranda in Shakespeare's *The Tempest,* witness to her father, the magician Prospero, the former duke of Milan. Although their island is idyllic in some respects, they are there because of an abuse of power, and there are abuses of power, enslavements, on the island as well. Miranda's wonder calls forth her father to abjure his magic and reenter the world.[23] I thought of the baby, in Toni Morrison's novel *Beloved,* whose witness of her mother, Sethe, is a constant reminder of the horrors and effects of slavery.[24]

These children, all in their own ways, have dipped into, or have been soaked in, what psychoanalyst Maurice Apprey calls "pooled communal memories."[25] All over the world there are communal memories of violence. Often the response to these memories is further violence. Those of us who work toward the transformation of violence think constantly of how to "transform the toxic errand of extinction, humiliation, massacre, a legacy of ashes," passed on over generations, to a "positive errand."[26]

It is not a simple matter. How can children honor their ancestors—their parents, grandparents, and beyond—and not use violent means to do so? What positive errand is thinkable if you are a Bosnian Muslim son and hear the story of your mother's rape in a Serbian camp? How does an African-American girl commit herself to a positive errand when she reads slave narratives and hears her own great-great-grandparents' stories?

What are the processes that transform legacies of violence in such a way that history is honored without repeating it? How do we respect the past, but, as Paul Ricoeur says about tradition, partner it with "innovation"? Ricouer cautions us that a "tradition remains living . . . only if it continues to be held in an unbroken process of reinterpretation. . . . The unfulfilled future of the past forms perhaps the richest part of tradition."[27] How do we reinterpret the past so that we fulfill the promise of the future? How do we link histories of violence to unrealized possibilities of peace in the past and bring to fruition in the present what was neglected—or couldn't be accomplished—in the past? How do we help the wounded living release their younger kin to repair, not avenge, relationships? And whose responsibility is it to create the conditions so that this can come to pass?

It belongs to all of us. Some who are less wounded may need to assume more responsibility, although those who are more wounded may be the most knowledgeable and credible about finding the way. Some will see the way, and some will recognize it when it is shown. We need to help each other to walk the way.

Dr. Xolela Mangcu is the executive director of the Steve Biko Foundation. Biko was a leader of the black consciousness movement in South Africa, a prominent antiapartheid activist, who was killed in custody in 1977 at the age of thirty-one. Dr. Mangcu writes about the day his daughter was a "confetti girl" at the wedding of Steve Biko's son, Nkosinathi. For his seven-year-old daughter the wedding, and her part in it, was simply the best day of her life. For Dr. Mangcu the day was rich and loaded with memory and meaning. At the wedding ceremony, looking around at the assembled crowd, he could not fail to see "symbolic images" of the day, twenty-four years before, when he had walked the same route as the wedding party, but to the church graveyard to bury Steve Biko. He remembered Nkosinathi's cry, "The whites have killed my father," even as, now, he admired the young man in his wedding suit.[28]

Dr. Mangcu wonders why he had the double vision: why the political memories of Steve Biko's tragic murder interlaced with the images of the young couple's and his own daughter's happiness. Archbishop Desmond Tutu, who spoke at the wedding, addressed his internal question. Tutu thanked Steve Biko for his son, who "through his marriage made it possible for us now to celebrate with tears of joy, and become ordinary again.[29] Tutu's formulation has proved useful to Dr. Mangcu. He was able to release his daughter to own both extraordinary stories of her father, and of others who were active in the antiapartheid struggle, and ordinary stories of a marriage.

Dr. Mangcu's short article shows one way. Letting the ordinary have a place alongside the extraordinary is a beginning. Releasing his daughter to her pure, unalloyed joy at the wedding—with no injunction to dip into the pooled communal memory of outrage, horror, or sorrow—is to accept that the conditions of her life are different than his were. This acceptance gives her permission to reinterpret the past, one expression of which is to be a child who links the history of apartheid through the touch of her father to her own future unblighted by it. How will this position her to live with white South Africans? What is her account that she will now place alongside those of her peers, of all colors and ethnicities in the New South Africa?

Can we witness our elders and ancestors so that they are certain that we understand, and then transform what we know into truths that heal, not incite?[30] Are there actions that end cycles of violence that do not entail reconciliation, when the effort to reconcile itself produces its own violation, coming prematurely, before there has been time to rest and heal from violence? Can we promote healing individually, collectively, and across groups with histories of enmity that promote peace without requiring reconciliation, promote tolerance without demanding forgiveness?

These are critical questions. I believe that the answer to all of them must be yes, and that compassionate witnessing is one way of enacting that affirmation. When we do compassionate witnessing, we are compelled to remember what the other wants us to remember. We are immersed in memories of the past for the purpose of fulfilling the future of the past in the present. This form of remembering does not "perpetuate hatred," as Elie Wiesel informs us, but undermines it. Wiesel's logic is straightforward. If one is true to memory, one rejects anything that might distort it, which hatred invariably does.[31] Thus memory and truth serve the past, the present, and the future.

Further, they direct us to each other. We create each other's hells and we must create each other's hope. Love may be the only solution, but hope is our shared imperative.

I used to think, as I am sure many others do, that feeling hope was my individual responsibility. I used to believe that I either had it or didn't; I was either hopeful or hopeless. I no longer accept any of these premises. Rather, I believe that hope happens when we see a pathway to effective action. Thus it is better understood as the responsibility of the community and something that we do together.[32]

Compassionate witnessing is one of the ways I do hope with others. The effects of hope are profound, as are the effects of hopelessness. Just as food, water, and security must be equitably distributed, so too must hope. Compassionate witnessing is a way we can contribute to the equitable distribution of hope, and work for justice for all.

Appendix One

Suggestions to Manage the Biological Psychological, Interpersonal, and Societal Consequences of Common Shock[1]

(These recommendations assume that you are currently safe)

The Biological Consequences of Common Shock

1. Learn to recognize how your body feels when it is experiencing stress. For instance, do you notice your heart beating faster, your breath feeling tight, a knot or butterflies in your stomach, your thoughts racing or slowed down, difficulty swallowing?
2. Use your breath as an anchor to feel calmer. Inhale slowly to a count of three, hold your breath to a count of three, and exhale to a count of three. Repeat this sequence until you notice you are breathing more easily.
3. Sometimes as a person releases pent-up stress from a common shock experience, the body trembles involuntarily. This is a natural and healthy response.
4. Make a list of ten activities that comfort you—for instance, listening to a particular piece of music or taking a hot shower. Keep the list in your wallet or someplace where it is always handy and do one activity each day.
5. Avoid overusing stimulants like caffeine, alcohol, sugar, or drugs, but do drink plenty of fluids and eat comforting, nutritious foods in moderation.
6. Balance vigorous exercise with relaxing exercise, e.g., running with stretching.

7. Take a warm shower or bath.
8. Try sitting on the ground. Many people find placing their bodies on the ground is comforting. If this is not possible, sit in a chair and feel the sensation of your buttocks and the backs of your legs on the chair.
9. Look at some object of natural beauty. Even one will do. Study a leaf, notice the way the light looks, look at a rock. Take a walk in a park or in an area where grass, plants, or trees grow.
10. Light a candle and dedicate the light to something or someone whose presence near you will be comforting.

The Psychological Consequences of Common Shock

1. Tell your experience to someone you trust. Don't worry if you are getting the details right; convey your overall sense of your experience.
2. Let yourself release the feelings you have. If you feel sadness, cry; if anger, yell.
3. Create an image for yourself that makes you feel part of a larger group. For instance, imagine that you are one animal in a large herd of animals or imagine that your hands are linked in a human chain that spans the globe. Use this image several times a day, perhaps before you do your breathing exercise.
4. Think of one small action that you can take, symbolic or actual, that makes you feel less helpless.
5. If you are feeling afraid in the present when you know you are actually safe, ask yourself the following questions: Am I safe now? How is the present moment different from the time when I was in danger? What can I do now to comfort myself?
6. Express yourself in an artistic medium: sing, draw, bang on plastic container "drums," dance, make a collage, etc.
7. If you feel shame, consider whether it is appropriate or not. This is a very hard idea to consider, but well worth it. If you feel ashamed of something you have done, think of a way you can make amends. Consider asking someone to help you figure this out, if it is too overwhelming to imagine what you might do to make amends. If you feel shame, but you don't believe that you have really done anything to deserve it, consider that someone may have "dumped"—transferred—his or her unbearable feelings of shame onto you. You may want to confront the person or,

again, create a ritual. For a ritual you might want to cleanse yourself of your undeserved shame by burning or burying a symbolic representation of it.

8. Do not expect a lot of yourself. Cut yourself slack.
9. Spend time with people who care about you.
10. Let others comfort you. If others need comfort, comfort them.
11. Hug friends and family members.
12. Give yourself time to heal.

Interpersonal Consequences of Common Shock

1. Silence: It is important to feel safe and to share your experience with at least one other person whom you trust to listen carefully and to decide with you what, if any, next steps you might take to feel better and/or to act in relation to the situation you have witnessed. In many situations it may seem impossible both to tell someone and maintain your own and/or others' safety. However, ultimately silence or secrecy seldom keeps people safe. These are difficult choices, but speaking out has a better chance of leading to improvement than silence.
2. Shattered Assumptions: Assumptions are not like glass; they are built out of experiences in the world with others and these experiences can change. When "shattered," with time, with support from others, and with distance from the experiences that produced the collapse of core beliefs, related ones will form. These will form in new ways to accommodate both prior and new experience. It is unlikely that you will emerge the same, which may produce its own interpersonal challenges. But the changes can usually be placed in a context that makes them understandable to others.
3. Inhibition of Self-Disclosure: There are often times when a person needs to talk, but others cannot bear the story he has to tell. This invariably creates a sense of isolation and may deepen grief and loss. As sad as this circumstance is, it is rarely total. You may have to manage your disappointment that the person you *most* want to talk to is unavailable, but there will usually be someone available. If no one you know is willing to listen to you, look in your area for support groups led by trained professionals. Group discussion can be very beneficial when your own support networks are depleted. Or, you can seek professional help. You can contact your state's professional organizations of psychology, social work,

marriage and family counseling, or psychiatry for referral information.

4. Problems of Fit: It is highly unlikely that any two people, even or especially life partners, will manage common shock identically, initially or over time. As painful as this can be, it is helpful to accept it as fact. Both parties should try to be clear and direct about their needs to their partner, friend, or family member and both should be candid in return about what they can and cannot provide. Try not to turn to people for something you know they cannot provide. Look for other sources of support. Trust that when the situation is more stable, the discoveries you have made regarding problems of fit can be discussed and that incremental changes in preferred directions can be made.

Societal Consequences of Common Shock

In a calm moment of reflection, ask yourself the following question: Has violence, retaliation, or revenge ever produced lasting peace and harmony in families, communities, or nations at any time or in any place in history?

Suggestions for Parents

These suggestions cannot cover all circumstances and will not be appropriate for all ages. They are meant to stimulate your own thoughts about how to assist a particular child in the particular circumstance you and your child are in.

1. The first task is to remember that you are your child's primary resource. Your child will be attuned to your feelings at a nonverbal as well as a verbal level. As best as you are able, try to achieve some measure of physical calm. Use the suggestions in the sections above to assist you with this. At all times monitor your own state of arousal as well as your child's. Use whatever physical means is age appropriate and acceptable to your child to induce physical calm, be it a hug or a light touch on the arm. If either you or your child is becoming more aroused as you try one of these suggestions, pause and slow down or stop what you are doing.
2. Like you, your child needs to feel safe above all else. Assuming that your child is now safe, reassure your child that this is so.

a. Help your child communicate what he has witnessed and what has been disturbing. In some situations accurate detail is important, but between parent and child, usually, you don't want to interrupt the flow of your child's speaking; and you are trying to listen for the overall sense of his experience, not grill him for accuracy. Remember that memory can be altered under extreme emotional arousal.
b. If your child can talk, let him tell you as often as he wishes about what he has witnessed, and in whatever medium works best: words, drawings, puppet play, or gestures. Older children may want to write in a journal.
c. Help your child recognize the physical signs or feelings that let him know he feels upset, unsafe, frightened, or angry. For example: What do you notice about how your body feels when you are frightened (unsafe, upset, etc.)?
d. Help your child identify what reduces the physical or emotional feelings of distress. For example: How does your body feel when you feel safe and comfortable? What kinds of things make you feel this way? Let's try a few things to see which ones work now. I'll make a list so that we have them for the future.

3. Establishing routines is essential to helping restore a child's biological and psychological integrity. Sleep is particularly vulnerable to disturbances and it is especially important to reestablish good sleep habits. Try to provide nutritious meals as well. This is a good time to help your child learn the foods he considers comfort foods. Make this a game. Is spinach a comfort food? Is ketchup a comfort food? What about applesauce? A young child might be able to identify two, and older children might be able to identify five or six comfort foods.
4. Your child may have many thoughts on her mind that are disturbing to her, and many questions. Try to be patient if she seems aloof. Let her know that you are there for her to talk about whatever she wants to discuss or ask. Depending on your child, you could gently probe. For example, what do you think about the most? What would you like to be thinking about? How can we help you turn the channel to the "station" you want to hear?
5. Conversely, if your child is badgering you with questions, be as patient as you possibly can. If it gets too much for you, enlist allies to help you with the child's questions. At some point you may want to say something like "I keep having lots of thoughts in my head about this, too, but I know that they will go away soon."

6. If your child feels helpless, think of one small action that she can take, symbolic or actual, that can make her feel less helpless.
7. Sometimes children blame themselves for aspects of situations they have witnessed. Your child may directly let you know this, or you may infer that this is the case. If you think this is happening, you can say, "What kinds of names are you calling yourself? What kinds of talk do you hear inside your head about you? Are they the kinds of names and is it the kind of talk you want to hear? If not, what might you prefer to be hearing?"
8. Children's emotions vary widely. Expressing emotions in a constructive way is helpful, even though it may be hard on parents to hear what our children feel. Parents can help young children manage the intensity of their feelings by being a container for them. Letting children know that nothing they think or feel is too difficult for you to hear is a great gift. Then, if it *is* overwhelming, share your feelings with someone else. You may need support to support your child.
9. Older children may be ambivalent about turning to parents rather than peers. Still, it is important to stay available, even if you feel rebuffed. Providing opportunities for adolescents to get together in guided discussion with adults in the community is a good strategy. Schools, churches, even sport teams can do this.
10. If possible, avoid lengthy separations from your child. Your reliable presence will be soothing. At the same time, you cannot always meet your child's needs, especially if he is more demanding than usual. Try to take responsibility for your own limits. You can try saying something like this: "I know you need me now, and I wish I could be here for you, but I am just too tired now. If I rest for a while, I will be able to give you my attention when I feel better."
11. Provide as much physical comfort as your child will permit. Hugging heals!
12. Assume that your child's behavior will regress. Be patient. Don't let your reaction to the regressed behavior—aggression, clinginess, whininess—make it even worse for both of you. Have faith that it will pass.
13. Build on your child's resources. When the time is appropriate, access his humor; provide age-appropriate responsibility and give positive feedback for success; support your child's efforts at making meaning of the experience. If spirituality is a source of comfort to your child, support this. Help your child to connect to other supportive adults.

14. One of the most challenging tasks for parents is how to balance protecting their children from their own distress without pulling out of an authentic relationship with them. While it is essential not to overwhelm your child with your own feelings, it is also crucial that your child know that you are fully present and not feel disconnected from you. Sharing your feelings in a way that helps your child feel connected to you is helpful.

Appendix Two

Witnessing Exercise

This is an exercise in which you can return to an event that was distressing and redo the outcome by changing how you behaved at the time. It is essential that you choose an event that is of low to moderate intensity or discomfort for you, since this is a self-guided exercise. Should you feel very upset as you return to the memory of the event or incident, stop. Either select another incident and try again or wait for another day to try the less intense distressing incident. Read the instructions all the way through once before starting at the beginning with step 1.

1. Think of one moment during an incident in which you witnessed something you did not want to see or hear. This may be a situation that arose between a person who was intentionally hurtful to someone else or a situation in which something happened to another person that was upsetting to watch. Or you may choose a moment in which you are the person to whom something happened, who was both a witness and a victim, as it were.
2. Let yourself reenter the scene. Where are you? Inside or outside? What do the surroundings look like? What do you see from where you are? How old are you? What are you doing? Are you sitting, standing, or lying down? What can you hear? What is the temperature? Are there any smells? What are you wearing? What are others in the scene doing? What are the expressions on their faces? If you could see your own expression what would you see?

3. Breathe regularly as you re-view the moment. On the in-breath, breathe in what you see or hear. On the out-breath, breathe out what you wish had been present at that moment, for instance, calm or caring or peacefulness. Do this for a few minutes until you feel calmer about what you are re-viewing.
4. Imagine yourself now, with all your abilities, resources, and gifts. Get a clear image of that self. Now imagine that this self is going to accompany you, in some way, to reenter the scene or situation.

If there was a person or persons who were perpetrators of harm, imagine that that they are no longer in the scene. If there was an event, like an accident, imagine that it is now over. Imagine that you can reenter the scene safely.

5. You can reenter the scene in at least one of four ways.
   a. You can use your current self to inform the actions, attitude, or intention of your younger self;
   b. You can use your current self to enter the scene and be present as a coach to your younger self, supporting and guiding your younger self's actions, attitude, or intention.
   c. You can use your current self to reenter the scene and be present in the scene as witness.
   d. You can bring another person into the scene with you as a supportive presence and compassionate witness to you.
6. Select the focus of your witnessing. Remember, you cannot make an incident not happen, but you can bring a new response to the incident.
7. Before you reenter the scene, think about what you want to do in the scene. Imagine what you are going to do. Or imagine how you want to be. To make it vivid, think about how old you are, where you are, indoors or outside. What do the surroundings look like? What can you see from where you are? Are you sitting or standing or lying down? What can you hear? Are there any smells? What are the others in the scene doing? What are the expressions on their faces? If you could see your own expression, what would you see?
8. Now see yourself, alone or with your companion, doing or being the way you want to be as a witness to the events in the incident. Watch the effects of your actions. What happens? What difference does it make? Now leave the scene. Reenter the present moment.

9. Now imagine telling someone you trust what you have just done. Tell this as if it has really happened. That is, tell the story of your original witnessing and then the story of what you did when you reentered the scene. Tell both with as much detail as you can. Notice the shift between the two kinds of witnessing experiences.
10. Debriefing. You may want to debrief this experience by yourself, thinking about it, walking around inside the new memory, writing about it, drawing or dancing it, or you may want to debrief with another person. Only share what feels comfortable to you to share.

Notes

Part One: What Is the Matter?

1. Hatley, J. *Suffering Witness: The Quandary of Responsibility After the Irreparable* (Albany: State University of New York Press, 2000), 3.

Chapter One: A Thousand Natural Shocks

1. The World Health Organization (WHO) defines violence as: "The intentional use of physical force or power, threatened or actual, against oneself, another person, or against a group or community, that either results in or has a high likelihood of resulting in injury, death, psychological harm, maldevelopment or deprivation." E. G. Krug et al., *World Report on Violence and Health, 5* (Geneva: World Health Organization, 2002).
2. See W. M. Byrd and L. A. Clayton, *An American Health Dilemma*, V. 2: *Race, Medicine, and Health Care in the United States 1900–2000* (New York: Routledge, 2002) for a comprehensive analysis of how racism affects health outcomes and participation in medicine for African-Americans. This is an example of structure violence.
3. J. Galtung, "Violence, Peace, and Peace Research," *Journal of Peace Research* 3 (1969), 171.
4. G. Becker, *Disrupted Lives: How People Create Meaning in a Chaotic World* (Berkeley: University of California Press, 1997).
5. N. Scheper-Hughes, "Peacetime Crime and the Violence of Everyday Life," *Ideas* 9 (1)(2002), 56–59.

6. E.G. Krug et al., *World Report on Violence and Health* (Geneva: World Health Organization, 2002).
7. See S.L. Buka et al., "Youth Exposure to Violence: Prevalence, Risks, and Consequences," *American Journal of Orthopsychiatry* 71 (3)(2001), 298–310, and M.B. Selner-O'Hagan et al., "Assessing Exposure to Violence in Urban Youth," *Journal of Child Psychology and Psychiatry and Allied Disciplines* 39(2) (1998), 215–224, for an excellent review of effects of witnessing violence on children and youth and a comprehensive discussion of measurement dilemmas regarding the assessment of witnessing violence. Work coming out of the Project on Human Development in Chicago Neighborhoods (PHDCN) is refining an instrument to assess effects of exposure to violence on child development. One continuing problem is that the concept of witnessing itself does not get separated out from the experience of being a victim or perpetrator of violence. For instance, in a 1996 guide for pediatricians on bullying, bullies and victims are discussed, but not witnesses. See C. Garrity and M.A. Baris, "Bullies and Victims; A Guide for Pediatricians," *Contemporary Pediatrics* (1996), 90. In an excellent review article on children's witnessing of adult domestic violence, Edleson draws distinctions about witnessing that are key, but which so far have gone untested in the literature. He rightly points out that the definition of witnessing violence must include seeing, hearing, or being used as part of it. See J.L. Edleson, "Children's Witnessing of Adult Domestic Violence," *Journal of Interpersonal* Violence 14 (8)(1999), 839–870.
8. B.J. Bushman and C.A. Anderson, "Media Violence and the American Public. Scientific Facts versus Media Misinformation," *American Psychologist* 56(6–7) (2001), 477–489. Media provide one of the major ways we witness acts of violence and violation. There are over 250 million television sets in use today in the United States alone (*http://www.techneglas.com/web2/whatnew/FAO.htm*): three out of four U.S. residents see at least one movie per year (*http://ww.mpaa.org/jack/2000/00 03 07.htm*): and Americans spend over $1.5 billion on video games (*http://www.njla.org/trivia.html*). There is clear scientific evidence from multiple kinds of quantitative and qualitative analyses that exposure to media violence, in the form of television, film, or video games, correlates with increases in aggressive behavior for children, adolescents, and adults (C.A. Anderson and B.J. Bushman, "The Effects of Media Violence on Society," *Science*, 295 [March 29, 2002], 2377). The associations are moderate, but if compared to other associations whose relationships we place confidence in, for instance the association between smoking and lung cancer, or the one between condom use and preventing the spread of STDs, this link falls in between in effect-size. Researchers lament that while good scientific evidence has accumulated over the decades of a link between media violence and aggressive behavior, and in 2000 six major professional societies signed a joint statement on the negative consequences of exposing children to media violence (Bushman and Anderson, 2001), news reports

have gotten weaker over time, suggesting that there is less to be concerned about than scientists believe the data show. Increasingly, scientists are scrutinizing the news media, asking why they deny the strong links between exposure to media violence and aggression. Some factors that have been mentioned are: economic interests (rock star Marilyn Manson was interviewed on NPR, October 12, 2002 and suggested that media cultivate fear to increase consumption of the products they advertise); a fairness doctrine, by which a minority opinion is overrepresented; and the failure of the scientific community to argue their case persuasively.

Yet another argument that has been proposed is that media believe that they are reflecting the level of violence that exists in the society. Film critic Michael Medved (quoted in Bushman and Anderson, 2001, 479) plays out this argument statistically: "If this were true, then why do so few people witness murders in real life but everybody sees them on TV and in the movies? The most violent ghetto isn't in South Central L.A. or Southeast Washington, D.C.; it's on television. About 350 characters appear each night on prime-time TV, but studies show an average of seven of these are murdered every night. If this rate applied in reality, then in just fifty days everyone in the United States would be killed and the last left could turn off the TV."

While we are regularly told that media exposure is linked to increases in aggressive behavior, there is less discussion of the dynamics of witnessing per se that are involved in viewing media violence. Lieutenant Colonel Dave Grossman, a former army ranger and paratrooper and currently a professor of military science at Arkansas State University, proposes that television, film, and video games apply military techniques that are used to overcome soldiers' resistance to kill in their programming. He believes that these techniques—classical conditioning, operant conditioning, and social learning and role models—work to desensitize a civilian population to killing without any of the safeguards that are in place in the military, such as killing only upon command and with considerable training to distinguish who is and who is not an appropriate target (Grossman, D. *On killing: The Psychological Cost of Learning to Kill in War and Society* [Boston: Little Brown, 1996]).

The lively debate about whether exposure to violent media is associated with aggressive behavior or, a new concern, whether television exposure to replays of terror attacks contributes to PTSD symptoms (W. E. Schlenger et al., "Psychological Reactions to Terrorist Attacks: Findings from the National Study of Americans' Reactions to September 11." *JAMA* 288[5] 2002, 581–588) is important and unlikely to go away. [Heins, M., and J. Cantor, *Violence and the Media: An Exploration of Cause, Éffect and First Amendment* (Nashville: First Amendment Center, 2001). *http://www.thefirstamendment.org/amicus%20briefs/aamaamicus.html*)

As I sift through the voluminous research and analyses in this area I am struck that I can find no discussion of possible effects of how particular content creates different witnessing positions for the viewer with regard to what they are seeing. For instance, if the viewer is left feeling helpless, does this have a different effect on subsequent behavior than if the viewer concludes her viewing feeling that justice has been served? I hope that by thinking about different witnessing positions and different qualities of witnessing, we may be able to refine studies and enter into a fruitful area of investigation. At the moment, unfortunately, the debate on the effects of media violence on aggression seems deadlocked. We need interdisciplinary fora and generative dialogue to address the pressing questions that witnessing media violence pose, questions that become even more urgent as the everyday violence that constitutes not just daily crime but also international conflict are brought into homes all over the world.

9. See S. Galea et al., "Psychological Sequelae of the September 11 Terrorist Attacks in New York City," *New England Journal of Medicine* 346(13) (2002), 982–987; B. A. van der Kolk, "Trauma and PTSD: Aftermaths of the WTC Disaster." *Medscape Mental Health*, 6 (5)(2001); Retrieved March, 2003 from the Web: *http://www.traumacenter.org/bvdk_interview.htm*; R. Yehuda, "Posttraumatic Stress Disorder," *New England Journal of Medicine*, 346(2) (2002), 108–114, and R. Yehuda et al., "Predicting the Development of Posttraumatic Stress Disorder from the Acute Response to a Traumatic Event," *Biological Psychiatry*, 44 (12)(1998) 1305–1313.
10. E.J. Nightingale, "APA Appoints Task Force to Coordinate and Address Trauma Issues," *Traumatic Stress Points* (Spring 2001), 7, *www.istss.org* and M.P.P. Root, "Reconstructing the Impact of Trauma on Personality," in (Ed.), L. S. Brown and M. Ballou, *Personality and Psychopathology: Feminist Reappraisals*, (New York: Guilford Press, 1992), 229–265.
11. M. B. Lykes, "Meaning Making in a Context of Genocide and Silencing." In M. B. Lykes et. al, (Ed.), *Myths About the Powerless: Contesting Social Inequalities* (Philadelphia: Temple University Press; 1996), 159–178. A. Kleinman, "Violence, Culture, and the Politics of Trauma." In A. Kleinman (Ed.), *Writing at the Margin: Discourse Between Anthropology and Medicine* (Berkeley: University of California Press, 1995), 173–192.
12. A. Kleinman, "Violence, Culture, and the Politics of Trauma." In A. Kleinman (Ed.), *Writing at the Margin: Discourse Between Anthropology and Medicine* (Berkeley: University of California Press, 1995), 173–192 and M. B. Pipher, *The Middle of Everywhere: the World's Refugees Come to Our Town*, 1st ed. (New York: Harcourt, 2002).
13. Elmarie Kotzé, personal communication, February, 2002.
14. A. Mutler, June 12, 2001. "Romanians Mesmerized by Toddler Who Fell Down a Well." Associated Press Newswires.
15. J. G. Silverman et al., "Dating Violence Against Adolescent Girls and Associated Substance Use, Unhealthy Weight Control, Sexual Risk Behavior, Pregnancy, and Suicidality," *JAMA* 286 (5)(2001), 572–579.
16. According to large-scale-survey research, 25 percent of women will experience this kind of intimate partner violence at some point in their lifetimes.

This number is startling in and of itself, but the way the number is expressed—25 percent of women—obscures the very phenomenon it represents. Men experience it too, only they are the perpetrators of the experience! Further, these women, as well as the people who know them, experience the aftermath, continuously or intermittently, for years. See J. G. Silverman et al., "Dating Violence Against Adolescent Girls and Associated Substance Use, Unhealthy Weight Control, Sexual Risk Behavior, Pregnancy, and Suicidality." *JAMA*, 286 (5) (2001), 572–579. In another study, based on data from 710 girls ages 14–17, researchers found that girls who experienced or were exposed to domestic violence were three times more likely to engage in risky sexual behavior. Witnessing violence had nearly as profound an effect on the young girls as being victimized did. G. Elliot et al., "The Encounter with Family Violence and Risky Sexual Activity Among Young Adolescent Females." *Journal of Violence and Victims*, 17 (5) (2002), 569–592.

17. The Surgeon General's report on youth violence in the same time period as the *JAMA* article contains the startling statistic that 15 to 30 percent of female youths report having committed a serious violent offense at some point in their lives by age seventeen and that male youths report a prevalence of serious violence by age seventeen of about 30 to 40 percent. It seems entirely plausible that the effects of experiencing and witnessing intimate partner violence stimulate some of this serious violent crime, much of it considered public violence. See Surgeon General, U.S. "The Magnitude of Youth Violence: A Report of the Surgeon General." Retrieved August 2, 2001 from the Web: *http://www.surgeongeneral.gov/library/youthviolence/chapter2/sec1.html*
18. This statement is generally true. Obviously, though, no one has found a way to measure suffering, and comparing suffering is not usually productive. Further, I have worked with many families in which members would agree that the witness to family violence suffered more than the victim, either in the short or long run.
19. See A. G. Miller, "Constructions of the Obedience Experiments: A Focus upon Domains of Relevance," *Journal of Social Issues*, 51 (3) (1995), 33–53 and A. G. Miller et al., "Perspective on obedience to authority: The Legacy of the Milgram Experiments," *Journal of Social Issues*, 51 (3) (1995), 1–19.
20. It has had a "towering impact" precisely because of the "sobering social issues" the study raises. See A. G. Miller et al., "Perspectives on Obedience to Authority: The Legacy of the Milgram Experiments," *Journal of Social Issues* 51 (3) (1995), 1–19.
21. M. L. Hoffman, *Empathy and Moral Development: Implications for Caring and Justice* (Cambridge, UK; New York: Cambridge University Press, 2000).
22. See M. C. Nussbaum, *Upheavals of Thought: The Intelligence of Emotions.* (Cambridge, UK; New York: Cambridge University Press, 2001.), for her discussion of empathy and its relation to compassion.

23. Garbarino, J. "The Effects of Community Violence of Children." In L. Balter and C. S. Tamis-LeMonda (Eds.), *Child Psychology: A Handbook of Contemporary Issues*, (Philadelphia: Psychology Press/Taylor & Francis, 1999), 412–425.
24. However desirable an empathic bridge may be, there are also pitfalls in creating one. It is crucial that in using our own experience to understand the experience of another that we do not erase or diminish difference. If we lose sight of difference, empathy degenerates into misunderstanding; we distort the empathic bridge with "leveling comparison." See D. LaCapra, *Representing the Holocaust: History, Theory, Trauma* (Ithaca: Cornell University Press, 1994), and K. Oliver, *Witnessing: Beyond Recognition* (Minneapolis: University of Minnesota Press, 2001).
25. I have worked in Kosovo under the auspices of the Kosovar Family Professional Educational Collaborative (KFPEC). The KFPEC is a partnership between the University of Prishtina School of Medicine and the American Family Therapy Academy (AFTA); the Center on Genocide, Psychiatry, and Witnessing at the University of Illinois at Chicago; the University of Chicago–affiliated Chicago Center for Family Health; and the International Trauma Studies Program of New York University. The KFPEC has sought to counter the effects of genocide and ethnic culturecide by strengthening protective family processes. Rather than provide direct mental-health services, it has bolstered the clinical competence of Kosovar mental-health professionals in conducting family-centered, community-based, resilience-focused consultations and therapies. This partnership seeks to build a Kosovar mental health system with the family as the key unit for mental health treatment.

    Kosovo is a land approximately the size of Kentucky with 1.8 million people, of whom 95 percent are Kosovar Albanian and 5 percent are Serbian in ethnicity. A 1999 study by the Centers for Disease Control and Prevention found that 62 percent of Albanian Kosovars had near encounters with death during the war, and 67 percent were at some point deprived of food and water. Eighty-two percent fled their homes, most to other countries, and over half witnessed murders or knew someone who was killed. These statistics came alive for me in virtually every interview I had during my two visits. B. L. Cardozo et al., "Mental Health, Social Functioning, and Attitudes of Kosovar Albanians Following the War in Kosovo." JAMA 284 (5) 2000, 569–577.
26. A vast number of people we met also had exposure to severe victimization and would certainly have met criteria for a diagnosis of trauma.
27. W. Shakespeare, and S. L. Wofford, *Hamlet: Complete, Authoritative Text with Biographical and Historical Contexts, Critical History, and Essays from Five Contemporary Critical Perspectives* (Boston: Bedford Books, 1994), lines 61–62.

Chapter Two: The Varieties of Witnessing Experience

1. T. Nhât Hanh, *The Witness Remains, Call Me by My True Names: The Collected Poems of Thich Nhât Hanh* (Berkeley: Parallax Press, 1999), 26.
2. B. MacQuarrie and M.R. Merrill, "Board Is Silent on Harassment Case Specifics: Lawyer Details Schoolgirl's Complaint," *The Boston Globe*, May 18, 2000, B1, B4.
3. N.D. Stein, *Classrooms and Courtrooms: Facing Sexual Harassment in K-12 Schools* (New York: Teachers College Press, 1999).
4. B. MacQuarrie and M.R. Merrill, "Board Is Silent on Harassment Case Specifics: Lawyer Details Schoolgirl's Complaint," *The Boston Globe*, May 18, 2000, B1, B4.
5. N.D. Stein, *Classrooms and Courtrooms: Facing Sexual Harassment in K-12 Schools* (New York: Teachers College Press, 1999).
6. Oftentimes the role of witness is not even acknowledged. In an article addressed to pediatricians to help them work with the problem of bullying, there is no mention of witnesses to bullying, which may be the most prevalent experience for children and youth. See C. Garrity and M.A. Baris, "Bullies and Victims: A Guide for Pediatricians," *Contemporary Pediatrics*, (February, 1996), 90.
7. For many people God is the witness, who sees, knows, and understands all. See J.L. Griffith and M.E. Griffith, *Encountering the Sacred in Psychotherapy: How to Talk with People About Their Spiritual Lives* (New York: Guilford Press, 2002).
8. There is less agreement among researchers about how to define witnessing than there is about how to define victimization. Because definitions of witnessing vary considerably, this means that findings about witnessing sometimes actually include what other researchers or clinicians, myself included, would consider victimization. One comprehensive review article on witnessing community violence that excluded studies that used definitions that would include data on victimization comes from the Project on Human Development in Chicago Neighborhoods (PHDCN). They found
   1. high rates of witnessing violence for urban youth; incomplete data for rural youth, but data suggestive of rates that were comparable to urban youth;
   2. fewer gender differences during early childhood, with increased rates of witnessing violence for males as children get older;
   3. clear links of poverty with rates of exposure to violence;
   4. increased risk of psychological, academic, social, and physical difficulties as well as an increased risk for committing violent acts themselves for youth exposed to high levels of violence.

   S.L. Buka et al., "Youth Exposure to Violence: Prevalence, Risks, and Consequences," *American Journal of Orthopsychiatry* 71 (3)(2001), 298–310.

For a review of children witnessing domestic violence see J. L. Edleson, "Children's Witnessing of Adult Domestic Violence," *Journal of Interpersonal Violence* 14 (8)(August 1999), 839–870.

9. Root, M.P.P. "Reconstructing the Impact of Trauma on Personality." In L. S. Brown and M. Ballou, (Eds.), *Personality and Psychopathology: Feminist Reappraisals* (New York: Guilford Press, 1992), 229–265.
10. For a definitive account of racism in the American health-care system, see W. M. Byrd and L. A. Clayton, *An American Health Dilemma*, V. 2: *Race, Medicine, and Health Care in the United States, 1900–2000* (New York: Routledge, 2002).
11. J. Gilligan, *Violence: Reflections on a National Epidemic* (New York: Vintage Books, 1997), 3.
12. Akhet Egyptology. April 28, 2002. Osiris and Isis. Akhet Egyptology. Retrieved, 2002, from the Web: *http://www.akhet.co.uk/isisosir.htm* and "The Gods of Egypt." *Theosophy*, 15(8) (1927), 353–360.
13. Deena Metzger, personal communication, Rowe, MA, 16–18, March 2001.
14. M.P.P. Root, "Reconstructing the Impact of Trauma on Personality," in L. S. Brown and M. Ballou, (Eds.), *Personality and Psychopathology: Feminist Reappraisals* (New York: Guilford Press, 1992), 242–246.
15. For an earlier version of this schema, see K. Weingarten, "Witnessing, Wonder, and Hope," *Family Process* 39 (4)(2000), 389–402.
16. S. Sontag, *Illness as Metaphor* (New York: Farrar, Straus & Giroux, 1978). For a multicultural perspective on truth telling and the end of life, see L. M. Candib, "Truth Telling and Advance Planning at the End of Life: Problems with Autonomy in a Multicultural World," *Families, Systems and Health* 20 (3)(2002), 213–228.
17. To send a story of your own to the witnessing archive, contact the archive at the Witnessing Project, Family Institute of Cambridge, 51 Kondazian Street, Watertown, MA 02459 or *www.witnessingproject.org*.
18. N. Mandela, *Long Walk to Freedom: The Autobiography of Nelson Mandela* (Boston: Little Brown, 1994).
19. N. Mandela, *Long Walk to Freedom: The Autobiography of Nelson Mandela* (Boston: Little Brown, 1994), 544.
20. N. Mandela, *Long Walk to Freedom: The Autobiography of Nelson Mandela* (Boston: Little Brown, 1994), 545.
21. P. Green, "Teaching Non-Violence in a Violence Addicted World," *Re-Vision: A Journal of Consciousness and Transformation* 20 (2)(1997), 43–46.
22. The following section draws on ideas from a number of sources. They are: B. Latané et al., *The Unresponsive Bystander: Why Doesn't He Help?* (New York: Appleton-Century Crofts, 1970); D. Olweus, *Bullying at School: What We Know and What We Can Do* (Oxford, UK; Cambridge, MA: Blackwell, 1993); F. Rochat and A. Modigliani, "The Ordinary Quality of Resistance: From Milgram's Laboratory to the Village of Le Cham-

bon," *Journal of Social Issues* 51 (3)(1995), 195–210; E. Staub, "The Psychology of Perpetrators and Bystanders," *Political Psychology* 6 (1)(1985), 61–85; E. Staub, "The Evolution of Bystanders, German Psychoanalysts, and Lessons for Today," *Political Psychology* 10 (1)(1989), 39–52; E. Staub, *The Roots of Evil: The Origins of Genocide and Other Group Violence* (Cambridge, UK: Cambridge University Press, 1989).

23. R. E. Cramer et al., "Subject Competence and Minimization of the Bystander Effect," *Journal of Applied Social Psychology* 18 (13)(1988), 1133–1148.
24. P. P. Hallie, *Lest Innocent Blood Be Shed: The Story of the Village of Le Chambon, and How Goodness Happened There*, (1st ed.) (New York: Harper & Row, 1979); F. Rochat and A. Modigliani, "The Ordinary Quality of Resistance: From Milgram's Laboratory to the Village of Le Chambon," *Journal of Social Issues* 51 (3)(1995), 195–210; and E. Staub, *The Roots of Evil: The Origins of Genocide and Other Group Violence* (Cambridge, UK; Cambridge University Press, 1989).
25. S. T. Shepela et al., "Courageous Resistance: A Special Case of Altruism," *Theory and Psychology* 9 (6)(1999), 787–805.
26. S. L. Bloom and M. Reichert, *Bearing Witness: Violence and Collective Responsibility* (New York: Haworth Maltreatment and Trauma Press, 1998); B. Latané et al., *The Unresponsive Bystander: Why Doesn't He Help?* (New York: Appleton-Century Crofts, 1970); F. Rochat and A. Modigliani, "The Ordinary Quality of Resistance: From Milgram's Laboratory to the Village of Le Chambon," *Journal of Social Issues* 51 (3)(1995), 195–210; E. Staub, *The Roots of Evil: The Origins of Genocide and Other Group Violence* (Cambridge, UK; New York: Cambridge University Press, 1989).
27. A. Wade, "Small Acts of Living: Everyday Resistance to Violence and Other Forms of Oppression," *Contemporary Family Therapy* 19 (1)(1997), 23–29; K. Weingarten, "The Small and the Ordinary: The Daily Practice of a Postmodern Narrative Therapy," *Family Process* 37 (3)(1998), 3–15.
28. For a discussion of four types of bully bystanders—"puppet masters," victim bystanders, avoidant bystanders, and ambivalent bystanders—see S. W. Twemlow et al., "An Innovative Psychodynamically Influenced Approach to Reduce School Violence," *Journal of the American Academy of Child and Adolescent Psychiatry* 40 (3)(2001), 377–379.
29. D. Olweus, *Bullying at School: What We Know and What We Can Do.* (Oxford, UK; Cambridge, MA: Blackwell, 1993); N. D. Stein, *Bullyproof: A Teacher's Guide on Teasing and Bullying for Use with Fourth and Fifth Grade Students* (Wellesley Center for Research on Women, 1996); Dulwich Centre Journal, *Taking the Hassle Out of School and Stories from Younger People* nos. 2 & 3, (Adelaide, Australia: Dulwich Centre Publications, 1998).
30. B. Latané et al., *The Unresponsive Bystander: Why Doesn't He Help?* (New York: Appleton-Century Crofts, 1970). This book describes numerous

negative constraints on helping in a group. First, we may fear that if we suggest a helpful action, we will not be supported but instead be ignored or judged. Second, once we are in a group, our sense of responsibility for taking-action diffuses. We may look toward others to observe what they are doing and if they are not acting, we may downgrade our sense that action is urgently required. Finally, if we are with a group and action is delayed, intervention is less likely. Inertia sets in. Not seeing others act may prompt a reconsideration of our belief that we should have acted as misguided, unfounded, foolish, or unwise. Knowing these constraints can help us deal more effectively with them.

Chapter Three: Consequences of Common Shock

1. S. Galea et al., "Psychological Sequelae of the September 11 Terrorist Attacks in New York City." *New England Journal of Medicine* 346 (13)(2002), 982–987; W.E. Schlenger et al., "Psychological Reactions to Terrorist Attacks: Findings from the National Study of Americans' Reactions to September 11," *JAMA*, 288 (5)(2002), 581–588; van der Kolk, B.A. 2001. Trauma and PTSD: Aftermaths of the WTC Disaster. Medscape Mental Health, 6 (5)(2001), retrieved March, 2003 from the Web: http://www.traumacenter.org/bvak_interview.htm
2. Judith Herman asserts that "Witnesses as well as victims are subject to the dialectic of trauma." J.L. Herman, *Trauma and Recovery* (New York, N.Y.: BasicBooks, 1992), 2.
3. D. Remnick, "From Our Correspondents: September 11, 2001," *The New Yorker*, September 24, 2001, 58.
4. E. Goode, "Stress from Attacks Will Chase Some into the Depths of Their Minds, and Stay," *The New York Times*, September 18, 2001, 1.
5. B.A. van der Kolk, Trauma and PTSD: Aftermaths of the WTC Disaster. Medscape Mental Health, 6 (5)(2001) retrieved March, 2003 from the Web:*http://www.traumacenter.org/bvdk_interview.htm*
6. The biological experience of common shock falls into a range of categories that researchers distinguish from one another, although there is not necessarily agreement about how to do this: shock, a stress response (R.S. Lazarus and S. Folkman, *Stress, Appraisal, and Coping* [New York: Springer Pub. Co. 1984]); a trauma response (P. Levin, "The Trauma Response," David Baldwin's Trauma Information Pages, 1989. Retrieved 08/07/2001, from the Web:*http://www.trauma-pages.com/t-facts.htm*): an acute stress disorder (American Psychiatric Association, *Diagnostic and Statistical Manual of Mental Disorders* [4th Edition] [Washington, D.C., 1994]); and acute or chronic posttraumatic stress disorder. American Psychiatric Association, *Diagnostic and Statistical Manual of Mental Disor-*

ders [4th Edition] [Washington, D.C., 1994]). Throughout this chapter and book, I will be explicit about which of these I am discussing, since in a fine-grain analysis of their biology or psychology there are significant differences among them.

7. R.S. Lazarus and S. Folkman, *Stress, Appraisal, and Coping* (New York: Springer Pub. Co., 1984).
8. Mid-range responses might be designated as a trauma response (see P. Levin, 1989, "The Trauma Response." David Baldwin's Trauma Information Pages. Retrieved 08/07/2001, from the Web: *http://www.traumapages.com/t-facts.htm*) or an acute stress disorder (American Psychiatric Association, *Diagnostic and Statistical Manual of Mental Disorders* [4th Edition] [Washington, D.C., 1994]).
9. American Psychiatric Association, *Diagnostic and Statistical Manual of Mental Disorder (4th Edition)* (Washington, D.C., 1994); R. Yehuda, "Post-traumatic Stress Disorder," *New England Journal of Medicine* 346 (2)(2002), 108–114.
10. J. Kabat-Zinn, *Full Catastrophe Living: Using the Wisdom of Your Body and Mind to Face Stress, Pain, and Illness* (New York: Delacorte Press, 1990) and B. Rothschild, *The Body Remembers: The Psychophysiology of Trauma and Trauma Treatment* (New York: Norton, 2000).
11. J.L. Herman, *Trauma and Recovery* (New York: BasicBooks, 1992); and M.P.P. Root, "Reconstructing the Impact of Trauma on Personality." In L.S. Brown and M. Ballou (Eds.), *Personality and Psychopathology: Feminist Reappraisals* (New York: Guilford Press, 1992), 229–265.
12. In general, those who will develop a trauma response from less direct exposure, say reading an account versus seeing or hearing, are those who are already sensitized, and have experienced a trauma response before. In relation to child witnesses to domestic violence, for instance, researchers contend that all the ways that children witness it—seeing, hearing, being used in it, and experiencing the aftermath—pose a risk of trauma to children. See J.L. Edleson, "Children's Witnessing of Adult Domestic Violence," *Journal of Interpersonal Violence* 14 (8)(1999), 839–870.
13. E. Fox et al., "Do Threatening Stimuli Draw or Hold Visual Attention in Subclinical Anxiety?" *Journal of Experimental Psychology: General* 130 (4)(2001), 681–700; and W.E. Schlenger et al., "Psychological Reactions to Terrorist Attacks: Findings from the National Study of Americans' Reactions to September 11," *JAMA*, 288 (5)(2001), 581–588.
14. C.A.I. Morgan "Startle Response in Individuals with PTSD." *NCP Clinical Quarterly*, 7 (4)(1997), 65, 67–69.
15. American Psychiatric Association, *Diagnostic and Statistical Manual of Mental Disorders* (4th Edition) (Washington, D.C., 1994).
16. S. Galea et al., "Psychological Sequelae of the September 11 Terrorist Attacks in New York City," *New England Journal of Medicine*, 346 (13)(2002), 982–987; van der Kolk, B.A. "Trauma and PTSD: Aftermaths of the WTC Disaster," *Medscape Mental Health*, 6 (5)(2001),

retrieved March 2003 from the Web: http://www.traumacenter.org/ bvdk_interview.htm.; and R. Yehuda, "Posttraumatic Stress Disorder," *New England Journal of Medicine*, 346 (2)(2002), 108–114.

17. J. G. Allen, *Traumatic Relationships and Serious Mental Disorders* (Chichester: John Wiley & Sons, 2001), citing Krystal, 1989.
18. J. G. Allen, *Traumatic Relationships and Serious Mental Disorders* (Chichester: John Wiley & Sons, 2001), 142.
19. P. A. Levine, *Waking the Tiger: Healing Trauma: The Innate Capacity to Transform Overwhelming Experiences* (Berkeley: North Atlantic Books, 1997).
20. There are still further alterations in the brain. Stress-induced changes in the body's dopaminergic system, a set of nerve pathways that regulate a number of neurological functions, decrease its tone, possibly contributing to the emotional flatness and depression associated with trauma.
21. B. A. van der Kolk, "Biological Considerations About Emotions, Trauma, Memory, and the Brain," In S. L. Ablon (Ed.), *Human Feelings: Explorations in Affect Development and Meaning* (Hillsdale, NJ: Analytic Press, 1993), 221–240.
22. J. G. Allen, "Traumatic Relationships and Serious Mental Disorders (Chichester: John Wiley & Sons, 2001), 149: "Sensitization is the process by which an initial severe stressor enhances subsequent responsiveness to a stressor of similar or lesser magnitude. . . . *Extreme, repeated, and intermittent stressors are most likely to result in sensitization*, although a single stressor may also do so." (Italics in original text.)
23. It is also true that some people who are exposed to violent events and interactions do not experience them as traumatic, and rather than being sensitized seem to be desensitized. See R.J.R. Blair, "Neurocognitive Models of Aggression, the Antisocial Personality Disorders, and Psychopathy," *Journal of Neurology, Neurosurgery and Psychiatry* 71 (6)(2002), 727–731.
24. There are many excellent books on trauma, some of which specifically address the experience of witnessing violence and violation. Other excellent books on trauma do not distinguish the victim from the witness experience. The following are accessible for a general reader. J. G. Allen, *Traumatic Relationships and Serious Mental Disorders* (Chichester: John Wiley & Sons, 2001); J. L. Herman, *Trauma and Recovery* (New York: Basic Books, 1992); and P. A. Levine, *Waking the Tiger: Healing Trauma: The Innate Capacity to Transform Overwhelming Experiences* (Berkeley: North Atlantic Books, 1997).
25. A. Kleinman, "Violence, Culture, and the Politics of Trauma," In A. Kleinman (Ed.), *Writing at the Margin: Discourse Between Anthropology and Medicine* (Berkeley: University of California Press, 1995), 173–192; and J. Zur, 1996. "From PTSD to voices in context: from an experience-far to an experience-near understanding of responses to war and atrocity across cultures." *International Journal of Social Psychiatry* 42 (4)(1996), 305–317.

26. M.B. Pipher, *The Middle of Everywhere: The World's Refugees Come to Our Town*, 1st ed. (New York: Harcourt, 2002).
27. R. Janoff-Bulman, *Shattered Assumptions: Towards a New Psychology of Trauma* (New York: Free Press, 1992); and M.P.P. Root, "Reconstructing the Impact of Trauma on Personality," In L.S. Brown and M. Ballou (Eds.), *Personality and Psychopathology: Feminist Reappraisals* (New York: Guilford Press, 1992), 229–265.
28. R. Janoff-Bulman, *Shattered Assumptions:Towards a New Psychology of Trauma* (New York: Free Press, 1992); and M.P.P. Root, "Reconstructing the Impact of Trauma on Personality," In L.S. Brown and M. Ballou (Eds.), *Personality and Psychopathology: Feminist Reappraisals* (New York: Guilford Press), 243.
29. Our experience is also made more complicated when we believe we have suffered and there is no external validation of this, either by those we know or by professionals who assign diagnoses of disorders through a diagnostic manual. For instance, currently, the principle professional diagnostic manual virtually ignores race-related stressors as provocations for psychological distress. See R.M. Scurfield, "Positive and Negative Aspects of Exposure to Racism and Trauma; Research, Assessment, and Treatment Implications," *NCP Clinical Quarterly* 10 (1)(2000), 1–10; and R.M. Scurfield and D.W. Mackey, "Racism, Trauma, and Positive Aspects of Exposure to Race-Related Experiences: Assessment and Treatment Implications," *Journal of Ethnic and Cultural Diversity in Social Work* 10 (1)(2000), 23–47. A decade ago, learning about the life-threatening illness of a loved one was not included in the manual as an event that could produce a trauma response.
30. Numbing is a natural analgesic; it helps people block out pain until their arousal system is more settled and able to take on the emotional work of making sense of what has happened to them. The numbing that is experienced by people who have PTSD is probably qualitatively different. Recent work suggests that there is a biological basis to this psychic numbing in which there is a stress-induced analgesia. See B.A. van der Kolk and J. Saporta, "The Biological Response to Psychic Trauma: Mechanisms and Treatment of Intrusion and Numbing," *Anxiety Research* 4 (3)(1991), 199–212, and B.A. van der Kolk, "Trauma and PTSD: Aftermaths of the WTC Disaster," *Medscape Mental Health* 6 (5)(2001). Retrieved from the Web: http:/; shwww.traumacenter.org/bvdk_interview.htm
31. D.L. Schacter, *Searching for Memory: The Brain, the Mind, and the Past*, 1st ed. (New York: Basic Books, 1996); 42. This section on elaborative encoding is based on material in this book.
32. G.H. Bower and H. Sivers, "Cognitive Impact of Traumatic Events," *Development and Psychopathology* 10 (4)(1998), 625–653. Chronicity of exposure and degree of threat will also interfere with encoding. For work on memory and sexual victimization, see L.M. Williams, "Recovered Memories of Abuse in Women with Documented Child Sexual Victimization

Histories," *Journal of Traumatic Stress* 8 (4)(1995), 649–673; L.M. Williams, " 'Recall of Childhood Trauma: A Prospective Study of Women's Memories of Child Sexual Abuse': Correction," *Journal of Consulting and Clinical Psychology* 63 (3)(1995), 343; and L.M. Williams and V.L. Banyard, "Gender and Recall of Child Sexual Abuse: A Prospective Study," J. Read (Ed.); D. Lindsay (Ed.), *Recollections of Trauma: Scientific Evidence and Clinical Practice*, NATO ASI series: Series A: Life sciences, 291 (1997), 371–377.

33. Material in this section is based on ideas about two kinds of memory, implicit and explicit. See J.G. Allen, *Traumatic Relationships and Serious Mental Disorders* (Chichester: John Wiley & Sons, 2001); B. Rothschild, *The Body Remembers: The Psychophysiology of Trauma and Trauma Treatment* (New York: Norton, 2000); D.L. Schacter, *Searching for Memory: The Brain, the Mind, and the Past*, (1st ed.) (New York: Basic Books, 1996); D.J. Siegel, *The Developing Mind: Toward a Neurobiology of Interpersonal Experience* (New York: Guilford Press, 1999); B.A. van der Kolk, "Biological Considerations About Emotions, Trauma, Memory, and the Brain," In S.L. Ablon (Ed.), *Human Feelings: Explorations in Affect Development and Meaning*, (Hillsdale, NJ: Analytic Press, 1993), 221–240. Cahill suggests that each time a PTSD patient re-experiences an episode of intrusive memory or a flashback, this may produce a stress hormone, thus strengthening the memory. See L. Cahill, "The Neurobiology of Emotionally Influenced Memory. Implications for Understanding Traumatic Memory," In R. Yehuda and A.C. McFarlane (Eds.), *Psychobiology of Posttraumatic Stress Disorder, Annals of the New York Academy of Sciences* (New York: New York Academy of Sciences, 1997), (821), 238–246.
34. B.M. Groves, *Children Who See Too Much: Lessons from the Child Witness to Violence Project* (Boston: Beacon Press, 2002).
35. R. Fivush, "Children's Recollections of Traumatic and Nontraumatic Events," *Development and Psychopathology* 10 (4)(1998), 699–716.
36. This material is based on my clinical experience and on R. Fivush, "Children's Recollections of Traumatic and Nontraumatic Events," *Development and Psychopathology* 10 (4)(1998), 699–716. I am not endorsing that a therapist impose a storyline on a client's memories. Most professional organizations that work with issues of trauma have guidelines to help therapists work with clients to minimize memory distortion. There are also numerous books and articles that deal with this subject. See for example, L. Berliner and J. Briere, "Trauma, Memory, and Clinical Practice," In L.M. Williams and V.L. Banyard (Eds.), *Trauma and Memory* (Thousand Oaks, CA: Sage Publications, 1999), 3–18; J. Briere, *Therapy for Adults Molested as Children: Beyond Survival* (New York: Springer Pub., 1996); D.P. Brown et al., *Memory, Trauma Treatment, and the Law* (New York: W.W. Norton, 1998); and C.A. Courtois, "Guidelines for the Treatment of Adults Abused or Possibly Abused as Children (with Attention to Issues of De-

layed/Recovered Memory," *American Journal of Psychotherapy* 51 (4)(1997), 497–510. However, it is the therapist's job to help clients make sense of their experience and, if possible, to create a coherent narrative about it.

37. J. W. Pennebaker, *Opening Up: The Healing Power of Expressing Emotions* (New York: Guilford Press, 1997).
38. B. Rothschild, *The Body Remembers: The Psychophysiology of Trauma and Trauma Treatment* (New York: Norton 2000), 62.
39. A. Morris and G. Maxwell, "The Practice of Family Group Conferences in New Zealand: Assessing the Place, Potential and Pitfalls of Restorative Justice," In A. Crawford and J. Goodey (Eds.), *Integrating a Victim Perspective Within Criminal Justice: International Debates* (Aldershot, UK; Brookfield, Vt.: Ashgate Publishing, 2000). This paper reports on an innovative project in New Zealand that addresses shame in youthful offenders. As part of the restorative justice movement (see Chapter Eight), Morris and Maxwell invite youth who admit to their offense to a family group conference in which they, members of their families, the victims, and their supporters, a representative of the police, and a manager of the process are all present. The goals of the conference, among others, are to learn about the effects of the offense on the victims and to make amends to them. Maxwell and Morris report that those youth who felt that they had made amends to their victims were less likely to be reconvicted of a crime six years later than those who had felt shamed by their conviction process.
40. M. J. Lewis, *Shame: The Exposed Self* (New York: Free Press, 1995).
41. B. A. van der Kolk, "Biological Considerations About Emotions, Trauma, Memory, and the Brain," In S. L. Ablon (Ed.), *Human Feelings: Explorations in Affect Development and Meaning* (Hillsdale, NJ: Analytic Press, 1993), 221–240.
42. D. G. Dutton, "Traumatic Origins of Intimate Rage," *Aggression and Violent Behavior* 4 (4)(1999), 431–447; J. Gilligan, *Violence: Reflections on a National Epidemic* (New York: Vintage Books, 1997); B. A. van der Kolk et al., *Traumatic Stress: The Effects of Overwhelming Experience on Mind, Body, and Society* (New York: Guilford Press, 1996); R. Yehuda, "Managing Anger and Aggression in Patients with Posttraumatic Stress Disorder," *Journal of Clinical Psychiatry*, 60 (Suppl 15) (1999), 33–37.
43. See M. Cimino, *The Deer Hunter* [VHS.] (Universal City, CA: MCA Home Video, 1991); and P. Roth, *The Human Stain* (Boston: Houghton Mifflin, 2000).
44. J. Gilligan, *Violence: Reflections on a National Epidemic* (New York: Vintage Books, 1997); M. J. Lewis, *Shame: The Exposed Self* (New York: Free Press, 1995); and H. B. Lewis, *The Role of Shame in Symptom Formation* (Hillsdale, N.J.: L. Erlbaum Associates, 1987).
45. A. J. Franklin and N. Boyd-Franklin, "Invisibility Syndrome: A Clinical Model of the Effects of Racism on African-American Males," *American*

Journal of Orthopsychiatry 70 (1)(2000), 33–41; S. P. Harrell, "A Multidimensional Conceptualization of Racism-Related Stress: Implications for the Well-Being of People of Color," *American Journal of Orthopsychiatry* 70 (1)(2000), 42–57; and C. M. Pierce, "Stress in the Workplace," In A. F. Coner-Edwards and J. Spurlock (Eds.), *Black Families in Crisis: The Middle Class* (New York: Brunner/Mazel, 1988), 27–34.

46. There are many cultural variations on how one expresses feelings, with whom, and in what circumstances. This sentence in the text is not an endorsement of any one way of making sense of one's experience, but rather a caution about the importance of finding a culturally appropriate way of doing so. Silencing of experience seems to be universally problematic for healthy functioning. See M. B. Lykes, "Meaning Making in a Context of Genocide and Silencing," In M. B. Lykes et al. (Ed.), *Myths About the Powerless: Contesting Social Inequalities* (Philadelphia: Temple University Press, 1996), 159–178; and D. Wilkinson, *Silence on the Mountain: Stories of Terror, Betrayal, and Forgetting in Guatemala* (Boston: Houghton Mifflin, 2002).
47. In some instances a failure to cooperate can be lethal. In an altogether different context, but related to the American premium on individualism, Joe Klein notes that before the September 11 attacks on America, efforts at creating a single coordinated agency between branches of government that tracked information about suspected terrorists consistently failed. In the same piece he quotes Richard Holbrooke as saying, "Bureaucracies have a natural tendency not to cooperate, coordinate, or consolidate with each other." J. Klein, "Closework," *The New Yorker*, October 1, 2001, 48.
48. N. Farwell and J. B. Cole, "Community as a Context of Healing," *International Journal of Mental Health* 30 (4)(2001), 19–41; J. Saul, "Terror and Trauma: Enhancing Family and Community Resilience," Paper presented at the American Family Therapy Academy, New York, June 29, 2002.
49. For a discussion of the intersection of silence within families and a conspiracy of silence in the social and political realms, see Y. Danieli, "Conclusions and Future Directions," in Y. Danieli (Ed.), *International Handbook of Multigenerational Legacies of Trauma* (New York: Plenum Press, 1998), 669–689.
50. Maria Root calls these "dimensions of security." M.P.P. Root, "Reconstructing the Impact of Trauma on Personality," In L. S. Brown and M. Ballou (Eds.), *Personality and Psychopathology: Feminist Reappraisals* (New York: Guilford Press, 1992), 251.
51. R. Janoff-Bulman, *Shattered Assumptions: Towards a New Psychology of Trauma* (New York: Free Press, 1992), 6.
52. J. W. Pennebaker, *Opening Up: The Healing Power of Expressing Emotions* (New York: Guilford Press, 1997).
53. J. W. Pennebaker and K. D. Harber, "A Social Stage Model of Collective Coping: The Loma Prieta Earthquake and the Persian Gulf War," *Journal of social Issues*, 49 (4)(1993), 125–145.

54. I discuss two of the three stages in their model. See J. W. Pennebaker and K. D. Harber, "A Social Stage Model of Collective Coping: The Loma Prieta Earthquake and the Persian Gulf War," *Journal of Social Issues* 49 (4)(193), 125–145.
55. J. G. Allen, *Traumatic Relationships and Serious Mental Disorders* (Chichester: John Wiley & Sons, 2001), 148–149.
56. For-powerful accounts of these complex relationships see F. Butterfield, *All God's Children: The Bosket Family and the American Tradition of Violence* (New York: Knopf, 1995); and A. Kotlowitz, *There Are No Children Here: The Story of Two Boys Growing Up in the Other America* (New York: Anchor Books, 1992).
57. S. L. Buka et al., "Youth Exposure to Violence: Prevalence, Risks, and Consequences," *American Journal of Orthopsychiatry* 71 (3)(2001), 298–310; J. P. Shonkoff et al., *From Neurons to Neighborhoods: The Science of Early Child Development* (Washington, D.C.: National Academy Press, 2000); M. B. Selner-O'Hagan et al., "Assessing Exposure to Violence in Urban Youth," *Journal of Child Psychology and Psychiatry and Allied Disciplines*, 39 (2)(1998), 215–224.
58. See S. L. Buka et al, "Youth Exposure to Violence: Prevalence, Risks, and Consequences," *American Journal of Orthopsychiatry*, 71 (3)(2001), 298–310; D. W. Foy and C. A. Goguen, "Community-Violence Related PTSD in Children and Adolescents," *PTSD Research Quarterly*, 9 (4)(1998), 1–3, J. Garbarino, "The Effects of Community Violence on Children," in L. Balter and C. S. Tarnis-LeMonda (Eds.), *Child Psychology: A Handbook of Contemporary Issues* (Philadelphia: Psychology Press/Taylor & Francis, 1999), 412–42; P. Martinez, and J. E. Richters, "The NIMH Community Violence Project: II. Children's Distress Symptoms Associated with Violence Exposure," *Psychiatry*, 56 (1) (1993), 22–35; Osofsky, J. D. *Children in a Violent Society* (New York: Guilford Press, 1997); Selner-O'Hagan, M. B. et al., "Assessing Exposure to Violence in Urban Youth," *Journal of Child Psychology and Psychiatry and Allied Disciplines* 39 (2) (1998), 215–224; J. P. Shonkoff et al., *From Neurons to Neighborhoods: The Science of Early Child Development* (Washington, D.C.: National Academy Press, 2000); M. I. Singer et al., "Adolescents' Exposure to Violence and Associated Symptoms of Psychological Trauma," *JAMA* 273 (6) (1995), 477–482, and B. S. Warner and M. D. Weist, "Urban Youth as Witnesses to Violence: Beginning Assessment and Treatment Efforts," *Journal of Youth and Adolescence*, 25 (3)(1996), 361–377.
59. J. D. Osofsky, "The Effects of Exposure to Violence on Young Children," *American Psychologist* 50 (9)(1995), 782–788; and J. D. Osofsky, *Children in a Violent Society* (New York: Guilford Press, 1997).
60. M. I. Singer et al., "Adolescents' Exposure to Violence and Associated Symptoms of Psychological Trauma," *JAMA* 273 (6)(1995), 477–482.
61. S. L. Buka et al., "Youth Exposure to Violence: Prevalence, Risks and Consequences," *American Journal of Orthopsychiatry*, 71 (3)(2001), 298–310.

62. K. M. Fitzpatrick and J. P. Boldizar, "The Prevalence and Consequences of Exposure to Violence Among African-American Youth," *Journal of the American Academy of Child and Adolescent Psychiatry*, 32 (2)(1993), 424–430.
63. J. Garbarino, "The Effects of Community Violence on Children," In L. Balter and C. S. Tamis-LeMonda (Eds.), *Child Psychology: A Handbook of Contemporary Issues* (Philadelphia: Psychology Press/Taylor & Francis, 1999), 412–425.
64. J. Garbarino, "The Effects of Community Violence on Children," In L. Balter and C. S. Tamis-LeMonda, (Eds.), *Child Psychology: A Handbook of Contemporary Issues* (Philadelphia: Psychology Press/Taylor & Francis, 1999), 418.
65. C. C. Bell and E. J. Jenkins, "Community Violence and Children on Chicago's Southside," *Psychiatry*, 56 (1)(1993), 46–54.
66. F. Earls, "Community Factors Supporting Child Mental Health," *Child and Adolescent Psychiatric Clinics of North America* 10 (4)(2001), 693–709; and D. Pelcovitz and S. J. Kaplan, "Child Witnesses of Violence Between Parents: Psychosocial Correlates and Implications for Treatment," *Child and Adolescent Psychiatric Clinics of North America*, 3 (4)(1994), 745–758.
67. F. Earls, "Community Factors Supporting Child Mental Health," *Child and Adolescent Psychiatric Clinics of North America*, 10 (4)(2001), 693–709.
68. B. M. Groves, *Children Who See Too Much: Lessons from the Child Witness to Violence Project* (Boston: Beacon Press, 2002) (See appendix in Groves's book for a list of resources); and D. Prothrow-Stith and M. Weissman, *Deadly Consequences* (New York: HarperCollins, 1991).
69. M. Harway et al., *What Causes Men's Violence Against Women?* (Thousand Oaks, CA: Sage Publications, 1999); E. G. Krug et al., *World Report on Violence and Health* (Geneva: World Health Organization, 2002); P. Tjaden and N. Thoennes, *Extent, Nature, and Consequences of Intimate Partner Violence: Findings From the National Violence Against Women Survey* (Washington, D.C.: U.S. Department of Justice, Office of Justice Programs, 2000).
70. See J. L. Edleson, "Children's Witnessing of Adult Domestic Violence," *Journal of Interpersonal Violence* 14 (8)(1999), 839–870; G. Elliott et al., "The Encounter with Family Violence and Risky Sexual Activity Among Young Adolescent Females," *Journal of Violence and Victims* 17 (5)(2002), 569–592; D. Pelcovitz and S. J. Kaplan, "Child Witnesses of Violence Between Parents: Psychosocial Correlates and Implications for Treatment," *Child and Adolescent Psychiatric Clinics of North America*, 3 (4)(1994), 745–758 and D. A. Wolfe et al., "Child Witnesses to Violence Between Parents: Critical Issues in Behavioral and Social Adjustment," *Journal of Abnormal Child Psychology*, 14 (1)(March 1986), 95–104.
71. See M. Harway et al., "What Causes Men's Violence Against Women?" (Thousand Oaks, CA: Sage Publications, 1999); and B. Richie, *Compelled*

to Crime: the Gender Entrapment of Battered Black Women (New York: Routledge, 1996).

72. B. Richie, *Compelled to Crime: The Gender Entrapment of Battered Black Women* (New York: Routledge, 1996); M. P. Root, 1996, "Women of Color and Traumatic Stress in Domestic Captivity: Gender and Race as Disempowering Statuses," In A. J. Marsella and M. J. Friedman et al. (Eds.), *Ethnocultural Aspects of Posttraumatic Stress Disorder: Issues, Research, and Clinical Applications* (Washington, D.C.: American Psychological Association, 1996), 363–387.
73. S. L. Wofford, "Introduction: Biological and Historical Contexts." In W. Shakespeare (S. L. Wofford, Ed.), *Hamlet: Complete, Authoritative Text with Biographical and Historical Contexts, Critical History, and Essays from Five Contemporary Critical Perspectives* (Boston: Bedford Books, 1994), 3–26.

Part Two: How Do We Pass Along Common Shock?

1. C. Sagan, *Pale Blue Dot: A Vision of the Human Future in Space*, 1st ed. (New York: Random House, 1994), 6.

Chapter Four: The Toll of Illness and Dying in Families

1. J. W. Pennebaker, *Opening Up: The Healing Power of Expressing Emotions* (New York: Guilford Press, 1997).
2. B. R. Sarason et al., "Close Personal Relationships and Health Outcomes: A Key to the Role of Social Support," In B. R. Sarason and S. Duck (Eds.), *Personal Relationships: Implications for Clinical and Community Psychology* (Chichester, England: John Wiley & Sons, 2001), 15–41; B. R. Sarason et al., *Social Support: An Interactional View* (New York: J. Wiley & Sons, 1990); and W. Stroebe and M. Stroebe, "The Social Psychology of Social Support," In E. T. Higgins and A. W. Kruglanski (Eds.), *Social Psychology: Handbook of Basic Principles* (New York: Guilford Press, 1996), 597–621. In addition to having positive psychological and interpersonal effects, social support has been found to lower physiological arousal and to reduce physiological reactivity to various types of challenges. See B. N. Uchino et al., "The Relationship Between Social Support and Physiological Processes: A Review with Emphasis on Underlying Mechanisms and Implications for Health," *Psychological Bulletin* 119 (3)(1996), 488–531.
3. The inclusion of this criterion did not occur until the 1994 edition of the diagnostic manual. See American Psychiatric Association, "Diagnostic

and Statistical Manual of Mental Disorders" (4th Edition) (Washington, D.C., 1994) and M. L. Stuber, "Psychiatric Sequelae in Seriously Ill Children and Their Families," *Consultation-Liaison Psychiatry* 19 (3)(1996), 481–493.

4. A. E. Kazak et al., "Assessing Posttraumatic Stress Related to Medical Illness and Treatment: The Impact of Traumatic Stressors Interview Schedule (ITSIS)," *Families, Systems and Health* 14 (3)(1996), 365–380.
5. R. Frost, "Home Burial," In R. Frost (E. C. Lathem, Ed.), *The Poetry of Robert Frost* (New York: Holt, Rinehart and Winston, 1969), 51–55.
6. K. Weingarten, "The Discourses of Intimacy: Adding a Social Constructionist and Feminist View," *Family Process* 30 (3) (1991), 285–305.
7. See citations in endnote 2.
8. E. Scarry, *The Body in Pain: The Making and Unmaking of the World* (New York: Oxford University Press, 1985).
9. M. Greenspan, " 'Exceptional' Mothering in a 'Normal' World," In C. T. García Coll et al., *Mothering Against the Odds: Diverse Voices of Contemporary Mothers* (New York: Guilford Press, 1998), 45.
10. K. Duff, *The Alchemy of Illness* (New York: Bell Tower, 1993), 82–83.
11. See J. W. Pennebaker, *Opening Up: The Healing Power of Expressing Emotions* (New York: Guilford Press, 1997); J. M. Smyth et al., "Effects of Writing About Stressful Experiences on Symptom Reduction in Patients with Asthma or Rheumatoid Arthritis: A Randomized Trial," *JAMA* 281 (14) (1999), 1304–1309; and J. M. Smyth, "Written Emotional Expression: Effect Sizes, Outcome Types, and Moderating Variables," *Journal of Consulting and Clinical Psychology* 66 (1)(1998), 174–184.
12. See endnote 1.
13. P. Penn, "Chronic Illness: Trauma, Language, and Writing: Breaking the Silence," *Family Process* 40 (1)(2001), 39. (Italics in the original.) This idea is an elaboration of Judith Herman's observation that the conflict between speaking and not speaking is the "central dialectic" of trauma. See J. L. Herman, *Trauma and Recovery* (New York: BasicBooks, 1992), 2.
14. P. Penn, "Chronic Illness: Trauma, Language, and Writing: Breaking the Silence," *Family Process* 40 (1)(2001), 50. (Italics in the original.)
15. L. Focht-Birkerts and W. R. Beardslee, "A Child's Experience of Parental Depression: Encouraging Relational Resilience in Families with Affective Illness," *Family Process* 39 (4)(2000), 417–434; and W. R. Beardslee, *Out of the Darkened Room: When a Parent is Depressed: Protecting the Children and Strengthening the Family*, 1st ed. (Boston: Little Brown, 2000). Their work is influenced by family systems theory and psychoanalysis, both of which emphasize the importance of emotional expression.
16. L. Focht-Birkerts and W. R. Beardslee, "A Child's Experience of Parental Depression: Encouraging Relational Resilience in Families with Affective Illness," *Family Process* 39 (4)(2000), 411. (Italics in the original.)
17. K. Weingarten, *The Mother's Voice: Strengthening Intimacy in Families*, 2nd ed. (New York: Guilford Press, 1997.

18. A.W. Frank, *The Wounded Storyteller: Body, Illness, and Ethics* (Chicago: University of Chicago Press, 1995); and A. Kleinman, *The Illness Narratives: Suffering, Healing, and the Human Condition* (New York: Basic Books, 1988). Race and gender also impose a major constraint on the illness narrative. On race, see W.M. Byrd and L.A. Clayton, *An American Health Dilemma*, V. 2: *Race, Medicine, and Health Care in the United States 1900–2000* (New York: Routledge, 2002). On gender, see J. Lorber, *Gender and the Social Construction of Illness* (Thousand Oaks, CA: Sage Publications, 1997).
19. The terms *progressive* and *regressive narrative* are drawn from K.J. Gergen, *Realities and Relationships: Soundings in Social Construction* (Cambridge, Mass.: Harvard University Press, 1994). The application to illness is work that I have done and can be found in K. Weingarten, "Making Sense of Illness Narratives: Braiding Theory, Practice, and the Embodied Life," In C. White (Ed.), *Working with the Stories of Women's Lives* (Adelaide, South Australia: Dulwich Centre Publications, 2001), 111–125.
20. K. Weingarten, "The Politics of Illness Narratives: Who Tells, Who Listens, and Who Cares?" Paper presented at the Narrative Therapy and Community Work Conference, Adelaide, South Australia, 1999, 113–126.
21. C.R. Figley, *Burnout in Families: The Systemic Costs of Caring* (Boca Raton, Fla.: CRC Press, 1998), 21.
22. S.B. Chatman, *Story and Discourse: Narrative Structure in Fiction and Film* (Ithaca, N.Y.: Cornell University Press, 1978).
23. I am indebted to the work of Michael White and David Epston for the ideas that stimulated my thinking about this ceremony. See M. White and D. Epston, *Narrative Means to Therapeutic Ends*, 1st ed. (New York: Norton, 1990) and J.C. Freeman et al., *Playful Approaches to Serious Problems: Narrative Therapy with Children and Their Families* (New York: Norton, 1997).
24. For another account of the events leading up to, and a description of, this ceremony, see K. Weingarten and M.E. Weingarten Worthen, "A Narrative Approach to Understanding the Illness Experiences of a Mother and Daughter," *Families, Systems and Health* 15 (1)(1997), 41–54.
25. K. Weingarten and M.E. Weingarten Worthen, "A Narrative Approach to Understanding the Illness Experiences of a Mother and Daughter," *Families, Systems and Health* 15 (1)(1997), 52.
26. K. Weingarten and ME. Weingarten Worthen, "A Narrative Approach to Understanding the Illness Experiences of a Mother and Daughter," *Families, Systems and Health* 15 (1)(1997), 52.
27. See endnote 1.
28. R. Shilts, *And the Band Played On: Politics, People, and the AIDS Epidemic* (New York: St. Martin's Press, 1987), 144.
29. S. Epstein, "The Construction of Lay Expertise: AIDS Activism and the Forging of Credibility in the Reform of Clinical Trials," *Science Technology and Human Values* 20 (4)(1995), 408–437; R. Pear, "AIDS at 20: Advocates for Patients Barged In, and the Federal Government Changed," *The*

New York Times, June 5, 2001, F3. In this country AIDS activism has met with many successes. Yearly deaths have declined significantly in the last few years, although some populations are seeing AIDS rates rise. People who thought they would die are now living healthy lives. And in the context of this chapter, fewer people are enrolled as team members to support and witness their friends and loved ones. This has lessened the burden on some communities, even as people remember the complexities and sacredness of their commitments to each other. (This last point is from a personal communication with Mike Ward, November, 2001.)

30. J. Agee, *A Death in the Family* (New York:Bantam, 1938), 191.
31. This article is no longer available at the Web site: *www.planet-therapy.com*
32. It is less common for communities to come together to assist families with dying itself. Nor is it always possible to name—or to agree upon—the moment that living transforms into dying. Linda Blachman founded and directs the Mothers' Living Stories Project, a project that helps mothers living with cancer record their life stories as a legacy for their children. Aware of the multiple sensitivities patients and family members may have to the idea of recording a life story, fearing that it signals an acceptance of death, Blachman suggests that people think of it as a "work in progress, rather than a summary of a life nearing completion." She has trained volunteers to listen to and record the mothers' stories, "empathetically witnessing, receiving, and holding the other's story, in all its complexity and suffering, grief and joy." Not surprisingly, the volunteer listeners reap great benefit as well. See L. Blachman, Mothers' Living Stories Project, 2002. Retrieved October 10, 2002, from the Web: ***http://www.motherslivingstories.org/***
33. In a series of articles in *The New York Times* in 2001–2002, one reporter focused her story on a rural community, Hlabisa, in Kwa Zulu Natal, which has the highest rate of HIV infection of any province in South Africa. "The virus is invisible, people here say, but its fingerprints are everywhere." R. L. Swarns, "South Africa's AIDS Vortex Engulfs a Rural Community," *The New York Times*, November 25, 2001, A1, A16.
34. M. Battle, *Reconciliation: The Ubuntu Theology of Desmond Tutu* (Cleveland, Ohio: Pilgrim Press, 1997), 1; and M.J. Bhengu, *Ubuntu: The Essence of Democracy* (Cape Town, South Africa: Novalis Press, 1996).
35. Conversations with AIDS and Care, " 'A Spirit on Its Own Is Easily Broken but Together We Will Not Break.' Communities Respond to HIV/AIDS, Diabetes, and Grief." *Dulwich Centre Newsletter* 3(1996), 7. This story was brought to the Dulwich Centre by Yvonne Sliep, Ph.D.
36. This is a project of Mrs. Magdalena Dladla of the Riverview Community.
37. Communities without Borders. Information about this NGO is available by contacting Dr. Richard Bail, MD, and MPH Consultant, UNAIDS/Internist, Harvard Vanguard Medical Center, Watertown, MA, 02472.

Chapter Five: Double Jeopardy or Do No Harm

1. In this incident there is a perceived interpersonal act of racism. However, these single episodes are systemwide and systemic phenomena. Blacks are disciplined disproportionately to their numbers. See P. Tosto, "When Race, Discipline Meet," *St. Paul Pioneer Press*, March 15, 2002, A1; and R. Denn, "Blacks Are Disciplined at Far Higher Rates than Other Students," *Seattle Post-Intelligencer*, March 15, 2002. In an investigation undertaken by the *Seattle Post-Intelligencer* of this issue, they found that the race of the students was a much larger factor in the differential discipline rates than, for example, nontraditional homes or poverty, R. Denn, *Seattle Post-Intelligencer*, March 15, 2002. "Blacks Are Disciplined at Far Higher Rates Than Other Students." 2002. Retrieved from the Web April, 2002: *http://seattlepi.nwsource.com/disciplinegap/61940newdiscipline12.shtml* A similar analysis can be made with regard to the health-care system. While individuals encounter racial discrimination, there is a systemwide problem in which people of color are systematically disadvantaged over whites. For a comprehensive analysis see W. M. Byrd and L. A. Clayton, *An American Health Dilemma*, V. 2: *Race, Medicine, and Health Care in the United States 1900–2000* (New York: Routledge, 2002).
2. M. R. Peterson, *At Personal Risk: Boundary Violations in Professional-Client Relationships*, 1st ed. (New York: Norton, 1992).
3. J. M. Violanti and D. Paton *Police Trauma: Psychological Aftermath of Civilian Combat* (Springfield, Ill.: Charles C. Thomas Publisher, 1999).
4. E. Newman and R. Simpson et al., in submission, "Trauma Exposure and Posttraumatic Stress Disorder among Photojournalists."
5. C. Hedges, *War Is a Force That Gives Us Meaning*, 1st Ed. (New York: Public Affairs, 2002).
6. N. D. Stein, *Classrooms and Courtrooms: Facing Sexual Harassment in K-12 Schools* (New York: Teachers College Press, 1999).
7. See endnote 6.
8. D. A. Friedman, *Jewish Pastoral Care: A Practical Handbook from Traditional and Contemporary Sources*. (Woodstock, Vt.: Jewish Lights Publishing, 2001), xi.
9. See J. Barbanel, "How the Study of Sexual Abuse by Priests Was Conducted," *The New York Times*, January 12, 2003, 21; and L. Goodstein, "Trail of Pain in Church Crisis Leads to Nearly Every Diocese," *The New York Times*, January 12, 2003, 1, 20, 21. A summary conducted nine months earlier reveals much lower numbers, reflecting the acceleration of disclosure following the public outcry against the Church and the support for victims; J. Zimmerman and J. B. Feister, "A Church in Crisis," *American Catholic*. Retrieved May 4 2002, from the Web: *http//www.americancatholic.org/News/ClergySexAbuse/*

10. J. Berry, *Lead Us Not into Temptation: Catholic Priests and the Sexual Abuse of Children*, 1st Illinois paperback ed. (Urbana: University of Illinois Press and *Globe* Newspaper, 2000); the investigative staff of *The Boston Globe, Betrayal: The Crisis in the Catholic Church* (Boston: Little Brown, 2002).
11. M. Bochenek et al., *Hatred in the Hallways: Violence and Discrimination Against Lesbian, Gay, Bisexual, and Transgender Students in U.S. Schools* (New York: Human Rights Watch, 2001).
12. M. Bochenek et al., *Hatred in the Hallways: Violence and Discrimination Against Lesbian, Gay, Bisexual, and Transgender Students in U.S. Schools* (New York: Human Rights Watch, 2001), 81.
13. R. Chen and E. Gilmore, *Interest Group on Death and Dying*, American Medical Student Association, 2002. Retrieved September 29, 2002, from the Web: *http://www.amsa.org/dd/*
14. R.E. Peschel and E.R. Peschel, *When a Doctor Hates a Patient, and Other Chapters in a Young Physician's Life* (Berkeley: University of California Press, 1986); and A.W. Frank, "Acts of Witness: Forms of Engagement in Illness." Paper presented at the Narrative Based Medicine, Cambridge, UK, September 3–4, 2001. I learned about this collection of essays in Arthur Frank's talk.
15. J.P. Wilson and J.D. Lindy, *Countertransference in the Treatment of PTSD* (New York: Guilford Press, 1994).
16. R.B. Thomas, *An Investigation of Empathic Stress Reactions Among Mental Health Professionals Working with Post Traumatic Stress Disorder* (Dissertation Abstracts International: Section B: the Sciences and Engineering: The Union Institute, 1999); and M.L. Hoffman, *Empathy and Moral Development: Implications for Caring and Justice* (Cambridge, UK: New York, Cambridge University Press, 2000). Hoffman uses the term *empathic distress*.
17. While there is a substantial literature on these reactions, as for other phenomena I discuss in this book, studies tend not to focus on the issues of witnessing or the witness per se.
18. There is a third form of empathic stress reaction, vicarious traumatization, a concept introduced in 1990 to account for the cumulative effect over time on people working with survivors of childhood sexual abuse. Helpers who develop therapeutic relationships with survivors of sexual abuse are exposed to the details of their abuse, which invariably consist of betrayals, failures of protection by people who should have and might have behaved differently, and violations of the victims' basic needs for safety, nurturance, trust, control, and esteem. Exposure to these stories confronts trauma therapists with the reality of human cruelty and the potential for harm befalling us or anyone we love.

    Empathic attunement to clients, while essential to doing the work, is the specific channel through which vicarious traumatization occurs. For it is precisely in the "taking in" of the client's experience that the therapist risks having her world view fundamentally and permanently altered. While secondary traumatic stress and vicarious traumatization share some features, vicarious traumatization develops over a longer period of time and represents permanent changes in the therapist's sense of herself and the world. The management of vicarious traumatization requires lifestyle changes, that is, a willingness to accept that trauma work demands certain ways of caring for the self in order to be of service to others. See I. L. McCann and L. A. Pearlman, "Vicarious Traumatization: A Framework for Understanding the Psychological Effects of Working with Victims," *Journal of Traumatic Stress* 3(1) (1990), 131–149; L. A. Pearlman and K. W. Saakvitne, "Treating Therapists with Vicarious Traumatization and Secondary Traumatic Stress Disorders," In C. R. Figley (Ed.), *Compassion Fatigue: Coping with Secondary Traumatic Stress Disorder in Those Who Treat the Traumatized* (New York: Brunner/Mazel 1995); L. A. Pearlman and K. W. Saakvitne, *Trauma and the Therapist: Countertransference and Vicarious Traumatization in Psychotherapy with Incest Survivors*, 1st ed. (New York: Norton, 1995), 150–177; and R. B. Thomas, *An Investigation of Empathic Stress Reactions Among Mental Health Professionals Working with Post Traumatic Stress Disorder* (Dissertation Abstracts International: Section B: the Sciences & Engineering: The Union Institute, 1999).

19. The term *burnout* was introduced in 1975. C. R. Figley, *Burnout in Families: The Systemic Costs of Caring* (Boca Raton, Fla.: CRC Press, 1998); C. Maslach, "What Have We Learned About Burnout and Health?" *Psychology and Health* 16 (5)(2001), 607–611; and A. M. Pines and E. Aronson, *Career Burnout: Causes and Cures* Free Press: New York, 1989).
20. Burnout consists of physical symptoms (fatigue, physical depletion, sleep disturbances, gastrointestinal ailments, and headaches); emotional symptoms (irritability, anxiety, guilt, helplessness, anger, and depression); behavioral symptoms (problems with concentration, aggression, pessimism, callousness, substance abuse); work-related symptoms (lowered job performance, tardiness, missed days of work); and interpersonal symptoms (hostility toward or distancing from co-workers and clients, poor communication, and lack of cooperation). See C. R. Figley, *Burnout in Families: the Systemic Costs of Caring* (Boca Raton, Fla.: CRC Press, 1998); C. Maslach, "What Have We Learned About Burnout and Health?" *Psychology and Health* 16 (5)(2001) 607–611; and W. B. Schaufeli et al., "On the Clinical Validity of the Maslach Burnout Inventory and the Burnout Measure," *Psychology and Health* 16 (5)(2001), 565–582.
21. R. D. Beaton, and S. A. Murphy, "Working with People in Crisis: Research Implications," In C. R. Figley (Ed.), *Compassion Fatigue: Coping with Secondary Traumatic Stress Disorder in Those Who Treat the Traumatized* (Brunner/Mazel Psychological Stress Series, No. 23) (Philadelphia: Brunner/Mazel, Inc., 1995), 51–81.
22. See Casey as quoted in R. A. Simpson and J. G Boggs, "An Exploratory Study of Traumatic Stress Among Newspaper Journalists," *Journalism and*

Communication Monographs (Spring 1999), 3; and C. Hedges, *War Is a Force That Gives Us Meaning*, 1st ed. (New York: Public Affairs, 2002).

23. C. Aiken, "Reporters Are Victims, Too," *Nieman Report* 50 (3)(1996), 30.
24. C. Howard et al., "Unspeakable Emotion: A Discursive Analysis of Police Talk About Reactions to Trauma," *Journal of Language and Social Psychology* 19 (3)(2000), 295–314; R. A. Simpson and J. G Boggs, "An Exploratory Study of Traumatic Stress Among Newspaper Journalists," *Journalism and Communication Monographs* (Spring 1999), 1–26; and A. C. Smith and S. Kleinman, "Managing Emotions in Medical School: Students' Contacts with the Living and the Dead," *Social Psychology Quarterly* 52 (1)(1989), 56–69.
25. C. Howard et al., "Unspeakable Emotion: A Discursive Analysis of Police Talk About Reactions to Trauma," *Journal of Language and Social Psychology* 19 (3)(2000), 295–314.
26. R. E. Peschel and E. R. Peschel, *When a Doctor Hates a Patient, and Other Chapters in a Young Physician's Life* (Berkeley: University of California Press, 1986); and M. R. Pogrebin and E. D. Poole, "Emotion Management: A Study of Police Response to Tragic Events," In M. G. Flaherty and C. Ellis (Eds.), *Social Perspectives on Emotion*, Vol. 3 (Stamford: JAI Press, Inc., 1995), 149–168.
27. B. M. Gassaway, "Making Sense of War: An Autobiographical Account of a Vietnam War Correspondent," *Journal of Applied Behavorial Science* 25 (4)(1989), 327–349.
28. R. Rosenblatt, "Rwanda Therapy," *The New Republic* (June 6, 1994), 16.
29. A. Feinstein and J. Owen, "Journalists, War, and Posttraumatic Stress Disorder," In Y. Danieli (Ed.), *Sharing the Front Line and the Back Hills: International Protectors and Providers: Peacekeepers, Humanitarian Aid Workers and the Media in the Midst of Crisis* (Amityville, NY: Baywood Publishing Co., Inc., 2002), 305–315.
30. J. Firth-Cozens, "Interventions to Improve Physicians' Well-being and Patient Care," *Social Science and Medicine* 52 (2)(2001), 215–222; and J. M. Violanti and D. Paton, *Police Trauma: Psychological Aftermath of Civilian Combat* (Springfield, Ill.: Charles C. Thomas Publisher, 1999).
31. T. J. Wachtel et al., "Physicians' Utilization of Health Care," *Journal of General Internal Medicine*, 10 (5)(1995), 261–265.
32. D. A. Lott, "Physician—Treat Thyself?" *Psychiatric Times* XVIII (12)(2001).
33. L. N. Blum, *Force Under Pressure: How Cops Live and Why They Die* (New York: Lantern Books, 2000); and J. M. Violanti and D. Paton, *Police Trauma: Psychological Aftermath of Civilian Combat* (Springfield, Ill.: Charles C. Thomas Publisher, 1999).
34. A. Cooper et al., "Dealing with the Trauma of Covering War: Excerpts from a Conference," *Nieman Reports* 53 (2)(1999), 24–25.
35. A. Cooper et al., "Dealing With the Trauma of Covering War: Excerpts from a Conference," *Nieman Reports* 53 (2)(1999), 24–25.

36. D. Gordon et al., "Photographing the War in Afghanistan," *The Connection* (Boston: WBUR, December 6, 2001).
37. D. Gordon et al., "Photographing the War in Afghanistan," *The Connection* (Boston: WBUR, 2001). Grossfield was referring to Kevin Carter, who committed suicide at age thirty-three, two months after winning the Pulitzer Prize. A white, English-speaking South African, he dedicated himself to exposing the brutality of the apartheid system. For years he covered violence in black townships with three other colleagues, one of whom died six days after Carter learned he had won the Pulitzer. Carter was plagued by many concerns at the time of his death, of which the "baggage" he carried from that one photograph was a single part. He was committed to grappling with issues that "most people just accept," wrote his sister about him. "The pain of his mission to open the eyes of the world to so many of the issues and injustices that tore at his soul eventually got to him." P. G. Randburg, letter. *Time*, October 3, 1994, 144.
38. A. R. Kates, *Copshock: Surviving Posttraumatic Stress Disorder* (PTSD) (Tucson: Holbrook Street Press, 1999); and W. M. Sotile and M. O. Sotile, "Today's Medical Marriage," Part 2, *JAMA* 277 (16)(1997), 1322.
39. A. Bovell, *Lantana* (R. Lawrence, Director), J. Chapman and S. Wells (Producer). Australia: Fandango.
40. R. Clark et al., "Racism as a Stressor for African Americans: A Biopsychosocial Model," *American Psychologist* 54 (10)(1999), 805–816, and R. M. Scurfield, "Positive and Negative Aspects of Exposure to Racism and Trauma: Research, Assessment, and Treatment Implications," *NCP Clinical Quarterly* 10 (1)(2000), 1–10.
41. R. N. Jacobs, *Race, Media, and the Crisis of Civil Society: From Watts to Rodney King* (Cambridge, UK; New York: Cambridge University Press, 2000). According to Jacobs, personal correspondence, August 9, 2002, Holliday originally offered the videotape to the LAPD, but they were not interested in talking to him.
42. D. Linder, *The Trials of Los Angeles Police Officers in Connection with the Beating of Rodney King*. University of Missouri—Kansas City Law School, 2001. Retrieved September 30, 2002, from the Web: *http://www.law.umkc.edu/faculty/projects/trials/lapd/lapdaccount.html*
43. See endnote 42.
44. D. Linder, "Excerpts from the LAPD Officers' Trial," University of Missouri—Kansas City, 1992. Retrieved September 30, 2002, from the Web: *http://www.law.umkc.edu/faculty/projects/trials/lapd/kingtranscripot.html*, 8.
45. C. J. Ogletree et al., *Beyond the Rodney King Story: An Investigation of Police Conduct in Minority Communities* (Boston: Northeastern University Press, 1995), xx.
46. R. N. Jacobs, *Race, Media, and the Crisis of Civil Society: From Watts to Rodney King* (Cambridge, UK; New York: Cambridge University Press, 2000), 101.

47. R. N. Jacobs, *Race, Media, and the Crisis of Civil Society: From Watts to Rodney King* (Cambridge, UK; New York: Cambridge University Press, 2000).
48. L. Romney, "LA Still Finding Its Way After '92 Riots," *The Boston Globe*, 2.
49. R. N. Jacobs, *Race, Media, and the Crisis of Civil Society: From Watts to Rodney King* (Cambridge, UK; New York: Cambridge University Press, 2000), 119, quoting the *Los Angeles Sentinel*, May 7, 1992, A7.
50. R. N. Jacobs, *Race, Media, and the Crisis of Civil Society: From Watts to Rodney King* (Cambridge, UK; New York: Cambridge University Press, 2000), 119, quoting the *Los Angeles Sentinel*, May 7, 1992, A7.
51. See endnote 47.
52. D. Linder, *Excerpts from the LAPD Officers' Trial*, University of Missouri—Kansas City. Retrieved September 30, 2002, from the Web: *http://www.law.umkc.edu/faculty/projects/ftrials/lapd/kingtranscript.html*
53. T. L. Beauchamp and J. F. Childress, *Principles of Biomedical Ethics*, 5th ed. (New York: Oxford University Press, 2001).
54. P. Applebome, "Front-Line Journalism—As History Unfolded," *Duke Magazine* 88 (1)(2001), 4.
55. See endnote 54.
56. See endnote 54.
57. G. Favre, September 20, *Forgetting Our Feelings*. Poynter.org. Retrieved 2001, from the Web: *http://www.poynter.org/Terrorism/greg7.htm*
58. C. R. Figley, *Compassion Fatigue: Coping with Secondary Traumatic Stress Disorder in Those Who Treat the Traumatized* (Philadelphia: Brunner/Mazel, Inc., 1995); L. A. Pearlman and K. W. Saakvitne, *Trauma and the Therapist: Countertransference and Vicarious Traumatization in Psychotherapy with Incest Survivors*, 1st ed. (New York: Norton, 1995); B. H. Stamm, *Secondary Traumatic Stress: Self-Care Issues for Clinicians, Researchers, and Educators* (Lutherville, Md.: Sidran Press, 1995); and J. P. Wilson and J. D. Lindy, *Countertransference in the Treatment of PTSD* (New York: Guilford Press, 1994).
59. H.J.M. Nouwen, *The Wounded Healer: Ministry in Contemporary Society*, 1st Image ed. (New York: Image Books, 1990).

Chapter Six: The Blindness of One's Heart

1. Homer, *The Odyssey*, trans. S. H. Butcher and A. Lang. Vol. XXII. The Harvard Classics (New York: P. F. Collier & Son, 1909–14).
2. The lines, not italicized, from the Butcher and Lang translation appear in the preface to Samuel Butler's translation. See Homer, *The Odyssey of Homer*, trans. Samuel Butler (Roslyn, New York: Walter J. Black, 1944), xiii.

3. This insight was inspired during a conversation with Patti Levin, LICSW, PsyD.
4. This phrase is drawn from C. Lasch, *Haven in a Heartless World: The Family Besieged* (New York: Basic Books, 1977).
5. The term *the Holocaust* is itself a controversial topic. The word *holocaust* first appeared in Middle English in the fourteenth century to refer to the act of sacrificing a male animal to God through burning it. *Holocaust* comes from the Greek word *holokauston*, which was a translation of a Hebrew word meaning "that which goes up" in smoke. The application of this word to the Nazis' destruction of the Jews of Europe occurred first around 1942, but wasn't used widely until the 1950s, when the phrase *the Holocaust* came into circulation. Also in the 1940s, another Hebrew word, *sho'ah,* was used to refer to the destruction of European Jewry. This word means "catastrophe." Some people consider the use of the term *the Holocaust*, which carries the meaning of religious sacrifice, to be sacrilegious, since the Nazis intended murder, not sacrifice. J. Hatley, *Suffering Witness: The Quandary of Responsibility After the Irreparable*, (Albany, State University of New York Press, 2000), 5–6; *Holocaust in American Heritage Dictionary of the English Language*; 4th ed. (Boston: Houghton Mifflin Company, 2000); I. Gutman, *Holocaust* in I. Gutman, (Ed.), *Encyclopedia of the Holocaust*, vol. 2 (New York: Macmillan Library Reference, 1995). I consider the naming of the destruction of European Jewry by the Nazis problematic. Although I share the sensibility that the implication of "burnt offering" in the term *the Holocaust* is offensive, I use this term in the book in preference to others, like *Shoah*, because it is the more common way to refer to these events. I did not want to use a term that might distance the reader from the material and I believe that a less familiar term runs that risk.
6. Y. Danieli, *International Handbook of Multigenerational Legacies of Trauma* (New York: Plenum Press, 1998).
7. A. Novak, *Prevention of Intergenerational Transmission of Effects of Trauma*, Presentation at ISTSS Conference (Santa Clarita, CA: Professional Programs, Inc., 2001), and J. Hackett, *Disturbance of the Inner Ear* (New York: Carroll & Graf, 2002). The narrator of this novel is the daughter of a Holocaust survivor and beautifully illustrates the vulnerability/resilence thesis.
8. Y. Danieli, "Psychotherapists' Participation in the Conspiracy of Silence About the Holocaust," *Psychoanalytic Psychology*, 1 (1)(1984), 23–43; and Y. Danieli, *International Handbook of Multigenerational Legacies of Trauma* (New York: Plenum Press, 1998). A literature search of two large catalogs, the on-line WorldCat and the Union Catalog of the Harvard Libraries, reveals a similar pattern. (These catalogs were selected because the Holocaust was used as a subject heading regardless of whether volumes were listed under this subject heading when they entered the catalog system. Since the term *the Holocaust* was not used widely until the 1950s, this is an important consideration.) Publications on the Holocaust drop from the 1940s to the 1950s and then double with each succeeding decade.

9. Initial studies of clinical samples of Holocaust survivors and their children reported psychological problems in both survivors and their offspring. As findings of disturbance in adjustment accumulated in the 1970s, many scientists, some of whom were children of survivors themselves, became concerned about the validity of the findings on methodological and philosophical grounds. Significant concerns were raised about biased samples without appropriate control groups, "reliance on anecdotal data, and presumption of psychopathology." N. Solkoff, "Children of Survivors of the Nazi Holocaust: A Critical Review of the Literature," *American Journal of Orthopsychiatry* 62 (3)(1992), 342. Likewise, scientists worried about the implications of finding "flaws" with survivors and their children. Might this collude with the Nazi agenda of showing the basic inferiority of the Jewish people? Would this give the impression that the Nazis had "won" after all, by causing permanent "damage" to those they had not murdered? N.C. Auerhahn and D. Laub, "Intergenerational Memory of the Holocaust," in Y. Danieli, (Ed.), *International Handbook of Multigenerational Legacies of Trauma.* (The Plenum Series on Stress and Coping) (New York: Plenum Press, 1998), 21–41; and R. Yehuda et al., "Phenomenology and Psychobiology of the Intergenerational Response to Trauma," In Y. Danieli, (Ed.), *International Handbook of Multigenerational Legacies of Trauma.* (The Plenum Series on Stress and Coping) (New York: Plenum Press, 1998), 639–655. Social scientists responded to these concerns by refining their methodologies and redoubling their efforts to design studies adequate to the complexities of the issues. As more work was done in this area, some scientists took it upon themselves periodically to review and analyze the entire body of research, leading to a new research agenda. N. Solkoff, "Children of Survivors of the Nazi Holocaust: A Critical Review of the Literature," *American Journal of Orthopsychiatry* 62 (3)(1992), 342–358; N.P. Kellerman, "Psychopathology in Children of Holocaust Survivors: A Review of the Research Literature," *Israel Journal of Psychiatry and Related Sciences* 38 (1)(2001), 36–46.
10. N. Solkoff, "Children of Survivors of the Nazi Holocaust: A Critical Review of the Literature," *American Journal of Orthopsychiatry* 62 (3)(1992), 342–358.
11. R. Yehuda et al., "Phenomenology and Psychobiology of the Intergenerational Response to Trauma," In Y. Danieli (Ed.), *International Handbook of Multigenerational Legacies of Trauma* (The Plenum Series on Stress and Coping) (New York: Plenum Press, 1998), 642.
12. Cortisol levels were measured by analyses of urine that had been collected over a twenty-four-hour period.
13. R. Yehuda et al., "Vulnerability to Posttraumatic Stress Disorder in Adult Offspring of Holocaust Survivors," *American Journal of Psychiatry*, 155(9)(1998), 1163–1171 and R. Yehuda et al., "Relationship Between Posttraumatic Stress Disorder Characteristics of Holocaust Survivors and

Their Adult Offspring," *American Journal of Psychiatry*, 155 (6)(1998), 841–843.

14. There are a number of memoirs and novels written by second-generation children of Holocaust survivors. See for example, H. Fremont, *After Long Silence: A Memoir* (New York: Delacorte Press, 1999); J. Hackett, *Disturbance of the Inner Ear*, (New York: Carroll & Graf, 2002); L. Kehoe, NB *Maus I & Maus II. In This Dark House: A Memoir* (New York: Schocken Books, 1995); S. Pilcer, *The Holocaust Kid* (New York: Dell, 2000); A. Spiegelman, *Maus II: A Survivor's Tale: And Here My Troubles Began,* 1st ed. (New York: Pantheon Books, 1991) and A. Spiegelman, *Maus I: A Survivor's Tale: My Father Bleeds History* (Rev. pbk. ed.) (New York: Pantheon Books, 1986).
15. A. Spiegelman, *Maus II: A Survivor's Tale: And Here My Troubles Began,* 1st ed. (New York: Pantheon Books, 1991); and A. Spiegelman *Maus: A Survivor's Tale: I: My Father Bleeds History* (Rev. pbk. ed.) (New York: Pantheon Books, 1986).
16. A. Spiegelman, *Maus: A Survivor's Tale: And Here My Troubles Began*, 1st ed. (New York: Pantheon Books, 1991), 16.
17. A. Spiegelman, *Maus II: A Survivor's Tale: And Here My Troubles Began,* 1st ed. (New York: Pantheon Books, 1991), 16.
18. A. Novac, and S. Hubert-Schneider, "Acquired Vulnerability: Comorbidity in a Patient Population of Adult Offspring of Holocaust Survivors," *American Journal of Forensic Psychiatry* 19 (2)(1998), 45–58. In fact, research on nonhuman primates, primarily monkeys—who share about 94 percent of their genes with humans—shows that there are several ways that monkeys do pass on preparedness to their children. One is through observation. Juvenile monkeys who had no previous fear of snakes learned permanently to fear snakes from observing another monkey, especially their mother, behave fearfully around one. Their fear response had both a psychological and a biological dimension. A second way preparedness is passed on is through deficits in maternal behavior. Mother monkeys who were stressed tended to have children who themselves overreacted both physiologically and behaviorally to stressors in their own environments. In addition, female monkeys who received deficient caretaking from their mothers as infants tended to pass these deficits on to their offspring in nearly identical ways. The third way that monkeys pass on preparedness, or transmit trauma to the next generation, is through prenatal mechanisms. Monkey offspring of mothers who were stressed while pregnant with them were more reactive to mildly stressful events and situations as juveniles and adolescents than their peers whose mothers had not been stressed during their pregnancies.

    All three ways produce similar consequences for offspring, a greater physiological and behavioral reactivity to "novelty and/or challenge" (635) in their environment. Theoretically, these three mechanisms might interact with each other and have cumulative effects. Primate researchers believe that these ways provide evidence that there is "cross-generation transmission of trauma." Given that our "closest primate relatives" pass psychological and biological effects of trauma to each other across the generations, and have probably been doing so for millions of years, it seems imperative that we understand this process as thoroughly as we can for our own species. See S. J. Suomi and S. Levine, "Psychobiology of Intergenerational Effects of Trauma: Evidence from Animal Studies," In Y. Danieli (Ed.), *International Handbook of Multigenerational Legacies of Trauma* (New York: Plenum Press, 1998), 623–638. (All quotes are taken from their chapter.)

19. R. Yehuda et al., "Vulnerability to Posttraumatic Stress Disorder in Adult Offspring of Holocaust Survivors," *American Journal of Psychiatry* 155 (9)(1998), 1163–1171; and R. Yehuda et al., "Relationship Between Posttraumatic Stress Disorder Characteristics of Holocaust Survivors and Their Adult Offspring," *American Journal of Psychiatry* 155 (6)(1998), 841–843.
20. E. B. Foa et al., "The Posttraumatic Cognitions Inventory (PTCI): Development and Validation," *Psychological Assessment*, 11 (3)(1991), 303–314.
21. A. Spiegelman, *Maus I: A Survivor's Tale: My Father Bleeds History*, Rev. pbk.). (New York: Pantheon Books, 1986), 16. Spiegelman sets off this episode, making it emblematic of a recurrent theme in his relationship to his father. Researchers have more prosaic ways of trying to assess the impact of such themes on large samples of people. Two Israeli studies looked at adult children of Holocaust survivors and their response to two quite different traumatic events to see whether prior experiences with their parents would confer vulnerability. In one study of soldiers who experienced combat-stress reactions during the 1982 Lebanon War, researchers found that the soldiers whose parents were Holocaust survivors had more intense and enduring posttraumatic symptoms that lasted longer than those of their peers with combat-stress reactions whose parents were not Holocaust survivors. Z. Soloman, "Transgenerational Effects of the Holocaust: The Israeli Research, Perspective," In Y. Danieli (Ed.), *International Handbook of Multigenerational Legacies of Trauma* (New York: Plenum Press, 1998)(1), 69–84, and Z. Solomon et al., "Combat-Related Posttraumatic Stress Disorder Among Second-Generation Holocaust Survivors: Preliminary Findings," *American Journal of Psychiatry* 145 (7)(1988), 865–868. In the other study Jewish women with breast cancer who were the children of Holocaust-survivor parents reacted with significantly more distress to their illness than Jewish women with breast cancer whose parents were not Holocaust survivors, although their attitudes toward coping with their cancer were equally functional. L. Baider et al., "Transmission of Response to Trauma? Second-Generation Holocaust Survivors' Reaction to Cancer," *American Journal of Psychiatry* 157 (6)(2000) 904–910.
22. J. Kaufman and E. Zigler, "Do Abused Children Become Abusive Parents?" *American Journal of Orthopsychiatry* 57 (2)(1987), 186–192.

23. J. Kaufman and E. Zigler, "Do Abused Children Become Abusive Parents?" *American Journal of Orthopsychiatry* 57 (2)(1987), 186–192; and A. Buchanan, "Intergenerational Child Maltreatment," In Y. Danieli, (Ed.), *International Handbook of Multigenerational Legacies of Trauma* (The Plenum Series on Stress and Coping) (New York: Plenum Press, 1998), 535–552.
24. A. Buchanan, "Intergenerational Child Maltreatment," In Y. Danieli, (Ed.), *International Handbook of Multigenerational Legacies of Trauma* (The Plenum Series on Stress and Coping) (New York: Plenum Press, 1998), 535–552.
25. D. Levinson, *Family Violence in Cross-Cultural Perspective* (Newbury Park, CA: Sage Publications, 1989.)
26. J. Kaufman and E. Zigler, "Do Abused Children Become Abusive Parents?" *American Journal of Orthopsychiatry* 57 (2) (1987), 186–192, quoting Straus, 1983.
27. See endnote 24.
28. J. Cassidy and P.R. Shaver, *Handbook of Attachment: Theory, Research, and Clinical Applications* (New York: Guilford Press, 1999).
29. F. Rothbaum et al., "Attachment and Culture: Security in the United States and Japan," *American Psychologist* 55 (10)(1993), 1093–1104.
30. S.H. Franzblau, "Historicizing Attachment Theory: Binding the Ties That Bind," *Feminism and Psychology* 9 (1)(1989), 22–31; and S.H. Franzblau, "Editor's Introduction: Attachment Theory," *Feminism and Psychology* 9 (1)(1999), 5–9.
31. J.G. Allen, *Traumatic Relationships and Serious Mental Disorders* (Chichester: John Wiley & Sons, 2001), 39.
32. The American Academy of Pediatrics lists witnessing intimate partner violence as a form of psychological maltreatment if it is severe or is repetitious. S.W. Kairys et al., "The Psychological Maltreatment of Children—Technical Report," *Pediatrics* 109 (4)(2002): e68. For a review of problems associated with witnessing domestic violence, see J.L. Edleson, "Children's Witnessing of Adult Domestic Violence," *Journal of Interpersonal Violence* 14 (8)(1999), 839–870. For a poetic rendering of the complexities of witnessing domestic violence, see "African Violets" in F. Marchant, *Full Moon Boat: Poems* (Saint Paul, Minn.: Graywolf Press, 2000).
33. C.H. Zeanah and P.D. Zeanah, "Intergenerational Transmission of Maltreatment: Insights from Attachment Theory and Research," *Psychiatry* (1989), 177–196.
34. The child's internal working model consists of explicit and implicit memory. See Chapter Three. However, the theory does not specifically address whether or not witnessing influences the child's internal working model, and if so, how.
35. See endnote 33.
36. P. Fonagy et al., "The Development of Violence and Crime as It Relates to Security of Attachment," In J.D. Osofsky, (Ed.), *Children in a Violent*

Society (New York: Guilford Press; 1999), 150–177; K. Lyons-Ruth and D. Jacobvitz, "Attachment Disorganization: Unresolved Loss, Relational Violence, and Lapses in Behavioral and Attentional Strategies," In J. Cassidy and P. R. Shaver, (Eds.), *Handbook of Attachment: Theory, Research, and Clinical Applications* (New York: Guilford Press, 1999), 520–554; and C. S. Widom, "Motivation and Mechanisms in the 'Cycle of Violence,'" In D. J. Hansen (Ed.), *Nebraska Symposium on Motivation* 46(1998). *Motivation and Child Maltreatment* (Lincoln: University of Nebraska Press, 1998), 1–37.

37. K. Lyons-Ruth and D. Jacobvitz, "Attachment Disorganization: Unresolved Loss, Relational Violence, and Lapses in Behavioral and Attentional Strategies," In J. Cassidy and P. R. Shaver (Eds.), *Handbook of Attachment: Theory, Research, and Clinical Applications* (New York: Guilford Press, 1999), 520–554.
38. J. G. Allen, *Traumatic Relationships and Serious Mental Disorders* (Chichester: John Wiley & Sons, 2001), 39; and E. A. Carlson, "A Prospective Longitudinal Study of Attachment Disorganization/Disorientation," *Child Development* 69 (4)(1998), 1107–1128.
39. D. J. Siegel, *The Developing Mind: Toward a Neurobiology of Interpersonal Experience* (New York: Guilford Press, 1999).
40. See endnote 39.
41. A. Novac and S. Hubert-Schneider, "Acquired Vulnerability: Comorbidity in a Patient Population of Adult Offspring of Holocaust Survivors," *American Journal of Forensic Psychiatry* 19 (2) 1998, 45–58. (This is a paraphrase of pages 50–52).
42. Andrei Novak, personal communication, August 2002.
43. E. A. Carlson, "A Prospective Longitudinal Study of Attachment Disorganization/Disorientation," *Child Development* 69 (4)(1998), 1107–1128.
44. It is also the case that some parents who mistreat their children do not have histories of having been abused or neglected themselves. Parents who have been exposed to violence and violation through other life circumstances—such as living in an unsafe neighborhood or war—may "pass" the residue of these experiences to their children by abusing or neglecting them.
45. Also, parents whose life circumstances are considered low, not high, in stress and who have good social support are less prone to maltreat their children. See J. Belsky, "Child Maltreatment: An Ecological Integration," *American Psychologist* 35 (4)(1980), 320–335.
46. J. G. Allen, 2001, *Traumatic Relationships and Serious Mental Disorders* (Chichester: John Wiley & Sons, 2001), 177, summarizing Kluft.
47. I am endebted to Regina Yando, Ph.D., for this observation.
48. B. Egeland and A. Susman-Stillman, "Dissociation as a Mediator of Child Abuse Across Generations," *Child Abuse and Neglect* (1996), 20(11)(1996), 1123–1132; and J. E. Oliver, "Intergenerational Transmission of Child Abuse: Rates, Research, and Clinical Implications," *American Journal of Psychiatry* 150 (9)(1993), 1315–1324.

49. J. G. Allen, *Traumatic Relationships and Serious Mental Disorders* (Chichester: John Wiley & Sons, 2001); B. Egeland and A. Susman-Stillman, "Dissociation as a Mediator of Child Abuse Across Generations," *Child Abuse and Neglect* 20 150 (9)(11)(1996), 1123–1132; and J. E. Oliver, "Intergenerational Transmission of Child Abuse: Rates, Research, and Clinical Implications," *American Journal of Psychiatry* (1993), 1315–1324.
50. K. Weingarten, "The Discourses of Intimacy: Adding a Social Constructionist and Feminist View," *Family Process* 30 (3)(1991), 285–305; and K. Weingarten, "A Consideration of Intimate and Nonintimate Interactions in Therapy" *Family Process* 31 (1991), 45–59.

Chapter Seven: Putting It All Together: Our Planet, Ourselves

1. J. Hackett, *Disturbance of the Inner Ear* (New York: Carroll & Graf, 2002).
2. J. Hackett, *Disturbance of the Inner Ear* (New York: Carroll & Graf, 2002); H. Schulman, *The Revisionist: A Novel*, 1st ed. (New York: Crown Publishers, 1998); and A. Spiegelman, *Maus I: A Survivor's Tale: My Father Bleeds History* (New York: Pantheon Books, 1986) and A. Spiegelman, *Maus II: A Survivor's Tale: And Here My Troubles Began* (1st ed) (New York: Pantheon Books, 1991).
3. M. R. Ancharoff et al., "The Legacy of Combat Trauma: Clinical Implications of Intergenerational Transmission," In Y. Danieli (Ed.), *International Handbook of Multigenerational Legacies of Trauma* (The Plenum Series on Stress and Coping) (New York: Plenum Press, 1998), 257–276; Y. Danieli, "Introduction: History and Conceptual Foundations," In Y. Danieli (Ed.), *International Handbook of Multigenerational Legacies of Trauma* (New York: Plenum Press, 1998), 1–17, and Y. Danieli "Conclusions and Future Directions," In Y. Danieli, (Ed.), *International Handbook of Multigenerational Legacies of Trauma* (New York: Plenum Press, 1998), 669–689.
4. M. R. Ancharoff et al., "The Legacy of Combat Trauma: Clinical Implications of Intergenerational Transmission," In Y. Danieli (Ed.), *International Handbook of Multigenerational Legacies of Trauma* (The Plenum Series on Stress and Coping) (New York: Plenum Press, 1998), 257–276.
5. My parents testified before the Senate Subcommittee to Investigate the Administration of the Internal Security Act and Other Internal Security Laws of the Committee of the Judiciary, United States Senate. These hearings, known as the Eastland hearings, were chaired by Senator James O. Eastland. J. G. Sourwine was the chief counsel.
6. The Rosenbergs' innocence or guilt is still debated. The recent declassification of documents related to the Venona Project has been convincing to some people of Ethel's absolute innocence of the government's charges

against her, and of the relatively minor role of Julius. Others are not persuaded of the accuracy of these documents. There is much for a contemporary audience to learn from this period. See M.B Garber and R.L. Walkowitz, *Secret Agents: the Rosenberg Case, McCarthyism, and Fifties America* (New York: Routledge, 1995); E. Schrecker, *The Age of McCarthyism: A Brief History with Documents*, 2nd ed. (Boston: Bedford/St. Martin's, 2002); S. Roberts, *The Brother: The Untold Story of Atomic Spy David Greenglass and How He Sent His Sister, Ethel Rosenberg, to the Electric Chair*, 1st ed. (New York: Random House, 2001); and *Secrets, Lies, and Atomic Spies; Nova*. Retrieved October 16, 2002 from the Web: *http://www.pbs.org/wgbh/nova/venona/*.

7. In the 1930s, participation in the Communist Party was common for socially progressive liberals.
8. E. Schrecker, *The Age of McCarthyism: A Brief History with Documents*, 2nd ed. (Boston: Bedford/St. Martin's, 2002).
9. R.M. Fried, *Nightmare in Red: The McCarthy Era in Perspective* (New York: Oxford University Press, 1990).
10. See references to projective identification in J.G. Allen, *Traumatic Relationships and Serious Mental Disorders* (Chichester: John Wiley & Sons, 2001); D. Rowland-Klein and R. Dunlop, "The Transmission of Trauma Across Generations: Identification with Parental Trauma in Children of Holocaust Survivors," *Australian and New Zealand Journal of Psychiatry* 32 (3)(June 1998), 358–369; and G. Hardtmann, "Children of Nazis: A Psychodynamic Perspective," In Y. Danieli (Ed.), *International Handbook of Multigenerational Legacies of Trauma* (The Plenum Series on Stress and Coping) (New York: Plenum Press, 1998), 85–95.
11. A. Shlaim, *The Iron Wall: Israel and the Arab World*, 1st ed. (New York: Norton, 2000).
12. See footnote 6.
13. E. Thomas and M. Isikoff, "Justice Kept in the Dark," *Newsweek*, December 10, 2001, 37.
14. Z. Solomon et al. "Combat-Related Posttraumatic Stress Disorder Among Second-Generation Holocaust Survivors: Preliminary Findings," *American Journal of Psychiatry* 145 (7)(1988), 865–868.
15. Silence feels different still when one belongs to a group whose experience of violence and violation is neither readily discussed within the family nor in the national community that imposed it, which is the case for Japanese Americans whose family members were evacuated and placed in internment camps following the attack on Pearl Harbor in 1941. See D.K. Nagata, "Intergenerational Effects of the Japanese American Internment," In Y. Danieli (Ed.), *International Handbook of Multigenerational Legacies of Trauma* (New York: Plenum Press, 1998), 125–146.
16. K. Weingarten, *The Mother's Voice: Strengthening Intimacy in Families* (New York: Guilford Press, 1997).

17. J. Gilligan, *Violence: Reflections on a National Epidemic* (New York: Vintage Books, 1997).
18. G. Kaufman, *Shame: The Power of Caring* (Rochester, Vt.: Schenkman Books, 1992).
19. E.G. Lindner, "Humiliation—Trauma That Has Been Overlooked: An Analysis Based on Fieldwork in Germany, Rwanda/Burundi, and Somalia," *Traumatology* (2001), 51–79; E.G. Lindner, "Humiliation and Human Rights: Mapping a Minefield," *Human Rights Review* 2 (2)(2001), 46–63; V.D. Volkan, *Bloodlines: From Ethnic Pride to Ethnic Terrorism*, 1st ed. (New York: Farrar, Straus & Giroux, 1997); V.D. Volkan, "The Tree Model: A Comprehensive Psychopolitical Approach to Unofficial Diplomacy and the Reduction of Ethnic Tension," *Mind and Human Interaction* 10 (3)(1999), 142–210; and V.D. Volkan, "Traumatized Societies and Psychological Care: Expanding the Concept of Preventive Medicine," *Mind and Human Interaction* 11 (3)(2000), 177–194.
20. Although societal mechanisms of trauma transfer are usually used to account for the passing of trauma from an older to a younger generation, there are some situations in which young people who were involved in political movements "traumatized" their parents due to the risks and dangers associated with their political activities. In these instances vertical transmission went "up" as well as "down" the generations. See M.A. Simpson, "The Second Bullet: Transgenerational Impacts of the Trauma of Conflict Within a South African and World Context," In Y. Danieli (Ed.), *International Handbook of Multigenerational Legacies of Trauma* (New York: Plenum Press, 1998), 487–512.
21. Linder sets forth four propositions that account for the ways that processes of humiliation between societies can set in motion large-scale violence, even genocide. First, some people must humble others. The response of those humbled will vary depending on the ideology that supports the cultural practices of humiliation and the prior social conditions that existed between the two groups. There may be acceptance tinged with resentment, a desire to return to social equality between the groups, or a motivation to "reverse the relationship and humble the dominant group" (Lindner, 2001a, 54). Second, if the ideology of human rights has pervaded the cultural consciousness, domination and humiliation by one group will be particularly onerous for the subordinated group. Third, the conditions for genocide as a means of reversing domination will be ripe in those societies undergoing a transition between accepting humiliation as normal and believing it violates human rights, and in societies in which existing hierarchical social structures are weakening. Fourth, societies will be better able to bear routine humiliation if they feel the respect of the world community; but, conversely, the experience of humiliation will become intolerable if they perceive that they are disrespected or have lost respect. This will engender more rage, adding to the accumulation of resentment and contributing to the impulse

toward retaliation. E. G. Lindner, "Humiliation and Human Rights: Mapping a Minefield," *Human Rights Review* 2 (2)(2001a), 46–63.

22. E. G. Lindner, "Humiliation—Trauma That Has Been Overlooked: An Analysis Based on Fieldwork in Germany, Rwanda/Burundi, and Somalia," *Traumatology* 7 (1)(2001), 51–79.
23. V. D. Volkan, *Bloodlines: From Ethnic Pride to Ethnic Terrorism*, 1st ed. (New York: Farrar, Straus & Giroux, 1997); V. D. Volkan, "The Tree Model: A Comprehensive Psychopolitical Approach to Unofficial Diplomacy and the Reduction of Ethnic Tension," *Mind and Human Interaction* 10 (3)(1999), 142–210; V. D. Volkan, "Traumatized Societies and Psychological Care: Expanding the Concept of Preventive Medicine," *Mind and Human Interaction* 11 (3)(2000), 177–194; and V. D. Volkan, "Transgenerational Transmissions and Chosen Traumas: An Aspect of Large-Group Identity," *Group Analysis* 34 (1)(2001), 79–97.
24. V. D. Volkan, "Transgenerational Transmissions and Chosen Traumas: An Aspect of Large-Group Identity," *Group Analysis* 34 (1)(2001), 87.
25. V. D. Volkan, "Transgenerational Transmissions and Chosen Traumas: An Aspect of Large-Group Identity," *Group Analysis* 34 (1)(2001), 88.
26. V. D. Volkan, "Transgenerational Transmissions and Chosen Traumas: An Aspect of Large-Group Identity," *Group Analysis* 34 (1)(2001), 89.
27. B. L. Cardozo et al. "Mental Health, Social Functioning, and Attitudes of Kosovar Albanians Following the War in Kosovo," *JAMA* 284 (5)(2000), 569–577.
28. P. Boss, *Ambiguous Loss: Learning to Live with Unresolved Grief* (Cambridge, Ma.: Harvard University Press, 1999).
29. There is no consensus about why NATO intervened in Kosovo and whether it was the "right" thing to do. Opinions vary on the right and the left as to whether the NATO campaign caused more suffering or brought it to an end. Most people agree that the Serbian government headed by Slobodon Milošović had systematically oppressed Albanian Kosovars beginning in 1989 and that Serbian atrocities (often followed by Kosovar Albanian counterattacks) were escalating in 1998. Commentators note that the massive scale of Serb crimes against humanity started after the NATO bombings began and that the NATO campaign in Kosovo did not seem to have any effect on stopping Serb military action. NATO began bombing Serbian targets in May; Milošović surrendered on June 3, 1999, and signed an agreement six days later, after seventy-eight days of NATO bombing. (See Knightley for a discussion of what caused Milošović to surrender.) These texts give a number of views of the NATO bombings. N. Chomsky, "In Retrospect: A Review of NATO's War over Kosovo," Part I; *Z Magazine*, April 2000, 19–24; N. Chomsky, "In Retrospect: A Review of NATO's War over Kosovo," Part II, *Z Magazine*, Part II; April 2000, 21–27; C. Hedges, *War Is a Force That Gives Us Meaning*, 1st ed. (New York: Publio Affairs, 2002); P. Knightley, *The First Casualty: The War Correspondent as Hero and Myth-maker from the Crimea to Kosovo*, Johns Hopkins Paper-

backs ed. (Baltimore: Johns Hopkins University Press, 2002); and S. Power, *A Problem from Hell: America and the Age of Genocide* (New York: Basic Books, 2002).

30. S. Power, *A Problem from Hell: America and the Age of Genocide* (New York: Basic Books, 2002).
31. Those who do include T. Judah, *Kosovo: War and Revenge* (New Haven: Yale University Press, 2000); S. Power, *A Problem from Hell: America and the-Age of Genocide* (New York: Basic Books, 2002); and V.D. Volkan, "Transgenerational Transmissions and Chosen Traumas: An Aspect of Large-Group Identity," *Group Analysis* 34 (1)(2001), 79–97. Others do not find this compelling. Hedges believes that the wars in the Balkans were "manufactured" and were "born out of the collapse of civil societies, perpetuated by fear, greed, and paranoia, and . . . run by gangsters, who rise up from the bottom of their own societies and terrorize all, including those they purport to protect." C. Hedges, *War Is a Force That Gives Us Meaning*, 1st ed. (New York: PublicAffairs, 2002), 20.
32. V.D. Volkan, "Transgenerational Transmissions and Chosen Traumas: An Aspect of Large-Group Identity," *Group Analysis* 34 (1)(2001), 79–97.
33. T. Judah, *Kosovo: War and Revenge* (New Haven: Yale University Press, 2002), 17–18, quoting T.A. Emmert, *Serbian Golgotha: Kosovo, 1389* (New York: Columbia University Press, 1990), 133.
34. S. Power, *A Problem from Hell: America and the Age of Genocide* (New York: Basic Books, 2002); and V.D. Volkan, "Transgenerational Transmissions and Chosen Traumas: An Aspect of Large-Group Identity," *Group Analysis* 34 (1)(2001), 79–97.
35. V.D. Volkan, "Transgenerational Transmissions and Chosen Traumas: An Aspect of Large-Group Identity," *Group Analysis*, 34 (1)(2001), 94, quoting Vulliamy, 1994, 51. This speech is widely reported as having stirred Serbian nationalistic fervor. In fact, a BBC and U.S. Department of Commerce translation of this speech does not reveal these themes. See BBC Summary of World Broadcasts, "Slobodon Milošović Addresses Rally at Gazimestan," Belgrade home service 1109 gmt 28, June 1989.
36. F. Pretorius, *The Anglo-Boer War, 1899–1902*, 2nd rev. ed. (Cape Town: Struik, 1998).
37. F. Pretorius, *The Anglo-Boer War, 1899–1902*, 2nd ed., (Cape Town: Struik, 1998), 81.
38. P. Levi, *The Drowned and the Saved* (New York: Summit Books, 1988); S. Power, *A Problem from Hell: America and the Age of Genocide* (New York: Basic Books, 2002); and E. Staub, *The Roots of Evil: The Origins of Genocide and Other Group Violence* (Cambridge, UK; New York: Cambridge University Press, 1989).
39. E. Staub, *The Roots of Evil: The Origins of Genocide and Other Group Violence* (Cambridge, UK; New York: Cambridge University Press, 1989), and V.D. Volkan, *Bloodlines: From Ethnic Pride to Ethnic Terrorism*, 1st ed. (New York: Farrar, Straus & Giroux, 1997).

40. This term was introduced by President George W. Bush in his State of the Union address in Washington, D.C., on January 29, 2002.
41. O. Botcharova, "Implementation of Track Two Diplomacy: Developing a Model of Forgiveness," In R. G. Helmick and R. I. Petersen (Eds.), *Forgiveness and Reconciliation: Religion, Public Policy and Conflict Transformation* (Philadelphia: Templeton Foundation Press, 2001), 269–293; I. Kogan, "Breaking the Cycle of Trauma: From the Individual to Society," *Mind and Human Interaction* 11 (1)(2002), 2–10; and V. D. Volkan, *Bloodlines: From Ethnic Pride to Ethnic Terrorism*, 1st ed. (New York: Farrar, Straus & Giroux, 1997).
42. O. Botcharova, "Implementation of Track Two Diplomacy: Developing a Model of Forgiveness," In R. G. Helmick and R. L. Petersen (Eds.), *Forgiveness and Reconciliation: Religion, Public Policy, and Conflict Transformation* (Philadelphia: Templeton Foundation Press, 2001), 269–293; J. Kliman and R. Llerena-Quinn, "Dehumanizing and Rehumanizing Responses to September 11," *Journal of Systemic Therapies* 21 (3)(2002), 8–18; and N. G. Sider, "At the Fork in the Road: Trauma Healing," *Conciliation Quarterly* 20 (2)(2001), 7–11.
43. M. Shahini, "Therapy, Tradition, and Myself," *AACAP News* 32 (4) (2001), 182.
44. K. Kollwitz and H. Kollwitz, *The Diary and Letters of Kaethe Kollwitz* (Evanston, Ill.: Northwestern University Press, 1988).
45. O. Botcharova, "Implementation of Track Two Diplomacy: Developing a Model of Forgiveness," In R. G. Helmick and R. L. Petersen (Eds.), *Forgiveness and Reconciliation: Religion, Public Policy and Conflict Transformation* (Philadelphia: Templeton Foundation Press, 2001), 288.
46. H. Klinger, *Family Dynamics and Intergenerational Transmission* (Penn Valley, Pa.: Transcending Trauma Project, 2001); and A. Novak, *Prevention of Intergenerational Transmission of Effects of Trauma* (Presentation at ISTSS-Conference) (Santa Clarita, CA: Professional Programs, Inc., 2001).
47. See P. Fonagy and M. Target, "Attachment and Reflective Function: Their Role in Self-Organization," *Development and Psychopathology* 9 (4)(1997), 679–700, regarding the consequences for individuals and society when an individual's mentalizing capacity is compromised.
48. S. Felman, and D. Laub, *Testimony: Crises of Witnessing in Literature, Psychoanalysis, and History* (New York; London: Routledge, 1992).
49. J. Hatley, *Suffering Witness: The Quandary of Responsibility After the Irreparable* (Albany: State University of New York Press, 2000).
50. In September 2002 I heard Arn Chorn-Pond, human rights activist and survivor of the Cambodian genocide, discuss how his ability to witness himself, and now thousands of others, developed from his having been witnessed. See also, S. Felman and D. Laub, *Testimony: Crises of Witnessing in Literature, Psychoanalysis, and History* (New York; London: Routledge, 1992); J. Hatley, *Suffering Witness: The Quandary of Responsibility*

after the Irreparable (Albany: State University of New York Press, 2001); Krog, A., *Country of My Skull* (New York: Random House, 1989); and L. L. Langer; *Holocaust Testimonies: the Ruins of Memory* (New Haven: Yale University Press, 1991).

51. W. G. James, and L. v. d. Vijver, *After the TRC: Reflections on Truth and Reconciliation in South Africa* (Athens: Ohio University Press, 2001), 64.
52. See endnote 51.
53. K. Weingarten, "The Discourses of Intimacy: Adding a Social Constructionist and Feminist View," *Family Process* 30 (3)(1991), 285–305; and K. Weingarten, "A Consideration of Intimate and Nonintimate Interactions in Therapy," *Family Process* 31 (1)(1992), 45–59.
54. For a discussion of the impact of parental silence in the context of war, see A. Dyregrov et al., "Children Exposed to Warfare: A Longitudinal Study," *Journal of Traumatic Stress*, 15 (1)(2002), 59–68.
55. D. Bar-On, *Legacy of Silence: Encounters with Children of the Third Reich* (Cambridge, Ma.: Harvard University Press, 1989); D. Blair, "Bicommunal Dialogue: Kosovar Albanian and Serb Young Adult Leaders. Peacebuilding in Action," (*Karuna Center Newsletter*, 2001); and V. D. Volkan, 1999, "The Tree Model: A Comprehensive Psychopolitical Approach to Unofficial Diplomacy and the Reduction of Ethnic Tension," *Mind and Human Interaction*, 10 (3)(1999), 142–210.
56. A. L. Berger, and N. Berger, *Second Generation Voices: Reflections by Children of Holocaust Survivors and Perpetrators*, 1st ed. (Syracuse, N.Y.: Syracuse University Press, 2001).
57. See article on this Web site for a description of a dialogue that brought together members of One by One, a group that sponsors dialogues between children and grandchildren of Holocaust survivors and Nazi perpetrators, and Bosnian Muslims and Serbs: P. Green, "An Infusion of Dialogues: Bosnians in Dialogue Meet Holocaust Descendants in Dialogue," The Karuna Center. Retrieved October 16, 2002, from the Web: *http://www.karunacenter.org*.
58. D. Blair, "Bi-communal dialogue: Kosovar Albanian and Serb young adult leaders. Peacebuilding in Action" (Karuna Center Newsletter, 2001); and D. Bar-On et al., "Who am I in relation to my past, in relation to the other? German and Israeli students confront the Holocaust and each other." In Y. Danieli (Ed.), *International Handbook of Multigenerational Legacies of Trauma*. (The Plenum Series on Stress and Coping) (New York, Plenum Press, 1998) 97–116.
59. K. Weingarten, "The Small and the Ordinary: The Daily Practice of a Postmodern Narrative Therapy," *Family Process, 37* (1): 3–15, 1998.
60. Aeschylus, and R. A. Lattimore, *Aeschylus I: Oresteia*, 1st Phoenix ed., (Chicago: University of Chicago Press, 1969).

Part Three: What We Can Do

1. D. Metzger, *Looking for the Faces of God* (Berkeley, Ca.: Parallax Press, 1989).

Chapter Eight: Foundations of Witnessing

1. *The Nation* (Nairobi), June 3, 2002, "Maasai's 'Ultimate Gift' Of Cows To US," All Africa. Retrieved August 4, 2002, from the Web: *http://allafrica. com/stories/200206030712.html*
2. M. Rosenberg, "Kenyan Villagers Honor 9–11 Victims," *The Associated Press*, June 3, 2002.
3. M. Delio, June 5, 2002, "How to Thank Kenya for 9/11 Cows." Wired. Retrieved August 4, 2002, from the Web: *http://www.wired.com/news/culture/0,1284,52984,00.html*
4. The Family of Firefighter Jeffrey James Olsen, July 17, 2002, "Thanks for the Cattle" Retrieved October 17, 2002 from the Web: *http://dual-boot-comp.com/14cattle/viewcomments.php*
5. As Michael Ignatieff observes: "What defines [humanity], the very identity we share as a species, is the fact that we are differentiated by race, religion, ethnicity, and individual difference. . . . A sense of otherness, of distinctness, is the very basis of the consciousness of our individuality. . . . To attack any one of these differences . . . is to attack the shared element that makes us what we are as a species. In this way of thinking we understand humanity, our common flesh and blood, as valuable to the degree that it allows us to elaborate the dignity and the honor that we give to our differences. . . ." See M. Ignatieff, "The Danger of a World Without Enemies. Lemkin's Word," *The New Republic*, February 21, 2001, 25.
6. I am not suggesting that the person who is responded to in this fashion has no reaction to it. These are different points.
7. In most states there are mandatory reporting laws that dictate what kinds of abuse and neglect must be reported, by whom, and to whom.
8. Joaquín Samayoa, quoted by Ignacio Martín-Baró, states that war produces dehumanization that impoverishes "a) the ability to think lucidly, b) the ability to communicate truthfully, c) sensitivity to the suffering of others, and d) hope." I. Martin-Baro, "Political Violence and War as Causes of Psychosocial Trauma in El Salvador," *International Journal of Mental Health* 18 (1)(1989), 140.
9. See Priam's encounter with Achilles after the latter has killed and defiled Priam's son, Hector. Homer and R.A. Lattimore, 1961, *The Iliad of*

Homer (Chicago: University of Chicago Press, 1961), 480–488. For a discussion of how shared sorrow can bridge enmity, see H. Kamya and D. Trimble, "Response to Injury: Toward Ethical Construction of the Other," *Journal of Systemic Therapies* 21 (3)(2002), 9–29.

10. P. Gobodo-Madikizela, "Remorse, Forgiveness, and Rehumanization: Stories from South Africa," *Journal of Humanistic Psychology* 42 (1)(2002), 7–32. This paper was written in the context of the TRC. See also, P. Gobodo-Madikizela, *A Human Being Died That Night: A South African Story of Forgiveness* (Boston: Houghton Mifflin, 2003).
11. E.M. Remarque, *All Quiet on the Western Front*, 1st Ballantine Books ed. (New York: Ballantine Books, 1982), 223.
12. D. Grossman, *On Killing: The Psychological Cost of Learning to Kill in War and Society* (Boston: Little Brown, 1996).
13. D. Grossman, *On Killing: The Psychological Cost of Learning to Kill in War and Society* (Boston: Little Brown, 1996), 160, quoting Peter Watson.
14. R.J. Sternberg, (*A Duplex Theory of Hate and its Development and its Application to Massacres and Genocide.* Unpublished manuscript, Yale University, New Haven, 2002), relates propaganda to the concept of hate. Propaganda is the antithesis of compassionate witnessing. A formal analysis of both would reveal that the structure, values, and purposes of each are radically dissimilar. See M. Underwood, December 4, 2001, "Political propaganda and persuasion: What is Propaganda?" Communication, Cultural and Media Studies. Retrieved October 17, 2002, from the Web: ***http://www.cultsock.ndirect.co.uk/MUHome/cshtml/propaganda/pol2. html***
15. Y. Landau, "Rehumanizing the 'Enemy' and Confronting Ourselves: Challenges for Educators in an Era of Peace," *Palestine-Israel Journal of Politics, Economics and Culture*, III (1)(Winter 1996), 65.
16. A search of one of the behavioral-science indexes reveals 108 articles on the subject of dehumanization, but only four on rehumanizing, of which P. Gobodo-Madikizela, "Remorse, Forgiveness, and Rehumanization: Stories from South Africa," *Journal of Humanistic Psychology* 42 (1)(2002), 7–32, is the one most relevant to this book.
17. S. Wright, *Quotes from Stephen Wright*, Eric S. Raymond Web site. Retrieved October 17, 2002, from the Web: ***http://www.tuxedo.org/~esr/fortunes/stephen-wright.html***
18. Two resources are P. Chödrön, *Good Medicine* (Boulder, Co.: Sounds True, 1999); and R. Sogyal et al., *The Tibetan Book of Living and Dying* (San Francisco: Harper San Francisco, 1992). Also Shambhala has an extensive selection of books, tapes, and videos on meditation. ***http://www.shambhala.com/***
19. R.J. Lifton, *The Broken Connection: On Death and the Continuity of Life* (New York: Simon & Schuster, 1979), 392.
20. J. Kabat-Zinn, *Full Catastrophe Living: Using the Wisdom of Your Body and Mind to Face Stress, Pain, and Illness* (New York: Delacorte Press, 1990).

21. A.H. Maslow, *Motivation and Personality*, 1st ed. (New York: Harper, 1954).
22. J.L. Herman, *Trauma and Recovery* (New York: BasicBooks, 1992).
23. S.T. Shepela et al., "Courageous Resistance: A Special Case of Altruism," *Theory and Psychology* 9 (6)(1999), 801.
24. S. T. Shepela et. al., "Courageous Resistance: A Special Case of Altruism," *Theory and Psychology* 9 (6)(1999), 790.
25. N. Eisenberg, "Empathy and Sympathy," In W. Damon, (Ed.), *Child Development Today and Tomorrow*. The Jossey-Bass Social and Behavioral Science Series (San Francisco, Ca.: Jossey-Bass, 1989), 137–154; M.L. Hoffman, *Empathy and Moral Development: Implications for Caring and Justice* (Cambridge, UK; New York, 2000); A. Kohn, 1990, *The Brighter Side of Human Nature: Altruism and Empathy in Everyday Life* (New York: Basic Books, 1990). To complicate matters, though, James Hatley suggests that in situations of extreme suffering, it is imperative not to confuse one's own suffering that comes from imagining the other's suffering with the person's suffering itself. He writes, "We suffer, so to speak, the impossibility of suffering the other's suffering." J. Hatley, *Suffering Witness: The Quandary of Responsibility After the Irreparable* (Albany: State University of New York Press, 2000), 5.
26. A. Kohn, *The Brighter Side of Human Nature: Altruism and Empathy in Everyday Life* (New York: Basic Books, 1990).
27. P. Fallon, "Ramadan for Non-Muslims," *Morning Edition* radio program: WBUR. Boston, December 7, 2001.
28. G. Svirsky, "Wanted: Living Rooms to Ransack." Jerusalem, Israel: e-mail, June 15, 2002.
29. See endnote no. 26.
30. N. Eisenberg, "Empathy and Sympathy," In W. Damon (Ed.), *Child Development Today and Tomorrow*. The Jossey-Bass Social and Behavioral Science Series (San Francisco, Ca.: Jossey-Bass, 1989), 137–154; M.L. Hoffman, *Empathy and Moral Development: Implications for Caring and Justice* (Cambridge, UK; New York: Cambridge University Press, 2000); and A. Kohn, *The Brighter Side of Human Nature: Altruism and Empathy in Everyday Life* (New York: Basic Books, 1990).
31. Impact Model Mugging: Strategies for Safe Living. Retrieved from the Web: *http://www.impactboston.com/*
32. *Aidos* "Ideas and Roots" 2001. Retrieved November 20, 2001, from the Web: *http://www.consultsos.com/pandora/aidos.htm*
33. M.P.O. Morford et al., *Classical Mythology* (New York: McKay 1977), 43.
34. J. Gilligan, *Violence: Reflections on a National Epidemic* (New York: Vintage Books, 1997); G. Kaufman, *Shame: The Power of Caring* (Rochester, Vt.: Schenkman Books, 1992); M.J. Lewis, *Shame: The Exposed Self* (New York: Free Press, 1995); and J.W. Mason et al., "Psychogenic Lowering of Urinary Cortisol Levels Linked to Increased Emotional Numbing and a Shame-Depressive Syndrome in Combat-Related Postraumatic Stress Disorder," *Psychosomatic Medicine* 63 (3)(2001), 387–401.

35. K. Duff, *The Alchemy of Illness* (New York: Bell Tower, 1993); and G. Kaufman, *Shame: The Power of Caring* (Rochester, Vt.: Schenkman Books, 1993).
36. H. B. Lewis, *Shame and Guilt in Neurosis* (New York: International Universities Press, 1971); and M. J. Lewis, *Shame: The Exposed Self* (New York: Free Press, 1995).
37. S. Wiesenthal et al., *The Sunflower: On the Possibilities and Limits of Forgiveness*, rev. and expanded, 2nd ed. (New York: Schocken Books, 1997), 130.
38. S. Batchelor, *Buddhism Without Beliefs: A Contemporary Guide to Awakening* (New York: Riverhead Books); and P. Chödrön, *When Things Fall Apart: Heart Advice for Difficult Times* 1st ed. (Boston: Shambhala, Distributed in the United States by Random House, 1997).
39. This conference was organized by Judith Thompson in cooperation with the Boston Center for Research in the 21st Century, Cambridge, Ma., September 2002.
40. D. Imbrogno, *Belfast Diary: Hanging Out with the Dalai Lama, IRA Victims, Former Paramilitaries, and Struggling Peacemakers in the Bombed and Barbed Wire Capital of Northern Ireland*. Hundred Mountain, 2001. Retrieved October 17, 2002, from the Web: *http://www.hundredmountain.com/Pages/pageone_stuff/winter_01/belfast1_winter01.html*
41. See D. McKittrick and D. McVea, *Making Sense of the Troubles: The Story of the Conflict in Northern Ireland* (Chicago: New Amsterdam Books, 2002).
42. Richard Moore, personal communication, September 2002.
43. M. C. Nussbaum, *Upheavals of Thought: The Intelligence of Emotions* (Cambridge, UK; New York: Cambridge University Press, 2001).
44. H. Kamya and D. Trimble, "Response to Injury: Toward Ethical Construction of the Other," *Journal of Systemic Therapies* 21 (3)(2002), 19–29; M. E. McCullough et al., "Vengefulness: Relationships with Forgiveness, Rumination, Well-being, and the Big Five," *Personality and Social Psychology Bulletin* 27 (5)(2001), 601–610; and R. J. Sternberg, *A Duplex Theory of Hate and its Development and its Application to Massacres and Genocide*. Unpublished manuscript, Yale University, New Haven, 2002.
45. W. Wink, *Engaging the Powers: Discernment and Resistance in a World of Domination* (Minneapolis: Fortress Press, 1992).
46. D. L. Smith-Christopher, *Subverting Hatred: The Challenge of Nonviolence in Religious Traditions* (New York: Orbis Books, 2000).
47. D. A. Doran, "Nigerian Women Signal End to Siege," *The Boston Globe*, July 17, 2002, A13.
48. M. Gandhi et al., *Gandhi on Nonviolence* (New York: New Directions, 2002), 15.
49. K. Waterson, "The Cantor and the Klansman." In J. Canfield and M. V.

Hansen and D. P. Elkins (Eds.), *Chicken Soup for the Jewish Soul: Stories to Open the Heart and Rekindle the Spirit* (Deerfield Beach, Fla.: Health Communications, 2001), 7–13.

50. K. Kraft, *Inner Peace, World Peace: Essays on Buddhism and Nonviolence* (Albany: State University of New York Press, 1992); T. Nhât Hanh and A. Kotler, *Being Peace* (Berkeley: Parallax Press, 1996); and D. L. Smith-Christopher, *Subverting Hatred: The Challenge of Nonviolence in Religious Traditions* (New York: Orbis Books, 2000). See also *ubuntu*, an African worldview in which a person is viewed as human "precisely in being enveloped in the community of other human beings." M. Battle, *Reconciliation: The Ubuntu Theology of Desmond Tutu* (Cleveland: Pilgrim Press, 1997), 39.
51. M. Gopin, *Between Eden and Armageddon: The Future of World Religions, Violence, and Peacemaking* (Oxford, UK; New York: Oxford University Press, 2000); M. Polner and N. Goodman, *The Challenge of Shalom: the Jewish Tradition of Peace and Justice* (Philadelphia: New Society Publishers, 1994); H. O. Thompson, *World Religions in War and Peace* (Jefferson, N.C.: McFarland, 1988); and W. Wink, *Engaging the Powers: Discernment and Resistance in a World of Domination* (Minneapolis: Fortress Press, 1992).
52. D. L. Smith-Christopher, *Subverting Hatred: The Challenge of Nonviolence in Religious Traditions* (New York: Orbis Books, 2000), 172.
53. D. Kaminer, D. J. Stein, I. Mbanga, and N. Zungu-Dirwayi, "Forgiveness: Toward an Integration of Theoretical Models," *Psychiatry: Interpersonal and Biological Processes* 63 (4)(2000), 344–357.
54. J. P. Pingleton, "The Role and Function of Forgiveness in the Psychotherapeutic Process," *Journal of Psychology and Theology*, 17 (1)(1989), 27–35.
55. J. North, "The 'Ideal' of Forgiveness: A Philosopher's Exploration," In Robert D. Enright and Joanna North (Eds.), *Exploring Forgiveness* (Madison: University of Wisconsin Press, 1998), 15–34.
56. E. N. Dorff, "The Elements of Forgiveness: A Jewish Approach," In E. L. Worthington, (Ed.), *Dimensions of Forgiveness: Psychological Research and Theological Perspectives* (Philadelphia: Templeton Foundation Press, 1998), 29–55.
57. A. Jenkins, M. Joy, and R. Hall, "Forgiveness and Child Sexual Abuse: A Matrix of Meanings," *The International Journal of Narrative Therapy and Community Work*, (1)(2002), 35–51.
58. M. S. Rye, K. I. Pargament, M. A. Ali, G. L. Beck, E. N. Dorff, C. Hallisey, V. Narayanan, and J. G. Williams, "Religious Perspectives on Forgiveness." In M. E. McCullough and K. I. Pargament et al. (Eds.), *Forgiveness: Theory, Research, and Practice* (New York: Guilford Press, 2000), 17–40.
59. E. Lomax, *The Railway Man: A POW's Searing Account of War, Brutality, and Forgiveness* (New York: Norton, 1995).

60. *Medical Foundation for the Care of Victims of Torture* 2002. Retrieved October 17, 2002, from the Web: *http://www.torturecare.org.uk/*
61. E. Lomax, *The Railway Man: A POW's Searing Account of War, Brutality, and Forgiveness* (New York: Norton, 1995), 239.
62. E. Lomax, *The Railway Man: A POW's Searing Account of War, Brutality, and Forgiveness* (New York: Norton, 1995), 251.
63. S. Wiesenthal, H. J. Cargas, and B. V. Fetterman, *The Sunflower: On the Possibilities and Limits of Forgiveness*, rev. and expanded, 2nd ed. (New York: Schocken Books, 1997).
64. E. Lomax, *The Railway Man: A POW's Searing Account of War, Brutality, and Forgiveness* (New York: Norton, 1995), 255.
65. J. Hatley, *Suffering Witness: The Quandary of Responsibility After the Irreparable* (Albany: State University of New York Press, 2000).
66. A. Jenkins et al., "Forgiveness and Child Sexual Abuse: A Matrix of Meanings," *The International Journal of Narrative Therapy and Community Work* 1, (2002) 35–51 and P. Gobodo-Madikizela, *A Human Being Died That Night: A South African Story of Forgiveness* (Boston: Houghton Mifflin, 2003).
67. S. Freedman, "Forgiveness and Reconciliation: The Importance of Understanding How They Differ," *Counseling and Values* 42 (3)(1998), 200–216.
68. T. Ashbrook, *Bringing Bereaved Israelis and Palestinians Together*. Radio program: *On Point*, WBUR Boston, March 20, 2002.
69. A. R. Chapman, "Truth Commissions as Instruments of Forgiveness and Reconciliation," In R. G. Helmick and R. L. Petersen, (Eds.), *Forgiveness and Reconciliation: Religion, Public Policy, and Conflict Transformation* (Philadelphia: Templeton Foundation Press, 2001), 247–267.
70. M. Snyder, *No Hole in the Flame: A Memoir on Love and Grief in Poetry and Prose* (Albuquerque: Wildflower Press, 2003).
71. M. Snyder, *No Hole in the Flame: A Memoir on Love and Grief in Poetry and Prose* (Albuquerque: Wildflower Press, 2003), 54.
72. M. Snyder, *No Hole in the Flame: A Memoir on Love and Grief in Poetry and Prose* (Albuquerque: Wildflower Press, 2003), 55.
73. M. Snyder, *No Hole in the Flame: A Memoir on Love and Grief in Poetry and Prose* (Albuquerque: Wildflower Press, 2003), 55.
74. A. W. Frank, "Just listening: Narrative and Deep Illness," *Families, Systems and Health*, 16 (3)(1998), 197–212; C. Hwoschinsky, *Listening with the Heart: A Guide For Compassionate Listening* (Indianola, Wa. MidEast Citizen Diplomacy, 2001); and K. Weingarten, "Radical Listening: Challenging Cultural Beliefs for and About Mothers," In K. Weingarten, (Ed.), *Cultural Resistance: Challenging Beliefs About Men, Women, and Therapy* (New York: Harrington Park Press/Haworth Press, 1995), 7–22.
75. J. S. Hirsch, *Riot and Remembrance: The Tulsa Race War and Its Legacy*

(Boston: Houghton Mifflin, 2002), and personal communication, July 2002.

76. W. S. Merwin, "Unchopping a Tree," In W. S. Merwin, (Ed.), *The Miner's Pale Children*, 1st ed. (New York: Antheneum, 2002); suggested by Lawrence Wechsler, quoted by M. Minow, *Between Vengeance and Forgiveness: Facing History After Genocide and Mass Violence* (Boston: Beacon Press, 1998), 62.
77. Or, yet another angle. Marius Schoon was an apartheid opponent who spent twelve years in prison for allegedly blowing up a police station in 1964. During the amnesty hearings of the Truth and Reconciliation Commission, Mr. Schoon actively fought amnesty for Craig Williamson, who admitted to planting the bomb that killed Mr. Schoon's wife and six-year-old daughter. During the hearings he remarked, "On the whole, I'm in favor of the Truth and Reconciliation Commission. I think it's going to bring about national reconciliation. In my case, it's not going to bring about personal reconciliation." D. G. McNeil, "Marius Schoon, 61, Is Dead; Foe of Apartheid Lost Family," *New York Times*, February 9, 1999, 31.
78. V. Goldner, "Generation and Gender: Normative and Covert Hierarchies," *Family Process* 27 (1)(1988), 17–31; V. Goldner et al., "Love and Violence: Gender Paradoxes in Volatile Attachments," *Family Process* 29 (4)(1990), 343–364; and R.T. Hare-Mustin, "A Feminist Approach to Family Therapy," *Family Process* 17 (2)(1978), 181–194.
79. S. Opotow, "Reconciliation in Times of Impunity: Challenges for Social Justice," *Social Justice Research* 14 (2)(2001), 149–170.
80. S. Opotow, "Reconciliation in Times of Impunity: Challenges for Social Justice," *Social Justice Research* 14 (2)(2001), 165.
81. E. Staub, "Preventing Genocide: Activating Bystanders, Helping Victims and the Creation of Caring," *Peace & Conflict: Journal of Peace Psychology*, (2/3)(1996), 189–200; and D. M. Tutu, "Without Forgiveness There Is No Future," In R. D. Enright and J. North, (Eds.), *Exploring Forgiveness* (Madison: University of Wisconsin Press, 1998).
82. M. Minow, *Between Vengeance and Forgiveness: Facing History After Genocide and Mass Violence* (Boston: Beacon Press, 1998), 147.
83. H. L. Brown, "The Navajo Nation's Peacemaker Division: An Integrated, Community-Based Dispute Resolution Forum," *American Indian Law Review* 24 (297)(2000), quoting Bill Donovan, "Peacemakers Do Justice to Navajos," *Arizona Republic*, April 5, 1993, A1. For a critique of Navajo peacemaking methods with regard to whether or not the procedure addresses feminist concerns that offender apologies are overvalued and that insufficient attention is paid to the societal conditions that support individual acts of batterers, see D. Coker, *Enhancing Autonomy for Battered Women: Lessons from Navajo Peacemaking* (The Regents of the University of California *UCLA Law Review* 47 [1], October 1999).

84. H.L. Brown, "The Navajo Nation's Peacemaker Division: An Integrated, Community-Based Dispute Resolution Forum," *American Indian Law Review* 24 (297)(2000), 2, quoting Robert Yazzie.
85. Restorative justice is an emerging justice paradigm that is being implemented all over the world. It was first used in Canada in 1974 and in the United States in 1977–78. Some methods focus on the victim and the offender, while others explicitly include the community as a stakeholder. For excellent discussions of restorative justice, see S.G. Bazemore and M. Schiff, *Restorative Community Justice: Repairing Harm and Transforming Communities* (Cincinnati: Anderson Pub. 2001); R. Claassen, *Restorative Justice—Fundamental Principles* (Center for Peacemaking and Conflict Studies, Fresno Pacific College, 1996). Retrieved September 2002, from the Web: *http://www.fresno.edu/pacs/rjprinc.html*; J. Consedine, *Restorative Justice: Healing the Effects of Crime*, rev ed. (Lyttelton, N.Z.: Ploughshares Publications, 1999); M. Forget, "Crime as Interpersonal Conflict: Reconciliation Between Victim and Offender." Paper presented at at the Dilemmas of Reconciliation conference, Fresno, Ca., June 1996; L. Kurki, "Restorative and Community Justice in the United States," *Crime and Justice: A Review of Research* 27 (2000), 235–304; D. Sullivan and L. Tifft, *Restorative Justice: Healing the Foundations of Our Everyday Lives* (Monsey, N.Y.: Willow Tree Press, 2001); and T. Wachtel and P. McCold, "Restorative Justice in Everyday Life," In H. Strang and J. Braithwaite, (Eds.), *Restorative Justice and Civil Society* (Cambridge, UK; New York: Cambridge University Press, 2001), 114–129. Of note, the South African Truth and Reconciliation Commission also has features in common with the restorative justice paradigm, see A.R. Chapman, "Truth Commissions as Instruments of Forgiveness and Reconciliation," In R.G. Helmick and R.L. Petersen (Eds.), *Forgiveness and Reconciliation: Religion, Public Policy, and Conflict Transformation* (Philadelphia: Templeton Foundation Press, 2001), 247–267; and M. Minow, *Between Vengeance and Forgiveness: Facing History After Genocide and Mass Violence* (Boston: Beacon Press, 1998).
86. Based on S. Sharpe, 2001; *Restorative Justice: A Vision for Healing and Change* (Edmonton: Mediation and Restorative Justice Centre, 2001).
87. A. Morris and G. Maxwell, "The Practice of Family Group Conferences in New Zealand: Assessing the Place, Potential and Pitfalls of Restorative Justice," In A. Crawford and J. Goodey (Eds.), *Integrating a Victim Perspective Within Criminal Justice: International Debates* (Brookfield Vt.: Aldershot, 2000).
88. Open House: A Center of Healing and Hope. 1995. *Holy Land Magazine*.
89. *Friends of Open House*. August 15, 2002. Newton, Ma. *http://www.openhouse.org.il*
90. Dalia Landau's response is a direct response to systemic violence, or what Sullivan and Tifft call the violence of power. D. Sullivan and L. Tifft.

2001. *Restorative Justice: Healing the Foundations of our Everyday Lives* (Monsey, N.Y.: Willow Tree Press, 2001), 121–138.
91. M.L. Hadley, *The Spiritual Roots of Restorative Justice* (Albany: State University of New York Press, 2001).
92. E.G. Krug et al., *World Report on Violence and Health* (Geneva: World Health Organization, 2002), 218.
93. R.J. Sampson et al., "Neighborhoods and Violent Crime: A Multilevel Study of Collective Efficacy," *Science*, 277 (5328)(1997), 918–924; and R.J. Sampson et al., "Beyond Social Capital: Spatial Dynamics of Collective Efficacy for Children," *American Sociological Review*, 64 (5)(1999), 633–660. The work of this group on collective efficacy for children is key. It suggests that stable neighborhoods are protective of children exposed to violence.
94. E.G. Krug et al., *World Report on Violence and Health* (Geneva: World Health Organization, 2002).
95. United Mine Workers of America, *Step by Step*. Preamble to the Constitution of the United Mine Workers of America, 1890. Retrieved October 17, 2002, from the Web: *http://www.musa.ca/Songs/step.html*
96. E.G. Krug et al., *World Report on Violence and Health* (Geneva: World Health Organization, 2002), 221.
97. See G. Rhine et al., *Wiping the Tears of Seven Generations* [VHS.] (San Francisco: Kifaru Productions, 1992). For a discussion of the American Indian identity in the context of multiple historical traumas, see H.N. Weaver and M.Y.H. Brave Heart, "Examining Two Facets of American Indian Identity: Exposure to Other Cultures and the Influence of Historical Trauma," *Journal of Human Behavior in the Social Environment* 2 (1–2)(1999), 19–33.
98. P. Harriman, "Young Lakota Riders Draw Strength from History," *The Argus Leader*, December 22, 2000.
99. E.G. D'Aquili, "Human Ceremonial Ritual and the Modulation of Aggression," *Zygon: Journal of Religion and Science* 20 (1)(1985), 22.
100. For an astute discussion of how community can inadvertently exclude and ways of thinking about community that address this propensity, see G. Pavlich, "The Force of the Community," In H. Strang and J. Braithwaite, (Eds.), *Restorative Justice and Civil Society* (Cambridge UK; New York: Cambridge University Press, 2001), 56–68.
101. Good Grief Program, Boston Medical Center: 1 BMC Place, MAT 5, Boston, Ma., 02118.
102. B. English, "Caring and Connecting in Face of Tragedy," *The Boston Globe*, November 14, 1999, South Weekly, 2.
103. See J. Saul, "2 Pillars are Crucial to Helping Children Adjust," *The New York Times*, September 11, 2002, A17. Saul is a psychologist and director of the International Trauma Studies Program at New York University and the father of two sons who attend P.S. 234. He has long been an advocate of family and community approaches to recovery from disasters. He points

out that the vast majority of funds for mental health services after the terrorist attacks went to the provision of mental health services for individuals, despite the wealth of research that supports the conclusion that family and community support are the most protective factors in preventing long-term mental health problems following disasters. See J. Saul, "Terror and Trauma: Enhancing Family and Community Resilience." Paper presented at the American Family Therapy Academy, New York, June 29, 2002.

104. M. R. Harvey, "An Ecological View of Psychological Trauma and Trauma Recovery," *Journal of Traumatic Stress*, 9 (1)(1996), 3–23.
105. N. Farwell and J. B. Cole, "Community as a Context of Healing," *International Journal of Mental Health*, 30 (4) (2001), 19–41.
106. R. L. Corcoran and K. E. Greisdorf, *Connecting Communities* (Washington, D.C.: Initiatives of Change, 2001).
107. S. S. Driggs, R. G. Wilson, and R. P. Winthrop, *Richmond's Monument Avenue* (Chapel Hill: University of North Carolina Press, 2001).
108. R. L. Corcoran and K. E. Greisdorf, *Connecting Communities* (Washington, D.C.: Initiatives of Change, 2001); and M. Henderson, "America's Unfinished Business," In M. Henderson (Ed.), *The Forgiveness Factor: Stories of Hope in a World of Conflict* (Salem, Or., Grosvenor Books, 1996) 197–214.
109. The King Center, "The Beloved Community of Martin Luther King, Jr." Retrieved September 29, 2002, from the Web: *http://www.thekingcenter.org/bc.html*
110. J. Hackett, "The Territory of Trauma: A Novelist Finds Herself in Unexpected Historical Territory, Confronting the Ethics and Politics of Her Art," *The Boston Review* (December 2001—January 2002), 23–27.
111. A. C. Rich, *Arts of the Possible: Essays and Conversations*, 1st ed. (New York: Norton, 2001), 141.
112. A. C. Rich, *Arts of the Possible: Essays and Conversations*, 1st ed. (New York: Norton, 2001), 142.
113. See endnote 112.
114. F. Marchant, "Comebacks and Counterweights," *Peacework* (2000), 16.
115. Marchant asks, "So what exactly is the kind of witness that poetry provides? Some clues might be found in the far reaches of the etymology of the word. Wit is more than cleverness, and the word has the aura of heightened awareness, as in keeping one's wits during a crisis. *Wit* in this sense of the word is basically unchanged from its meaning (and spelling) in Old and Middle English. In the deep background of the Old English *wit* is the Indo-European root, *weid*, which gives us *wis*, as in our *wisdom* and *wise* . . ." F. Marchant, "Night Visions," *The Journal of Public Affairs, In Press*.
116. F. Marchant, "A Sense of the Sleight-of-Hand," *Peacework* (2002), 7.
117. S. Heaney, *The Redress of Poetry* (New York: Farrar, Straus & Giroux, 1995), 3.
118. S. Heaney, *The Redress of Poetry* (New York: Farrar, Straus & Giroux,

1995), 10; and F. Marchant, "Comebacks and Counterweights," *Peacework* (2000), 16–17.

119. See M. Binelli, "Bruce Springsteen's American Gospel," *Rolling Stone*, August 22, 2002 62–68, 94; and K. Loder, review of Bruce Springsteen's *The Rising*, (August 22, 2002), 81–82.
120. See R. E. Thomas, and J. Rappaport, "Art as Community Narrative: A Resource for Social Change," In M. B. Lykes et al., (Ed.), *Myths About the Powerless: Contesting Social Inequalities* (Philadelphia: Temple University Press, 1996), 317–336; and A. Patchett, *Bel Canto: A Novel*, 1st Perennial ed. (New York: HarperPerennial, 2002). Patchett eloquently describes how music transforms violence during a protracted hostage seige.
121. M. Martin, "HIV/AIDS in South Africa—Can the Visual Arts Make a Difference?" Paper presented at the conference AIDS in South Africa: The Social Expression of a Pandemic, Wellesley College, April 19–20, 2002.
122. G. Mendel, *A Broken Landscape: HIV and AIDS in Africa* (London: Network Photographers, 2001).
123. See endnote 121.
124. J. Morgan, "Boxes and Remembering in the Time of AIDS," *Dulwich Center Journal* 4 (2000), 45–48.
125. See endnote 121.
126. K. Weingarten, "Witnessing, Wonder, and Hope," *Family Process* 39 (4) (2000), 389–402.
127. V. Klinkenborg, "The Quiet Consolation of the Material World," *The New York Times*, September 22, 2001, 24.
128. I have read books about prison life and know that even in solitary confinement people have found nature available, either imaginatively or in reality, for instance developing relationships with cockroaches. At the same time, other books suggest that there are times in prisons where nature is absolutely missing. See I. Ratushinskaia, *Grey Is the Color of Hope*, 1st American ed. (New York: Knopf, 1988).

Chapter Nine: Steps to Compassionate Witnessing

1. E. Wiesel, *From the Kingdom of Memory: Reminiscences* (New York: Summit Books, 1990), 235.
2. A. Wade, "Small Acts of Living: Everyday Resistance to Violence and Other Forms of Oppression," *Contemporary Family Therapy* 19 (1)(1997), 23–29.
3. Victor Turner, as cited by Barbara Myerhoff, uses the term *re-membering* to refer to the "reaggregation of one's members, the figures who properly belong to one's life story, one's own prior selves, the significant others without

which the story cannot be completed." B. G. Myerhoff, "Re-membered Lives," *Parabola* 5 (1) (1980), 77. I have been strongly influenced in my clinical work by Michael White's work with re-membering practices, based on his interpretation of Myerhoff's work. M. White, *Narratives of Therapists' Lives* (Adelaide, S.A.: Dulwich Centre Publications, 1997). Here, I am thinking about witnessing as a process that re-members qualities of ours, not people.

4. The material in the section that follows has been influenced by a number of sources. I want to acknowledge my collaboration with Sallyann Roth, M.S.W., with whom I co-taught at the Family Institute of Cambridge for over a decade. Together, we spent many hours thinking together about listening. Two exercises that we codeveloped appear in K. Weingarten, "The Small and the Ordinary: The Daily Practice of a Postmodern Narrative Therapy," *Family Process* 37 (1)(1998), 3–15. Ideas are also drawn from K. Weingarten, "Radical Listening: Challenging Cultural Beliefs for and about Mothers," In K. Weingarten, (Ed.) *Cultural Resistance: Challenging Beliefs About Men, Women, and Therapy* (New York: Harrington Park Press/ Haworth Press, 1995), 7–22; and C. Hwoschinsky, *Listening with the Heart: A Guide for Compassionate Listening* (Indianola, Wa., MidEast Citizen Diplomacy, 2001).
5. C. Hwoschinsky, *Listening with the Heart: A Guide for Compassionate Listening* (Indianola, Wa.: MidEast Citizen Diplomacy, 2001).
6. H. Anderson and H. Goolishian, "The Client Is the Expert: A Not-Knowing Approach to Therapy," In S. McNamee and K. J. Gergen (Eds.), *Therapy as Social Construction. Inquiries in Social Construction* (Thousand Oaks, Ca.: Sage Publications, 1992), 25–39; and H. Anderson, *Conversation, Language, and Possibilities: A Postmodern Approach to Therapy*, 1st ed. (New York: Basic Books, 1997).
7. V. Satir, *Peoplemaking* (Palo Alto: California Science and Behavior Books, 1972), 49.
8. A. W. Frank, "Just Listening: Narrative and Deep Illness," *Families, Systems and Health*, 16 (3)(1998), 197–212.
9. Casa Myrna Vasquez is the largest provider of comprehensive services to battered women and children in New England. The Mothers and Sons program (MAS), where this work was carried out, is the first residential program in New England where women with teenage sons and their siblings can be served. (Casa Myrna Vasquez, P.O. Box 180019, Boston, Ma. 02118).
10. N. C. Auerhahn and D. Laub, "Intergenerational Memory of the Holocaust," In Y. Danieli, (Ed.), *International Handbook of Multigenerational Legacies of Trauma* (The Plenum Series on Stress and Coping) (New York: Plenum Press, 1998), 68.
11. C. Hwoschinsky, *Listening with the Heart: A Guide for Compassionate Listening* (Indianola, Wa., MidEast Citizen Diplomacy, 2001), 64.

12. A. Morgan, *What is Narrative Therapy?: An Easy-to-Read Introduction* (Adelaide, South Australia: Dulwich Centre Publications, 2000).
13. His question points to what Michael White calls the "absent but implicit." M. White, "Re-engaging with History: The Absent but Implicit," In M. White, (Ed.), *Reflections on Narrative Practice: Essays and Interviews* (Adelaide, South Australia: Dulwich Centre Publications, 2000).
14. Michael White is the codeveloper with David Epston, a therapist from New Zealand, of a form of therapy called narrative therapy. He first introduced me to the clinical application of witnessing ideas. See M. White, *Reauthoring Lives: Interviews and Essays* (Adelaide, South Australia: Dulwich Centre Publications, 1995).
15. These three areas of response may be useful in a wide variety of contexts we don't usually think of as opportunities for witnessing, but which do provide such possibilities, for instance in making toasts or writing condolence letters or thank-you cards.
16. L. Hogan et al., *Intimate Nature: The Bond Between Women and Animals* (New York: Fawcett Columbine, 1998), 162.
17. In the aftermath of September 11 in the United States, many constituencies in this country and abroad took great pains to make the point that now more Americans knew what it felt like to live in fear. This point was made by Palestinians and Israelis, advocates for battered women living in shelters in the United States, African-Americans and prisoners, among others, in the hopes of helping people who had previously had the privilege of living without fear make the connection between their current feelings of fear and the daily experience of others. It is a crucial point, although an uncomfortable one, to take in. Hopefully, acknowledging these inequities motivates us to work for equity in those arenas over which we do, individually, have control.
18. S. Felman and D. Laub, *Testimony: Crises of Witnessing in Literature, Psychoanalysis, and History* (New York; London: Routledge, 1992), 82.
19. The difference between knowing and understanding is not trivial. Laub speculates that had it been possible to witness effectively, the course of the Holocaust would have been changed and "the 'final solution' could not have been carried out to the extent that it was, in full view of the civilized world," S. Felman and D. Laub, *Testimony: Crises of Witnessing in Literature, Psychoanalysis, and History* (New York; London; Routledge, 1992), 84. For another perspective on this, see also M.R. Beschloss, *The Conquerors: Roosevelt, Truman, and the Destruction of Hitler's Germany, 1941–1945* (New York: Simon & Schuster 2002), regarding revelations about what F.D. Roosevelt knew and decisions he made about bombing Auschwitz. This still raises the questions of whether FDR fully understood the Nazi-perpetrated horrors.
20. K. Adams, *Journal to the Self: 22 Paths to Personal Growth* (New York: Warner Books, 1990).
21. J.W. Pennebaker, *Opening Up: The Healing Power of Expressing Emo-*

tions (New York: Guilford Press, 1997); and J. W. Pennebaker, "The Effects of Traumatic Disclosure on Physical and Mental Health: The Values of Writing and Talking About Upsetting Events," *International Journal of Emergency Mental Health* 1 (1)(1999), 9–18.

22. J. W. Pennebaker, *Opening Up: The Healing Power of Expressing Emotions* (New York: Guilford Press, 1997), 103; and J. W. Pennebaker, "The Effects of Traumatic Disclosure on Physical and Mental Health: The Values of Writing and Talking About Upsetting Events," *International Journal of Emergency Mental Health* 1 (1)(1999), 9–18.
23. J. M. Smyth, "Written Emotional Expression: Effect Sizes, Outcome Types, and Moderating Variables," *Journal of Consulting and Clinical Psychology* 66 (1)(1998), 174–184.
24. T. Nhât Hanh and A. Kotler, *Being Peace* (Berkeley: Parallax Press, 1996), 4.
25. A variety of claims have been made with regard to the health and mental health benefits of meditation for people with diverse presenting problems, from adolescents to the aged. For a sample of some of this work, see J. Andresen, "Meditation Meets Behavioural Medicine: The Story of Experimental Research on Meditation," *Journal of Consciousness Studies* 7 (11–12)(2002), 17–73; J. Kabat-Zinn, "Indra's Net at Work: The Mainstreaming of Dharma Practice in Society," G. Watson and S. Batchelor (Eds.); et al., *The Psychology of Awakening: Buddhism, Science, and Our Day-to-Day Lives* (York, Me., S. Weiser, 2000), 225–249; and D. K. Reibel et al., "Mindfulness-Based Stress Reduction and Health-Related Quality of Life in a Heterogeneous Patient Population," *General Hospital Psychiatry*, 23 (4)(2001), 183–192.
26. S. Salzberg, *Loving-kindness: The Revolutionary Art of Happiness*, 1st ed. (Boston: Shambhala, 1995), 21.
27. S. Salzberg, *Loving-kindness: The Revolutionary Art of Happiness*, 1st ed. (Boston: Shambhala, 1995), 18.
28. C. Gall, "Kosovo Albanians Cheer the Return of a Doctor Freed in Serbia," *The New York Times*, November 2, 2000, A13.
29. M. Savic, "Activist Visits Kosovo Albanian Prisoners in Belgrade," *The Boston Globe*, November 10, 2000, A10.
30. UNIFEM, 2002, The Millenium Peace Prize for Women: 2001 peace prize recipient's biography—Flora Brovina. UNIFEM/UNDP. Retrieved in 2002 from the Web: *http://www.undp.org/unifem/mpprize/brovinabio.html*
31. K. P. Davison et al., "Who Talks? The Social Psychology of Illness Support Groups," *American Psychologist*, 55 (2)(2000), 205–217.
32. OSCE Kosovo Verification Mission, 1999. *Kosovo/Kosova As Seen, As Told—Djakovica/Gjakova*. OSCE. Retrieved October 16, 2002, from the Web: *http://www.osce.org/kosovo/documents/reports/hr/part1/p5dja.htm*
33. A. R. Chapman, "Truth Commissions as Instruments of Forgiveness and Reconciliation," In R. G. Helmick and R. L. Petersen (Eds.), *Forgiveness and Reconciliation: Religion, Public Policy and Conflict Transformation*

(Philadelphia: Templeton Foundation Press, 2001), 247–267; P. B. Hayner, "Fifteen Truth Commissions: 1974–1994," *Human Rights Quarterly*, 16(1994), 597–655; and M. Minow, *Between Vengeance and Forgiveness: Facing History After Genocide and Mass Violence* (Boston: Beacon Press, 1998).

34. M. Minow, *Between Vengeance and Forgiveness: Facing History After Genocide and Mass Violence* (Boston: Beacon Press, 1998).
35. F. Reid and D. Hoffman, *Long Night's Journey into Day* (San Francisco: Iris Films; California Newsreel; in association with Cinemax Reel Life, 2000). (A film about the TRC); A. R. Chapman, "Truth Commissions as Instruments of Forgiveness and Reconciliation," In R. G. Helmick and R. L. Petersen, (Eds.), *Forgiveness and Reconciliation: Religion, Public Policy and Conflict Transformation* (Philadelphia: Templeton Foundation Press, 2001), 247–267; W. G. James, and L.v.d. Vijver, *After the TRC: Reflections on Truth and Reconciliation in South Africa* (Athens: Ohio University Press, 2001); and A. Krog, *Country of My Skull* (New York: Random House, 1999).
36. A. Krog *Country of My Skull* (New York: Random House, 1999), 43.
37. A. Krog *Country of My Skull* (New York: Random House, 1999), 57.
38. F. Reid and D. Hoffman, *Long Night's Journey into Day* (San Francisco: Iris Films; California Newsreel; in Association with Cinemax Reel Life, 2000).
39. A.R. Chapman, "Truth Commissions as Instruments of Forgiveness and Reconciliation," In R. G. Helmick and R. L. Petersen, (Eds.), *Forgiveness and Reconciliation: Religion, Public Policy and Conflict Transformation* (Philadelphia: Templeton Foundation Press, 2001), 247–267; W. G. James and L.v.d. Vijver, *After the TRC: Reflections on Truth and Reconciliation in South Africa* (Athens: Ohio University Press, 2001); A. Krog, *Country of My Skull* (New York: Random House, 1999).
40. A. Krog, *Country of My Skull* (New York: Random House, 1999), 142.
41. *Frontline, The Long Walk of Nelson Mandela*, 1999. WGBH/Frontline. Retrieved October 16, 2002, from the Web: *http://www.pbs.org/wgbh/pages/frontline/shows/mandela/*
42. See endnote 41.
43. A. Jenkins et al., "Forgiveness and Child Sexual Abuse: A Matrix of Meanings," *The International Journal of Narrative Therapy and Community Work* 1(2002), 35–51.
44. A. Jenkins et al., "Forgiveness and Child Sexual Abuse: A Matrix of Meanings," *The International Journal of Narrative Therapy and Community Work* 1(2002), 50.
45. J. Hatley, *Suffering Witness: The Quandary of Responsibility After the Irreparable* (Albany: State University of New York Press, 2000), 5.
46. J. Karski, "Jan Karski's Account," *Literature of the Holocaust*. Retrieved September 30, 2002, from the Web: *hhtp://www.english.upenn.edu/~afilreis/Holocaust/karski.html*

47. C. Lanzmann, *Shoah: An Oral History of the Holocaust: The Complete Text of the Film*, 1st American ed. (New York: Pantheon Books, 1985), 174.
48. J. Karski, "Jan Karski's Account," *Literature of the Holocaust*. Retrieved September 30, 2002, from the Web: *http://www.english.upenn.edu/~afilreis/Holocaust/karski.html*
49. M.T. Kaufman, "Jan Karski Dies at 86; Warned West About Holocaust," *The New York Times*, July 15, 2000, Section C15.
50. M.T. Kaufman, "Jan Karski Dies at 86; Warned West About Holocaust," *The New York Times*, July 15, 2000, 15; and M.R. Beschloss, *The Conquerors: Roosevelt, Truman and the Destruction of Hitler's Germany, 1941–1945*, (New York: Simon & Schuster, 2002).
51. S. Felman and D. Laub, *Testimony: Crises of Witnessing in Literature, Psychoanalysis, and History* (New York, London: Routledge, 1992), 238.
52. P. Gourevitch, "Genocide in Our Time," U.S. Institute of Peace, 1998. Retrieved October 16, 2002, from the Web: *http://www.usip.org/pubs/pw/1298/profile.html*
53. S. Power, "Bystanders to Genocide: Why the United States Let the Rwandan Tragedy Happen," *The Atlantic Monthly*, September 2001; and S. Power, *A Problem from Hell: America and the Age of Genocide* (New York: Basic Books, 2002) for another account of the United States actions/inactions regarding Rwanda.
54. P. Gourevitch, *We Wish to Inform You That Tomorrow We Will Be Killed with Our Families: Stories from Rwanda* (New York: Farrar, Straus & Giroux, 1998), 170.
55. Motherland Nigeria, *Historical Government*. Motherland Nigeria Web site, 2002. Retreived September 7, 2002, from Web: *http://www.motherland-nigeria.com/govthistory.html*
56. J. Breneman, "Harvard Grad Tells of Nigeria Nightmare," *Cambridge Chronicle*, May 1997, 11.
57. Cambridge City Council. May 19, 1997. Resolution on Nigeria. Cambridge, Ma.
58. S. Salzberg, *Loving-kindness: The Revolutionary Art of Happiness*, 1st ed. (Boston: Shambhala, 1995), 37.
59. S. Salzberg, *Loving-kindness: The Revolutionary Art of Happiness*, 1st ed. (Boston: Shambhala, 1995), 37.
60. T. Nhât Hanh and A. Kotler, *Being Peace* (Berkeley: Parallax Press, 1996), 35.

Chapter Ten: Repairing the World, Transforming Violence

1. All quoted material is from L. Erdrich, "The Shawl," *The New Yorker*, March 5, 2001, 84–87. (*Chippewa* is an English name for the Anishinaabeg people.)

2. For an eloquent meditation on love as the only means of survival when "Thanatos is ascendent," see C. Hedges, *War Is a Force That Gives Us Meaning*, 1st ed. (New York: Public Affairs, 2002), 184.
3. For a profound and disturbing history of the relationship between government policy and press censorship from the Crimean War to the present see P. Knightley, *The First Casualty: The War Correspondent as Hero and Myth-maker from the Crimea to Kosovo* (Baltimore: Johns Hopkins University Press, 2002). Hedges's experience as a war correspondent in the last fifteen years supports Knightley's perspective. C. Hedges, *War Is a Force That Gives Us Meaning*, 1st ed. (New York: Public Affairs, 2002).
4. D.L. Schacter, *Searching for Memory: The Brain, the Mind and the Past*, 1st ed. (New York: Basic Books, 1996).
5. K. Weingarten, *The Mother's Voice: Strengthening Intimacy in Families* (2nd ed.) (New York: Guilford Press, 1997).
6. J.L. Griffith and M.E. Griffith, *Encountering the Sacred in Psychotherapy: How to Talk with People About Their Spiritual Lives* (New York: Guilford Press, 2002).
7. These couplets are described in J.L. Griffith and M.E. Griffith, *Encountering the Sacred in Psychotherapy: How to Talk with People About Their Spiritual Lives* (New York: Guilford Press, 2002), 267–268.
8. J. Rilling et al., "A Neural Basis for Social Cooperation," *Neuron* 35 (2) (2002), 395–405.
9. S.E. Taylor et al., "Biobehavioral Responses to Stress in Females: Tend-and-Befriend, Not Fight-or-Flight," *Psychological Review* 107 (3) (2002), 411–429; and S.E. Taylor, *The Tending Instinct: How Nurturing Is Essential for Who We Are and How We Live*, 1st ed. (New York: Times Books, 2002).
10. See endnote 9.
11. A.B. Newberg and E.G. d'Aquili, "The Neuropsychology of Religious and Spiritual Experience," *Journal of Consciousness Studies* 7(2002), 11–12.
12. A.B. Newberg et al., *Why God Won't Go Away: Brain Science and the Biology of Belief*, 1st ed. (New York: Ballantine Books, 2001).
13. M. Csikszentmihalyi, *Finding Flow: The Psychology of Engagement with Everyday Life* (New York: Basic Books, 1997).
14. A.I. Solzhenitsyn, *The Gulag Archipelago, 1918–1956: An Experiment in Literary Investigation*, 1st ed. (New York: Harper & Row, 1974).
15. M. Twain, 2002, "The War Prayer," BoondocksNet. Retrieved September 3, 2002, from the Web: *http://www.boondocksnet.com-/ai/wain/war_prayer.html*
16. D. Bar-Tal, "Why Does Fear Override Hope in Societies Engulfed by Intractable Conflict, as It Does in the Israeli Society?" *Political Psychology* 22 (3)(2001), 604; and H. Kamya and D. Trimble, "Response to Injury: Toward Ethical Construction of the Other," *Journal of Systemic Therapies* 21 (3)(2002), 19–29.

17. D. Bar-Tal, "Why Does Fear Override Hope in Societies Engulfed by Intractable Conflict, as It Does in the Israeli Society?" *Political Psychology* 22 (3)(2001), 601–627.
18. I am indebted to John A. Sargent, M.D., for suggesting this idea. Personal communication, May 10, 2002.
19. P. Knightly, *The First Casualty: The War Correspondent as Hero and Myth-maker from the Crimea to Kosovo* (Baltimore: Johns Hopkins University Press, 2002).
20. By telling, I do not only mean speaking. People of different cultures and ages tell stories in a wide variety of ways. For instance, children's stories told through play or art vividly reveal their suffering and struggles. J. C. Freeman et al., *Playful Approaches to Serious Problems: Narrative Therapy with Children and Their Families* (New York: Norton, 1997); and E. Kotzé and E. Morkel, *Matchboxes, Butterflies, and Angry Foots* (Pretoria: Ethics Alive, 2002). Compassionate witnessing practices can be culturally and developmentally appropriate.
21. On July 16, 2002, the IRA published an open letter of apology for the "deaths and injuries" of noncombatants and acknowledged the "grief and pain" of the relatives of combatants who had died. BBC News, "Accept IRA Apology, Urges Sinn Fein." BBC, July 17, 2002. Retrieved July 17, 2002, from the Web: *http://news.bbc.co.uk/1/hi/uk/northern_ireland/2132847.stm*
22. E. M. Remarque, *All Quiet on the Western Front*, 1st Ballantine Books ed. (New York: Ballantine Books, 1982), 263–264.
23. H. C. Goddard, *The Meaning of Shakespeare* (Chicago: University of Chicago Press, 1960).
24. T. Morrison, *Beloved: A Novel* (New York: Plume, 1987).
25. M. Apprey, "Reinventing the Self in the Face of Received Transgenerational Hatred in the African American Community," *Journal of Applied Psychoanalytic Studies* 1 (2)(1999), 32.
26. M. Apprey, "Reinventing the Self in the Face of Received Transgenerational Hatred in the African American Community," *Journal of Applied Psychoanalytic Studies*, 1 (2)(1999), 33.
27. P. Ricoeur, "Reflections on a New Ethos for Europe," In P. Ricoeur and R. Kearney (Eds.), *Paul Ricoeur: the Hermeneutics of Action* (Thousand Oaks, Ca.: Sage Publications, 1996), 8.
28. X. Mangcu, "A Wedding Story," *South Africa Development Fund*, Fall 2001.
29. See endnote 28.
30. D. Bar-On, *Fear and hope: Three Generations of the Holocaust* (Cambridge, Ma.: Harvard University Press, 1995).
31. E. Wiesel, *From the Kingdom of Memory: Reminiscences* (New York: Summit Books, 1990), 201.
32. K. Weingarten, "Witnessing, Wonder, and Hope," *Family Process*, 39 (4)(2000), 389–402.

Appendix One

1. Brohl, *Working with Traumatized Children: A Handbook for Healing* (Washington, D.C.: CWLA Books, 1996); R. H. Gurwitch et. al., "What to Expect After Trauma: Possible Reactions in Elementary School Students," *American Psychological Association* (2001). Retrieved 10/18/2001, from the Web: *http://www.apa.org/practice/ptguidelines.html*; P. Levin, "The Trauma Response," David Baldwin's Trauma Information Pages. Retrieved August 7, 2001, from the Web: *http://www.trauma-pages.com/t-facts.htm*; P. A. Levine, *Waking the Tiger: Healing Trauma: The Innate Capacity to Transform Overwhelming Experiences* (Berkeley: North Atlantic Books, 1997); B. F. Meltz, "Children Need Time to Cope with Trauma," *The Boston Globe*, September 20, 2001; American Psychological Association, "Managing Traumatic Stress: Tips for Recovering from Disasters and Other Traumatic Events." American Psychological Association Web site. Retrieved September 17, 2001, from the Web: *http://helping.apa.org/daily/traumatic-stress.html*; B. Rothschild, *The Body Remembers: The Psychophysiology of Trauma and Trauma treatment* (New York: Norton: 2000).

Bibliography

Adams, K. 1990. *Journal to the Self: 22 Paths to Personal Growth*. New York: Warner Books.

Aeschylus, and R. A. Lattimore. 1969. *Aeschylus I: Oresteia* (1st Phoenix ed.). Chicago: University of Chicago Press.

Agee, J. 1938. *A Death in the Family*. New York: Bantam.

Aiken, C. 1996. "Reporters Are Victims, Too." *Nieman Report*, 50(3): 30–32.

Akhet Egyptology. 2002, April 28. *Osiris and Isis*. Akhet Egyptology. Retrieved, 2002, from the Web: http://www.akhet.co.uk/isisosir.htm

Akinyela, M. 2002. "Decolonizing Our Lives: Divining a Postcolonial Therapy." *The International Journal of Narrative Therapy and Community Work*, 2, 32–43.

Akinyela, M. 2002. Reparations: Repairing Relationships and Honouring Ancestry. *The International Journal of Narrative Therapy and Community Work*, 2, 45–49.

Albeck, J. H. 1994. "Intergenerational Consequences of Trauma: Reframing Traps in Treatment Theory—A Second Generation Perspective." In M. B. Williams and J. F. Sommer (Eds.), *Handbook of Posttraumatic Therapy*. Westport, CT: Greenwood Press, 106–125.

Albom, M. 1997. *Tuesdays with Morrie: An Old Man, a Young Man, and Life's Greatest Lesson* (1st ed.). New York: Doubleday.

Alexander, C. 1999. "Police Psychological Burnout and Trauma." In J. M. Violanti and D. Paton (Eds.), *Police Trauma: Psychological Aftermath of Civilian Combat*. Springfield, IL. Charles C. Thomas, 54–64.

Allen, J. G. 2001. *Traumatic Relationships and Serious Mental Disorders*. Chichester: John Wiley & Sons.

Allende, I. 1996. *Paula* (1st HarperPerennial ed.). New York: HarperPerennial.

Altman, R. 1996. *Waking Up, Fighting Back: The Politics of Breast Cancer*. Boston: Little Brown.

American Civil Liberties Union. January 22, 2002. *The USA Patriot Act: A Civil Liberties Briefing*. Retrieved February 1, 2002, from the Web: *http://www.aclu-mass.org/legal/USApatriotact.html*

American Heritage Dictionary of the English Language: Fourth Edition. 2000. Boston: Houghton Mifflin Company.

American Psychiatric Association. *Diagnostic and Statistical Manual of Mental Disorders* (4th ed.). Washington, D.C.: American Psychiatric Association.

American Psychological Association. 2001. *Handling Anxiety in the Face of the Anthrax Scare*. Retrieved November 9, 2001, from the Web: *http://helping.apa.org/daily/anthrax.html*

American Psychological Association. 2001. *Managing Traumatic Stress: Tips for Recovering From Disasters and Other Traumatic Events*. American Psychological Association. Retrieved September 14, 2001, from the Web: *http://helping.apa.org/daily/traumaticstress.html*

Amnesty International USA. 1996. *United States of America: Police Brutality and Excessive Force in the New York City Police Department*. New York: Amnesty International USA.

Amundson, A. 2001, November 24. *Letter to President Bush*. Voices in the Wilderness. Retrieved 2001 from the Web: *http://www.nonviolence.org/vitw/AALetter%20to%20Bush.html*

An Crann. "The Tree." 2000. *Bear in Mind: Stories of the Troubles*. Belfast: Lagan Press.

Ancharoff, M. R., J. F. Munroe, and L. M. Fisher. 1998. "The Legacy of Combat Trauma: Clinical Implications of Intergenerational Transmission." In Y. Danieli (Ed.), *International Handbook of Multigenerational Legacies of Trauma*. The Plenum Series on Stress and Coping. New York: Plenum Press, 257–276.

Anderson, C. A., and B. J. Bushman. 2002. "The Effects of Media Violence on Society." *Science*, 295: 2377–2379.

Anderson, H. 1997. *Conversation, Language, and Possibilities: A Postmodern Approach to Therapy* (1st ed.). New York: Basic Books.

Anderson, H., and H. Goolishian. 1992. "The Client Is the Expert: A Not-Knowing Approach to Therapy," In S. McNamee and K. J. Gergen (Eds.), *Therapy as Social Construction. Inquiries in Social Construction*. Thousand Oaks, CA: Sage Publications, 25–39.

Anderson, H., and H. A. Goolishian. 1988. "Human Systems as Linguistic Systems: Preliminary and Evolving Ideas About the Implications for Clinical Theory." *Family Process*, 27(4): 371–393.

Anderson, M., J. Kaufman, T. R. Simon, L. Barrios, L. Paulozzi, G. Ryan, R. Hammond, W. Modzeleski, T. Feucht, L. Potter, and School-Associated Violent Deaths Study Group. 2001. "School-Associated Violent Deaths in the United States, 1994–1999." *JAMA*, 286(21): 2695–2702.

Andresen, J. 2000. "Meditation Meets Behavioural Medicine: The Story of Experimental Research on Meditation." *Journal of Consciousness Studies*, 7(11–12), 17–73.

Angier, N. 2002, 09/10/2002. "How Brain, and Spirit, Adapt to a 9/11 World." *The New York Times*, Section F, 1.

Appiah, A., and A. Gutmann. 1996. *Color Conscious: The Political Morality of Race*. Princeton, N.J.: Princeton University Press.

Applebome, P. 2001. "Front-Line Journalism—As History Unfolded." *Duke Magazine*, 88 (1), 4.

Apprey, M. 1999. "Reinventing the Self in the Face of Received Transgenerational Hatred in the African American Community." *Journal of Applied Psychoanalytic Studies*, 1(2), 131–143.

Ashbrook, T. March 20, 2002. *Bringing Bereaved Israelis and Palestinians Together*. Boston: WBUR—*On Point*.

Auerhahn, N. C., and D. Laub. 1998. "Intergenerational Memory of the Holocaust." In Y. Danieli, (Ed.), *International Handbook of Multigenerational Legacies of Trauma*. The Plenum Series on Stress and Coping. New York: Plenum Press, 21–41.

Baider, L., T. Peretz, P. E. Hadani, S. Perry, R. Avramov, and A. K. De-Nour. 2000. "Transmission of Response to Trauma? Second-Generation Holocaust Survivors' Reaction to Cancer." *American Journal of Psychiatry*, 157(6): 904–910.

Banuazizi, A. 1996. "Psychology, the Distant Other, and the Dialectics of Change in Non-Western Societies." In M. B. Lykes et al. (Ed.), *Myths About the Powerless: Contesting Social Inequalities*. Philadelphia: Temple University Press, 179–197.

Barbanel, J. January 12, 2002. "How the Study of Sexual Abuse by Priests Was Conducted." *The New York Times*, Section A, 21.

Barber, B. K. 2001. "Political Violence, Social Integration, and Youth Functioning: Palestinian Youth from the Intifada." *Journal of Community Psychology*, 29(3), 259–280.

Barna Research Online. 2002. "Survey Provides Profile of Protestant Pastors." Barna Research Online. Retrieved June 3, 2002, from the Web: *http//www.barna.org/cgi-bin/PagePressRelease.asp?PressReleaseID20*

Barnett, R. C., L. Biener, and G. K. Baruch. 1987. *Gender and Stress*. New York Free Press: London.

Bar-On, D. 1989. *Legacy of Silence: Encounters with Children of the Third Reich*. Cambridge, MA: Harvard University Press.

Bar-On, D. 1995. *Fear and Hope: Three Generations of the Holocaust*, Cambridge, MA: Harvard University Press.

Bar-On, D. 1996. "Attempting to Overcome the Intergenerational Transmission of Trauma: Dialogue Between Descendants of Victims and of Perpetrators." In R. J. Apfel and B. Simon (Eds.), *Minefields in their Hearts: The Mental Health of Children in War and Communal Violence*. New Haven: Yale University Press, 165–188.

Bar-On, D. 1999. *The Indescribable and the Undiscussable: Reconstructing Human Discourse After Trauma*. Budapest, Hungary: Central European University Press; Ithaca N.Y.: Distributed in the United States by Cornell University Press.

Bar-On, D., T. Ostrovsky, and D. Fromer. 1998. "'Who Am I in Relation to My Past, in Relation to the Other?' German and Israeli Students Confront the Holocaust and Each Other." In Y. Danieli, (Ed.), *International Handbook of Multigenerational Legacies of Trauma*. The Plenum Series on Stress and Coping. New York: Plenum Press, 97–116.

Bar-Tal, D. 2001. "Why Does Fear Override Hope in Societies Engulfed by Intractable Conflict, as It Does in the Israeli Society?" *Political Psychology*, 22(3): 601–627.

Batchelor, S. 1997. *Buddhism Without Beliefs: A Contemporary Guide to Awakening*. New York: Riverhead Books.

Battle, M. 1997. *Reconciliation: The Ubuntu Theology of Desmond Tutu*. Cleveland, Ohio: Pilgrim Press.

Bayley, J. 1999. *Elegy for Iris*, (1st ed.): New York: St. Martin's Press.

Bazemore, S. G., and M. Schiff. 2001. *Restorative Community Justice: Repairing Harm and Transforming Communities*. Cincinnati: Anderson Pub.

BBC News. July 17, 2002. "Accept IRA Apology, Urges Sinn Fein." BBC. Retrieved July 17, 2002, from the Web: *http://news.bbc.co.uk/1/hi/uk/northern_ireland/2132847.stm*

Beardslee, W. R. 2002. *Out of the Darkened Room: When a Parent is Depressed: Protecting the Children and Strengthening the Family* (1st ed.). Boston: Little Brown.

Bearison, D. J. 1991. *"They Never Want to Tell You": Children Talk About Cancer*. Cambridge, MA: Harvard University Press.

Beaton, R. D., and S. A. Murphy. 1995. "Working with People in Crisis: Research Implications." In C. R. Figley (Ed.), *Compassion Fatigue: Coping with Secondary Traumatic Stress Disorder in Those Who Treat the Traumatized*. Brunner/Mazel Psychological Stress Series, No. 23. Philadelphia: Brunner/Mazel, Inc. 51–81.

Beauchamp, T. L., and J. F. Childress. 2001. *Principles of Biomedical Ethics*, 5th ed. Cambridge, UK; New York: Oxford University Press.

Becker, G. 1997. *Disrupted Lives: How People Create Meaning in a Chaotic World*. Berkeley: University of California Press.

Becker, J. V., and J. A. Hunter. 1997. "Understanding and Treating Child and Adolescent Sexual Offenders." In T. H. Ollendick and R. J. Prinz (Eds.), *Advances in Clinical Child Psychology*, 19. New York: Plenum Press, 177–197.

Beckham, J. C., S. D. Moore, and V. Reynolds. 2000. "Interpersonal Hostility and Violence in Vietnam Combat Veterans with Chronic Posttraumatic Stress Disorder: A Review of Theoretical Models and Empirical Evidence." *Aggression and Violent Behavior* 5(5): 451–466.

Behar, R. 1996. *The Vulnerable Observer: Anthropology That Breaks Your Heart*. Boston: Beacon Press.

Bell, C. C., and E. J. Jenkins. 1993. "Community Violence and Children on Chicago's Southside." *Psychiatry*, 56(1): 46–54.

Belsky, J. 1980. "Child Maltreatment: An Ecological Integration." *American Psychologist*, 35(4), 320–335.

Benson, H., and M. Stark. 1996. *Timeless Healing: The Power and Biology of Belief*. New York: Scribner.

Benzein, E., and B.I. Saveman. 1998. "One Step Towards the Understanding of Hope: a Concept Analysis." *International Journal of Nursing Studies*, 35(6): 322–329.

Berger, A.L., and N. Berger. 2001. *Second Generation Voices: Reflections by Children of Holocaust Survivors and Perpetrators* (1st ed.). Syracuse, NY: Syracuse University Press.

Berliner, L., and J. Briere. 1999. "Trauma, Memory, and Clinical Practice." In L.M. Williams and V.L. Banyard (Eds.), *Trauma and Memory*. Thousand Oaks, CA: Sage Publications, 3–18.

Berry, J. 2000. *Lead Us Not into Temptation: Catholic Priests and the Sexual Abuse of Children* (1st Illinois paperback ed.). Urbana: University of Illinois Press.

Beschloss, M.R. 2002. *The Conquerors: Roosevelt, Truman, and the Destruction of Hitler's Germany, 1941–1945*. New York: Simon & Schu-ster.

Bhengu, M.J. 1996. *Ubuntu: The Essence of Democracy*. Cape Town, South Africa: Novalis Press.

Binelli, M. 2002, August 22. "Bruce Springsteen's American Gospel." *Rolling Stone*, 62–68, 94.

Birns, B. 1999. "Attachment Theory Revisited: Challenging Conceptual and Methodological Sacred Cows." *Feminism and Psychology*, 9(1), 10–21.

Blachman, L. 2002. *Mothers' Living Stories Project*. Retrieved October 10, 2002, from the Web: *http://www.motherslivingstories.org/*

Blair, D. 2001. "Bi-Communal Dialogue: Kosovar Albanian and Serb Young Adult Leaders." *Peacebuilding in Action—Karuna Center Newsletter*.

Blair, R.J.R. 2001. "Neurocognitive Models of Aggression, the Antisocial Personality Disorders, and Psychopathy." *Journal of Neurology, Neurosurgery, and Psychiatry*, 71(6): 727–731.

Bliwise, N.G. 1999. "Securing Attachment Theory's Potential." *Feminism and Psychology*, 9(1), 43–52.

Bloom, P. 2000. *Buddhist Acts of Compassion*. Berkeley: Conari Press.

Bloom, S.L. 1997. *Creating Sanctuary: Toward the Evolution of Sane Societies*. New York: Routledge.

Bloom, S.L., and M. Reichert. 1998. *Bearing Witness: Violence and Collective Responsibility*. New York: Haworth Maltreatment and Trauma Press.

Blum, L.N. 2000. *Force Under Pressure: How Cops Live and Why They Die*. New York: Lantern Books.

Blumenfeld, L. 2002. *Revenge: A Story of Hope*. New York: Simon & Schuster.

Bochenek, M., A.W. Brown. 2001. *Hatred in the Hallways: Violence and Discrimination Against Lesbian, Gay, Bisexual, and Transgender Students in U.S. Schools*. New York: Human Rights Watch.

Bolen, J.S. 1996. *Close to the Bone: Life-threatening Illness and the Search for Meaning*. New York: Scribner.

Boss, P. 1999. *Ambiguous Loss: Learning to Live with Unresolved Grief*. Cambridge, MA: Harvard University Press.

Boston Globe Investigative Staff. 2002. *Betrayal The Crisis in the Catholic Church*. Boston: Little, Brown.

Botcharova, O. 2001. "Implementation of Track-Two Diplomacy: Developing a Model of Forgiveness." In R. G. Helmick and R. L. Petersen (Eds.), *Forgiveness and Reconciliation: Religion, Public Policy, and Conflict Transformation*. Philadelphia: Templeton Foundation Press, 269–293.

Bovell, A. 2001. *Lantana* (R. Lawrence, Director). J. Chapman and S. Wells (Producers). Australia: Fandango.

Bower, G. H. and H. Sivers. 1998. "Cognitive Impact of Traumatic Events." *Development and Psychopathology*, 10(4): 625–653.

Boyd-Franklin, N., A. J. Franklin, and P. Toussaint. 2000. *Boys into Men: Raising Our African American Teenage Sons*. New York: Dutton.

Brack, P., and B. Brack. 1990. *Moms Don't Get Sick* (1st ed.). Aberdeen, SD: Melius Pub. Corp.

Brehony, K. A. 1999. *Ordinary Grace: An Examination of the Roots of Compassion, Altruism, and Empathy, and the Ordinary Individuals Who Help Others in Extraordinary Ways*. New York: Riverhead Books.

Bremner, J. D., and M. Narayan. 1998. "The Effects of Stress on Memory and the Hippocampus Throughout the Life Cycle: Implications for Childhood Development and Aging." *Development and Psychopathology*, 10(4): 871–885.

Breneman, J. May, 1997. "Harvard Grad Tells of Nigeria Nightmare." *Cambridge Chronicle*, 11.

Briere, J. 1996. *Therapy for Adults Molested as Children: Beyond Survival*. New York: Springer Pub.

Brody, J. E. June 5, 2001. "When Death Sentences are Reprieved." *The New York Times*, 5.

Brody, L. 1999. *Gender, Emotion, and the Family*. Cambridge, MA: Harvard University Press.

Broome, B. J. 1993. "Managing Differences in Conflict Resolution: The Role of Relational Empathy." In D.J.D. Sandole and H.V.D. Merwe (Eds.), *Conflict Resolution theory and Practice: Integration and Application*. Manchester, UK: New York, 95–111.

Brown, D. P., A. W. Scheflin, and D. C Hammond. 1998. *Memory, Trauma Treatment, and the Law*. New York: Norton.

Brown, H. L. 2000. "The Navajo Nation's Peacemaker Division: An Integrated, Community-Based Dispute Resolution Forum." *American Indian Law Review*, 24(297).

Brown, J. 1988. "Of Mice and Memory." *Oral History Review*, 16(1) 91–109.

Brown; L. S. 1997. "The Private Practice of Subversion: Psychology as Tikkun Olam." *American Psychologist*, 52(4). 449–462.

Broyard, A. 1993. *Intoxicated by my Illness: And Other Writings on Life and Death*. New York: Fawcett Columbine.

Broz, S. 2002. *Good People in an Evil Time* (E.E. Bursac, trans.). Sarajevo: Other Press.

Buber, M., W.A. Kaufmann (Ed.). 1970. *I and Thou*. New York: Scribner.

Buchanan, A. 1998. "Intergenerational Child Maltreatment." In Y. Danieli (Ed.), *International Handbook of Multigenerational Legacies of Trauma*. The Plenum Series on Stress and Coping. New York: Plenum Press, 535–552.

Buka, S.L.; T.L. Stichick, I. Birdthistle, and F.J. Earls. 2001. "Youth Exposure to Violence: Prevalence, Risks and Consequences." *American Journal of Orthopsychiatry*, 71(3): 298–310.

Burrow, R.J. 2000. "Personal-Communitarianism and the Beloved Community." *Encounter*, 61(1): 21–43.

Burton, J.W. 1993. *Conflict: Human Needs Theory*. Basingstoke: Macmillan.

Bushman, B.J., and C.A. Anderson. 2001. "Media Violence and the American Public: Scientific Facts versus Media Misinformation." *American Psychologist*, 56(6–7): 477–489.

Butler, S., and B. Rosenblum. 1991. *Cancer in Two Voices*. San Francisco: Spinsters Book Co.

Butner, B.K., H. Burley, and A.F. Marbley. 2000. "Coping with the Unexpected: Black Faculty at Predominately White Institutions." *Journal of Black Studies*, 30(3): 453–462.

Butterfield, F. 1995. *All God's Children: The Bosket Family and the American Tradition of Violence*. New York: Knopf.

Butts, J., and J. Travis. 2002. "The Rise and Fall of American Youth Violence: 1980 to 2000." *Urban Institute*, (March). 1–18.

Byrd, W.M., and L.A. Clayton. 2002. *An American Health Dilemma, V. 2: Race, Medicine and Health Care in the United States 1900–2000*. New York: Routledge.

Cahill, K.M. 1999. *A Framework for Survival: Health, Human Rights, and Humanitarian Assistance in Conflicts and Disasters*. New York: Routledge.

Cahill, L. 1997. "The Neurobiology of Emotionally Influenced Memory. Implications for Understanding Traumatic Memory." In R. Yehuda and A.C. McFarlane (Eds.), *Psychobiology of Posttraumatic Stress Disorder. Annals of the New York Academy of Sciences*, (821). New York: New York Academy of Sciences, 238–246.

Cairns, D.L. 1993. *Aidos: The Psychology and Ethics of Honour and Shame in Ancient Greek Literature*. New York: Oxford Clarendon Press.

Cambridge City Council. May 19, 1997. "Resolution on Nigeria." Cambridge, MA.

Candib, L.M. 2002. "Truth Telling and Advance Planning at the End of Life: Problems with Autonomy in a Multi-Cultural World" *Families, Systems & Health*, 20(3): 213–228.

Cardozo, B.L., A. Vergara, F. Agani, and C.A. Gotway. 2000. "Mental Health, Social Functioning, and Attitudes of Kosovar Albanians Following the War in Kosovo." *JAMA*, 284(5): 569–577.

Carlson, E.A. 1998. "A Prospective Longitudinal Study of Attachment Disorganization/Disorientation." *Child Development*, 69(4): 1107–1128.

Carter, L.S., L.A. Weithorn, and R.E. Behrman. 1999. "Domestic Violence and Children: Analysis and Recommendations." *Future of Children*, 9(3): 4–20.

Cassidy, J., and P.R. Shaver. 1999. *Handbook of Attachment: Theory, Research, and Clinical Applications*. New York: Guilford Press.

Catherall, D. 1995. "Preventing Institutional Secondary Traumatic Stress Disorder." In C.R. Figley (Ed.), *Compassion Fatigue: Coping with Secondary Traumatic Stress Disorder in Those Who Treat the Traumatized*. Brunner/Mazel Psychological Stress Series, No. 23. Philadelphia: Brunner/Mazel, Inc., 232–247.

Cerney, M.S. 1995. "Treating the 'heroic treaters.'" In C.R. Figley (Ed.), *Compassion Fatigue: Coping with Secondary Traumatic Stress Disorder in Those Who Treat the Traumatized*, Brunner/Mazel Psychological Stress Series, No. 23. Philadelphia: Brunner/Mazel, Inc., 131–149.

Chapman, A.R. 2001. Truth Commissions as Instruments of Forgiveness and Reconciliation. In R.G. Helmick and R.L. Petersen (Eds.), *Forgiveness and Reconciliation: Religion, Public Policy and Conflict Transformation*. Philadelphia: Templeton Foundation Press, 247–267.

Chappell, D.W. 1999. *Buddhist Peacework: Creating Cultures of Peace*. Somerville, MA; Wisdom Publications, in association with Boston Research Center for the 21st Century.

Charmaz, K. 1983. "Loss of Self: A Fundamental Form of Suffering in the Chronically Ill." *Sociology of Health and Illness*, 5(2): 168–195.

Chen, R., and E. Gilmore. 2002. *Interest Group on Death and Dying*. American Medical Student Association. Retrieved September 29, 2002, from the Web: *http://www.amsa.org/dd/*

Chiel, S., and H. Dreher. 2000. *For Thou Art with Me: The Healing Power of Psalms*. Emmaus, PA: Daybreak.

Chinmoy, S. 1996. *Commentaries on the Vedas, the Upanishads, and the Bhagavad Gita: The Three Branches of India's Life-Tree*. Jamaica, NY: Aum Publications.

Chödrön, P. 1997. *When Things Fall Apart: Heart Advice for Difficult Times* (1st ed.). Boston: Shambhala.

Chödrön, P. 1999. *Good Medicine*. Boulder, CO: Sounds True.

Chomsky, N. 2000, April. "In Retrospect: A Review of NATO's War over Kosovo," Part I. Z *Magazine*, 19–24.

Chomsky, N. 2000, April. "In Retrospect: A Review of NATO's War over Kosovo," Part II. Z *Magazine*, 21–27.

Chomsky, N. 2001. 9–11. New York: Seven Stories Press.

Christy, C.A., and H. Voigt. 1994. "Bystander Responses to Public Episodes of Child Abuse." *Journal of Applied Social Psychology*, 24(9): 824–847.

Ciaramicoli, A.P., and K. Ketcham. 2000. *The Power of Empathy: A Practical Guide to Creating Intimacy, Self-Understanding, and Lasting Love in Your Life*. New York: Dutton.

Cicchetti, D. and N. Garmezy. 1993. "Prospects and Promises in the Study of Resilience." *Development and Psychopathology*, 5(4): 497–502.

Cimino, M. 1991. *The Deer Hunter* [VHS]. Universal City, CA: MCA Home Video.

Claassen, R. 1996. *Restorative Justice—Fundamental Principles*. Center for Peacemaking and Conflict Studies Fresno Pacific College. Retrieved September 2002 from the Web: *http://www.fresno.edu/pacs/rjprinc.html*

Claassen, R. 1996. *Whether Crime or Misbehavior, Restorative Justice Principles Provide Guidance on How to Respond*. Center for Peacemaking and Conflict Studies Fresno Pacific College. Retrieved September 2002 from the Web: *http://www.fresno.edu/pacs/docs/dtrl.html*

Claassen, R. 1996. *What is Forgiveness? The Peacemaking Model*. Center for Peacemaking and Conflict Studies Fresno Pacific College. Retrieved September 2002 from the Web: *http://www.fresno.edu/pacs/docs/restj2.shtml*

Clark, M. E. 1993. "Symptoms of Cultural Pathologies: A Hypothesis." In D.J.D. Sandole and H.V.D. Merwe (Eds.), *Conflict Resolution Theory and Practice: Integration and Application*. Manchester, UK: New York, 43–54.

Clark, R., N. B. Anderson, V. R. Clark, and D. R. Williams. 1999. "Racism as a Stressor for African Americans. A Biopsychosocial Model." *American Psychologist*, 54(10): 805–816.

Clarkson, P. 1987. "The Bystander Role." *Transactional Analysis Journal*, 17(3): 82–87.

Cleary, R. J. 1999. "Bowlby's Theory of Attachment and Loss: A Feminist Reconsideration." *Feminism and Psychology*, 9(1), 32–42.

Clendinnen, I. 1999. *Reading the Holocaust*. Cambridge, UK; New York: Cambridge University Press.

Coffin, W. S. 1999. "The Politics of Compassion." In W. S. Coffin (Ed.), *The Heart Is a Little to the Left: Essays on Public Morality*. Hanover, NH: University Press of New England [for] Dartmouth College, 9–25.

Cohen, M. S. 1999. "Families Coping with Childhood Chronic Illness: A Research Review." *Families, Systems and Health*, 17(2): 149–164.

Coker, D. 1999. "Enhancing Autonomy for Battered Women: Lessons from Navajo Peacemaking." *The Regents of the University of California UCLA Law Review*, 47 UCLA L. Rev.(1).

Coner-Edwards, A. F., and J. Spurlock. 1988. *Black Families in Crisis: The Middle Class*. New York: Brunner/Mazel.

Consedine, J. 1999. *Restorative Justice: Healing the Effects of Crime* (Rev. ed.). Lyttelton, N.Z.: Ploughshares Publications.

Cook, J. M. 2001. "Posttraumatic Stress Disorder in Older Adults." PTSD *Research Quarterly*, 12(3): 1–3.

Cooper, A., S. Sullivan, E. Neuffer, J. Nachtwey, and L. Cockburn. 1999. "Dealing with the Trauma of Covering War: Excerpts from a Conference." *Nieman Reports*, 53(2): 24–26.

Corcoran, R. L., and K. E. Greisdorf. 2001. *Connecting Communities*. Washington, DC: Initiatives of Change.

Cordova, M.J., M.A. Andrykowski, D.E. Kenady, P.C. McGrath, D.A. Sloan, and W.H. Redd. 1995. "Frequency and Correlates of Posttraumatic-Stress-Disorder–Like Symptoms After Treatment for Breast Cancer." *Journal of Consulting and Clinical Psychology*, 63(6): 981–986.

Cose, E. 1993. *The Rage of a Privileged Class*. New York: HarperCollins.

Coté, W.E., and R. Simpson. 2000. *Covering Violence: A Guide to Ethical Reporting About Victims and Trauma*. New York: Columbia University Press.

Cotton, K. 1997. *Developing Empathy in Children and Youth*. Northwest Regional Educational Laboratory. Retrieved September 2001 from the Web: *http://www.nwrel.org/scpd/sirs/7/cul3.html*

Courtois, C.A. 1997. "Guidelines for the Treatment of Adults Abused or Possibly Abused as Children (with Attention to Issues of Delayed/Recovered Memory)." *American Journal of Psychotherapy*, 51(4): 497–510.

Cousins, N. 1979. *Anatomy of an Illness as Perceived by the Patient: Reflections on Healing and Regeneration*. New York: Bantam.

Cox, G. 1985. *Bearing Witness: Quaker Process and a Culture of Peace*. Wallingford, PA: Pendle Hill Publications.

Cramer, R.E., M.R. McMaster, P.A. Bartell, and M. Dragna. 1988. "Subject Competence and Minimization of the Bystander Effect." *Journal of Applied Social Psychology*, 18(13): 1133–1148.

Cross, W.E., Jr. 1998. "Black Psychological Functioning and the Legacy of Slavery: Myths and Realities." In Y. Danieli (Ed.), *International Handbook of Multigenerational Legacies of Trauma*. The Plenum Series on Stress and Coping. New York: Plenum Press, 387–400.

Csikszentmihalyi, M. 1997. *Finding Flow: The Psychology of Engagement with Everyday Life*. New York: Basic Books, Inc.

Cummings, E.M. 1998. "Children Exposed to Marital Conflict and Violence: Conceptual and Theoretical Directions." Holden, G.W., R. Geffner et al. (Eds.), *Children Exposed to Marital Violence: Theory, Research, and Applied Issues*. APA Science Volumes. Washington, DC: American Psychological Association, 55–93.

Daniel, J.H. 2000. "The Courage to Hear: African American Women's Memories of Racial Trauma." In L.C. Jackson and B. Greene (Eds.), *Psychotherapy with African-American Women: Innovations in Psychodynamic Perspective and Practices*. New York: Guilford Press, 126–144.

Danieli, Y. 1984. "Psychotherapists' Participation in the Conspiracy of Silence About the Holocaust." *Psychoanalytic Psychology*, 1(1), 23–42.

Danieli, Y. 1998. *International Handbook of Multigenerational Legacies of Trauma*. The Plenum Series on Stress and Coping. New York: Plenum Press.

Danieli, Y. 1998. "Introduction: History and Conceptual Foundations." In Y. Danieli (Ed.), *International Handbook of Multigenerational Legacies of Trauma*. The Plenum Series on Stress and Coping. New York: Plenum Press, 1–17.

Danieli, Y. 1998. "Conclusions and Future Directions." In Y. Danieli (Ed.), *In-*

ternational Handbook of Multigenerational Legacies of Trauma. The Plenum Series on Stress and Coping. New York: Plenum Press, 669–689.

Danieli, Y. 2002. *Sharing the Front Line and the Back Hills: International Protectors and Providers: Peacekeepers, Humanitarian Aid Workers, and the Media in the Midst of Crisis.* Amityville, NY: Baywood Pub. Co.

D'Aquili, E. G. 1985. "Human Ceremonial Ritual and the Modulation of Aggression." *Zygon: Journal of Religion and Science,* 20(1):21–30.

D'Aulaire, I. and E. P. D'Aulaire. 1962. *Book of Greek Myths.* Garden City, NY: Doubleday.

Davison, K. P., and J. W. Pennebaker. 1996. "Social Psychosomatics." In E. T. Higgins and A. W. Kruglanski (Eds.), *Social Psychology: Handbook of Basic Principles.* New York: Guilford Press, 102–130.

Davison, K. P., J. W. Pennebaker, and S. S. Dickerson. 2000. "Who Talks? The Social Psychology of Illness Support Groups." *American Psychologist,* 55(2): 205–217.

Delbo, C. 1995. *Auschwitz and After.* New Haven: Yale University Press.

Delbo, C. 2001. *Days and Memory.* Evanston, IL: Marlboro Press.

Delbo, M. 2002, June 5. "How to Thank Kenya for 9/11 Cows." *Wired.* Retrieved August 4, 2002, from the Web: *http://www.wired.com/news/culture/0, 1284, 52984,00.html*

Denn, R. 2002, March 15. "Blacks Are Disciplined at Far Higher Rates than Other Students." *Seattle Post-Intelligencer.* Retrieved April 2002 from the Web: *http://seattlepi.nwsource.com/disciplinegap/61970_newdiscipline12.shtml*

Diamond, L. 2001. *The Peace Book: 108 Simple Ways to Create a More Peaceful World.* Berkeley: Conari Press.

Dineen, T. 2000, July 13. "The Solitary, Tortured Nobility of Romeo Dallaire." *The Ottawa Citizen.* Retrieved April 2002 from the Web: *http://tanadineen.com/columnist/columns/Dallaire.htm*

Doherty, W. J., and S. K. Burge. 1989. "Divorce Among Physicians. Comparisons with Other Occupational Groups." *JAMA,* 261(16): 2374–2377.

Doran, D. A. 2002, July 17. "Nigerian Women Signal End to Siege." *The Boston Globe,* Section A, 13.

Doran, D. A. July 18, 2002. "Nigerian Women Occupy Oil Plants." *The Boston Globe,* Section A, 19.

Dorff, E. N. 1998. "The Elements of Forgiveness: A Jewish Approach." In E. L. Worthington (Ed.), *Dimensions of Forgiveness: Psychological Research and Theological Perspectives.* Philadelphia: Templeton Foundation Press, 29–55.

Draimin, B. H. C. Levine, & L. McKelvy. 1998. "AIDS and Its Traumatic Effects on Families." In Y. Danieli (Ed.), *International Handbook of Multigenerational Legacies of Trauma.* The Plenum Series on Stress and Coping. New York: Plenum Press, 587–601.

Dray, P. 2002. *At the Hands of Persons Unknown: The Lynching of Black America.* New York: Random House.

Driggs, S. S., R. G. Wilson, R. P. Winthop, The Historic Monument Avenue and Fan District Foundation. 2001. *Richmond's Monument Avenue*. Chapel Hill: University of North Carolina Press.

Duff, K. 1993. *The Alchemy of Illness*. New York: Bell Tower.

Dulmus, C. N. and J. S. Wodarski. 2000. "Trauma-Related Symptomatology Among Children of Parents Victimized by Urban Community Violence." *American Journal of Orthopsychiatry*, 70(2): 272–277.

Dulwich Centre Journal. 2000. "Living Positive Lives." No. 4, Adelaide, South Australia: Dulwich Centre Publications.

Dulwich Centre Journal. 2000. "Narrative Therapy and Community Work: A Conference Collection." Nos. 1 & 2, Adelaide, South Australia: Dulwich Centre Publications.

Dulwich Centre Journal. 1998. "Taking the Hassle Out of School: and stories from younger people." Nos 2 & 3, Adelaide, South Australia: Dulwich Centre Publications.

Dulwich Centre Newsletter. 1995. "Reclaiming Our Stories, Reclaiming Our Lives." No. 1, Adelaide, South Australia: Dulwich Centre Publications.

Dunning, C. 1999. "Postintervention Strategies to Reduce Police Trauma: A Paradigm Shift." In J. M. Violanti and D. Paton (Eds.), *Police Trauma: Psychological Aftermath of Civilian Combat*. Springfield, IL: Charles C. Thomas, 269–289.

Dupree, C. September, 2002. "Inhibited Killers: Hair-Trigger Temperaments." *Harvard Magazine*, September–October 2002, 12–14.

Duran, E., B. Duran, M.Y.H. Brave Heart, and S. Yellow Horse-Davis. 1998. "Healing the American Indian Soul Wound." In Y. Danieli (Ed.), *International Handbook of Multigenerational Legacies of Trauma*. The Plenum Series on Stress and Coping. New York: Plenum Press, 341–351.

Dutton, D. G. 1999. "Traumatic Origins of Intimate Rage." *Aggression and Violent Behavior*, 4(4): 431–447.

Dutton, M. A., and F. L. Rubinstein. 1995. "Working with People with PTSD: Research Implications." In C. R. Figley (Ed.), *Compassion Fatigue: Coping with Secondary Traumatic Stress Disorder in Those Who Treat the Traumatized*. Brunner/Mazel psychological stress series, No. 23. Philadelphia: Brunner/Mazel, Inc, 82–100.

Dwyer, S. 1999. "Reconciliation for Realists." *Ethics and International Affairs*, 13 (spring), 81–98.

Dyregrov, A., R. Gjestad, and M. Raundalen. 2002. "Children Exposed to Warfare: A Longitudinal Study." *Journal of Traumatic Stress*, 15 (1): 59–68.

Earls, F. 2001. "Community Factors Supporting Child Mental Health." *Child and Adolescent Psychiatric Clinics of North America*, 10(4), 693–709.

Eck, D. L. 1993. *Encountering God: A Spiritual Journal from Bozeman to Banaras*. Boston: Beacon Press.

Eck, D. L. 2001. *A New Religious America: How a "Christian Country" Has Now Become the World's Most Religiously Diverse Nation*. San Francisco: Harper.

Edleson, J. L. 1999. "Children's Witnessing of Adult Domestic Violence." *Journal of Interpersonal Violence*, 14(8), 839–870.

Egeland, B., and A. Susman-Stillman. 1996. "Dissociation as a Mediator of Child Abuse Across Generations." *Child Abuse and Neglect*, 20(11), 1123–1132.

Eggers, D. 2000. *A Heartbreaking Work of Staggering Genius*. New York: Simon & Schuster.

Ehlich, P. J., L. Roemer, and R. T. Litz. 1997. "PTSD After a Peacekeeping Mission." *American Journal of Psychiatry*, 154(9), 1319–1320.

Eisenberg, M. G., L. C. Sutkin, and M. A. Jansen. 1984. *Chronic Illness and Disability Through the Life Span: Effects on Self and Family*. New York: Springer Pub. Co.

Eisenberg, N. 1989. "Empathy and Sympathy." In W. Damon (Ed.), *Child Development Today and Tomorrow*. The Jossey-Bass Social and Behavioral Science Series. San Francisco: Jossey-Bass, 137–154.

Ell, K. 1996. "Social Networks, Social Support, and Coping with Serious Illness: The Family Connection." *Social Science and Medicine*, 42(2), 173–183.

Elliott, G., R. Avery, E. Fishman, and B. Hoshiko. 2002. "The Encounter with Family Violence and Risky Sexual Activity Among Young Adolescent Females." *Journal of Violence and Victims*, 17(5), 569–592.

Ellis, G.F.R. 2001. "Afterward: Exploring the Unique Role of Forgiveness." In R. G. Helmick and R. L. Petersen (Eds.), *Forgiveness and Reconciliation: Religion, Public Policy and Conflict Transformation*. Philadelphia: Templeton Foundation Press, 385–400.

Elms, A. C. 1995. "Obedience in Retrospect." *Journal of Social Issues*. 51(3), 21–31.

English, B. 1999, November 14. "Caring and Connecting in Face of Tragedy." *The Boston Globe*, South Weekly, 2.

Enloe, C. H. 2000. *Maneuvers: The International Politics of Militarizing Women's Lives*. Berkeley: University of California Press.

Enright, R. D., S. Freedman, and J. Rique. 1998. "The Psychology of Interpersonal Forgiveness." In R. D. Enright and J. North (Eds.), *Exploring Forgiveness*. Madison: University of Wisconsin Press, 46–62.

Enright, R. D., and J. North (Eds.). 1998. *Exploring Forgiveness*: Madison: University of Wisconsin Press.

Ensler, E. 2001. *Necessary Targets: A Story of Women and War*. New York: Villard.

Epstein, H. 1988. *Children of the Holocaust: Conversations with Sons and Daughters of Survivors*. New York: Penguin Books.

Epstein, J., and L. H. Lefkovitz. 2001. *Shaping Losses: Cultural Memory and the Holocaust*. Urbana: University of Illinois Press.

Epstein, S. 1995. "The Construction of Lay Expertise: AIDS Activism and the Forging of Credibility in the Reform of Clinical Trials." *Science, Technology, and Human Values*, 20 (4), 408–437.

Erdrich, L. March 5, 2001. "The Shawl." *The New Yorker*, 84–87.
Erlanger, S. November 10, 2000. "A Freed Albanian Visits Restive Serbian Prisons." *The New York Times*, Section A, 14.
Esposito, J. L. 2002. *Unholy War: Terror in the Name of Islam*. Oxford; New York: Oxford University Press.
Eth, S., R. S. and Pynoos, A. 1985. *Posttraumatic Stress Disorder in Children*. Washington, DC: American Psychiatric Press.
Eve, N. 2000. *The Family Orchard: A Novel* (1st ed.). New York: Knopf.
Fadiman, A. 1997. *The Spirit Catches You and You Fall Down: A Hmong Child, Her American Doctors, and the Collision of Two Cultures*. New York: Farrar, Straus & Giroux.
Fakhry, M. 2000. *Islamic Philosophy, Theology, and Mysticism: A Short Introduction*. Oxford: Oneworld.
Fallon, P. December 7, 2001. *Ramadan for Non-Muslims*. Boston: Morning Edition, WBUR.
Famularo, R., R. Kinscherff, and T. Fenton. 1990. "Symptom Differences in Acute and Chronic Presentation of Childhood Posttraumatic Stress Disorder." *Child Abuse and Neglect*, 14(3), 439–444.
Farragher, T. July 2, 2001. "Vengeance at Dachau: In Dark Footnote to Death Camps Liberation, U.S. Soldiers Shocked by Holocaust Executed Nazi SS Troops." *The Boston Globe*, Section A, 1.
Farren, P. 1995. *Keepin' On: Political Journalism, Personal Illness and Community*. Boston: The Community Church of Boston.
Farwell, N., and J. B. Cole. 2001. "Community as a Context of Healing." *International Journal of Mental Health*, 30(4), 19–41.
Favre, G. 2001, September 20. *Forgetting Our Feelings*. Poynter.org. Retrieved 2001 from the Web: *http://www.poynter.org/Terrorism/greg7.htm*
Federal Bureau of Investigation, Association of State Uniform Crime Reporting Programs, Northeastern University, Center for Applied Social Research, and Criminal Justice Information Services Division of the FBI. 1990. *Hate Crime Statistics: A Resource Book*. Washington, DC: The Federal Bureau of Investigation.
Fein, H. 1994. "Reading the Second Text: Meanings and Misuses of the Holocaust." In M. Polner and N. Goodman (Eds.), *The Challenge of Shalom: The Jewish Tradition of Peace and Justice*. Philadelphia: New Society Publishers, 71–81.
Feinstein, A., and J. Owen. 2002. "Journalists, War, and Posttraumatic Stress Disorder." In Y. Danieli (Ed.), *Sharing the Front Line and the Back Hills: International Protectors and Providers: Peacekeepers, Humanitarian Aid Workers, and the Media in the Midst of Crisis*. Amityville, NY: Baywood Publishing Co., Inc. 305–315.
Feld, S. L. and D. T. Robinson. 1998. "Secondary Bystander Effects on Intimate Violence: When Norms of Restraint Reduce Deterrence." *Journal of Social and Personal Relationships*, 15(2), 277–285.

Felman, S., and D. Laub. 1992. *Testimony: Crises of Witnessing in Literature, Psychoanalysis, and History*. New York: Routledge.

Felsen, I. 1998. "Transgenerational Transmission of Effects of the Holocaust: The North American Research Perspective." In Y. Danieli (Ed.), *International Handbook of Multigenerational Legacies of Trauma*. The Plenum Series on Stress and Coping. New York: Plenum Press, 43–68.

Fenton, Z. E. 1998. "Domestic Violence In Black and White: Racialized Gender Stereotypes in Gender Violence." *Columbia Journal of Gender and Law*, 8: 10–31.

Figley, C. R. 1995. *Compassion Fatigue: Coping with Secondary Traumatic Stress Disorder in Those Who Treat the Traumatized*. Bruner/Mazel Psychological Stress Series, No. 23. Philadelphia: Brunner/Mazel, Inc.

Figley, C. R. 1995. "Introduction." In C. R. Figley (Ed.), *Compassion Fatigue: Coping with Secondary Traumatic Stress Disorder in Those Who Treat the Traumatized*. Brunner/Mazel Psychological Stress Series, No. 23. Philadelphia Brunner/Mazel, Inc., 82–100.

Figley, C. R. 1995. "Compassion Fatigue as Secondary Stress Disorder: An Overview." In C. R. Figley (Ed.), *Compassion Fatigue: Coping with Secondary Traumatic Stress Disorder in Those Who Treat the Traumatized*. Brunner/Mazel Psychological Stress Series, No. 23. Philadelphia: Brunner/Mazel, Inc. 1–20.

Figley, C. R. 1995. Epilogue: "The Transmission of Trauma." In C. R. Figley (Ed.), *Compassion Fatigue: Coping with Secondary Traumatic Stress Disorder in Those Who Treat the Traumatized*. Brunner/Mazel Psychological Stress Series, No. 23. Philadelphia: Brunner/Mazel, Inc, 248–254.

Figley, C. R. 1998. *Burnout in Families: The Systemic Costs of Caring*. Boca Raton, FL: CRC Press.

Figley, C. R. 1999. "Police Compassion Fatigue: Theory, Research, Assessment, Treatment, and Prevention." In J. M. Violanti and D. Paton (Eds.), *Police Trauma: Psychological Aftermath of Civilian Combat*. Springfield, IL: Charles C. Thomas, 269–289.

Fincham, F. D. 2000. "The Kiss of the Porcupines: From Attributing Responsibility to Forgiving." *Personal Relationships*. 7(1), 1–23.

Fine, M., et al. 1996. "Insisting on Innocence: Accounts of Accountability by Abusive Men." In M. B. Lykes, et. al (Ed.), *Myths About the Powerless: Contesting Social Inequalities*. Philadelphia: Temple University Press, 128–158.

Fineman, M., and R. Mykitiuk. 1994. *The Public Nature of Private Violence: the Discovery of Domestic Abuse*. New York: Routledge.

Finkelstein, N. G., and R. B. Birn. 1998. *A Nation on Trial: The Goldhagen Thesis and Historical Truth*. New York: Henry Holt.

Firth-Cozens, J. 2001. "Interventions to Improve Physicians' Well-being and Patient Care." *Social Science and Medicine*, 52(2), 215–222.

Fischer, K. 2002. *Pathways to Aggression Through Inhibited Temperament and*

Parental Violence. Harvard Graduate School of Education. Retrieved August 23, 2002, from the Web: *http://www.gse.harvard.edu/news/features/fischersummary.html*

Fitzpatrick, K. M., and J. P. Boldizar. 1993. "The Prevalence and Consequences of Exposure to Violence Among African-American Youth." *Journal of the American Academy of Child and Adolescent Psychiatry*, 32(2), 424–430.

Fivush, R. 1998. "Children's Recollections of Traumatic and Nontraumatic Events." *Development and Psychopathology*, 10(4), 699–716.

Flam, N., J. Offel, and A. Eilberg. *Acts of Loving-Kindness: A Training Manual for Bikkur Holim*. San Francisco: The National Center for Jewish Healing.

Flanigan, B. 1998. "Forgivers and the Unforgivable." In R. D. Enright and J. North (Eds.), *Exploring Forgiveness*. Madison: University of Wisconsin Press, 95–105.

Fletcher, R. H. and S. W. Fletcher. 1993. "Here Come the Couples." *Annals of Internal Medicine*, 119(7 Pt 1), 628–630.

Foa, E. B., A. Ehlers, D. M. Clark, D. F. Tolin, and S. M. Orsillo. 1999. "The Posttraumatic Cognitions Inventory (PTCI): Development and Validation." *Psychological Assessment*, 11(3), 303–314.

Foa, E. B., T. M. Keane, and M. J. Friedman 2000. *Effective Treatments for PTSD: Practice Guidelines from the International Society for Traumatic Stress Studies*. New York: Guilford Press.

Focht, L., and W. R. Beardslee. 1996. " 'Speech After Long Silence': The Use of Narrative Therapy in a Preventive Intervention for Children of Parents with Affective Disorder." *Family Process*, 35(4), 407–422.

Focht-Birkerts, L. and W. R. Beardslee. 2000. "A Child's Experience of Parental Depression: Encouraging Relational Resilience in Families with Affective Illness." *Family Process*, 39(4), 417–434.

Fonagy, P. and M. Target. 1997. "Attachment and Reflective Function: Their Role in Self-Organization." *Development and Psychopathology*, 9(4), 679–700.

Fonagy, P., M. Target, M. Steele, and H. Steele. 1997. "The Development of Violence and Crime as It Relates to Security of Attachment." In J. D. Osofsky (Ed.), *Children in a Violent Society*. New York: Guilford Press, 150–177.

Forché, C. 1993. *Against Forgetting: Twentieth-Century Poetry of Witness*. New York: Norton.

Forget, M. 1996, June. *Crime as Interpersonal Conflict: Reconciliation Between Victim and Offender*. Paper presented at the Dilemmas of Reconciliation Conference, Fresno, CA.

Foucault, M. 1965. *Madness and Civilization: A History of Insanity in the Age of Reason*. New York: Vintage Books.

Foucault, M. and C. Gordon. 1980. *Power/Knowledge: Selected Interviews and Other Writings, 1972–1977*. New York: Pantheon Books.

Fow, N. R. 1996. "The Phenomenology of Forgiveness and Reconciliation." *Journal of Phenomenological Psychology*, 27(2), 219–233.

Fox, E., R. Russo, R. Bowles and K. Dutton. 2001. "Do Threatening Stimuli

Draw or Hold Visual Attention in Subclinical Anxiety?" *Journal of Experimental Psychology: General*, 130(4): 681–700.

Foy, D.W. and C.A. Goguen. 1998. "Community-Violence Related PTSD in Children and Adolescents." *PTSD Research Quarterly*, 9(4), 1–3.

Frank, A.W. 1995. *The Wounded Storyteller: Body, Illness, and Ethics*. Chicago: University of Chicago Press.

Frank, A.W. 1997. "Enacting Illness Stories: When, What, and Why." In H.L. Nelson (Ed.), *Stories and Their Limits: Narrative Approaches to Bioethics*. New York: Routledge, 31–49.

Frank, A.W. 1997. "Illness as Moral Occasion: Restoring Agency to Ill People." *Health*, 1(2), 131–148.

Frank, A.W. 1998. "Stories of Illness as Care of the Self: A Foucauldian Dialogue." *Health*, 2(3), 329–348.

Frank, A.W. 1998. "Just Listening: Narrative and Deep Illness." *Families, Systems, and Health*, 16(3), 197–212.

Frank, A.W. 2001, September 3–4. *Acts of Witness: Forms of Engagement in Illness*. Paper presented at the Narrative Based Medicine Conference, Cambridge, UK.

Frank, E. and A.D. Dingle. 1999. "Self-Reported Depression and Suicide Attempts Among U.S. Women Physicians." *American Journal of Psychiatry*, 156(12), 1887–1894.

Frank, J.D. 1972. *Persuasion and Healing: A Comparative Study of Psychotherapy*. New York: Schocken Books.

Franklin, A.J., and N. Boyd-Franklin. 2000. "Invisibility Syndrome: A Clinical Model of the Effects of Racism on African-American Males." *American Journal of Orthopsychiatry*, 70(1), 33–41.

Franzblau, S.H. 1999. "Historicizing Attachment Theory: Binding the Ties That Bind." *Feminism and Psychology*, 9(1), 22–31.

Franzblau, S.H. 1999. Editor's Introduction: "Attachment Theory." *Feminism and Psychology*, 9(1), 5–9.

Fredrickson, G.M. 2002. *Racism: A Short History*. Princeton, N.J.: Princeton University Press.

Freedman, J. and G. Combs, 1996. *Narrative Therapy: The Social Construction of Preferred Realities*. New York: Norton.

Freedman, S. 1998. "Forgiveness and Reconciliation: The Importance of Understanding How They Differ." *Counseling and Values*, 42(3): 200–216.

Freeman, J.C., D. Epston, and D. Lobovits. 1997. *Playful Approaches to Serious Problems: Narrative Therapy with Children and Their Families*. New York: Norton.

Freire, P. 1970. *Pedagogy of the Oppressed*. New York: Herder and Herder.

Fremont, H. 1999. *After Long Silence: A Memoir*. New York: Delacorte Press.

Freudenberger, H.J. 1986. "Chemical Abuse Among Psychologists: Symptoms, Causes, and Treatment Issues." In R.R. Kilburg and P.E. Nathan et al. (Eds.), *Professionals in Distress: Issues, Syndromes, and Solutions in Psychology*. Washington, DC: American Psychological Association, 135–152.

Freudenheim, M. June 7, 2001. "Price of Success in AIDS Treatment; Hospitals Confront New Therapy." *The New York Times*, Section C, 1.

Fried, R. M. 1990. *Nightmare in Red: The McCarthy Era in Perspective*. New York: Oxford University Press.

Friedman, D. A. 2001. *Jewish Pastoral Care: A Practical Handbook from Traditional and Contemporary Sources*. Woodstock, VT: Jewish Lights Publishing.

Frontline. 1999. *The Long Walk of Nelson Mandela*. WGBH/Frontline. Retrieved October 16, 2002, from the Web: *http://www.pbs.org/wgbh/pages/frontline/shows/mandela/*

Frost, R. 1969. "Home Burial." In R. Frost and E. C. Lathem (Eds.), *The Poetry of Robert Frost*. New York: Holt, Rinehart & Winston, 51–55.

Galea, S., J. Ahern, H. Resnick, D. Kilpatrick, M. Bucuvalas, J. Gold, and D. Vlahov. 2002. "Psychological Sequelae of the September 11 Terrorist Attacks in New York City." *New England Journal of Medicine*, 346(13): 982–987.

Gall, C. 2000, November 2. "Kosovo Albanians Cheer the Return of a Doctor Freed in Serbia." *The New York Times*, Section A, 13.

Galtung, J. 1969. "Violence, Peace, and Peace Research." *Journal of Peace Research*, 3, 167–191.

Gandhi, M., trans. M. H. Desai, 1957. *An Autobiography: The Story of My Experiments with Truth*. Boston: Beacon Press.

Gandhi, M., T. Merton (Ed.). 1965. *Gandhi on Nonviolence*. New York: New Directions.

Garbarino, J. 1999. "The Effects of Community Violence on Children." In L. Balter and C. S. Tamis-LeMonda (Eds.), *Child Psychology: A Handbook of Contemporary Issues*. Philadelphia: Psychology Press/Taylor & Francis, 412–425.

Garber, M. B. and R. L. Walkowitz. 1995. *Secret Agents: The Rosenberg Case, McCarthyism, and Fifties America*. New York: Routledge.

García Coll, C. T., J. L. Surrey, and K. Weingarten. 1998. *Mothering Against the Odds: Diverse Voices of Contemporary Mothers*. New York: Guilford Press.

Garrity, C. and M. A. Baris. 1996. "Bullies and Victims: A Guide for Pediatricians." *Contemporary Pediatrics*, February, 90.

Gassaway, B. M. 1989. "Making Sense of War: An Autobiographical Account of a Vietnam War Correspondent." *Journal of Applied Behavioral Science*, 25(4), 327–349.

Gay, Lesbian and Straight Education Network. 2000. *Youth Suicide*. GLSEN. Retrieved May 10, 2000, from the Web: *http://www.glsen.org/pages/sections/library/reference/011.article*

Gay, Lesbian and Straight Education Network. 2000. *New Study Highlights Violence Against Gay and Lesbian People*. GLSEN. Retrieved May 10, 2000, from the Web: *http://www.glsen.org/pages/sections/library/reference/013.article*

George, A. R. and L. Marks. 1998. *Hope: Photographs*. New York: Thames and Hudson.

Gergen, K. J. 1985. "The Social Constructionist Movement in Modern Psychology." *American Psychologist*, 40(3), 266–275.

Gergen, K. J. 1988. "If Persons Are Texts." In S. B. Messer and L. A. Sass, et al. (Eds.) *Hermeneutics and Psychological Theory: Interpretive Perspectives on Personality, Psychotherapy, and Psychopathology*. Rutgers Symposia on Applied Psychology, 2. New Brunswick, NJ: Rutgers University Press, 28–51.

Gergen, K. J. 1991. *The Saturated Self: Dilemmas of Identity in Contemporary Life*. New York: Basic Books.

Gergen, K. J. 1994. *Realities and Relationships: Soundings in Social Construction*. Cambridge, MA: Harvard University Press.

Gergen, K. J., and M. M. Gergen. 1983. "Narratives of the Self." In T. R. Sarbin and K. E. Scheibe (Eds.), *Studies in Social Identity*. New York: Praeger, 254–273.

Gil, D. G. 1996. "Preventing Violence in a Structurally Violent Society: Mission, Impossible." *American Journal of Orthopsychiatry*, 66(1), 77–84.

Gilbert, S. M. 1995. *Wrongful Death: A Medical Tragedy*. New York: Norton.

Gilligan, J. 1997. *Violence: Reflections on a National Epidemic*. New York: Vintage Books.

Glassman, B. 1998. *Bearing Witness: A Zen Master's Lessons in Making Peace*. New York: Bell Tower.

Gobodo-Madikizela, P. 2002. "Remorse, Forgiveness, and Rehumanization: Stories from South Africa." *Journal of Humanistic Psychology*, 42(1), 7–32.

Gobodo-Madikizela, P. 2003. *A Human Being Died That Night: A South African Story of Forgiveness*. Boston: Houghton Mifflin.

Goddard, H. C. 1960. *The Meaning of Shakespeare*. Chicago: University of Chicago Press.

Goldhagen, D. J. 1996. *Hitler's Willing Executioners: Ordinary Germans and the Holocaust*. New York: Knopf.

Goldner, V., P. Penn, M. Sheinberg, and G. Walker. 1990. "Love and Violence: Gender Paradoxes in Volatile Attachments." *Family Process*, 29(4), 343–364.

Goldstone, R. 2000. *For Humanity: Reflections of a War Crimes Investigator*. New Haven: Yale University Press.

Good, M.-J. D. 1992. *Pain as Human Experience: An Anthropological Perspective*. Berkeley: University of California Press.

Goode, E. September 18, 2001. "Stress from Attacks Will Chase Some into the Depths of Their Minds, and Stay." *The New York Times*, B1.

Goode, E. August 21, 2002. "Program to Cover Psychiatric Help for 9/11 Families." *The New York Times*, A1.

Goodstein, L. January 12, 2003. "Trail of Pain in Church Crisis Leads to Nearly Every Diocese." *The New York Times*, A1.

Gopin, M. 2000. *Between Eden and Armageddon: The Future of World Religions, Violence, and Peacemaking*. Oxford, UK, New York: Oxford University Press.

Gopin, M. 2002. *Holy War, Holy Peace: How Religion Can Bring Peace to the Middle East*. Auckland; New York: Oxford University Press.

Gordon, D., T. Hicks, and S. Grossfield. December 6, 2001. "Photographing the War in Afghanistan," *The Connection*. Boston: WBUR.

Gottschalk, L.A., J. Fronczek, and M.S. Buchsbaum. 1993. "The Cerebral Neurobiology of Hope and Hopelessness." *Psychiatry*, 56(3), 270–281.

Gourevitch, P. 1998. *We Wish to Inform You That Tomorrow We Will Be Killed with Our Families: Stories from Rwanda*. New York: Farrar, Straus & Giroux.

Gourevitch, P. 1998. *Genocide in Our Time*. U.S. Institute of Peace. Retrieved October 16, 2002, from the Web: *http://www.usip.org/pubs/pw/1298/profile.html*

Grabmeier, J. 2001, December 12. *Former Caregivers Still Show Psychological Ills Years After Caregiving Ends*. Ohio State University. Retrieved October 5, 2002, from the Web: *http://www.osu.edu/researchnews/archive/formcare.htm*

Grady, D. 2001, June 5. "AIDS AT 20; Volunteers Submit to Science." *The New York Times*, F4.

Grady, D. 2001, June 5. "Scientists Shifting Strategies in Quest for an AIDS Vaccine." *The New York Times*, Section F, 1.

Grattan, M. 2000. *Reconciliation: Essays on Australian Reconciliation*. Melbourne: Bookman Press.

Graves, R. 1968. *The Greek Myths*. New York: Penguin Books.

Grealy, L. 1994. *Autobiography of a Face*. Boston: Houghton Mifflin.

Green, A.H: 1998. "Factors Contributing to the Generational Transmission of Child Maltreatment." *Journal of the American Academy of Child and Adolescent Psychiatry*, 37(12), 1334–1336.

Green, B.L., S.A. Epstein, J.L. Krupnick, and J.H. Rowland. 1997. "Trauma and Medical Illness: Assessing Trauma-Related Disorders in Medical Settings." In J.P. Wilson and T.M. Keane (Eds.), *Assessing Psychological Trauma and PTSD*. New York: Guilford Press, 160–191.

Green, P. 1997. "Teaching Nonviolence in a Violence-Addicted World." *ReVision: A Journal of Consciousness and Transformation*, 20(2), 43–46.

Green, P. 2000. *An Infusion of Dialogues: Bosnians in Dialogue Meet Holocaust Descendants in Dialogue*. The Karuna Center. Retrieved October 16, 2002, from the Web: *http://www.karunacenter.org/article-aninfusion.html*

Greenspan, M. 1980. "Responses to the Holocaust." *Jewish Currents*, October: 20–39.

Griffin, S. 1992. *A Chorus of Stones: The Private Life of War*. New York: Doubleday.

Griffith, J.L., and M.E. Griffith. 1994. *The Body Speaks: Therapeutic Dialogues for Mind-Body Problems*. New York: BasicBooks.

Griffith, J. L. and M. E. Griffith. 2002. *Encountering the Sacred in Psychotherapy: How to Talk with People About Their Spiritual Lives*. New York: Guilford Press.

Groopman, J. September 17, 2001. "God on the Brain." *The New Yorker*, 165–168.

Grossman, D. 1996. *On Killing: The Psychological Cost of Learning to Kill in War and Society*. Boston: Little Brown.

Groves, B. M. 2002. *Children Who See Too Much: Lessons from the Child Witness to Violence Project*. Boston: Beacon Press.

Gudas, L. S. 2002. "Grief Work with Children and Families Following Traumatic Death and Loss." *Massachusetts Psychological Association*, 46(1), 5–7.

Gurevitch, Z. D. 1989. "The Power of Not Understanding: The Meeting of Conflicting Identities." *Journal of Applied Behavioral Science*, 25(2), 161–173:

Gurwitch, R. H., et. al. 2001. *What to Expect After Trauma: Possible Reactions in Elementary School Students*. American Psychological Association. Retrieved October 18, 2001, from the Web: *http://www.apa.org/practice/pt-guidelines.html*

Gusman, F. D., J. Stewart, et al. 1996. "A Multicultural Developmental Approach for Treating Trauma." In A. J. Marsella (Ed.), *Ethnocultural Aspects of Posttraumatic Stress Disorder: Issues, Research, and Clinical Applications* (1st ed.). Washington, DC: American Psychological Association, 439–457.

Guterson, D. 1995. *Snow Falling on Cedars* (1st Vintage contemporaries ed.). New York: Vintage Books.

Gutman, I. 1995. "Holocaust." In I. Gutman (Ed.), *Encyclopedia of the Holocaust* (2). New York: Macmillan Library Reference.

Gutman, R. 1993. *A Witness to Genocide: The 1993 Pulitzer Prize-winning Dispatches on the "Ethnic cleansing" of Bosnia*. New York: Macmillan.

Gutman, R., D. Rieff, and K. Anderson. 1999. *Crimes of War: What the Public Should Know*. New York: Norton.

Hacker, A. 1995. *Two Nations: Black and White, Separate, Hostile, Unequal*. New York: Ballantine Books.

Hackett, J. 2001. "The Territory of Trauma: A Novelist Finds Herself in Unexpected Historical Territory, Confronting the Ethics and Politics of Her Art." *The Boston Review* (December 2001–January 2002), 23–27.

Hackett, J. 2002. *Disturbance of the Inner Ear*. New York: Carroll & Graf.

Hadley, M. L. 2001. *The Spiritual Roots of Restorative Justice*. Albany: State University of New York Press.

Hallie, P. P. 1979. *Lest Innocent Blood Be Shed: The Story of the Village of Le Chambon, and How Goodness Happened There* (1st ed.). New York: Harper & Row.

Halling, S. 1994. "Shame and Forgiveness." *Humanistic Psychologist*, 22(1), 74–80.

Hamner, M. B. 1994. "Exacerbation of Posttraumatic Stress Disorder Symptoms with Medical Illness." *General Hospital Psychiatry*, 16(2): 135–137.

Harber, K.D. and J.W. Pennebaker. 1992. "Overcoming Traumatic Memories." In S.A. Christianson (Ed.), *The Handbook of Emotion and Memory: Research and Theory*. Hillsdale, NJ: Lawrence Erlbaum Associates, Inc., 359–387.

Hardtmann, G. 1998. "Children of Nazis: A Psychodynamic Perspective." In Y. Danieli (Ed.), *International Handbook of Multigenerational Legacies of Trauma*. The Plenum Series on Stress and Coping. New York: Plenum Press, 85–95.

Hargrove, A.C. 1988. *Getting Better*. Minneapolis: CompCare Publishers.

Harrell, S.P. 2000. "A Multidimensional Conceptualization of Racism-Related Stress: Implications for the Well-Being of People of Color." *American Journal of Orthopsychiatry*, 70(1), 42–57.

Harriman, P. 2000, December 22. "Young Lakota Riders Draw Strength from History." *The Argus Leader*. Retrieved from the Web: *http://www.argusleader.com/specialsections/2000/bigfoot/articleII.shtml*

Harris, C.J. 1995. "Sensory-Based Therapy for Crisis Counselors." In C.R. Figley (Ed.), *Compassion Fatigue: Coping with Secondary Traumatic Stress Disorder in Those Who Treat the Traumatized*. Brunner/Mazel Psychological Stress Series, No. 23. Philadelphia: Brunner/Mazel, Inc., 101–114.

Haruf, K. 2000. *Plainsong*. New York: Vintage Books.

Harvey, M.R. 1996. "An Ecological View of Psychological Trauma and Trauma Recovery." *Journal of Traumatic Stress*, 9(1), 3–23.

Harway, M., J.M. O'Neil, and J.R. Biden. 1999. *What Causes Men's Violence Against Women?* Thousand Oaks, CA: Sage Publications.

Hatley, J. 2000. *Suffering Witness: The Quandary of Responsibility After the Irreparable*. Albany: State University of New York Press.

Haugen, G.A. 1999. *Good News About Injustice: A Witness of Courage in a Hurting World*. Downers Grove, IL: InterVarsity Press.

Hayner, P.B. 1994. "Fifteen Truth Commissions: 1974–1994." *Human Rights Quarterly*, 16, 597–655.

Heaney, S. 1995. *The Redress of Poetry*. New York: Farrar, Straus & Giroux.

Hedges, C. 2002. *War Is a Force That Gives Us Meaning* (1st ed.). New York: Public Affairs.

Heins, M. and J. Cantor. 2001. *Violence and the Media: An Exploration of Cause, Effect, and the First Amendment*. Nashville, TN: First Amendment Center.

Heins, M., D. Greene, and B. Joseph. *Brief Amici Curiae of Scholars and Authors in the Field of Media and Communications in Support of the Plaintiffs-Appellants: Henry Jenkins, Richard Rhodes, Jib Fowles, Robert Horwitz, Ellen Seiter, Donna Gaines, Vivian Sobchack, Constance Penley*. The First Amendment Project. Retrieved September 7, 2002, from the Web: *http://www.thefirstamendment.org/amicus%20briefs/aamaamicus.htm*

Helmick, R.G. and R.L. Petersen. 2001. *Forgiveness and Reconciliation: Religion, Public Policy and Conflict Transformation*. Philadelphia: Templeton Foundation Press.

Henderson, M. 1996. *The Forgiveness Factor: Stories of Hope in a World of Conflict*. Salem, OR: Grosvenor Books.

Henderson, M. 1999. *Forgiveness: Breaking the Chain of Hate*. Wilsonville, OR: BookPartners.

Herman, J. L. 1992. *Trauma and Recovery*. New York: Basic Books.

Hirsch, J. S. 2002. *Riot and Remembrance: the Tulsa Race War and Its Legacy*. Boston: Houghton Mifflin.

Hirsch, M. 1992/1993. "Family Pictures: Maus, Mourning, and Postmemory." *Discourse: Theoretical Studies on Media and Culture*, 15(2), 3–29.

Hoffman, C. 1997. *Grant Proposal—Cambridge Youth Peace and Justice Corps*. Cambridge, MA: Cambridge Peace Commission.

Hoffman, M. L. 2000. *Empathy and Moral Development: Implications for Caring and Justice*. Cambridge, UK; New York: Cambridge University Press.

Hogan, L., D. Metzger, and B. Peterson. 1998. *Intimate Nature: The Bond Between Women and Animals*. New York: Fawcett Columbine.

Hojat, M. 1989. "Divorce Among Physicians." *JAMA*, 262(18), 2540.

Holden, G. W., R. Geffner, and E. N. Jouriles (Eds.). 1998. *Children Exposed to Marital Violence: Theory, Research, and Applied Issues*: Washington, DC: American Psychological Association.

Holden, G. W., J. D. Stein, K. L. Ritchie, S. D. Harris, and E. N. Jouriles. 1998. "Parenting Behaviors and Beliefs of Battered Women," In Holden, G. W., and R. Geffner et al. (Eds). *Children Exposed to Marital Violence: Theory, Research, and Applied Issues*. APA science volumes. Washington, DC, U.S.: American Psychological Association, 289–334.

Holmes, M. M., S. J. Mudlaff, C. Pillo 2000. *A Terrible Thing Happened*. Washington, DC: Magination Press.

Homer. 1944. *The Odyssey of Homer*, trans. Samuel Butler. Roslyn, New York: Walter J. Black.

Homer. 1909. *The Odyssey of Homer*, trans. S. H. Butcher and A. Lang. New York: P. F. Collier & Son.

Homer. 1961. *The Iliad of Homer*, trans. R. A. Lattimore. Chicago: Univ. of Chicago Press.

Homer. 1967. *The Odyssey of Homer*, trans. R. A. Lattimore. New York: Harper & Row.

Hood, B., and King, Rachel (Ed.). 2002. *Not in Our Name*. Cambridge, MA: Murder Victims' Families for Reconciliation.

Horowitz, M. J. 1997. *Stress Response Syndromes: PTSD, Grief, and Adjustment Disorders*. Northvale, NJ: J. Aronson.

House, J. S., D. Umberson, and K. R. Landis. 1988. "Structures and Processes of Social Support." *Annual Review of Sociology*, 14, 293–318.

Howard, C., K. Tuffin, and C. Stephens. 2000. "Unspeakable Emotion: A Discursive Analysis of Police Talk About Reactions to Trauma." *Journal of Language and Social Psychology*, 19(3), 295–314.

Hwoschinsky, C. 2001. *Listening with the Heart: A Guide for Compassionate Listening*. Indianola, WA: MidEast Citizen Diplomacy.

Hynes, S. L. 1997. *The Soldiers' Tale: Bearing Witness to Modern War*. New York: A. Lane.

Ignatieff, M. February 21, 2001. "The Danger of a World Without Enemies. Lemkin's Word." *The New Republic*, 25.

Imbrogno, D. 2001. *Belfast Diary: Hanging Out with the Dalai Lama, IRA Victims, Former Paramilitaries, and Struggling Peacemakers in the Bombed and Barbed Wire Capital of Northern Ireland*. Hundred Mountain. Retrieved October 17, 2002, from the Web: *http://www.hundred-mountain.com/Pages/pageone_stuff/winter_01/belfast1_winter01.html*

Initiatives of Change. 2001. *Connecting Communities for Reconciliation and Justice* (Conference Report). Howard University, June 20–24.

Inoue, Y. 1982. *Chronicle of My Mother*. New York: Kodanasha America.

Jackson, R. 2000. "Terzanelle of Kosovo Fields." In R. Jackson, *Heartwall*. Amherst: University of Massachusetts Press.

Jackson, V. 2002. "In Our Own Voice: African-American Stories of Oppression, Survival, and Recovery in Mental Health Systems." *The International Journal of Narrative Therapy and Community Work*, 2: 11–31.

Jacobs, R. N. 2000. *Race, Media, and the Crisis of Civil Society: From Watts to Rodney King*. Cambridge, UK. New York: Cambridge University Press.

James, W. G., and L. v. d. Vijver. 2001. *After the TRC: Reflections on Truth and Reconciliation in South Africa*. Athens: Ohio University Press.

Janoff-Bulman, R. 1992. *Shattered Assumptions: Towards a New Psychology of Trauma*. New York: Free Press.

Jenkins, A., M. Joy, and R. Hall. 2002. "Forgiveness and Child Sexual Abuse: A Matrix of Meanings." *The International Journal of Narrative Therapy and Community Work*, 1: 35–51.

Johnson, J. G., P. Cohen, E. M. Smailes, S. Kasen, and J. S. Brook. 2002. "Television Viewing and Aggressive Behavior During Adolescence and Adulthood." *Science*, 295(5564): 2468–2471.

Jordan, J. V. 2000. "The Role of Mutual Empathy in Relational/Cultural Therapy." *Journal of Clinical Psychology* 56(8), 1005–1016.

Jordan, J. V., J. L. Surrey, and A. G. Kaplan. 1983. *Women and Empathy* (82–02). Wellesley, MA.

Joyce, J. 1992. *Dubliners*. London, England: Penguin Books.

Judah, T. 2000. *Kosovo: War and Revenge*. New Haven: Yale University Press.

Jurgensen, G. and A. Hunter. 1999. *The Disappearance*. New York: Norton.

Kabat-Zinn, J. 2000. "Indra's Net at Work: The Mainstreaming of Dharma Practice in Society." In G. Watson, S. Batchelor, et al. (Eds.) *The Psychology of Awakening: Buddhism, Science, and Our Day-to-Day Lives*. York, ME: S. Weiser, 225–249.

Kabat-Zinn, J. and University of Massachusetts Medical Center Worcester Stress Reduction Clinic. 1990. *Full Catastrophe Living: Using the Wisdom of Your Body and Mind to Face Stress, Pain, and Illness*. New York: Delacorte Press.

Kairys, S.W., C.F. Johnson, and Committee on Child Abuse and Neglect. 2002. "The Psychological Maltreatment of Children—Technical Report." *Pediatrics*, 109(4), e68.

Kaminer, D., D.J. Stein, I. Mbanga, and N. Zungu-Dirwayi. 2000. "Forgiveness: Toward an Integration of Theoretical Models." *Psychiatry: Interpersonal and Biological Processes*, 63(4), 344–357.

Kaminer, D., D.J. Stein, I. Mbanga, and N. Zungu-Dirwayi. 2001. "The Truth and Reconciliation Commission in South Africa: Relation to Psychiatric Status and Forgiveness among Survivors of Human Rights Abuses." *British Journal of Psychiatry*, 178, 373–377.

Kamya, H. and D. Trimble. 2002. "Response to Injury: Toward Ethical Construction of the Other." *Journal of Systemic Therapies*, 21(3), 19–29.

Karski, J. *Jan Karski's Account*. Literature of the Holocaust. Retrieved September 30, 2002, from the Web: *http://www.english.upenn.edu/~afilreis/Holocaust/karski.html.*

Kashani, J.H., and W.D. Allan. 1998. *The Impact of Family Violence on Children and Adolescents*. Thousand Oaks, CA: Sage Publications.

Kasper, A.S. and S.J. Ferguson. 2000. *Breast Cancer: Society Shapes an Epidemic*. New York: St. Martin's Press.

Kates, A.R. 1999. *Copshock: Surviving Posttraumatic Stress Disorder* (PTSD). Tucson, AZ: Holbrook Street Press.

Kaufman, G. 1992. *Shame: The Power of Caring*. Rochester, VT: Schenkman Books.

Kaufman, J. and E. Zigler. 1987. "Do Abused Children Become Abusive Parents?" *American Journal of Orthopsychiatry*, 57(2), 186–192.

Kaufman, M.T. July 15, 2000. "Jan Karski Dies at 86; Warned West About Holocaust." *The New York Times*, Section C, 15.

Kayser, K., M. Sormanti, and E. Strainchamps. 1999. "Women Coping with Cancer: The Influence of Relationship Factors on Psychosocial Adjustment." *Psychology of Women Quarterly*, 23(4), 725–739.

Kazak, A.E., L.P. Barakat, K. Meeske, D. Christakis, et al. 1997. "Posttraumatic Stress, Family Functioning, and Social Support in Survivors of Childhood Leukemia and their Mothers and Fathers." *Journal of Consulting and Clinical Psychology*, 65(1), 120–129.

Kazak, A.E., M.L. Stuber, L.P. Barakat, and K. Meeske. 1996. "Assessing Posttraumatic Stress Related to Medical Illness and Treatment: The Impact of Traumatic Stressors Interview Schedule (ITSIS)." *Families, Systems and Health*, 14(3), 365–380.

Kehoe, L. 1995. *In This Dark House: A Memoir*. New York: Schocken.

Keise, C. 1992. *Sugar and Spice?: Bullying in Single-Sex Schools*. Stoke-on-Trent: Trentham Books.

Kellerman, N.P. 2001. "Psychopathology in Children of Holocaust Survivors: A Review of the Research Literature." *Israel Journal of Psychiatry and Related Sciences*, 38(1), 36–46.

Kendler, K.S. 1988. "Indirect Vertical Cultural Transmission: A Model for Nongenetic Parental Influences on the Liability to Psychiatric Illness." *American Journal of Psychiatry*, 145(6), 657–665.

Kimelman, R. 1968. "Nonviolence in the Talmud." *Judaism*, 17, 316–334.

Kincaid, J. 1997. *My Brother*. New York: Farrar, Straus & Giroux.

King, M.L., Jr. 1995. "Pilgrimage to Nonviolence." In S. Lynd and A. Lynd (Eds.), Nonviolence in America: *A Documentary History* (Rev ed.). Maryknoll, NY: Orbis Books, 209–220.

Kirkup, P.A. 1993. "Some Religious Perspectives on Forgiveness and Settling Differences." *Mediation Quarterly*, 11(1), 79–94.

Kivel, P. 1996. *Uprooting Racism: How White People Can Work for Racial Justice*. Gabriola Island, BC: New Society Publishers.

Klain, E. 1998. "Intergenerational Aspects of the Conflict in the Former Yugoslavia." In Y. Danieli (Ed.), *International Handbook of Multigenerational Legacies of Trauma*. The Plenum Series on Stress and Coping. New York: Plenum Press, 279–298.

Klass, P. 1990. *Other Women's Children*. New York: Random House.

Klein, J. 2001, October 1. "Closework." *The New Yorker*, 44–49.

Kleinman, A. 1988. *The Illness Narratives: Suffering, Healing, and the Human Condition*. New York: Basic Books.

Kleinman, A. 1995. *Writing at the Margin: Discourse Between Anthropology and Medicine*. Berkeley: University of California Press.

Klemperer, V. 1999. *I Will Bear Witness: A Diary of the Nazi Years 1942–1945*. New York: Random House.

Kliman, J. and R. Llerena-Quinn. 2002. "Dehumanizing and Rehumanizing Rèsponses to September 11." *Journal of Systemic Therapies*, 21(3), 8–18.

Klinger, H. 2001. *Family Dynamics and Intergenerational Transmission*. Penn Valley, PA: Transcending Trauma Project.

Klinkenborg, V. 2001, September 22. "The Quiet Consolation of the Material World." *The New York Times*, A24.

Knightley, P. 2002. *The First Casualty: The War Correspondent as Hero and Myth-maker from the Crimea to Kosovo*. Baltimore, MD: Johns Hopkins University Press.

Kogan, I. 2000. "Breaking the Cycle of Trauma: From the Individual to Society." *Mind and Human Interaction*, 11(1): 2–10.

Kohn, A. 1990. *The Brighter Side of Human Nature: Altruism and Empathy in Everyday Life*. New York: Basic Books.

Kolata, G. 2001, June 5. "On Research Frontier, Basic Questions." *The New York Times*, Section F 1.

Kollwitz, K. and H. Kollwitz. 1988. *The Diary and Letters of Kaethe Kollwitz*. Ill.: Northwestern University Press.

Koocher, G.P. and B.L. MacDonald. 1992. "Preventive Intervention and Family Coping with a Child's Life-Threatening or Terminal Illness." In T.J. Akamatsu and M.A.P. Stephens et al. (Eds.), *Family Health Psychology*. Series in applied psychology: Social issues and questions. Washington, DC: Hemisphere Publishing Corp., 67–86.

Koren, D., I. Arnon, P. Lavie, and E. Klein, 2002. "Sleep Complaints as Early Predictors of Posttraumatic Stress Disorder: A 1-Year Prospective Study of Injured Survivors of Motor Vehicle Accidents." *American Journal of Psychiatry*, 159(5): 855–857.

Kotlowitz, A. 1992. *There Are No Children Here: The Story of Two Boys Growing Up in the Other America*. New York: Anchor Books.

Kotzé, E. and E. Morkel. 2002. *Matchboxes, Butterflies and Angry Foots*. Pretoria: Ethics Alive.

Kotzé, D., J. Myburg, and J. Roux. 2002. *Ethical Ways of Being*. Pretoria: Ethics Alive.

Kozol, J. 1995. *Amazing Grace: The Lives of Children and the Conscience of a Nation*. New York: Crown.

Kraft, K. 1992. *Inner Peace, World Peace: Essays on Buddhism and Nonviolence*. Albany: State University of New York Press.

Krog, A. 1999. *Country of My Skull*. New York: Random House.

Krug, E. G. et al. 2002. *World Report on Violence and Health*. Geneva: World Health Organization.

Krystal, J. H. and L. M. Nagy et al. 1998. "Initial Clinical Evidence of Genetic Contributions to Posttraumatic Stress Disorder." In Y. Danieli (Ed.), *International Handbook of Multigenerational Legacies of Trauma*. The Plenum Series on Stress and Coping. New York: Plenum Press, 657–667.

Kübler-Ross, E. 1969. *On Death and Dying*. New York: Macmillan.

Kurki, L. 2000. "Restorative and Community Justice in the United States." *Crime and Justice: A Review of Research*, 27: 235–304.

Kwan, R., and R. Levy. 2002. *A Primer on Resident Working Hours: Everything You Always Wanted to Know but Were Afraid to Ask!* (2nd ed.). Reston, VA: American Medical Student Association.

Kyi, A.S.S., and A. Clements. 1997. *The Voice of Hope*. New York: Seven Stories Press.

LaCapra, D. 1994. *Representing the Holocaust: History, Theory, Trauma*. Ithaca: Cornell University Press.

LaCapra, D. 2001. *Writing History, Writing Trauma*. Baltimore: Johns Hopkins University Press.

Lamb, S. 1996. *The Trouble with Blame: Victims, Perpetrators, and Responsibility*. Cambridge, MA: Harvard University Press.

Landau, D. January 14, 1988. "A Letter to a Deportee." *The Jerusalem Post*.

Landau, Y. 1996. "Rehumanizing the 'Enemy' and Confronting Ourselves: Challenges for Educators in an Era of Peace." *Palestine-Israel Journal of Politics, Economics and Culture*, III(1).

Langer, L. L. 1991. *Holocaust Testimonies: The Ruins of Memory*. New Haven: Yale University Press.

Lanzmann, C. 1985. *Shoah: An Oral History of the Holocaust: The Complete Text of the Film* (1st American ed.). New York: Pantheon Books.
Lapsley, F. M. 2002. "The Healing of Memories." *The International Journal of Narrative Therapy and Community Work*, 2, 72–75.
Lasch, C. 1977. *Haven in a Heartless World: The Family Besieged.* New York: Basic Books.
Latané, B. and J. M. Darley, 1970. *The Unresponsive Bystander: Why Doesn't He Help?* New York: Appleton-Century Crofts.
Laub, D. 1991. "Truth and Testimony: The Process and the Struggle." *American Imago*, 48(1), 75–91.
Lauer, J. C. and R. H. Lauer. 1986. *Till Death Do Us Part: A Study and Guide to Long-Term Marriage.* New York: Harrington Park Press.
Lazarre, J. 1998. *Wet Earth and Dreams: A Narrative of Grief and Recovery.* Durham, NC: Duke University Press.
Lazarus, R. S. and S. Folkman. 1984. *Stress, Appraisal, and Coping.* New York: Springer Pub. Co.
Lederach, J. P. October 24, 2001. *Quo Vadis? Reframing Terror from the Perspective of Conflict Resolution.* Paper presented at the Townhall Meeting, University of California, Irvine.
Lederach, J. P. 2001. "Five Qualities of Practice in Support." In R. G. Helmick and R. L. Petersen (Eds.), *Forgiveness and Reconciliation: Religion, Public Policy, and Conflict Transformation.* Philadelphia: Templeton Foundation Press, 183–193.
Lerner, M. O. 1996. *Choices in Healing: Integrating the Best of Conventional and Complementary Approaches to Cancer.* Cambridge, MA: MIT Press.
Levi, P. 1988. *The Drowned and the Saved.* New York: Summit Books.
Levi, P. 1996. *Survival in Auschwitz: The Nazi Assault on Humanity.* New York: Simon & Schuster.
Levin, P. 1989. *The Trauma Response.* David Baldwin's Trauma Information Pages. Retrieved August 7, 2001, from the Web: *http://www.trauma-pages.com/t-facts.htm*
Lévinas, E. and P. Nemo. 1985. *Ethics and Infinity.* Pittsburgh: Duquense University Press.
Levine, P. A. 1997. *Waking the Tiger: Healing Trauma: the Innate Capacity to Transform Overwhelming Experiences.* Berkeley, CA: North Atlantic Books.
Levinson, D. 1989. *Family Violence in Cross-Cultural Perspective.* Newbury Park, CA: Sage Publications.
Lewis, H. B. 1971. *Shame and Guilt in Neurosis.* New York: International Universities Press.
Lewis, H. B. 1987. *The Role of Shame in Symptom Formation.* Hillsdale, NJ: L. Erlbaum Associates.
Lewis, M. J. 1995. *Shame: The Exposed Self.* New York: Free Press.
Lifton, R. J. 1979. *The Broken Connection: On Death and the Continuity of Life.* New York: Simon & Schuster.

Lifton, R. J. 1993. *The Protean Self: Human Resilience in an Age of Fragmentation.* New York: Basic Books.

Linder, D. 1992. *Excerpts from the LAPD Officers' Trial.* University of Missouri-Kansas City. Retrieved September 30, 2002, from the Web: *http://www.law.umkc.edu/faculty/projects/ftrials/lapd/kingtranscript.html*

Linder, D. 2001. *The Trials of Los Angeles Police Officers' in Connection with the Beating of Rodney King.* UMKC Law School. Retrieved September 30, 2002, from the Web: *http://www.law.umkc.edu/faculty/projects/ftrials/lapd/lapdaccount.html*

Lindner, E. G. 2000. "Were Ordinary Germans Hitler's 'Willing Executioners'?" *IDEA: A Journal of Social Issues,* 5(1), Retrieved March, 2002 from the Web: *http://www.ideajournal.com/lindner-willing-executioners.html*

Lindner, E. G. 2001. "Humiliation—Trauma That Has Been Overlooked: An Analysis Based on Fieldwork in Germany, Rwanda/Burundi, and Somalia." *Traumatology,* 7(1), 51–79.

Lindner, E. G. 2001. "Humiliation and Human Rights: Mapping a Minefield." *Human Rights Review,* 2(2), 46–63.

Litz, B. T., S. M. Orsillo, M. Friedman, P. Ehlich, et al. 1997. "Posttraumatic Stress Disorder Associated with Peacekeeping Duty in Somalia for U.S. Military Personnel." *American Journal of Psychiatry,* 154(2): 178–184.

Loder, K. August 22, 2002. Review of Bruce Springsteen's *The Rising. Rolling Stone,* 81–82.

Loeber, R., J. D. Burke, and B. B. Lahey. 2002. "What Are Adolescent Antecedents to Antisocial Personality Disorder?" *Criminal Behaviour and Mental Health.* 12(1), 24–36.

Lomax, E. 1995. *The Railway Man: A POW's Searing Account of War, Brutality, and Forgiveness.* New York: Norton.

Lorber, J. 1997. *Gender and the Social Construction of Illness.* Thousand Oaks, CA: Sage Publications.

Lorde, A. 1980. *The Cancer Journals.* Argyle, NY: Spinsters Ink.

Lorentzen, L. A. and J. E. Turpin. 1998. *The Women and War Reader.* New York: New York University Press.

Lott, D. A. 2001. "Physician—Treat Thyself?" *Psychiatric Times,* XVIII(12).

Love, S. M. and K. Lindsey. 1990. *Dr. Susan Love's Breast Book.* Reading, MA: Addison-Wesley.

Luce, A., J. Firth-Cozens, S. Midgley, and C. Burges. 2002. "After the Omagh Bomb: Posttraumatic Stress Disorder in Health Service Staff." *Journal of Traumatic Stress,* 15(1), 27–30.

Luhrmann, T. M. 2000. *Of Two Minds: The Growing Disorder in American Psychiatry.* New York: Knopf.

Lykes, M. B. 1996. *Myths About the Powerless: Contesting Social Inequalities.* Philadelphia: Temple University Press.

Lyle, R. R. and D. R. Gehart. 2000. "The Narrative of Ethics and the Ethics of Narrative: The Implications for Ricoeur's Narrative Model for Family Therapy." *Journal of Systemic Therapies,* 19(4), 73–89.

Lynch, J. W., G. A. Kaplan, and S. J. Shema. 1997. "Cumulative Impact of Sustained Economic Hardship on Physical, Cognitive, Psychological, and Social Functioning." *New England Journal of Medicine*, 337(26), 1889–1895.

Lynd, S. and A. Lynd. 1995. *Nonviolence in America: A Documentary History* (Rev. ed.). Maryknoll, NY: Orbis Books.

Lyons-Ruth, K. and D. Jacobvitz. 1999. "Attachment Disorganization: Unresolved Loss, Relational Violence, and Lapses in Behavioral and Attentional Strategies." In J. Cassidy and P. R. Shaver (Eds.), *Handbook of Attachment: Theory, Research, and Clinical Applications*. New York: Guilford Press, 520–554.

Macleod, S. September 12, 1994. "The Life and Death of Kevin Carter." *Time* magazine, 144.

MacQuarrie, B. and M. R. Merrill. May 18, 2000. "Board Is Silent on Harassment Case Specifics: Lawyer Details Schoolgirl's Complaint." *The Boston Globe*, B1, 4.

Magona, S. 1999. *Mother to Mother*. Boston: Beacon Press.

Maguire, K. May 22, 1997. "Students Appeal for Nigeria Boycott, City Council Takes Action." *Cambridge Chronicle*, 5.

Maier, S. F. and L. R. Watkins. 2000. "The Neurobiology of Stressor Controllability." In M.E.P. Seligman, J. Gillham (Eds.). *The Science of Optimism and Hope: Research Essays in Honor of Martin E. P. Seligman*. Philadelphia: Templeton Foundation Press, 41–56.

Mairs, N. 1996. *Carnal Acts: Essays*. Boston: Beacon Press.

Mandela, N. 1994. *Long Walk to Freedom: The Autobiography of Nelson Mandela*. Boston: Little Brown.

Mangcu, X. 2001. A Wedding Story. *South Africa Development Fund*, Fall.

Manne, S. L., K. Du Hamel, K. Gallelli, K. Sorgen, and W. H. Redd. 1998. Posttraumatic Stress Disorder Among Mothers of Pediatric Cancer Survivors: Diagnosis, Comorbidity, and Utility of the PTSD Checklist as a Screening Instrument. *Journal of Pediatric Psychology*, 23(6), 357–366.

Marchant, F. 1992. "Anima Mundi: In the Landscape of Nightmare." *Harvard Review*, 1(1), 92–96.

Marchant, F. 2000. *Full Moon Boat: Poems*. Saint Paul: Graywolf Press.

Marchant, F. July–August 2000. "Comebacks and Counterweights." *Peacework*: 16–17.

Marchant, F. July–August 2002. "A Sense of the Sleight-of-Hand." *Peacework*: 7–8.

Marchant, F. 2003. "Night Vision." *Public Affairs*. In Press.

Marcom, M. A. 2001. *Three Apples Fell from Heaven*. New York: Riverhead Books.

Marsella, A. J. 1996. *Ethnocultural Aspects of Posttraumatic Stress Disorder: Issues, Research, and Clinical Applications*. Washington, DC: American Psychological Association.

Martin, M. April 19–20, 2002. *HIV/AIDS in South Africa—Can the Visual Arts Make a Difference?* Paper presented at the AIDS in South Africa: The Social Expression of a Pandemic Conference, Wellesley College, Wellesley, MA.

Martín-Baró, I. 1989. "Political Violence and War as Causes of Psychosocial Trauma in El Salvador." *International Journal of Mental Health*, 18(1), 3–20.

Martín-Baró, I., A. Aron, and S. Corne. 1994. *Writings for a Liberation Psychology*. Cambridge, MA: Harvard University Press.

Martinez, P. and J. E. Richters. 1993. The NIMH Community Violence Project: II "Children's Distress Symptoms Associated with Violence Exposure." *Psychiatry*, 56(1), 22–35.

Maslach, C. 2001. "What Have we Learned About Burnout and Health?" *Psychology and Health*, 16(5), 607–611.

Maslow, A. H. 1954. *Motivation and Personality* (1st ed.). New York: Harper.

Mason, J. W., S. Wang, R. Yehuda, S. Riney, D. S. Charney, and S. M. Southwick. 2001. "Psychogenic Lowering of Urinary Cortisol Levels Linked to Increased Emotional Numbing and a Shame-depressive Syndrome in Combat-Related Posttraumatic Stress Disorder." *Psychosomatic Medicine*, 63(3), 387–401.

Masri, M. 2001. *Frontiers of Dreams and Fears* (M. Masri, Director). M. Masri (Producer). San Francisco: Independent Television Service.

Masten, A. S. 2001. "Ordinary Magic: Resilience Processes in Development." *American Psychologist*, 56(3), 227–238.

Mayou, R. A. and K. A. Smith. 1997. "Posttraumatic Symptoms Following Medical Illness and Treatment." *Journal of Psychosomatic Research*, 43(2), 121–123.

McCammon, S. L. and E. J. Allison. 1995. "Debriefing and Treating Emergency Workers." In C. R. Figley (Ed.), *Compassion Fatigue: Coping with Secondary Traumatic Stress Disorder in Those Who Treat the Traumatized*. Brunner/Mazel psychological stress series, No. 23. Philadelphia: Brunner/Mazel, Inc., 115–130.

McCann, I. L. and L. A. Pearlman, 1990. "Vicarious Traumatization: A Framework for Understanding the Psychological Effects of Working with Victims."*Journal of Traumatic Stress*, 3(1), 131–149.

McCullough, M. E., C. G. Bellah, S. D. Kilpatrick, and J. L. Johnson. 2001. "Vengefulness: Relationships with Forgiveness, Rumination, Well-Being, and the Big Five." *Personality and Social Psychology Bulletin*, 27(5), 601–610.

McCullough, M. E., K. I. Pargament, and C. E. Thoresen. 2000. *Forgiveness: Theory, Research, and Practice*. New York: Guilford Press.

McEwan, I. 1997. *Enduring Love: A Novel*. New York: Anchor Books.

McEwan, I. 2002. *Atonement: A Novel*. New York: Nan A. Talese/Doubleday.

McKittrick, D. and D. McVea. 2002. *Making Sense of the Troubles: The Story of the Conflict in Northern Ireland*. Chicago: New Amsterdam Books.

McNeil, D. G. 1999. "Marius Schoon, 61, Is Dead; Foe of Apartheid Lost Family." *The New York Times*, 31.

Meeropol, M. 1995. *The Significance of the Rosenberg Case*. Poughkeepsie: Vassar College. Retrieved April 2002 from the Web: *http://www.webcom.com/~pease/collections/disputes/matthew_vassar_lecture.htm*

Meeus, W.H.J. and Q.A.W. Raaijmakers. 1995. "Obedience in Modern Society: The Utrecht Studies." *Journal of Social Issues*, 51(3), 155–175.

Meiring, P. 1999. *Chronicle of the Truth Commission: A Journey Through the Past and Present—into the Future of South Africa*. Vanderbijlpark: Carpe Diem Books.

Meltz, B.F. September 21, 2001. "Children Need Time to Cope with Trauma."*The Boston Globe*, Living Section, 1.

Mendel, G. 2001. *A Broken Landscape: HIV and AIDS in Africa*. London: Network Photographers.

Merker, H. 2000. *Listening: Ways of Hearing in a Silent World*. Dallas: Southern Methodist University Press.

Merwin, W. S. 1970. "Unchopping a Tree." In W. S. Merwin (Ed.), *The Miner's Pale Children* (1st ed.). New York: Atheneum.

Metzger, D. 1989. *Looking for the Faces of God*. Berkeley: Parallax Press.

Metzger, D. 2000. *The Other Hand: A Novel*. Los Angeles: Red Hen Press.

Mid East Citizen Diplomacy. 2002. *Compassionate Listening Project*. Mid East Citizen Diplomacy. Retrieved September 28, 2002, from the Web: *http://www.mideastdiplomacy.org/clp.html*

Miller, A.G. 1995. "Constructions of the Obedience Experiments: A Focus upon Domains of Relevance." *Journal of Social Issues*, 51(3), 33–53.

Miller, A. G., B. E. Collins, and D. E. Brief. 1995. "Perspectives on Obedience to Authority: The Legacy of the Milgram Experiments." *Journal of Social Issues*, 51(3), 1–19.

Minot, S. 1998. *Evening* (1st ed.). New York: Knopf.

Minow, M. 1998. *Between Vengeance and Forgiveness: Facing History After Genocide and Mass Violence*. Boston: Beacon Press.

Mitchell, K. J., D. Finkelhor, and J. Wolak. 2001. "Risk Factors for and Impact of Online Sexual Solicitation of Youth." *JAMA*, 285(23), 3011–3014.

Monaghan-Blout, S. 1996. "Reexamining Assumptions About Trauma and Resilience: Implications for Intervention." *Psychotherapy in Private Practice*, 15(4), 45–68.

Montville, J. V. 1993. "The Healing Function in Political Conflict Resolution." In D.J.D. Sandole and H.v.d. Merwe (Eds.), *Conflict Resolution Theory and Practice: Integration and Application*. Manchester, UK; New York, 112–127.

Moore, L. 1998. *Birds of America: Stories*. New York: A Knopf.

Morford, M.P.O. and R. J. Lenardon. 1977. *Classical Mythology*. New York: McKay.

Morgan, A. 2000. *What Is Narrative Therapy?: An Easy-to-Read Introduction*. Adelaide, South Australia: Dulwich Centre Publications.

Morgan, C.A.I. 1997. "Startle Response in Individuals with PTSD." *NCP Clinical Quarterly*, 7(4), 65, 67–69.
Morgan, J. 2000. "Boxes and Remembering in the Time of AIDS." *Dulwich Centre Journal*, 4, 45–48.
Morgan, J. 2002. *Beyond Bereavement: Memory Boxes—Opening Up Alternative Stories and Building a Research Infrastructure*. Cape Town: ASRU Seminar Series.
Morris, A. and Maxwell, G. 2000. "The Practice of Family Group Conferences in New Zealand: Assessing the Place, Potential and Pitfalls of Restorative Justice." In A. Crawford and J. Goodey (Eds.), *Integrating a Victim Perspective Within Criminal Justice; International Debates*. Aldershot, UK: Brookfield, VT: Ashgate Publishing Co.
Morrison, D. 2002, April 11. *Classroom Management Linked to Lesser Teen Alienation from School*. University of Minnesota. Retrieved September 30, 2002, from the Web: *http://www.eurekalert.org/pub_releases/2002-04/uom-cml040902.php*.
Morrison, T. 1987. *Beloved: A Novel*. New York: Plume.
Morrison, T. 2002. *Sula*. New York: Knopf.
Morse, J.M. and B. Doberneck. 1995. "Delineating the Concept of Hope." *Image—the Journal of Nursing Scholarship*, 27(4), 277–285.
Mosher, B. 1995. *Visionaries*. Maryknoll, NY: Orbis Books.
Motherland Nigeria. 2002. *Historical Government*. Motherland Nigeria. Retrieved September 7, 2002, from the Web: *http://www.motherlandnigeria.com/govt_history.html*
Mulvey, E.P. and E. Cauffman. 2001. "The Inherent Limits of Predicting School Violence." *American Psychologist*, 56(10), 797–802.
Munroe, J.F. and J. Shay, et. al. 1995. "Preventing Compassion Fatigue: A Team Treatment Model." In C.R. Figley (Ed.), *Compassion Fatigue: Coping with Secondary Traumatic Stress Disorder in Those Who Treat the Traumatized*. New York: Brunner/Mazel, 209–231.
Mussen, P. and N. Eisenberg. 2001. "Prosocial Development in Context." In A.C. Bohart and D.J. Stipek (Eds.), *Constructive and Destructive Behavior: Implications for Family, School, and Society* (1st ed.). Washington, DC: American Psychological Association, 103–126.
Mutler, A. 2001, June 12. "Romanians Mesmerized by Toddler Who Fell Down a Well." Associated Press Newswires.
Myerhoff, B.G. 1980. "Re-membered Lives." *Parabola*, 5(1), 74–77.
Nader, K.O. 1998. "Violence: Effects of Parents' Previous Trauma on Currently Traumatized Children." In Y. Danieli (Ed.), *International Handbook of Multigenerational Legacies of Trauma*. The Plenum Series on Stress and Coping. New York: Plenum Press, 571–583.
Nader, K.O., R.S. Pynoos, L.A. Fairbanks, M. al-Ajeel, and A. al-Asfour. 1993. "A Preliminary Study of PTSD and Grief Among the Children of Kuwait Following the Gulf Crisis." *British Journal of Clinical Psychology*, 32(Pt 4), 407–416.

Nagata, D. K. 1998. "Intergenerational Effects of the Japanese-American Internment." In Y. Danieli (Ed.), *International Handbook of Multigenerational Legacies of Trauma*. The Plenum Series on Stress and Coping. New York: Plenum Press, 125–146.

Nagler, M. N. 2001. *Is There No Other Way?: The Search for a Nonviolent Future*. Berkeley: Berkeley Hills Books.

Najavits, L. 2002. *Seeking Safety: A Treatment Manual for PTSD and Substance Abuse*. New York: Guilford Press.

Nelson, B. S. and K. L. Schwerdtfeger. 2002. "Trauma to One Family Member Affects Entire Family." *Traumatic Stress Points*, 16(3), 7, 11.

Nelson, C. A. and L. J. Carver. 1998. "The Effects of Stress and Trauma on Brain and Memory: A View from Developmental Cognitive Neuroscience." *Development and Psychopathology*, 10(4), 793–809.

Neuffer, E. 2001. *The Key to My Neighbor's House: Seeking Justice in Bosnia and Rwanda* (1st ed.). New York: Picador.

Newberg, A. B. and E. G. D'Aquili. 1998. "The Neuropsychology of Spiritual Experience." In H. G. Koenig (Ed.), *Handbook of Religion and Mental Health*, San Diego, CA, US: Academic Press, Inc, 75–94.

Newberg, A. B. and E. G. D'Aquili. 2000. "The Neuropsychology of Religious and Spiritual Experience." *Journal of Consciousness Studies*, 7, 11–12.

Newberg, A. B., E. G. D'Aquili, and V. Rause. 2001. *Why God Won't Go Away: Brain Science and the Biology of Belief* (1st ed.). New York: Ballantine Books.

Newman, E. 2002. "The Bridge Between Sorrow and Knowledge: Journalists and Traumatic Stress." In Y. Danieli (Ed.), *Sharing the Front Line and the Back Hills: International Protectors and Providers: Peacekeepers, Humanitarian Aid Workers, and the Media in the Midst of Crisis*. Amityville, NY: Baywood Pub. Co., 316–322.

Newman, E. and R. Simpson, et al. in submission. "Trauma Exposure and Posttraumatic Stress Disorder Among Photojournalists."

Nhât Hanh, T. 1999. *Call Me by My True Names: The Collected Poems of Thich Nhât Hanh*. Berkeley: Parallax Press.

Nhât Hanh, T. 1999. "The Witness Remains." In *Call Me By My True Names: The Collected Poems of Thich Nhât Hanh* Berkeley: Parallax Press, 260.

Nhât Hanh, T. 1999. "Please Call Me by My True Names." *In Call Me by My True Names: The Collected Poems of Thich Nhât Hanh*. Berkeley: Parallax Press, 72.

Nhât Hanh, T. and A. Kotler. 1996. *Being Peace*. Berkeley: Parallax Press.

Nichols, T. and C. Jacques 1995. "Family Reunions: Communities Celebrate New Possibilities." In S. Friedman (Ed.), *The Reflecting Team in Action: Collaborative Practice in Family Therapy*. New York, NY: Guilford Press, 314–330.

Nightingale, E. J. 2001. *APA Appoints Task Force to Coordinate and Address Trauma Issues*. American Psychological Association. Retrieved September 30, 2002, from the Web: *http://www.istss.org/Pubs/TS/Spring01/Task-Force.htm*

Nolan, A. 2001. *Jesus Before Christianity* (25th anniversary ed.). Maryknoll, NY: Orbis Books.

Norris, F. 2002. "Psychosocial Consequences of Disasters." *PTSD Research Quarterly*. 13(2), 1–3.

North, J. 1998. "The 'Ideal' of Forgiveness: A Philosopher's Exploration." In R.D. Enright and J. North, (Eds.). *Exploring Forgiveness*. Madison: University of Wisconsin Press, 15–34.

Nouwen, H.J.M. 1990. *The Wounded Healer: Ministry in Contemporary Society* (1st Image ed.). New York: Image Books.

Novac, A. and S. Hubert-Schneider. "Acquired Vulnerability: Comorbidity in a Patient Population of Adult Offspring of Holocaust Survivors." *American Journal of Forensic Psychiatry*, 19(2), 45–58.

Novak, A. 2001. *Prevention of Intergenerational Transmission of Effects of Trauma*. Paper presented at ISTSS conference. Santa Clarita, CA: Professional Programs, Inc.

Novak, P. 1995. *The World's Wisdom: Sacred Texts of the World's Religions*. San Francisco: Harper.

Nunn, K.P. 1996. "Personal Hopefulness: A Conceptual Review of the Relevance of the Perceived Future to Psychiatry." *British Journal of Medical Psychology*, 69(3), 227–245.

Nussbaum, M.C. 2000. *Women and Human Development: The Capabilities Approach*. Cambridge, UK; New York: Cambridge University Press.

Nussbaum, M.C. 2001. *Upheavals of Thought: The Intelligence of Emotions*. Cambridge, UK; New York: Cambridge University Press.

Ochberg, F. 1996. "A Primer on Covering Victims." *Nieman Reports*, 1(3), 21–26.

O'Connor, T., February 24, 2001. *Police Stress and Employee Assistance Programs*. Department of Justice Studies North Carolina Wesleyan. Retrieved 2002, from the Web: *http://faculty.ncwc.edu/toconnor/417/417lect 09.htm*

Ofer, D. and L.J. Weitzman. 1998. *Women in the Holocaust*. New Haven: Yale University Press.

Ogletree, C.J., Harvard Law School Criminal Justice Institute, National Association for the Advancement of Colored People, and William Monroe Trotter Institute. 1995. *Beyond the Rodney King Story: An Investigation of Police Conduct in Minority Communities*. Boston: Northeastern University Press.

Oktay, J.S. and C.A. Walter. 1991. *Breast Cancer in the Life Course: Women's Experiences*. New York: Springer Pub. Co.

Oliver, J.E. 1993. "Intergenerational Transmission of Child Abuse: Rates, Research, and Clinical Implications." *American Journal of Psychiatry*, 150(9), 1315–1324.

Oliver, K. 2001. *Witnessing: Beyond Recognition*. Minneapolis: University of Minnesota Press.

Olweus, D. 1993. *Bullying at School: What We Know and What We Can Do*. Oxford, UK; Cambridge, MA: Blackwell.

Opotow, S. 2001. "Reconciliation in Times of Impunity: Challenges for Social Justice." *Social Justice Research*, 14(2), 149–170.

OSCE Kosovo "Verification Mission." 1999. *Kosovo/Kosova as Seen, as Told—Djakovica/Gjakova*. OSCE. Retrieved October 16, 2002, from the Web: *http//www.osce.org/kosovo/documents/reports/hr/part1/p5dja.htm*

Osofsky, J. D. 1995. "The Effects of Exposure to Violence on Young Children." *American Psychologist*, 50(9), 782–788.

Osofsky, J. D. 1997. *Children in a Violent Society*. New York: Guilford Press.

Ovnic, K. 2002. *Emory Brain Imaging Studies Reveal Biological Basis for Human Coopération*. EurekAlert. Retrieved July 8, 2002, from the Web: *http://www.eurekalert.org/pub_releases/2002-07/euhs-ebi071602.php*

Panzarino, C. 1994. *The Me in the Mirror*. Seattle: Seal Press Distributed by Publishers Group West.

Park, F. 1996. *Clergy Sexual Abuse*. Connecticut Sexual Assault Crisis Services, Inc. Newsletter. Retrieved September 30, 2002, from the Web: *http://www.advocateweb.org/cease/csa.htm*

Patchett, A. 2001. *Bel Canto: A Novel* (1st ed.). New York:HarperCollins.

Paul, N. L. 1967. "The Use of Empathy in the Resolution of Grief." *Perspectives in Biology and Medicine*, 11(1), 153–168.

Pavlich, G. 2001. "The Force of the Community." In H. Strang and J. Braithwaite (Eds.), *Restorative Justice and Civil Society*. Cambridge, UK; New York: Cambridge University Press, 56–68.

Pear, R. 2001, June 5. "AIDS at 20; Advocates for Patients Barged In, and the Federal Government Changed." *The New York Times*, F3.

Pearl, M. 2002, April 19. "Why Good Hearts Must Go Public." *The New York Times*, Section A, 27.

Pearlman, L. A. and Saakvitne, K. W. 1995. "Treating Therapists with Vicarious Traumatization and Secondary Traumatic Stress Disorders." In C. R. Figley (Ed.), *Compassion Fatigue: Coping with Secondary Traumatic Stress Disorder in Those Who Treat the Traumatized*. New York: Brunner/Mazel, 150–177.

Pearlman, L. A. and K. W. Saakvitne. 1995. *Trauma and the Therapist: Countertransference and Vicarious Traumatization in Psychotherapy with Incest Survivors* (1st ed.). New York: Norton.

Pelcovitz, D., B. Goldenberg, S. Kaplan, M. Weinblatt, F. Mandel, B. Meyers, and V. Vinciguerra. 1996. "Posttraumatic Stress Disorder in Mothers of Pediatric Cancer Survivors." *Psychosomatics*, 37(2), 116–126.

Pelcovitz, D. and S. J. Kaplan. 1994. "Child Witnesses of Violence Between Parents: Psychosocial Correlates and Implications for Treatment." *Child and Adolescent Psychiatric Clinics of North America*, 3(4), 745–758.

Peled, E., P. G. Jaffe, and J. L. Edleson. 1995. *Ending the Cycle of Violence: Community Responses to Children of Battered Women*. Thousand Oaks, CA: Sage Publications.

Penn, P. 2001. *So Close*. Fort Lee, NJ: CavanKerry Press.

Penn, P. 2001. "Chronic Illness: Trauma, Language, and Writing: Breaking the Silence." *Family Process*, 40(1), 33–52.

Penn, P. and M. Frankfurt. 1994. "Creating a Participant Text: Writing, Multiple Voices, Narrative Multiplicity." *Family Process*, 33(3): 217–231.

Pennebaker, J. W. 1993. "Social Mechanisms of Constraint." In D. M. Wegner and J. W. Pennebaker (Eds.), *Handbook of Mental Control*. Englewood Cliffs, NJ: Prentice Hall, 200–219.

Pennebaker, J. W. 1997. *Opening Up: The Healing Power of Expressing Emotions*. New York: Guilford Press.

Pennebaker, J. W. 1999. "The Effects of Traumatic Disclosure on Physical and Mental Health: The Values of Writing and Talking About Upsetting Events." *International Journal of Emergency Mental Health*, 1(1), 9–18.

Pennebaker, J. W. and K. D. Harber. 1993. "A Social Stage Model of Collective Coping: The Loma Prieta Earthquake and the Persian Gulf War." *Journal of Social Issues*, 49(4), 125–145.

Peschel, R. E. and E. R. Peschel. 1986. *When a Doctor Hates a Patient, and Other Chapters in a Young Physician's Life*. Berkeley: University of California Press.

Peterson, M. R. 1992. *At Personal Risk: Boundary Violations in Professional Client Relationships* (1st ed.). New York: Norton.

Pfefferbaum, B., S. J. Nixon, R. S. Krug, R. D. Tivis, V. L. Moore, J. M. Brown, R. S. Pynoos, D. Foy, and R. H. Gurwitch. 1999. "Clinical Needs Assessment of Middle and High School Students Following the 1995 Oklahoma City Bombing." *American Journal of Psychiatry*, 156(7), 1069–1074.

Pierce, C. M. 1988. "Stress in the Workplace." In A. F. Coner-Edwards and J. Spurlock (Eds.), *Black Families in Crisis: The Middle Class*. New York: Brunner/Mazel, 27–34.

Pierce, C. M. B. R. Sarason, and I. G. Sarason. 1996. "Conceptualizing and Assessing Social Support in the Context of the Family." In G. R. Pierce, B. R. Sarason, and I. G. Sarason (Eds.), *Handbook of Social Support and the Family*. New York: Plenum Press, 3–23.

Pierce, R. F. 2001. *Report of Investigation of Citizen Complaints to MBTA Police Department*. Boston: Goulston & Storrs.

Pilcer, S. 2002. *The Holocaust Kid*. New York: Dell.

Pines, A. M. and E. Aronson. 1989. *Career Burnout: Causes and Cures*. New York: Free Press; London: Collier Macmillan.

Pingleton, J. P. 1989. "The Role and Function of Forgiveness in the Psychotherapeutic Process." *Journal of Psychology and Theology*, 17(1), 27–35.

Pipher, M. B. 2002. *The Middle of Everywhere: The World's Refugees Come to Our Town* (1st ed.). New York: Harcourt.

Pogrebin, M. R. and E. D. Poole. 1995. "Emotion Management: A Study of Police Response to Tragic Events." In M. G. Flaherty and C. Ellis (Eds.), *Social Perspectives on Emotion*, Vol. 3 Stamford, CT: JAI Press, Inc., 149–168.

Pollack, M. H., K. T. Brady, R. D. Marshall, and R. Yehuda. 2001. "Trauma and Stress: Diagnosis and Treatment." *Journal of Clinical Psychiatry*, 62(11), 906–915.

Polner, M., and N. Goodman. 1994. *The Challenge of Shalom: The Jewish Tradition of Peace and Justice*. Philadelphia: New Society Publishers.

Pope, K. S. 1990. "Therapist-Patient Sexual Involvement: A Review of the Research." *Clinical Psychology Review*, 10(4), 477–490.

Power, S. 2002. *A Problem from Hell: America and the Age of Genocide*. New York: Basic Books.

Power, S. September, 2001. "Bystanders to Genocide: Why the United States Let the Rwandan Tragedy Happen."*The Atlantic Monthly*, 84–108.

Pretorius, F. 1998. *The Anglo-Boer War*, 1899–1902 (2nd rev. ed.). Cape Town: Struik.

Prothrow-Stith. D. and M. Weissman. 1991. *Deadly Consequences*. New York: HarperCollins.

Punamaeki, R.-L. 1989. "Factors Affecting the Mental Health of Palestinian Children Exposed to Political Violence." *International Journal of Mental Health*, 18(2), 63–79.

Quittner, A. L., L. C. Opipari, D. L. Espelage, B. Carter, N. Eid, and H. Eigen. 1998. "Role Strain in Couples with and without a Child with a Chronic Illness: Associations with Marital Satisfaction, Intimacy, and Daily Mood." *Health Psychology*, 17(2), 112–124.

Ramsay, M.A.E. 2000. *Physician Fatigue*. Baylor University Medical Center. Retrieved September 2002 from the Web: *http://www.baylorhealth.com/proceedings/13_2/13_2 ramsay_cme.htm*

Randburg, P. G. 1994, October 3. Letter, *Time* magazine, 144.

Ratushinskaia, I. 1988. *Grey is the Color of Hope* (1st American ed.). New York: Knopf.

Reddy, M. T. 1996. *Everyday Acts Against Racism: Raising Children in a Multiracial World*. Seattle: Seal Press.

Reibel, D. K., J. M. Greeson, G. C. Brainard, and S. Rosenzweig. 2001. "Mindfulness-Based Stress Reduction and Health-Related Quality of Life in a Heterogeneous Patient Population." *General Hospital Psychiatry*, 23(4), 183–192.

Reid, F. and D. Hoffman 2000. *Long Night's Journey into Day*. Iris Films, United States.

Reilly, I. 2000. "Legacy: People and Poets in Northern Ireland." *Australian and New Zealand Journal of Family Therapy*, 21(3), 162–166.

Remarque, E. M. 1982. *All Quiet on the Western Front* (1st Ballantine Books ed.). New York: Ballantine Books.

Remnick, D. September 24, 2001. "From Our Correspondents: September 11, 2001." *The New Yorker*, 58.

Rezendes, M. and M. Carroll. January 26, 2002. "Accusers' Accounts Tell of Abuse and Its Scars." *The Boston Globe*, A12.

Rhine G., F. D. Moreno, P. Cousineau, and H. Fixico. 1992. *Wiping the Tears of Seven Generations* [VHS.]. San Francisco: Kifaru Productions.

Ribadeneira, D. April 3, 1999. Power of Forgiveness Unites Pastor and the Man Who Killed His Son. *The Boston Globe*, B2.

Rich, A. C. 1993. *What Is Found There: Notebooks on Poetry and Politics.* New York: W. W. Norton.

Rich, A. C. 2001. *Arts of the Possible: Essays and Conversations* (1st ed.). New York: W. W. Norton.

Richards, J. L. 2000. *Angles of Reflection: Logic and a Mother's Love.* New York: W. H. Freeman.

Richie, B. 1996. *Compelled to Crime: The Gender Entrapment of Battered Black Women.* New York: Routledge.

Ricoeur, P. 1996. "Reflections on a New Ethos for Europe." In R. Kearney (Ed.), *Paul Ricoeur: The Hermeneutics of Action.* Thousand Oaks, CA: Sage Publications, 3–13.

Rilling, J., D. Gutman, T. Zeh, G. Pagnoni, G. Berns, and C. Kilts. 2002. "A Neural Basis for Social Cooperation." *Neuron*, 35(2), 395–405.

Roberts, S. 2001. *The Brother: The Untold Story of Atomic Spy David Greenglass and How He Sent His Sister, Ethel Rosenberg, to the Electric Chair* (1st ed.). New York: Random House.

Robinson, H. M., M. R. Sigman, and J. P. Wilson. 1997. "Duty-Related Stressors and PTSD Symptoms in Suburban Police Officers." *Psychological Reports*, 81(3), 835–845.

Rochat, F. and A. Modigliani. 1995. "The Ordinary Quality of Resistance: From Milgram's Laboratory to the Village of Le Chambon." *Journal of Social Issues*, 51(3), 195–210.

Rogers, A. G. 1995. *A Shining Affliction: A Story of Harm and Healing in Psychotherapy.* New York: Viking.

Rolland, J. S. 1994. *Families, Illness, and Disability: An Integrative Treatment Model.* New York: Basic Books.

Rollman, B. L., L. A. Mead, N. Y. Wang, and M. J. Klag. 1997. "Medical Speciality and the Incidence of Divorce." *New England Journal of Medicine*, 336(11), 800–803.

Romney, L. 2002. "LA Still Finding Its Way After '92 Riots." *The Boston Globe*, A2.

Root, M. P. 1996. "Women of Color and Traumatic Stress in 'Domestic Captivity': Gender and Race as Disempowering Statuses." In A. J. Marsella and M. J. Friedman, et al. (Eds.), *Ethnocultural Aspects of Posttraumatic Stress Disorder: Issues, Research, and Clinical Applications.* Washington, DC: American Psychological Association, 363–387.

Root, M.P.P. 1992. "Reconstructing the Impact of Trauma on Personality." In L. S. Brown and M. Ballou (Eds.), *Personality and Psychopathology: Feminist Reappraisals.* New York: Guilford Press, 229–265.

Rosenberg, M. 2002, June 3. "Kenyan Villagers Honor 9-11 Victims." The Associated Press.

Rosenblatt, R. 1994, June 6. "Rwanda Therapy." *The New Republic*, 14.

Rosenheck, R. and A. Fontana. 1998. "Warrior Fathers and Warriors Sons:

Intergenerational Aspects of Trauma." In Y. Danieli (Ed.), *International Handbook of Multigenerational Legacies of Trauma*. The Plenum Series on Stress and Coping. New York: Plenum Press, 225–242.

Rosenman, S. 1998. "Compassionate Heroes, Bystanders, and the Reformation of Society." *Journal of Psychohistory*, 26(2): 610–624.

Rosser, R. 1997. "Effects of Disaster on Helpers." In D. Black and Royal College of Psychiatrists (Eds.), *Psychological Trauma: A Developmental Approach*. London: Royal College of Psychiatrists, 326–338.

Roth, P. 2000. *The Human Stain*. Boston: Houghton Mifflin.

Roth, S. and M. J. Friedman. 1997. *Childhood Trauma Remembered: A Report on the Current Scientific Knowledge Base and Its Applications*. Northbrook, IL: The International Society for Traumatic Stress Studies.

Rothbaum, F., J. Weisz, M. Pott, K. Miyake, and G. Morelli. 1993. "Attachment and Culture: Security in the United States and Japan." *American Psychologist*, 55(10): 1093–1104.

Rothschild, B. 2000. *The Body Remembers: The Psychophysiology of Trauma and Trauma Treatment*. New York: Norton.

Rowland-Klein, D. and R. Dunlop. 1998. "The Transmission of Trauma Across Generations: Identification with Parental Trauma in Children of Holocaust Survivors." *Australian and New Zealand Journal of Psychiatry*, 32(3): 358–369.

Rutter, P. 1989. *Sex in the Forbidden Zone: When Men in Power—Therapists, Doctors, Clergy, Teachers, and Others—Betray Women's Trust* (1st ed.). Los Angeles: J. P. Tarcher.

Ruzek, J. and P. Watson. 2001. "Early Intervention to Prevent PTSD and Other Trauma-Related Problems." *PTSD Research Quarterly*, 12(4): 1–7.

Rye, M. S., K. I. Pargament, M. A. Ali, G. L. Beck, E. N. Dorff, C. Hallisey, V. Narayanan, and J. G. Williams. 2000. "Religious Perspectives on Forgiveness." In M. E. McCullough, K. I. Pargament et al., (Eds.), *Forgiveness: Theory, Research, and Practice*. New York: Guilford Press, 17–40.

Saakvitne, K. W. and L. A. Pearlman. 1996. *Transforming the Pain: A Workbook on Vicarious Traumatization*. New York: Norton.

Saaraj, E. 2002. "Compassionate Listening Journal." *MidEast Citizen Diplomacy*. Retrieved June 12, 2002, from the Web: *www.mideastdiplomacy.org*.

Sagan, C. 1994. *Pale Blue Dot: A Vision of the Human Future in Space* (1st ed.). New York: Random House.

Said, E. W. 2001, October 22. "The Clash of Ignorance." *The Nation*, 11–13.

Salovey, P., A. J. Rothman, J. B. Detweiler, and W. T. Steward. 2000. "Emotional States and Physical Health." *American Psychologist*, 55(1): 110–121.

Salzberg, S. 1995. *Loving-Kindness: The Revolutionary Art of Happiness* (1st ed.). Boston: Shambhala.

Salzberg, S. 2002. *Faith: Trusting Your Own Deepest Experience*. New York: Riverhead Books.

Sampson, E. E. 2000. "Reinterpreting Individualism and Collectivism: Their Religious Roots and Monologic Versus Dialogic Person-Other Relationship." *American Psychologist*, 55(12): 1425–1432.

Sampson, R. J., J. D. Morenoff, and F. Earls. 1999. "Beyond Social Capital: Spatial Dynamics of Collective Efficacy for Children." *American Sociological Review*, 64(5): 633–660.

Sampson, R. J., S. W. Raudenbush, and F. Earls. 1997. "Neighborhoods and Violent Crime: A Multilevel Study of Collective Efficacy." *Science*, 227(5328): 918–924.

Sandage, S. J., E. L. Worthington, Jr., T. L. Hight, and J. W. Berry. 2000. "Seeking Forgiveness: Theoretical Context and an Initial Empirical Study." *Journal of Psychology and Theology*, 28(1): 21–35.

Sapolsky, R. M. 1996. "Why Stress Is Bad for Your Brain." *Science*, 273(5276): 749–750.

Sarason, B. R., I. G. Sarason, and R.A.R. Gurung. 2001. "Close Personal Relationships and Health Outcomes: A Key to the Role of Social Support." In B. R. Sarason and S. Duck (Eds.), *Personal Relationships: Implications for Clinical and Community Psychology*. Chichester, UK: John Wiley & Sons, Ltd., 15–41.

Sarason, B. R., I. G. Sarason, and G. R. Pierce. 1990. *Social Support: An Interactional View*. New York: J. Wiley & Sons.

Satha-Anand, C. 1990. "The Nonviolent Crescent: Eight Theses on Muslim Nonviolent Action." In R. Crow, and P. Grant and S. E. Ibrahim (Eds.), *Arab Nonviolent Political Struggle in the Middle East*. Boulder: L. Rienner Publishers, 7–26.

Satir, V. 1972. *Peoplemaking*. Palo Alto: California Science and Behavior Books.

Saul, J. September 11, 2002. "2 Pillars Are Crucial to Helping Children Adjust." *The New York Times*, A17.

Saul, J. 2002, June 29. "Terror and Trauma: Enhancing Family and Community Resilience." Paper presented at the American Family Therapy Academy, New York.

Savic, M. 2000, November 10. "Activist Visits Kosovo Albanian Prisoners in Belgrade." *The Boston Globe*, A10.

Saxton, M. and F. Howe. 1987. *With Wings: An Anthology of Literature by and about Women with Disabilities*. New York: Feminist Press at the City University of New York.

Scarry, E. 1985. *The Body in Pain: The Making and Unmaking of the World*. New York: Oxford University Press.

Schacter, D. L. 1996. *Searching for Memory: The Brain, the Mind, and the Past* (1st ed.). New York: Basic Books.

Schaufeli, W. B., A. B. Bakker, K. Hoogduin, C. Schaap, and A. Kladler. 2001. "On the Clinical Validity of the Maslach Burnout Inventory and the Burnout Measure." *Psychology and Health*, 16(5), 565–582.

Scheeringa, M. S. and C. H. Zeanah. 1995. "Symptom Expression and Trauma Variables in Children Under Forty-Eight Months of Age." *Infant Mental Health Journal*, 16(4): 259–270.

Scheper-Hughes, N. 1998. "Undoing: Social Suffering and the Politics of Remorse in the New South Africa." *Social Justice*, 25(4) 114–142.

Scheper-Hughes, N. 2002. "Peace Time Crimes and the Violence of Everyday Life." *Ideas*, 9(1): 56–59.

Schlenger, W. E., J. M. Caddell, L. Ebert, B. K. Jordan, K. M. Rourke, D. Wilson, L. Thalji, J. M. Dennis, J. A. Fairbank, and R. A. Kulka. 2002. "Psychological Reactions to Terrorist Attacks: Findings from the National Study of Americans' Reactions to September 11." *JAMA*, 288(5), 581–588.

Schore, A. N. 1994. *Affect Regulation and the Origin of the Self: The Neurobiology of Emotional Development*. Hillsdale, NJ: L. Erlbaum Associates.

Schrecker, E. 2002. *The Age of McCarthyism: A Brief History with Documents* (2nd ed.). Boston: Bedford/St. Martin's.

Schuler, M. 1992. *Freedom from Violence: Women's Strategies from Around the World*. New York: OEF International Distributed by UNIFEM.

Schulman, H. 1998. *The Revisionist: A Novel* (1st ed.). New York: Crown Publishers.

Schulz, R. 1978. *The Psychology of Death, Dying, and Bereavement*. Reading, MA: Addison-Wesley Pub. Co.

Schulz, R., and A. L. Quittner. 1998. "Caregiving for Children and Adults with Chronic Conditions: Introduction to the Special Issue." *Health Psychology*, 17(2): 107–111.

Scott, K. M. 2000. "A Perennial Mourning: Identity Conflict and the Transgenerational Transmission of Trauma Within the African-American Community." *Mind and Human Interaction*, 11(1), 11–26.

Scurfield, R. M. 2000. "Positive and Negative Aspects of Exposure to Racism and Trauma: Research, Assessment, and Treatment Implications." *NCP Clinical Quarterly*, 10(1), 1–10.

Scurfield, R. M. and D. W. Mackey. 2001. "Racism, Trauma and Positive Aspects of Exposure to Race-Related Experiences: Assessment and Treatment Implications." *Journal of Ethnic and Cultural Diversity in Social Work*, 10(1), 23–47.

Sebald, W. G. 2001. *Austerlitz* (1st ed.). New York: Random House.

Sebold, A. 2002. *The Lovely Bones: A Novel* (1st ed.). Boston: Little Brown.

Segraves, K. and T. R. Segraves. 1967. "When the Physician's Marriage Is in Trouble." *Medical Aspects of Human Sexuality*. June: 148–159.

Seligman, M.E.P., J. Gillham, and Optimism Hope Symposium. 2000. *The Science of Optimism and Hope: Research Essays in Honor of Martin E. P. Seligman*. Philadelphia: Templeton Foundation Press.

Sells, J. N. and T. D. Hargrave. 1998. "Forgiveness: A Review of the Theoretical and Empirical Literature." *Journal of Family Therapy*, 20(1), 21–36.

Selner-O'Hagan, M. B., D. J. Kindlon, S. L. Buka, S. W. Raudenbush, and F. J. Earls. 1998. "Assessing Exposure to Violence in Urban Youth." *Journal of Child Psychology and Psychiatry and Allied Disciplines*, 39(2), 215–224.

Sereny, G. 2001. *The Healing Wound: Experiences and Reflections on Germany*, 1938–2001 (1st American ed.). New York: Norton.

Shabad, P. 1993. "Repetition and Incomplete Mourning: The Intergenerational Transmission of Traumatic Themes." *Psychoanalytic Psychology*, 10(1), 61–75.

Shahini, M. 2001. "Therapy, Tradition, and Myself." *AACAP News*, 32(4), 181–182.

Shakespeare, W., and S. L. Wofford. 1994. *Hamlet: Complete, Authoritative Text with Biographical and Historical Contexts, Critical History, and Essays from Five Contemporary Critical Perspectives*. Boston: Bedford Books.

Shalev, A. Y. 2001. "Treating Survivors in the Acute Aftermath of Traumatic Events." Unpublished, manuscript available from author.

Shapiro, D. 2000. *Mom's Marijuana: Insights About Living*. New York: Harmony Books.

Shapiro, E. R. 1994. *Grief as a Family Process: A Developmental Approach to Clinical Practice*. New York: Guilford Press.

Shapiro, J. P. 1993. *No Pity: People with Disabilities Forging a New Civil Rights Movement* (1st ed.). New York: Times Books.

Sharpe, S. 2001. *Restorative Justice: A Vision for Healing and Change*. Edmonton: Mediation and Restorative Justice Centre.

Shay, J. 1994. *Achilles in Vietnam: Combat Trauma and the Undoing of Character*. New York: Atheneum.

Shear, M. K. and K. Smith-Caroff. 2002. "Traumatic Loss and the Syndrome of Complicated Grief." *PTSD Research Quarterly*, 13(1), 1–8.

Shearing, C. 2001. "Transforming Security: A South African Experiment." In H. Strang and J. Braithwaite (Eds.), *Restorative Justice and Civil Society*. Cambridge, UK; New York: Cambridge University Press, 14–34.

Sheinberg, M. and P. Fraenkel. 2001. *The Relational Trauma of Incest: A Family-Based Approach to Treatment*. New York: Guilford Press.

Shepela, S. T., J. Cook, E. Horlitz, R. Leal, S. Luciano, E. Lutfy, C. Miller, G. Mitchell, and E. Worden. 1999. "Courageous Resistance: A Special Case of Altruism." *Theory and Psychology*, 9(6), 787–805.

Shields, C. 2002. *Unless* (1st ed.). London: New York.

Shilts, R. 1987. *And the Band Played On: Politics, People, and the AIDS Epidemic*. New York: St. Martin's Press.

Shlaim, A. 2000. *The Iron Wall: Israel and the Arab World* (1st ed.). New York: Norton.

Shonkoff, J. P., D. Phillips, and National Research Council Committee on Integrating the Science of Early Childhood Development. 2000. *From Neurons to Neighborhoods: The Science of Early Child Development*. Washington, DC: National Academy Press.

Shriver, D.W., Jr. 1998. "Is There Forgiveness in Politics? Germany, Vietnam, and America." In R.D. Enright and J. North (Eds.), *Exploring Forgiveness*. Madison: University of Wisconsin Press, 131–149.

Sider, N.G. 2001. "At the Fork in the Road: Trauma Healing." *Conciliation Quarterly*, 20(2), 7–11.

Siegel, D.J. 1999. *The Developing Mind: Toward a Neurobiology of Interpersonal Experience*. New York: Guilford Press.

Siegel, J. 2002. *The Five Generations of the House of Atreus, and Its Curse*. Dr. J. Classics. Retrieved September 30, 2002, from the Web: *http://www.drjclassics.com/drj/IH/house%20of%20atreus.htm*

Silverman, J.G., A. Raj, L.A. Mucci, and J.E. Hathaway. 2001. "Dating Violence Against Adolescent Girls and Associated Substance Use, Unhealthy Weight Control, Sexual Risk Behavior, Pregnancy, and Suicidality." *JAMA*, 286(5), 572–579.

Simons, R.L. and C. Johnson. 1998. "An Examination of Competing Explanations for the Intergenerational Transmission of Domestic Violence." In Y. Danieli (Ed.), *International Handbook of Multigenerational Legacies of Trauma*. Plenum Series on Stress and Coping. New York: Plenum Press, 553–570.

Simpson, M.A. 1998. "The Second Bullet: Transgenerational Impacts of the Trauma of Conflict Within a South African and World Context." In Y. Danieli (Ed.), *International Handbook of Multigenerational Legacies of Trauma*. Plenum Series on Stress and Coping. New York: Plenum Press, 487–512.

Simpson, R.A. and J.G. Boggs. 1999. "An Exploratory Study of Traumatic Stress Among Newspaper Journalists." *Journalism and Communication Monographs*, Spring, 1–26.

Singer, M. 2002, May 20. "A Year of Trouble." *The New Yorker*, 42.

Singer, M.I., T.M. Anglin, L.Y. Song, and L. Lunghofer. 1995. "Adolescents' Exposure to Violence and Associated Symptoms of Psychological Trauma." *JAMA*, 273 (6), 477–482.

Slabbert, F.V.Z. 2001. "Truth Without Reconciliation, Reconciliation Without Truth." In W.G. James and L.v.d. Vijver (Eds.), *After the TRC: Reflections on Truth and Reconciliation in South Africa*. Athens: Ohio University Press, 67–72.

Slater, L. 1996. *Welcome to My Country* (1st U S ed.). New York: Random House.

Slattery, M., M.R. Alderson, and J.S. Bryant. 1986. "The Occupational Risks of Alcoholism." *International Journal of the Addictions*, 21(8), 929–936.

Slovo, G. 2002. *Red Dust* (1st American ed.). New York: Norton.

Smith, A.C. and S. Kleinman. 1989. "Managing Emotions in Medical School: Students' Contacts with the Living and the Dead." *Social Psychology Quarterly*, 52(1), 56–69.

Smith, A.D. 1994. *Twilight Los Angeles, 1992: On the Road: A Search for American Character* (1st ed.). New York: Anchor Books.

Smith, H. 1993. *Forgotten Truth: The Common Vision of the World's Religions* (1st HarperCollins paperback ed.). San Francisco: Harper San Francisco.

Smith-Christopher, D.L. 2000. *Subverting Hatred: The Challenge of Nonviolence in Religious Traditions*. New York: Orbis Books.

Snyder, C.R. 1997. *Hope for the Journey: Helping Children Through Good Times and Bad*. Boulder: Westview Press.

Snyder, C.R. 1999. *Coping: The Psychology of What Works*. New York: Oxford University Press.

Snyder, C.R. 2000. *Handbook of Hope: Theory, Measures, and Applications*. San Diego: Academic Press, Inc.

Snyder, C.R., S.C. Sympson, F.C. Ybasco, T.F. Borders, M.A. Babyak, and R.L. Higgins. 1996. "Development and Validation of the State Hope Scale." *Journal of Personality and Social Psychology*, 70(2), 321–335.

Snyder, M. 2003. *No Hole in the Flame: A Memoir on Love and Grief in Poetry and Prose*. Albuquerque, NM: Wildflower Press.

Sobecks, N.W., A.C. Justice, S. Hinze, H.T. Chirayath, R.J. Lasek, M.M. Chren, J. Aucott, B. Juknialis, R. Fortinsky, S. Youngner, and C.S. Landefeld. 1999. "When Doctors Marry Doctors: A Survey Exploring the Professional and Family Lives of Young Physicians." *Annals of Internal Medicine*, 130, 312–319.

Sogyal, R., P.D. Gaffney, and A. Harvey. 1992. *The Tibetan Book of Living and Dying*. San Francisco: Harper San Francisco.

Solkoff, N. 1992. "Children of Survivors of the Nazi Holocaust: A Critical Review of the Literature." *American Journal of Othopsychiatry* 62(3), 342–358.

Soloman, Z. 1998. "Transgenerational Effects of the Holocaust: The Israeli Research Perspective." In Y. Danieli (Ed.), *International Handbook of Multigenerational Legacies of Trauma*. Plenum Series on Stress and Coping. New York: Plenum Press, 69–84.

Solomon, Z., M. Kotler, and M. Mikulincer. 1988. "Combat-Related Posttraumatic Stress Disorder Among Second-Generation Holocaust Survivors: Preliminary Findings." *American Journal of Psychiatry*, 145(7); 865–868.

Solzhenitsyn, A.I. 1974. *The Gulag Archipelago, 1918–1956: An Experiment in Literary Investigation* (1st ed.). New York: Harper & Row.

Sonneck, G. and R. Wagner. 1996. "Suicide and Burnout of Physicians." *Omega—Journal of Death and Dying*, 33(3), 255–263.

Sontag, S. 1978. *Illness as Metaphor*. New York: Farrar, Straus & Giroux.

Sorensen, T. and B. Snow. 1991. "How Children Tell: The Process of Disclosure in Child Sexual Abuse." *Child Welfare*, 70(1), 3–15.

Sotile, W.M. and M.O. Sotile. 1997. "Today's Medical Marriage," Part 1. *JAMA*, 277(15), 1180.

Sotile, W.M. and M.O. Sotile. 1997. "Today's Medical Marriage," Part 2. *JAMA*. 277(16), 1322.

Spender, D. 1980. *Man-Made Language*. London; Boston: Routledge.

Spiegelman, A. 1986. *Maus I: A Survivor's Tale: My Father Bleeds History* (1st ed.). New York: Pantheon Books.

Spiegelman, A. 1991. *Maus II: A Survivor's Tale: And Here My Troubles Began* (1st ed.). New York: Pantheon Books.

Spiro, H.M., et. al. 1993. *Empathy and the Practice of Medicine: Beyond Pills and the Scalpel*. New Haven: Yale University Press.

Stamm, B.H. 1997. "Work-Related Secondary Traumatic Stress." *PTSD Research Quarterly*, 8(2), 1–6.

Stamm, B.H. 1999. *Secondary Traumatic Stress: Self-Care Issues for Clinicians, Researchers, and Educators* (2nd ed.). Lutherville, MD: Sidran Press.

Stassen, G.H. 1998. *Just Peacemaking: Ten Practices for Abolishing War*. Cleveland: Pilgrim Press.

Staub, E. 1985. "The Psychology of Perpetrators and Bystanders." *Political Psychology*, 6(1), 61–85.

Staub, E. 1989. *The Roots of Evil: The Origins of Genocide and Other Group Violence*. Cambridge, UK; New York: Cambridge University Press.

Staub, E. 1989. "The Evolution of Bystanders, German Psychoanalysts, and Lessons for Today." *Political Psychology*, 10(1), 39–52.

Staub, E. 1996. "Preventing Genocide: Activating Bystanders, Helping Victims, and the Creation of Caring," *Peace & Conflict: Journal of Peace Psychology*, ([2T]), 189–200.

Staub, E. 2000. "Genocide and Mass Killing: Origins, Prevention, Healing, and Reconciliation." *Political Psychology*, 21(2), 367–382.

Staub, E. and L.A. Pearlman. 2001. "Healing, Reconciliation, and Forgiving after Genocide and Other Collective Violence." In R.G. Helmick and R.L. Petersen (Eds.), *Forgiveness and Reconciliation: Religion, Public Policy and Conflict Transformation*. Philadelphia: Templeton Foundation Press, 195–217.

Stein, M.B., C. Koverola, C. Hanna, M.G. Torchia, and B. McClarty. 1997. "Hippocampal Volume in Women Victimized by Childhood Sexual Abuse." *Psychological Medicine*, 27(4), 951–959.

Stein, N.D. 1996. "Bullyproof: A Teacher's Guide on Teasing and Bullying for Use with Fourth and Fifth Grade Students." Wellesley Center for Research on Women, Wellesley, MA.

Stein, N.D. 1999. *Classrooms and Courtrooms: Facing Sexual Harassment in K-12 Schools*. New York: Teachers College Press.

Steingraber, S. 1997. *Living Downstream: An Ecologist Looks at Cancer and the Environment*. Reading, MA: Addison-Wesley Publishing.

Sternberg, R.J. 2002. *A Duplex Theory of Hate and Its Development and Its Application to Massacres and Genocide*. Unpublished manuscript, Yale University, New Haven.

Steward, M.S., K. Bussey, G.S. Goodman, and K.J. Saywitz. 1993. "Implications of Developmental Research for Interviewing Children." *Child Abuse and Neglect*, 17(1), 25–37.

Strang, H. and J. Braithwaite (Eds.). 2001. *Restorative Justice and Civil Society*. Cambridge, UK: Cambridge University Press.

Streufert, S. and F. M. Gengo (Eds.). 1993. *Effects of Drugs on Human Functioning*. Basel, Switzerland: Karger AG.

Stroebe, W. and M. Stroebe. 1996. "The Social Psychology of Social Support." In E. T. Higgins and A. W. Kruglanski (Eds.), *Social Psychology: Handbook of Basic Principles*. New York: Guilford Press, 597–621.

Stuber, M. L. 1996. "Psychiatric Sequelae in Seriously Ill Children and Their Families." *Consultation-Liaison Psychiatry*, 19(3), 481–493.

Stuber, M. L., A. E. Kazak, K. Meeske, and L. Barakat. 1998. "Is Posttraumatic Stress a Viable Model for Understanding Responses to Childhood Cancer?" *Child and Adolescent Psychiatric Clinics of North America*, 7(1), 169–182.

Stuber, M. L., A. E. Kazak, K. Meeske, L. Barakat, D. Guthrie, H. Garnier, R. Pynoos, and A. Meadows. 1997. "Predictors of Posttraumatic Stress Symptoms in Childhood Cancer Survivors." *Pediatrics*, 100(6), 958–964.

Sullivan, D. and L. Tifft. 2001. *Restorative Justice. Healing the Foundations of our Everyday Lives*. Monsey, NY: Willow Tree Press.

Suomi, S. J. and S. Levine. 1998. "Psychobiology of Intergenerational Effects of Trauma: Evidence from Animal Studies." In Y. Danieli (Ed.), *International Handbook of Multigenerational Legacies of Trauma*. Plenum Series on Stress and Coping. New York: Plenum Press, 623–638.

Surgeon General, U.S. "The Magnitude of Youth Violence." Surgeon General of the United States of America. Retrieved August 2, 2001, from the Web: *http://www.surgeongeneral.gov/library/youthviolence/chapter2/sec1.html*

Svirsky, G. June 15, 2002. "Wanted: Living Rooms to Ransack." Jerusalem, Israel: e-mail.

Swarns, R. L. November 25, 2001. "South Africa's AIDS Vortex Engulfs a Rural Community." *The New York Times*, A1, 16.

Tatum, B. D. 1997. *"Why Are All the Black Kids Sitting Together in the Cafeteria?" and Other Conversations About Race*. New York: Basic Books.

Taylor, S. E. 2002. *The Tending Instinct: How Nurturing Is Essential for Who We Are and How We Live* (1st ed.). New York: Times Books.

Taylor, S. E., L. C. Klein, B. P. Lewis, T. L. Gruenewald, R.A.R. Gurung, and J. A. Updegraff. 2000. "Biobehavioral Responses to Stress in Females:
Tend-and-Befriend, Not Fight-or-Flight." *Psychological Review*, 107(3), 411–429.

Teicher, M. H. 2002. "Scars That Won't Heal: The Neurobiology of Child Abuse." *Scientific American*, 286(3), 68–75.

The King Center. *The Beloved Community of Martin Luther King, Jr.* Retrieved September 29, 2002, from the Web: *http://www.thekingcenter.org/bc.html*

The Nation (Nairobi). June 3, 2002. "Maasai's 'Ultimate Gift' Of Cows to US." All Africa. Retrieved August 4, 2002, from the Web: *http://allafrica.com/stories/200206030712.html*

The New York Times. September 11, 2002. "Counting the Consequences in Figures and Facts." *The New York Times*, A16.

The Pew Research Center for the People and the Press. 1999, December 28. "Columbine Shooting Biggest News Draw of 1999." The Pew Research Center for the People and the Press. Retrieved September, 2002, from the Web: *http://people-press.org/reports/display.php3?ReportID=48*

The Schumacher Group. 2002, August. *Emergency Physician Shift Work*. The Schumacher Group. Retrieved September 30, 2002, from the Web: *http://www.tsged.com/Newsletters/Emergency_Physician_Shift_Work.htm*

Thomas, E. and M. Isikoff. December 10, 2001. "Justice Kept in the Dark." *Newsweek*, 37.

Thomas, R.B. 1999. *An Investigation of Empathic Stress Reactions Among Mental Health Professionals Working with Posttraumatic Stress Disorder*. (Dissertation Abstracts International: Section B: the Sciences and Engineering.) The Union Institute.

Thomas, R.E. and J. Rappaport. 1996. "Art as Community Narrative: A Resource for Social Change." In M.B. Lykes et al. (Ed.), *Myths About the Powerless: Contesting Social Inequalities*. Philadelphia: Temple University Press, 317–336.

Thompson, B.W. 1996. "'A way outa no way': Eating Problems Among African-American, Latina, and White Women." In E.N. Chow and D.Y. Wilkinson et al. (Eds.), *Race, Class, and Gender: Common Bonds, Different Voices. Gender and Society Readers*. Thousand Oaks, CA: Sage Publications, 52–69.

Thompson, H.O. 1988. *World Religions in War and Peace*. Jefferson, NC: McFarland.

Thompson, J. 1999. "Deep Community: Finding Family in the World." *Futures*, 31, 511–517.

Thompson, M., C.O. Grace, and L.J. Cohen. 2001. *Best Friends, Worst Enemies: Understanding the Social Lives of Children*. New York: Ballantine Books.

Thomson, J.A. 2000. "Terror, Tears, and Timelessness: Individual and Group Responses to Trauma." *Mind and Human Interaction*, 11(3), 162–176.

Thoresen, C.E., and A.H.S. Harris. 2002. "Spirituality and Health: What's the Evidence and What's Needed?" *Annals of Behavioral Medicine*, 24(1), 3–13.

Tisak, M.S. and J. Tisak. 1996. "Expectations and Judgments Regarding Bystanders' and Victims' Responses to Peer Aggression Among Early Adolescents." *Journal of Adolescence*, 19(4), 383–392.

Tittensor, J. 1984. *Year One: A Record*. New York:Penguin Books.

Tjaden, P. and N. Thoennes. 2000. *Extent, Nature, and Consequences of Intimate-Partner Violence: Findings from the National Violence Against Women Survey*. Washington, U.S. Department of Justice, Office of Justice Programs.

Tocqueville, A. 1966. *Democracy in America* (1st ed.). New York: Harper & Row.

Todd, J. L. and J. Worell. 2000. "Resilience in Low-Income, Employed, African-American Women." *Psychology of Women Quarterly*, 24(2), 119–128.

Toobin, J. 2001, November 5. Crackdown. *The New Yorker*, 56–61.

Tosto, P. 2002, May 6. "When Race, Discipline Meet." *St. Paul Pioneer Press*, Section A, 1.

Toth, S. L., and D. Cicchetti. 1998. "Remembering, Forgetting, and the Effects of Trauma on Memory: A Developmental Psychopathology Perspective." *Development and Psychopathology*, 10(4), 589–605.

Tovar, J. and P. Montgomery. 2002. *Symbols and Ceremonies as Instruments of Change*. Paper presented at the Narrative Therapy and Community Work Conference, June 21–24, Atlanta, GA.

Trickett, P. K. and C. J. Schellenbach. 1998. *Violence Against Children in the Family and the Community* (1st ed.). Washington, DC: American Psychological Association.

Trinkoff, A. M. and C. L. Storr. 1998. "Substance Use Among Nurses: Differences Between Specialties." *American Journal of Public Health*, 88(4), 581–585.

Tutu, D. M. 1998. "Forward: Without Forgiveness There Is No Future." In R. D. Enright and J. North (Eds.), *Exploring Forgiveness*. Madison: University of Wisconsin Press, xiii–xiv.

Tutu, D. M. 2001. "Foreword." In R. G. Helmick and R. L. Petersen (Eds.), *Forgiveness and Reconciliation: Religion, Public Policy and Conflict Transformation*. Philadelphia: Templeton Foundation Press, ix–xiii.

Twain, M. 2002. "The War Prayer" BoondocksNet. Retrieved September 3, 2002, from the Web: *http://www.boondocksnet.com/ai/twain/war_prayer.html*

Twemlow, S. W. 2001. "Training Psychotherapists in Attributes of Mind from Zen and Psychoanalytic Perspectives, Part I: Core Principles, Emptiness, Impermanence, and Paradox." *American Journal of Psychotherapy*, 55(1), 1–21:

Twemlow, S. W. 2001. "Training Psychotherapists in Attributes of Mind from Zen, and Psychoanalytic Perspectives, Part II: Attention, Here and Now, Nonattachment, and Compassion." *American Journal of Psychotherapy*, 55(1), 22–39.

Twemlow, S. W., P. Fonagy, and F. C. Sacco. 2001. "An Innovative Psychodynamically Influenced Approach to Reduce School Violence." *Journal of the American Academy of Child and Adolescent Psychiatry*, 40(3), 377–379.

Uchino, B. N., J. T. Cacioppo, and J. K. Kiecolt-Glaser. 1996. "The Relationship Between Social Support and Physiological Processes: A Review with Emphasis on Underlying Mechanisms and Implications for Health." *Psychological Bulletin*, 119(3), 488–531.

Underwood, M. 2001, December 4. *Political Propaganda and Persuasion: What Is Propaganda?* Communication, Cultural, and Media Studies. Retrieved October 17, 2002, from the Web: *http://www.cultsock.ndirect.co.uk/MUHome/cshtml/propaganda/po12.html*

UNESCO. 1989. *The Seville Statement*. UNESCO. Retrieved September 14, 2002, from the Web: *http://www.unesco.org/cpp/uk/declarations/seville.pdf*

UNIFEM. 2002. *The Millenium Peace Prize for Women: 2001 Peace Prize Recipients Biography—Flora Brovina*. UNIFEM/UNDP. Retrieved in 2002 from the Web: *http://www.undp.org/unifem/mpprize/brovinabio.html*

United Mine Workers of America. 1890. *Step by Step*. Preamble to the Constitution of the United Mine Workers of America. Retrieved October 17, 2002, from the Web: *http://www.musa.ca/Songs/step.html*

United States Congress Senate Committee on the Judiciary. 1955. "Recruiting for Espionage. In Subcommittee to Investigate the Administration of the Internal Security Act and Other Internal Security Laws of the Committee of the Judiciary of the United States Senate," *Strategy and Tactics of World Communism*. Washington: U.S. Govt. Print. Office.

United States Department of Justice and United States Department of Education. 2000. *Annual Report on School Safety: 2000*. Washington, DC: U.S. Department of Education and U.S. Department of Justice.

United States Department of Justice—Bureau of Justice Statistics. 2001. *Criminal Victimization 2000: Changes 1999–2000 with trends 1993–2000*. Washington, DC: United States Department of Justice.

United States Institute of Peace Library. May 31, 2002. *Truth Commissions*. United States Institute of Peace. Retrieved September 30, 2002, from the Web: *http://www.usip.org/library/truth.html*

University of San Diego History Department. 2002. *Cold War Espionage*. Retrieved February 8, 2002, from the Web: *http://history.acusd.edu/gen/20th/coldwarspies.html*

Valent, P. 1995. "Survival Strategies: A Framework for Understanding Secondary Traumatic Stress and Coping in Helpers." In C.R. Figley (Ed.), *Compassion Fatigue: Coping with Secondary Traumatic Stress Disorder in Those Who Treat the Traumatized*. Brunner/Mazel Psychological Stress Series, No. 23. Philadelphia: Brunner/Mazel, Inc., 21–50.

van der Kolk, B.A. 1993. "Biological Considerations About Emotions, Trauma, Memory, and the Brain." In S.L. Ablon (Ed.), *Human Feelings: Explorations in Affect Development and Meaning*. Hillsdale, NJ: Analytic Press, 221–240.

van der Kolk, B.A. 1994. *Trauma and Memory: The Flexibility of Memory and the Engraving of Trauma*. Retrieved September 30, 2002, from the Web: *http://www.trauma-pages.com/vanderk4.htm*

van der Kolk, B.A. 2001. "Trauma and PTSD: Aftermaths of the WTC Disaster." *Medscape Mental Health*, 6(5). Retrieved March, 2003 from the Web: *http://www.traumacenter.org/bvdk_interview.htm*

van der Kolk, B.A. and R. Fisler. 1995. *Dissociation and the Fragmentary Nature of Traumatic Memories: Overview and Exploratory Study*. Retrieved September 30, 2002, from the Web: *http://www.traumapages.com/vanderk2.htm*

van der Kolk, B. A., N. Herron, and A. Hostetler. 1994. "The History of Trauma in Psychiatry." *Psychiatric Clinics of North America*, 17(3), 583–600.

van der Kolk, B. A., A. C. McFarlane, and L. Weisæth. 1996. *Traumatic Stress: The Effects of Overwhelming Experience on Mind, Body, and Society*. New York: Guilford Press.

van der Kolk, B. A. and J. Saporta. 1991. "The Biological Response to Psychic Trauma: Mechanisms and Treatment of Intrusion and Numbing." *Anxiety Research*, 4(3), 199–212.

van Zyl, S. 1999. "An Interview with Gillian Straker on the Truth and Reconciliation Commission in South Africa." *Psychoanalytic Dialogues*, 9(2), 245–274.

Villani, S. 2001. "Impact of Media on Children and Adolescents: A Ten-Year Review of the Research." *Journal of the American Academy of Child and Adolescent Psychiatry*, 40(4), 392–401.

Villarosa, L. 2001, June 5. "AIDS at 20; One Disease, Lived Six Different Ways." *The New York Times*, F6.

Violanti, J. M. and D. Paton. 1999. *Police Trauma: Psychological Aftermath of Civilian Combat*. Springfield, IL: Charles C. Thomas Publisher.

Volkan, V. D. 1997. *Bloodlines: From Ethnic Pride to Ethnic Terrorism* (1st ed.). New York: Farrar, Straus & Giroux.

Volkan, V. D. 1999. "The Tree Model: A Comprehensive Psychopolitical Approach to Unofficial Diplomacy and the Reduction of Ethnic Tension." *Mind and Human Interaction*, 10(3), 142–210.

Volkan, V. D. 2000. "Traumatized Societies and Psychological Care: Expanding the Concept of Preventive Medicine." *Mind and Human Interaction*, 11(3), 177–194.

Volkan, V. D. 2001. "Transgenerational Transmissions and Chosen Traumas: An Aspect of Large-Group Identity." *Group Analysis*, 34(1), 79–97.

Wachtel, T. and P. McCold. 2001. "Restorative Justice in Everyday Life." In H. Strang and J. Braithwaite (Eds.), *Restorative Justice and Civil Society*. Cambridge, UK; New York: Cambridge University Press, 114–129.

Wachtel, T. J., V. L. Wilcox, A. W. Moulton, D. Tammaro, and M. D. Stein. 1995. "Physicians' Utilization of Health Care." *Journal of General Internal Medicine*, 10(5), 261–265.

Wade, A. 1997. "Small Acts of Living: Everyday Resistance to Violence and Other Forms of Oppression." *Contemporary Family Therapy*, 19(1), 23–39.

Walker, A. 1976. *Meridian* (1st ed.). New York: Harcourt Brace Jovanovich.

Walker, A. 1982. *The Color Purple: A Novel* (1st ed.). New York: Harcourt Brace Jovanovich.

Walsh, F. 1998. *Strengthening Family Resilience*. New York: Guilford Press.

Walsh, F. 1999. *Spiritual Resources in Family Therapy*. New York: Guilford Press.

Walsh, F. and C. M. Anderson. 1988. *Chronic Disorders and the Family*. New York: Haworth Press.

Walsh, F. and M. McGoldrick. 1991. *Living Beyond Loss: Death in the Family* (1st ed.). New York: Norton.

Warner, B. S. and M. D. Weist. 1996. "Urban Youth as Witnesses to Violence: Beginning Assessment and Treatment Efforts." *Journal of Youth and Adolescence*. 25(3), 361–377.

Waterson, K. 2001. "The Cantor and the Klansman." In J. Canfield, M. V. Hansen, and D. P. Elkins (Eds.), *Chicken Soup for the Jewish Soul: Stories to Open the Heart and Rekindle the Spirit*. Deerfield Beach, FL: Health Communications, 7–13.

Weaver, H. N. and M.Y.H. Brave Heart. 1999. "Examining Two Facets of American Indian Identity: Exposure to Other Cultures and the Influence of Historical Trauma." *Journal of Human Behavior in the Social Environment*, 2(1–2), 19–33.

Weingarten, K. 1991. "The Discourses of Intimacy: Adding a Social Constructionist and Feminist View." *Family Process*, 30(3), 285–305.

Weingarten, K. 1992. "A Consideration of Intimate and Nonintimate Interactions in Therapy." *Family Process*, 31(1), 45–59.

Weingarten, K. 1994. *The Mother's Voice: Strengthening Intimacy in Families* (1st ed.). New York: Harcourt Brace.

Weingarten, K. 1995. "Radical Listening: Challenging Cultural Beliefs For and About Mothers." In K. Weingarten (Ed.), *Cultural Resistance: Challenging Beliefs About Men, Women, and Therapy*. New York: Harrington Park Press/Haworth Press, 7–22.

Weingarten, K. 1997. *The Mother's Voice: Strengthening Intimacy in Families* (2nd ed.) New York: Guilford Press.

Weingarten, K. 1998. "The Small and the Ordinary: The Daily Practice of a Postmodern Narrative Therapy." *Family Process*, 37(1), 3–15.

Weingarten, K. 1999. "Stretching to Meet What's Given: Opportunities for a Spiritual Practice." In F. Walsh (Ed.), *Spiritual Resources in Family Therapy*. New York: Guilford Press. 240–255.

Weingarten, K. 1999. *The Politics of Illness Narratives: Who Tells, Who Listens, and Who Cares?* Paper presented at the Narrative Therapy and Community Work Conference, Adelaide, South Australia.

Weingarten, K. 2000. "Witnessing, Wonder, and Hope." *Family Process*, 39(4), 389–402.

Weingarten, K. 2000. "Using the Internet to Build Social Support: Implications for Well-being and Hope." *Families, Systems, and Health*, 18(2), 157–160.

Weingarten, K. 2001. "Making Sense of Illness Narratives: Braiding Theory, Practice, and the Embodied Life." In C. White (Ed.), *Working with the Stories of Women's Lives*. Adelaide, South Australia: Dulwich Centre Publications, 111–125, and *http://www.dulwichcentre.com.au/kaethearticle.html*

Weingarten, K. and M. E. Weingarten Worthen. 1997. "A Narrative Approach to Understanding the Illness Experiences of a Mother and Daughter." *Families, Systems and Health*, 15(1), 41–54.

Weingarten, V. 1968. *Mrs. Beneker: A Novel.* New York: Simon & Schuster.

Weingarten, V. 1969. *A Loving Wife* (1st ed.). New York: Knopf.

Weingarten, V. 1972. *A Woman of Feeling* (1st ed.). New York: Knopf.

Weingarten, V. 1976. *Half a Marriage* (1st ed.). New York: Knopf.

Weingarten, V. 1978. *Intimations of Mortality* (1st ed.). New York: Knopf.

Weiss, M. and S. Weiss. 2000. "Second Generation to Holocaust Survivors: Enhanced Differentiation of Trauma Transmission." *American Journal of Psychotherapy*, 54(3): 372–385.

Wellisch, D.K. and A. Hoffman. 1998. "Daughters of Breast Cancer Patients: Genetic Legacies and Traumas." In Y. Danieli (Ed.), *International Handbook of Multigenerational Legacies of Trauma.* The Plenum Series on Stress and Coping. New York: Plenum Press, 603–619.

Whal, J. 2002. *28th June 1914—The Assassination of Archduke Franz Ferdinand.* Retrieved April 22, 2002, from the Web: *http://212.67.202.71/~johnwhal/timeline/assasin.htm*

Whealin, J.M., C.A. Morgan, and G. Hazlett. 2001. "The Role of Military Studies in Enhancing Our Understanding of PTSD." *PTSD Research Quarterly*, 12(1), 1–7.

White, J.L. and J.H. Cones. 1999. *Black Man Emerging: Facing the Past and Seizing a Future in America.* New York: W.H. Freeman.

White, M. 1988. "Saying Hullo Again: The Incorporation of the Lost Relationship in the Resolution of Grief." *Dulwich Centre Newsletter*, Spring 1988, 29–36.

White, M. 1995. *Reauthoring Lives: Interviews and Essays.* Adelaide, South Australia: Dulwich Centre Publications.

White, M. 2000. "Reengaging with History: The Absent but Implicit." In M. White (Ed.), *Reflections on Narrative Practice: Essays and Interviews.* Adelaide South Australia: Dulwich Centre Publications, 35–59.

White, M. and D. Epston. 1990. *Narrative Means to Therapeutic Ends* (1st ed.). New York: Norton.

Widom, C.S. 1999. "Posttraumatic Stress Disorder in Abused and Neglected Children Grown Up." *American Journal of Psychiatry*, 156(8), 1223–1229.

Widom, C.S. 2000. "Motivation and Mechanisms in the 'Cycle of Violence.'" In D.J. Hansen (Ed.), *Nebraska Symposium on Motivation, Vol. 46, 1998: Motivation and Child Maltreatment.* Lincoln: University of Nebraska Press, 1–37.

Wiesel, E. 1986. *The Nobel Acceptance Speech by Elie Wiesel in Oslo on December 10, 1986.* Elie Wiesel Foundation. Retrieved October 17, 2002, from the Web: *http://www.eliewieselfoundation.org/ElieWiesel/Nobel_Speech.htm*

Wiesel, E. 1990. *From the Kingdom of Memory: Reminiscences.* New York: Summit Books.

Wiesenthal, S., H. J. Cargas, and B. V. Fetterman. 1997. *The Sunflower: On the Possibilities and Limits of Forgiveness* (Rev. and expanded, 2nd ed.). New York: Schocken.

Wilkinson, D. 2002. *Silence on the Mountain: Stories of Terror, Betrayal, and Forgetting in Guatemala*. Boston: Houghton Mifflin.

Williams, L. M. 1995. "Recovered Memories of Abuse in Women with Documented Child Sexual Victimization Histories." *Journal of Traumatic Stress*, 8(4), 649–673.

Williams, L. M. 1995. "Recall of Childhood Trauma: A Prospective Study of Women's Memories of Child Sexual Abuse": Correction. *Journal of Consulting and Clinical Psychology*, 63(3), 343.

Williams, L. M. and V. L. Banyard. 1997. "Gender and Recall of Child Sexual Abuse: A Prospective Study," in J. D. Read and S. Lindsay (Eds.). (1997). *Recollections of Trauma: Scientific Evidence and Clinical Practice*. NATO ASI series: Series A: Life sciences. (291), 371–377.

Williams, L. M. and V. L. Banyard. 1997. "Perspectives on Adult Memories of Childhood Sexual Abuse: A Research Review." L. J. Dickstein, M. B. Riba, et al. (Eds.) *American Psychiatric Press Review of Psychiatry*, (16), Washington, DC, American Psychiatric Press, 123–151.

Williams, P. J. 1991. *The Alchemy of Race and Rights*. Cambridge, MA.: Harvard University Press.

Wilson, A., 1991. *World Scripture: A Comparative Anthology of Sacred Texts*. New York: International Religious Foundation Distributed by Paragon House.

Wilson, J. P. and J. D. Lindy. 1994. *Countertransference in the Treatment of PTSD*. New York: Guilford Press.

Winfield, N. December 16, 1999. "UN Failed Rwanda, Ignored Evidence of Genocide, Report Says." Global Policy Forum. Retrieved September 30, 2002, from the Web: *http://www.globalpolicy.org/security/issues/rwanda/rpt1299.htm*

Wink, W. 1992. *Engaging the Powers: Discernment and Resistance in a World of Domination*. Minneapolis: Fortress Press.

Wink, W. 2001/2002. "Can Love Save the World? *Yes!*" (Winter). Retrieved from the Web: *http://www.futurenet.org/20spirituality/wink.htm*

Wiseman, R. 2002. *Queen Bees and Wannabes: Helping Your Daughter Survive Cliques, Gossip, Boyfriends, and Other Realities of Adolescence* (1st ed.). New York: Crown Publishers.

Wittman, J. 1993. *Breast Cancer Journal: A Century of Petals*. Golden, CO: Fulcrum Pub.

Wolfe, D.A., L. Zak, S.K. Wilson, and P. Jaffe. 1986. "Child Witnesses to Violence Between Parents: Critical Issues in Behavioral and Social Adjustment." *Journal of Abnormal Child Psychology*, 14(1) Mar 1986, 95–104.

Worthen, M. 2001. "Growing Up with My Body: A Young Woman's Complicates Identity." In C. White (Ed.), *Working with the Stories of Women's Lives*. Adelaide, South Australia: Dulwich Centre Publications, 127–132.

Worthington, E. L. 1998. "An Empathy-Humility-Commitment Model of Forgiveness Applied Within Family Dyads." *Journal of Family Therapy*, 20(1), 59–76.

Worthington, E. L. 1998. *Dimensions of Forgiveness: Psychological Research and Theological Perspectives*. Philadelphia: Templeton Foundation Press.

Worthington, E. L., Jr. and D. T. Drinkard. 2000. "Promoting Reconciliation Through Psychoeducational and Therapeutic Interventions." *Journal of Marital and Family Therapy*, 26(1), 93–101.

Worthington, E. L., Jr., T. A. Kurusu, W. Collins, J. W. Berry, J. S. Ripley, and S. N. Baier. 2000. "Forgiving Usually Takes Time: A Lesson Learned by Studying Interventions to Promote Forgiveness." *Journal of Psychology and Theology*, 28(1), 3–20.

Wright, L. M., W. L. Watson, and J. M. Bell. 1996. *Beliefs: The Heart of Healing in Families and Illness*. New York: Basic Books.

Wright, S. 2002. "Quotes from Stephen Wright." Eric S. Raymond. Retrieved October 17, 2002, from the Web: *http://www.tuxedo.org/~esr/fortunes/stephen-wright.html*

Yassen, J. 1995. "Preventing Secondary Traumatic Stress Disorder." In C. R. Figley (Ed.), *Compassion Fatigue: Coping with Secondary Traumatic Stress Disorder in Those Who Treat the Traumatized*. Brunner/Mazel Psychological Stress Series. No. 23. Philadelphia: Brunner/Mazel, Inc., 178–208.

Yehuda, R. 1999. "Managing Anger and Aggression in Patients with Posttraumatic Stress Disorder." *Journal of Clinical Psychiatry*, 60(Suppl 15), 33–37.

Yehuda, R. 2002. "Posttraumatic Stress Disorder." *New England Journal of Medicine*, 346(2), 108–114.

Yehuda, R., L. M. Bieter, J. Schmeidler, D. H. Aferiat, I. Breslau, and S. Dolan. 2000. "Low Cortisol and Risk for PTSD in Adult Offspring of Holocaust Survivors." *American Journal of Psychiatry*, 157(8), 1252–1259.

Yehuda, R., S. L. Halligan, and R. Grossman. 2001. "Childhood Trauma and Risk for PTSD: Relationship to Intergenerational Effects of Trauma, Parental PTSD, and Cortisol Excretion." *Development and Psychopathology*, 13(3), 733–753.

Yehuda, R. and A. C. McFarlane (Eds.). 1997. *Psychobiology of Posttraumatic Stress Disorder*. New York: New York Academy of Sciences.

Yehuda, R., A. C. McFarlane, and A. Y. Shalev. 1998. "Predicting the Development of Posttraumatic Stress Disorder from the Acute Response to a Traumatic Event." *Biological Psychiatry*, 44(12), 1305–1313.

Yehuda, R., J. Schmeidler, A. Elkin, S. Wilson, L. Siever, K. Binder-Brynes, M. Wainberg, and D. Aferiot. 1998. "Phenomenology and Psychobiology of the Intergenerational Response to Trauma." In Y. Danieli (Ed.), *International Handbook of Multigenerational Legacies of Trauma*. The Plenum Series on Stress and Coping. New York: Plenum Press, 639–655.

Yehuda, R., J. Schmeidler, E. L. Giller, Jr., L. J. Siever, and K. Binder-Brynes. 1998. "Relationship Between Posttraumatic Stress Disorder Characteristics of Holocaust Survivors and Their Adult Offspring." *American Journal of Psychiatry*, 155(6), 841–843.

Yehuda, R., J. Schmeidler, M. Wainberg, K. Binder-Brynes, and T. Duvdevani. 1998. "Vulnerability to Posttraumatic Stress Disorder in Adult Offspring of Holocaust Survivors." *American Journal of Psychiatry*, 155(9), 1163–1171.

Young-Eisendrath, P. 1996. *The Gifts of Suffering: Finding Insight, Compassion, and Renewal*. Reading, MA: Addison-Wesley.

Zangrando, R.L. 1991. "About Lynching." Modern American Poetry. Retrieved August 6, 2001, from the Web: *http://www.english.uiuc.edu/maps/poets/g_l/lynching/lynching.htm*

Zeanah, C.H. and M.S. Scheeringa. 1997. "The Experience and Effects of Violence in Infancy," In J.D. Osofsky, (Ed). *Children in a Violent Society*. New York: Guilford Press.

Zeanah, C.H. and P.D. Zeanah. 1989. "Intergenerational Transmission of Maltreatment: Insights from Attachment Theory and Research." *Psychiatry*, 52(2), 177–196.

Zehr, H. 1995. *Changing Lenses: A New Focus for Crime and Justice*. Scottdale, PA: Herald Press.

Zimmerman, J. and J.B. Feister. 2002. *A Church in Crisis*. American Catholic. Retrieved May 4, 2002, from the Web: *http://www.americancatholic.org/News/ClergySexAbuse/*

Zimmerman, J.M. and V. Coyle. 1996. *The Way of Council*. Las Vegas, NV: Bramble Books.

Zinn, H. 2002. *Terrorism and War*. New York: Seven Stories Press.

Zugar, A. 2001, June 5. "A Veteran's Long Journey on the Front Line of AIDS." *The New York Times*, A1.

Zur, J. 1996. "From PTSD to Voices in Context: From an 'Experience-Far' to an 'Experience-near' Understanding of Responses to War and Atrocity Across Cultures." *International Journal of Social Psychiatry*, 42(4), 305–317.

Zuravin, S., C. McMillen, D. DePanfilis, and C. Risley-Curtiss. 1996. "The Intergenerational Cycle of Child Maltreatment: Continuity Versus Discontinuity." *Journal of Interpersonal Violence*, 11(3), 315–334.

Index

Acknowledgments

This book rests on the foundation of scholarship it has been my privilege to read. No one who studies violence is immune from the effects of being immersed in it. The authors I read provided accompaniment as they led me to empathic awareness of horrific, violent predicaments. I am profoundly grateful for the inspiration of the body of work that has been written by people committed to alleviating the suffering that violence and violation cause. While the Notes and Bibliography record the many scholars and writers whose work has informed mine, I wish to acknowledge the work of several people in particular: Yael Danieli, Thich Nhât Hanh, Judith Herman, James Gilligan, Dori Laub, Martha Minow, Samantha Power, Ervin Staub, Bessel van der Kolk, and Vamik Volkan.

My colleagues Michael White, Peggy Penn, and David Epston have had a major influence on my clinical and theoretical work. Their approaches to witnessing have inspired my own. Decades of collaboration with Carol Becker and Sallyann Roth have been influential in my work. Work with colleagues in Kosovo and South Africa has also been enormously meaningful to me and informs this book. I especially thank Ferid Agani, Pumla Gobodo-Madikizela, Elmarie Kotzé, Dirk Kotzé, Elize Morkel, Frida Rundell, Suzanne Shuda, Yvonne Sliep, Mita Solomon, Aferdita Uka, Shqipe Ukshini, and Jusuf Ulaj. Colleagues in other settings have also been supportive: Geraldine Eastler, Marsha Hanssen, Deborah Haynor, John Hubbell, Julie Kahn, Margie McGraw, Ruthie Rodhe, Monica Roizner, Vivian Torres, Mike Ward, and Jennifer Wittlin.

Deena Metzger helped me see the place from which this book needed to be written and believe that I could do it.

I have been incredibly fortunate to work with an agent and an editor who both understood this book. Each has been willing to match me e-mail for e-mail . . . which is no mean feat. They are both blessed with excellent judgment and skills to communicate this effectively. Mitch Hoffman, my editor, has steered this book faithfully toward its mission. His ear for tone has been an unerring guide. My agent, James Levine, has been a steady, wise companion through the entire gamut of publishing this book. I am profoundly grateful to them both.

Andrei Novak, Ron Jacobs, and Judith Herman read and commented on portions of the manuscript, for which they have my gratitude. John Sargent read the entire first draft of the manuscript and shared his insight and wisdom with me. I relied on his opinion when my own wavered. Corky Becker, Laura Benkov, Rachel Hare-Mustin, Peggy Penn, Jan Surrey, and Patti Levin gave helpful comments on the second draft that informed my revisions. Maria Root read the entire manuscript and offered her thoughtful professional critique of it. Regina Yando worked as closely with me on the revisions of this manuscript as she did thirty years earlier on my dissertation. Our long friendship includes her devoted intellectual mentorship of which I am the most fortunate beneficiary. Should there be remaining errors, despite wonderful help, the responsibility for them is mine.

Steven Brion-Meisels, Jan Cooper, Luise Erdmann, Frances Kadinoff, Kathleen Lancaster, Mary Kay Magistad, the Reverend Allie Perry, and Claire Willis all offered assistance and support at different phases. Jenny Bernstein-Rangan and Bette Tsouprake have kept body and soul together. I received technical assistance from five people: Jehanzeb Mansurali Baldiwala entered hundreds of references into a database; Senta Burton enthusiastically pitched in with locating references at the eleventh hour; Michelle Eberle offered invaluable assistance locating articles online; Debra Gustafson scoured Boston libraries to find obscure references for me; and Miranda Worthen spent scores of hours assembling the bibliography.

Writing this book has been a grueling process and many friends have offered sustenance along the way, including Glenda Alderman, Laura Benkov, Holly Bishop, Rene Brant, Victoria Dickerson, Melissa Elliott, Abigail Erdmann, Miriam Greenspan, Elmarie Kotzé, Dirk Kotzé, Kathleen Lancaster, Peggy Penn, Yvonne Sliep, and Jan Surrey. Corky Becker, Patti Levin, and Lois Natchez have sustained me in ways that are impossible to enumerate and which have made all the difference.

My parents, Violet and Victor Weingarten, have been close to me throughout the work on this book. I believe that they would have understood that this book is also a tribute to them. I hope it honors their memories.

My sister, Jan Greenberg, has supported me and this book in many ways. I have relied on her wisdom and humor such that life without her seems unimaginable.

My children, Miranda Worthen and Ben Worthen, helped with verve, creativity, and skillfulness at different phases of the book's completion. In the last few months of writing this book, Miranda was available to talk an idea through or hear a passage. Her on-the-spot consults were always helpful and also a great pleasure. Miranda's work in the area of human rights has inspired my own. Ben Worthen gave me invaluable and timely advice to help revise the manuscript. It is a compliment to him that I was often bursting with pride the more radical the changes he proposed. His humor was also in fine form, which made consulting him a double gift. My children are steady companions; our intimacy a source of immense pride and fulfillment.

Hilary Worthen, my husband, partner, and love of my life, has held faith through it all. His support of this book and me has spanned the widest possible gamut. He is an intrepid witness. This book is also for you.

About the Author

Dr. Kaethe Weingarten has been on the faculty of the Harvard Medical School since 1981, where she is now Associate Clinical Professor of Psychology in the Department of Psychiatry. She also teaches at the Family Institute of Cambridge, which sponsors the Witnessing Project, which she founded and directs. Dr. Weingarten has taught across the United States and in Africa, Australia, Canada, Europe, and New Zealand. She lives in Newton, Massachusetts.